SCHOLARLY WRITING

SCHOLARLY WRITING

IDEAS, EXAMPLES, AND EXECUTION

THIRD EDITION

Jessica Lynn Wherry
ASSOCIATE PROFESSOR OF LAW, LEGAL PRACTICE
GEORGETOWN UNIVERSITY LAW CENTER

Kristen E. Murray
PROFESSOR OF LAW
TEMPLE UNIVERSITY, BEASLEY SCHOOL OF LAW

CAROLINA ACADEMIC PRESS
Durham, North Carolina

Library of Congress Cataloging-in-Publication Data

Names: Wherry, Jessica Lynn, author. | Murray, Kristen E., author.
Title: Scholarly writing : ideas, examples, and execution / by Jessica Lynn
    Wherry and Kristen E. Murray.
Description: Third edition. | Durham, North Carolina : Carolina Academic
    Press, LLC, [2019] | Includes bibliographical references and index.
Identifiers: LCCN 2018042350 | ISBN 9781531013707 (alk. paper)
Subjects: LCSH: Legal composition. | Academic writing.
Classification: LCC KF250 .C528 2019 | DDC 808.06/634--dc23
LC record available at https://lccn.loc.gov/2018042350

eISBN 978-1-5310-1371-4

CAROLINA ACADEMIC PRESS, LLC
700 Kent Street
Durham, North Carolina 27701
Telephone (919) 489-7486
Fax (919) 493-5668
www.cap-press.com

Printed in the United States of America

To our parents,
the best teachers
we know,
and to
the kids in our lives
who share our love of learning.

CONTENTS

ACKNOWLEDGMENTS

We are indebted to many people who offered advice, support, encouragement, and feedback as we worked through our own writing process.

We continued to benefit from invaluable research help from several past research assistants. For this third edition, we had research assistance from Katie Ott. Our research assistants for the second edition were Sarah Krantz, Evan Sills, and Peter Smyth. Ben Grillot, Joe Pollak, Dave Schneider, and Lindsey Welsford provided research help for the first edition. Many student authors offered us use of their published and unpublished papers (and early notes, outlines, and drafts) to use as examples in the book. We thank them, especially the eleven authors whose work we used in this edition—Chris Bruno, Monica DiFonzo, Shaina Elias, Nathaniel Guest, Katy Ho, Natalie Hrubos, Emily Kimmelman, Jordan Schwartz, Jessie Shields, Peter Smyth, and Collin Swan.

Special thanks to the librarians at Temple University, Beasley School of Law, who provided research support and their own thoughts about student scholarly research. We are grateful to law librarian Andrew Lang for his review of our text, his suggested edits, and his attention to detail. We continue to benefit from the help we received on previous editions: in particular, thanks to Julie Eidman and Amy Feddema of Thomson Reuters and Elan Kleis and Natalie Timmers of LexisNexis for their advice and feedback for the first edition. For the research updates in the second edition, we again thank Natalie Timmers; we also thank Michael Heinlein, Charles Mikesell, and Alyson Paulick of Thomson Reuters.

Thank you to Georgetown Law Dean William Treanor and Temple University, Beasley School of Law Dean Gregory Mandel for the research support that allowed us to write this third edition.

Our family and friends offered unwavering support and enthusiastic cheerleading as we worked on all the editions of this book, and our mothers lent us their keen proofreading eyes so that we could follow our own advice about finishing.

Finally, we also owe a debt to the many legal writing students who have passed through our classrooms over our years of teaching. We thank you for inspiring us to write this book, and for all the lessons you taught us over the years. In particular, we thank the Fall 2017 Introduction to Scholarly Note Writing class at Georgetown, for your enthusiasm, insightfulness, and good humor.

FOREWORD

As an academic, few experiences are more gratifying than learning that a student's thesis, note, or paper has been accepted for publication. (If the student also won a large writing competition cash prize, so much the better.) At the opposite end of the spectrum, few tasks are more dispiriting than watching students toil for months only to produce unsatisfying work that, for all the right reasons, will never be published.

In our profession, strong writing skills prove tremendously helpful and, in many jobs, constitute the price of admission. As attorneys, the written word is the coin of our realm. Not surprisingly, the best student writers in our law schools enjoy a competitive advantage in the entry-level job market. In legal offices, strong writers quickly find themselves involved in the most challenging and important work. Quite simply, experience suggests that the best writers find that their skills offer them a fast track to professional opportunity and success.

The required first-year law school curriculum typically includes a highly structured and often formalistic introduction to the fundamentals of legal research and writing. To make matters worse, first-year students often fail to appreciate—at the time—the importance of these courses and the need to master these foundational skills. Conversely, most law students embark upon their initial, upper-level scholarly writing experience with minimal faculty guidance concerning the writing process and a focus almost exclusively on the subject matter of their research. Inadequate preparation for the enterprise leads many students to underestimate and, thus, under-invest in, their scholarly writing projects. It's frustrating to see students squander this opportunity, because writing articles or scholarly papers offers students the chance to spread their wings in terms of their research, analysis, and writing.

Nonetheless, a surprisingly small number of law students actually publish research papers. While the previous generation's proliferation of journals has expanded the number of student notes and comments published, students that publish remain the exception, not the rule. That's a shame. Performing in-depth, open-ended research offers a glimpse into the level of effort commonly expended by practitioners, particularly on large and important matters. Indeed, almost every step in the creation and—more importantly, the effort to achieve—perfection of a research paper helps prepare a law student to counsel, advocate, and communicate effectively in practice. Moreover, publication enhances student authors' credentials by demonstrating a facility in critical skills (research, analysis, and writing), signaling an interest and a certain level of expertise in a subject-matter area, while adding eye-catching fodder to student resumes. In addition, publishable student papers may generate income (with steadily increasing sums on offer in numerous writing competitions) and, at times, provide students the opportunity to hone their advocacy and persuasion skills by presenting their research to knowledgeable audiences.

Still, the reality remains. Daunting impediments deter students from pursuing publication. Of course, writing publishable papers requires hard work. Huge amounts of time must be expended and, all too often, holiday breaks and weekends must be sacrificed. (The dominant law school trend to truncate the academic semester, from fifteen to fourteen, and, increasingly, thirteen weeks only exacerbates the challenge students face.) The structure and rhythm of law school work—ranging from syllabi and a convenient textbook to frequent class meetings and timed examinations—does not apply. The shared experience—with colleagues preparing, reviewing, and, frequently, bemoaning identical material—is lacking. As many academics realize, producing serious, worthwhile scholarship can prove a lonely experience.

Looking back, I remain immensely grateful to the mentors who guided me through the process of conceptualizing, researching, organizing, polishing, submitting, and publishing my student work. (To Glenn George, Charles Koch, Jules Rothlein, and David Shipley, *thanks again!*) Alas, few law students are lucky enough to find so many gifted teachers and role models available and willing to shepherd them through the process. As a result, most students embark upon their quest to produce scholarly work—an output with which they have limited familiarity—ill-equipped for their journey.

Supervising legions of LL.M. candidates as they struggle to complete a thesis, J.D. students attempting to fulfill the note requirement that dominates their 2L *Law Review* or *Journal* experience, and J.D. and LL.M. candidates writing seminar papers (often to fulfill a mandatory upper-level writing requirement) or independent research and writing projects serves as a potent reminder that the *process* that leads to publishable legal research is not for the faint of heart. Faced with such a challenge, any type of helpful lifeline is a welcome sight.

Over the years, I worked with colleagues to draft, expand, and improve a set of thesis guidelines and advice for students, but this merely scratched the surface. Two early works, one by Eugene Volokh, and the other by Elizabeth Fajans and Mary R. Falk, now both in their fifth edition, made students' lives easier. The publication of Murray and Wherry's SCHOLARLY WRITING, now in its third edition, offers students a wealth of choices. What I appreciate most about Murray and Wherry's SCHOLARLY WRITING is that it guides the student each step of the way. Moreover, Murray and Wherry do not simply try to *tell* the student how to overcome each hurdle, they *anticipate* challenges, offer alternative solutions, and *show* the student various examples of how to improve and what to aspire to.

Having said that, my purpose here is not to compare and contrast these three tools, but to leave no doubt in law students' minds that consulting (nay, embracing) one or more of them will dramatically enhance their likelihood of success, whatever their endeavor. After more than two decades of working with student journal editors (and, alas, serving as an academic dean), I find it remarkable how few law schools, *Law Reviews*, and *Journals* recommend, let alone require, that students consult one or more of these texts. While history, tradition, or faculty largess may explain the legal academy's unique phenomenon of student management of *Law Reviews* and *Journals* (as opposed to the more common and, arguably, credible peer review model), nothing justifies the all-too-common sink-or-swim pedagogy associated with student note and comment writing. Surely, the best students figure it out, and many produce excellent pieces. Meanwhile, far more fail, and most never again attempt to publish their work. Today, that's unnecessary.

I strongly recommend Murray and Wherry's SCHOLARLY WRITING to law students and the faculty who mentor them. I can say—without reservation— that this book, and, more specifically, the method it espouses, has changed my life for the better. For more than twenty years, I have supervised a large cadre of LL.M. thesis candidates, while simultaneously serving as the faculty advisor to the leading journal in my field. Since our students began a structured instructional program employing this book (and, again, its methodology), our students have:

- Consistently chosen better thesis, note, and paper topics;
- Written better theses, notes, and papers;
- Published more theses and articles in leading journals;

- Published more student notes in our school's journals;
- Won *a lot* more money in writing competitions; and (I would be remiss if I failed to mention) ...
- Complained less about the thesis, note, and paper-writing process.

I could stop there. But I would be remiss if—in addressing my colleagues in the legal academy—I failed to mention how much more I enjoy reading and reviewing student theses, notes, and article drafts today. To my colleagues and friends, Kristen and Jessica, on behalf of myself, my colleagues, and my past, present, and future students: *Thank you!*

Steven L. Schooner
Nash & Cibinic Professor of Government Procurement Law
George Washington University
Washington, D.C.
November 2018

ABOUT THIS BOOK

We would like to start by congratulating you. Perhaps you were recently selected to be a member of your law school's law review or other legal journal. Maybe you are about to embark on an LL.M. program in a specialized area of law. Or your achievement could be that you finished your first (or even second) year of law school. Any of these reasons, and any other reason that has led you to this book, is congratulations-worthy!

If you are reading this book, you are about to begin the process of writing a scholarly legal research paper. Your scholarly writing project may take a variety of shapes and meet a variety of purposes. Perhaps your school requires an upper-level legal research paper to graduate with a J.D., a requirement that may be satisfied by writing a note or comment for your journal, writing a paper in a seminar class, or working on an independent writing project. Or maybe you are an LL.M. student tasked with writing a thesis to satisfy your LL.M. program requirements. Whatever your assignment is called, do not be confused by the various names. In this book, we generally use "scholarly writing project" and "scholarly paper," but if your professor talks about a legal research paper or other variation, we have you covered.

For many students, the scholarly paper is their biggest challenge in law school because the project is so large in scope and requires mostly independent work. We developed this book to provide guidance and support as you work on your scholarly writing project. Over several years of teaching scholarly writing, we have worked with hundreds of students writing papers on a wide variety of topics and surveyed law review and law journal student-editors to find out what criteria student-editors use in making publication decisions. Based on this experience and information, we have developed a process that works for all students writing on any topic. Put your fears aside; this book will take you through the process step by step!

Taking on a scholarly writing project is daunting, but it is also your opportunity to tell the world about your ideas and why your ideas are right, or at least worth considering. You might have a thoughtful idea you want to share with the legal community or the world; you might have stumbled across something in your work in other classes or in reading the latest news and something does not sit right with you. You think there must be a solution, or a better way to deal with a problem. Your scholarly writing project gives you an outlet for developing and sharing these ideas. It is also an opportunity for you to develop expertise on a topic, which you can use to guide your academic or professional career.

We have incorporated real samples of student scholarly writing throughout the book to illustrate many of the concepts we discuss. In our experience, looking at well-executed student papers can help you in crafting your own scholarly paper. We use eight student scholarly papers as examples throughout the book: Chris Bruno's paper on parental rights,[1] Monica DiFonzo's paper on art theft,[2] Shaina Elias's paper on deportation of alien widows,[3] Nathaniel Guest's paper on historical property rights,[4] Natalie Hrubos's paper on agreements to arbitrate employment discrimination claims,[5] Emily Kimmelman's paper on discharge of student loan debt,[6] Jessie Shields's paper on partial verdicts,[7] and Collin Swan's paper on personal services contracts.[8] We encourage you to read the full-text versions of one (or more) of these papers if you are interested in the

---

1. Christopher Bruno, Note, *A Right to Decide Not to be a Legal Father: Gonzales v. Carhart and the Acceptance of Emotional Harm as a Constitutionally Protected Interest*, 77 Geo. Wash. L. Rev. 141 (2008).

2. Monica R. DiFonzo, Note, *"Think you can steal our Caravaggio and get away with it? Think again." An Analysis of the Italian Cultural Property Model*, 44 Geo. Wash. Int'l L. Rev. 539 (2012).

3. Shaina N. Elias, Note, *From Bereavement to Banishment: The Deportation of Surviving Alien Spouses Under the "Widow Penalty,"* 77 Geo. Wash. L. Rev. 172 (2008).

4. Nathaniel Guest, Comment and Note, *Putting History on a Stone Foundation: Toward Legal Rights for Historic Property*, 18 Temp. Pol. & Civ. Rts. L. Rev. 699 (2009).

5. Natalie Hrubos, Note, *Agreements to Arbitrate Employment Discrimination Claims: Pyett Illustrates Need to Re-forest the Legal Landscape*, 18 Temp. Pol. & Civ. Rts. L. Rev. 281 (2008).

6. Emily Kimmelman, Comment, *Student Loans: Path to Success or Road to the Abyss? An Argument to Reform the Student Loan Discharge Exception*, 89 Temp. L. Rev. 155 (2016).

7. Jessie D. Shields, Comment, *On the Subject of Partial Verdicts: A Series of Practical Questions Answered for District Court Judges*, 88 Temp. L. Rev. 579 (2016).

8. Collin D. Swan, Note, *Dead Letter Prohibitions and Policy Failures: Applying Government Ethics Standards to Personal Services Contractors*, 80 Geo. Wash. L. Rev. 668 (2012).

topic to help you get a sense of what a scholarly paper looks like.[9] We have also included three annotated full-text notes in the Appendix to give you a comprehensive illustration of the concepts we discuss throughout the book.[10]

Scattered throughout the book are a series of sidebars called "Bright Ideas" and "Tech Talk." Bright Ideas are intended to give you practical tips for particular concepts or steps in the scholarly writing process. Tech Talk (new in this edition) points out places where you might use a specific app or technology-based shortcut to help with the writing process. You can easily identify the Bright Ideas throughout the book because they are set off with a shining light bulb icon, while Tech Talk is identified by a computer screen icon.

We have also included quizzes and checklists throughout the book. The quizzes are not designed to test whether you read the chapter, but to help you determine where you are in the writing process, what issues you may want to discuss with your professor or supervisor, and whether you are ready to move on to the next stage in the process. The checklists are intended to help you track your own progress and make sure you will meet the next deadline.

We hope this book helps you have a positive experience while working on your scholarly writing paper. We wrote this book to offer guidance and support to you, no matter the context—in a scholarly writing class using this book as a course text, in a seminar or other class using this book as a reference or course supplement, as a self-teaching guide throughout an independent writing process, or any other scenario. The book offers advice to students who are working alone, working with a supervisor, or working within a small peer-review group. No matter what framework you are working in and no matter how many resources you have at your disposal, you will likely find yourself doing the bulk of the work on your own. Whether you need some direction, some inspiration, or want to see an example of how another student approached a scholarly writing project, this book can serve as a helpful guide.

---

9. Throughout the book, we use examples from the students' draft papers (which are on file with the authors) as well as the published versions. We have omitted both citations to the papers and citations contained within the papers in favor of a clean presentation. If you are interested in the sources the students relied on in their papers, please consult the full-text published versions.

10. Katy (Yin Yee) Ho, *Defining the Contours of an Ethical Duty of Technological Competence*, 30 Geo. J. Legal. Ethics 853 (2017); Jordan Schwartz, State Executive Emergency Powers and the Second Amendment: A Call for Judicial Courage During a State Emergency (unpublished note) (on file with authors); Peter K. Smyth, A Functionalist Recommendation for Business Methods Patents: A Note on *Bilski* (unpublished case note) (on file with authors).

SCHOLARLY WRITING

CHAPTER 1

INTRODUCTION TO SCHOLARLY WRITING

Most law schools require upper-level and graduate-level students to write a thoughtful scholarly piece through a student-run journal, a research seminar, or an independent legal research and writing project. These scholarly writing projects call upon student authors to demonstrate their abilities in advanced legal research and sophisticated legal analysis to develop and defend a thesis on a legal topic.

Your first step is to mentally prepare yourself to work through the process of writing a scholarly paper. Writing a scholarly paper is a long-term project that requires a great deal of effort; you need to develop your ideas and understand your topic to be able to successfully complete your scholarly paper. Think of it as you would any activity that requires a long training period, such as running a marathon, losing weight, or entering a competitive hot dog eating contest. You would not just wake up one Saturday morning and decide to run a marathon with no training or preparation. If your goal is to lose 50 pounds, you cannot lose it all in one day. Similarly, you have little chance of doing well at competitive hot dog eating if you do not get your body used to consuming lots of dogs fast, and get control over your gag reflex. All of these endeavors require planning and preparation.

A good way to get started is to think ahead and consider what awaits you at the end—what will your finished paper look like? One way to visualize your own scholarly paper is to read samples of student-written scholarly papers to get a concrete sense of your end goal. Start with the full-text versions of the samples used in this book or look at the most recently published volume of

uploaded to webcourses for students

your journal.[1] If you are in a seminar class or a thesis program, your professor may have sample papers from former students to share with you. There might also be student notes cited in casebooks from your favorite classes, which you may find particularly interesting because of your interest and background in the area. Looking at completed student works can make you familiar with the expectations for this type of writing, including typical organization, length, and number of footnotes. As you read through these papers, think about things you like or dislike about them, and file these reactions in your mind to guide your thinking about your own scholarly paper.

If you take the time to prepare and train for your scholarly project, the experience can be enjoyable—or at least not miserable! This chapter starts at the planning and preparation stage and takes you through the basics you should know before you begin work on your scholarly project, including the considerations you should keep in mind throughout your project. We conclude this chapter with a description of the scholarly writing process, as an overview to the material covered in this book.

Approaching Your Scholarly Writing Project

You are probably familiar with practical legal writing from previous coursework, work experience, or both. In practical legal writing, you are almost always arguing about how the law should be applied to a particular set of facts, or for an outcome based on that application. Your arguments are, for the most part, bound by existing law, unless you are in the rare situation where you are arguing for an exception or a rule change.

Constructing a scholarly paper is different from writing memoranda, briefs, and client letters because it is your opportunity to put forth your own thoughts on a topic of your choice. The challenge, however, is that to do this you must become an expert on the idea you plan to write about. It may be helpful for you to think about your previous writing projects, and understand how this scholarly writing project is similar or different. During past academic experiences, you may have written an advanced research paper where you had to come up with an original idea and then explain and defend it; this type of project is similar to the scholarly writing task you have in front of you. If your habit has been to write a paper the night before it was due or to take a weekend to write a paper start to finish, know that you will not be able to complete this

---

1. For full citation information for the sample papers cited throughout this book, see About This Book.

type of project in that time frame. You will do yourself a disservice if you fail to recognize the nature of this project and the time and effort it will take to successfully complete it.

As a starting point, a scholarly paper needs both a topic and a thesis to become a project worth writing. Your topic is, of course, the subject area or legal issue your paper addresses. A thesis is a statement of your position on the topic. You need to say something original in a scholarly paper, not just offer an explanation or synthesis of a legal issue. In scholarly writing, the law is just your starting point; what you do with it or say about it is boundless. Thus, a scholarly paper is not only an opportunity for you to choose what to write about, but to choose what you want to say about a topic. That is the beauty of this project; it is yours to say what you want to say. You just have to be sure to say something concrete, thoughtful, and new, or in other words, have a thesis.

Ideally, your thesis will be a one-sentence statement of your position: a statement that includes the basis for the position you have taken and why your position is valid. A thesis can take a variety of forms including an argument for why something should be changed, why something has happened, how to solve a problem, or why an existing solution will not work. You should start thinking about your topic and thesis as two different things. We will return to this in greater detail in Chapter 2.

Variations on Scholarly Papers

There are many terms used to describe a piece of scholarly writing, beyond the generic terms "scholarly paper" or "legal research paper," typically used if you are writing a paper for a law school class. If you are writing for a journal, you might be writing a note or a comment. There are fewer forms of scholarly papers than there are terms to describe them simply because different publishers use different terms for the same type of paper. Generally, papers published in law reviews and journals fall into one of two broad categories: non-student-written and student-written. Non-student authors include law professors, practitioners, judges, and other post-J.D. authors.[2] These non-student authors' scholarly papers are generally published as articles, but may also

---

2. *See, e.g.*, Nestor M. Davidson, *The Problem of Equality in Takings*, 102 Nw. U. L. Rev. 1 (2008) (professor); Richard A. Posner, *Pragmatism Versus Purposivism in First Amendment Analysis*, 54 Stan. L. Rev. 737 (2002) (judge).

be published as essays.[3] Law reviews and journals may publish other types of writing including book reviews and commentaries on recent cases.[4]

As a student-author, how do you know what type of paper you are writing? Some commonly used terms for a student-written scholarly paper are Note, Comment, Case Note, Case Comment, Essay, and to some extent, Article.[5] For example, if you look at the Table of Contents in a recent *Temple Law Review*, you will see the student work categorized as Comments and the non-student work categorized as Articles,[6] but if you look at the *Georgetown Law Journal*, you will see the same type of student scholarly work categorized as Notes and the non-student works categorized as Articles.[7] Thus, journals may use the terms "note" and "comment" interchangeably. The only real difference between these papers and "articles" is authorship, although articles are often longer than notes and comments, and law reviews commonly publish more notes or comments than articles per issue.[8]

A scholarly paper that is focused on a discussion and analysis of a recent case is called a Case Note or Case Comment.[9] Students may be assigned a par-

---

3. *See, e.g.,* John F. Duffy, *Are Administrative Patent Judges Unconstitutional?*, 77 Geo. Wash. L. Rev. 904 (2009).

4. *See, e.g.,* Peter H. Schuck, *Is a Competent Federal Government Becoming Oxymoronic?*, 77 Geo. Wash. L. Rev. 973 (2009) (book review); Recent Case, *Constitutional Law—Free Speech—D.C. Circuit Upholds Access Restriction to Military-Run Newspapers on Forum Analysis Grounds.*—Bryant v. Gates, 532 F.3d 888 (D.C. Cir. 2008), 122 Harv. L. Rev. 2250 (2009).

5. *Harvard Law Review, Columbia Law Review, New York University Law Review, Cornell Law Review, Texas Law Review, Michigan Law Review, and Stanford Law Review* use "Note" to describe student written pieces while *California Law Review, University of Pennsylvania Law Review, University of Chicago Law Review, UCLA Law Review, and Northwestern Law Review* use "Comment." *Yale Law Journal* uses both "Note" and "Comment" to describe student-written pieces.

6. *See, e.g.,* David A. Nagdeman, Comment, *Sovereign Ephemera: State Standing Against the Federal Government for Injuries to Quasi-Sovereign Interests*, 90 Temp. L. Rev. 53 (2017); Gary M. Lucas, Jr., *Voter Psychology and the Carbon Tax*, 90 Temp. L. Rev. 1 (2017) (article).

7. *See, e.g.,* William Yeatman, *An Empirical Defense of* Auer *Step Zero*, 106 Geo. L.J. 515 (2018) (note), Joy Radice, *The Juvenile Record Myth*, 106 Geo. L.J. 365 (2018) (article).

8. Articles generally range from 23,000 words to 36,000 words, and notes or comments generally range from 10,000 words to 16,000 words. *See, e.g.,* Mark Angehr, Comment, *The International Court of Justice's Advisory Jurisdiction and the Review of Security Council and General Assembly Resolutions*, 103 Nw. U. L. Rev. 1007 (2009) (comment; approximately 14,000 words); Robert P. Merges & Jeffrey M. Kuhn, *An Estoppel Doctrine for Patented Standards*, 97 Cal. L. Rev. 1 (2009) (article; approximately 23,500 words).

9. *See, e.g.,* Recent Case, *Immigration Law—Administrative Adjudication—Third and Seventh Circuits Condemn Pattern of Error in Immigration Courts.*—Wang v. Attorney

what type of paper are you writing?

ticular case and told to write an analysis of the opinion including a summary of the case and the author's view of its potential effects. These papers are likely restricted in content, but they do require a thesis. Also keep in mind that case notes and case comments may be published as "notes" or "comments," just as Natalie's Case Note was published as a Note.

An Essay is a term used for relatively shorter scholarly pieces, and essays may be written by professors, practitioners, judges, or students.[10] Some law reviews require their members to write both a note or comment, and an essay. Essays generally have the same research and attribution requirements as notes or articles. The primary distinction between these types of projects is that an essay is shorter than a note or article.[11] Based on a review of several recently published essays, we can tell you that generally an essay is half the length of an average note. Individual journals may set specific limits. Essays may also be published as a group where numerous authors weigh in on a predefined topic. Many journals now also publish an online-only accompaniment with a variety of essays, articles, and commentary.

The term "thesis" (when referring to a full-blown paper) in the law school context is generally reserved for LL.M. scholarly works. If selected for publication, a thesis would likely be categorized as an article,[12] rather than a note or comment, because even though the thesis is a student-written work, the author is a post-J.D. student.

Simple enough, right? There are a few other things to keep in mind with these basic categorical distinctions. Student-written works published by non-journal members may be categorized as articles because notes or comments are reserved for the journal's student members. This depends on the journal's internal publication procedures. Also, keep in mind that you may try to publish your piece after graduation, which may put your scholarly paper into the "articles" category, even though you wrote the paper as a student.

General, 423 F.3d 260 (3d Cir. 2005), and Benslimane v. Gonzales, 430 F.3d 828 (7th Cir. 2005), 119 HARV. L. REV. 2596 (2006).

10. *See, e.g.*, Anthony V. Alfieri, *(Un)Covering Identity in Civil Rights and Poverty Law*, 121 HARV. L. REV. 805 (2008) (professor); Julian Helisek, *The Fault, Dear PCAOB, Lies Not In the Appointments Clause, But In the Removal Power, That You Are Unconstitutional*, 77 GEO. WASH. L. REV. 1063 (2009) (student).

11. Student-written essays generally range from 5,000 words to 8,000 words and professor-written essays are usually, though not always, longer. *See, e.g.*, Helisek, *supra* note 10 (approximately 7,000 words); Duffy, *supra* note 3 (approximately 8,700 words); Alfieri, *supra* note 10 (approximately 16,300 words).

12. *See, e.g.*, Karen DaPonte Thornton, *Fine-Tuning Acquisition Reform's Favorite Procurement Vehicle, the Indefinite Delivery Contract*, 31 PUB. CONT. L.J. 383 (2002).

Does any of this matter? For the most part, not really! If you are unsure whether you are writing a note, a comment, a case note, or an article, there is no need to panic. They are all variations of the same thing: a scholarly paper that follows the basic structure we discuss throughout the book. We use the term "note" to discuss student-authored scholarly papers. Where appropriate, we will refer to the other types of scholarly papers when there is something specific worth mentioning. Keep in mind any restrictions you have on your project, such as seminar topic or length, and adjust our guidance as needed to meet those restrictions. Generally speaking, you can take our guidance on writing a scholarly paper and apply it in whatever context you are writing your scholarly project.

What Else Should I Know Before Beginning My Scholarly Writing Project?

Here, we offer guidance on supervisory resources, audiences, project planning, and personal motivation. We will cover these concepts in more detail in later chapters, but we introduce them now to help you understand your project's framework.

Supervisory Resources

The amount of supervisory oversight given to your paper will vary. Most students who earn academic credit for their scholarly writing project will receive some type of faculty supervision. A faculty supervisor may be assigned to you, or you may have to go recruit a faculty supervisor yourself. In a seminar course, you will have a professor who is an expert on the seminar topic area, but the seminar classes will probably not cover the writing process. Your professor's priority will be to cover the substantive issues of the seminar, not to teach writing. In other contexts, such as writing a thesis or a journal note, you may have a designated co-requisite course to address the writing process, and then also have a faculty advisor working with you on the substantive aspects of your paper. You may also have a senior student working with you on your scholarly project, especially if you are writing a note for a law journal. If you are writing a paper for a journal that is entirely student-run and non-credit bearing, you may have no formal faculty oversight; the student supervisor may be the only authority you have.

As soon as you learn that you are writing a scholarly paper, find out what level of faculty supervision or advising you will receive. If you are writing a paper in a seminar, find out how involved your professor will be in your writing project. For example, you may have to get approval on a topic, but then work independently on the paper. If you are writing a paper as an independent writing project, a thesis, or a journal note, find out whether an advisor is assigned to you or you are responsible for seeking out someone who will agree to be your advisor.

Finding an advisor on your own can be a challenge, but it can be beneficial to have the ability to control who is working with you on your paper. Do not just ask anyone; ask someone you want to work with. Maybe you got to know one of your professors through office hours and you enjoyed that one-on-one time with the professor. Maybe you have an interest in writing on an international law topic and there is a world-renowned international law expert on your school's faculty. You will spend a lot of time working with your advisor, so make this a thoughtful decision.

You should also think about the type of relationship you want to have with your advisor. You can think about advisor-advisee relationships as three general types: heavy-handed, barely-there, and a hybrid. The heavy-handed advisor will want to be actively involved in your scholarly writing process and may even direct you on your topic and thesis. A heavy-handed advisor may be less flexible in letting you develop your ideas, and instead stick to predetermined thoughts, ideas, or conclusions based on his expertise in the area. A heavy-handed advisor will also set interim deadlines, and expect you to meet them with high quality submissions.

There are both drawbacks and advantages to a heavy-handed advisor. The heavy-handedness may seem somewhat paternalistic to you, but it is intended solely to help you complete this large and lengthy project. A heavy-handed advisor is also likely to be a strong cheerleader for you when you do come up with a great thesis and turn in a quality draft, letting you know you are doing good work and giving you constructive guidance to move forward. Truth is, a heavy-handed advisor is probably hard to come by; if you get an advisor this interested and engaged, you should consider yourself lucky.

The barely-there advisor is going to be fairly laid back during your scholarly writing process. The barely-there advisor will be interested in the final product, but not so much in the interim work along the way. Likewise, the advisor may let you figure things out on your own and work at a pace that is comfortable for you. This independence gives you flexibility and control over the development of your scholarly writing project. Still, the barely-there advisor will read the final paper and grade it, but you might not get as much guidance and support as you need or want. You may even find someone who is willing to be your advisor, and is up front about the fact that she will grade the project but will not be available much during the writing process.

A hybrid advisor is probably an ideal supervisor for many students, striking a balance between the heavy-handed and barely-there advisors. The hybrid advisor probably knows when to back off and let the student figure things out, and also knows when to give the student specific directions for moving forward. The hybrid advisor may not be able to provide detailed comments on every interim assignment, but the advisor will take care to provide the student with enough to keep the student on the right track.

Start talking to possible advisors only after you have thought about the characteristics of these three types of advisors and evaluated what you want out of an advisor-advisee relationship. Be honest with yourself and with the professors; the advisor-advisee relationship is for you. True, advisors can have rewarding experiences working closely with students (we can attest to that!), but finding a good advisor is not about making the advisor happy. Take the time to talk to different professors and avoid rushing around at the last minute when you might just settle for anyone who agrees. We further discuss the relationship between you and your supervisor in Chapter 6.

🔆 Ask other students about their experiences working with professors on seminar papers, journal notes, theses, and independent writing projects.

Primary and Secondary Audiences

Scholarly writing involves both primary and secondary audiences. Your primary audience includes all the people who are required to read your paper, for a variety of reasons: your professor grading your paper, peers in your seminar class or on your journal, or journal editors. This is the ultimate audience you need to satisfy. You need to know and meet their expectations on everything from arguments and assertions to technical and formatting matters.

You can be less concerned with the expectations of your secondary audience, but be mindful that various secondary audiences can exist. For example, your secondary audience includes people who read your paper just because it sounds interesting to them. Your secondary audience may include practitioners if your paper is published in a practitioner-directed journal. Students, professors, and research assistants may read your published paper when doing their own research. Potential employers may review your paper as part of your application. Finally, your family and friends may also want to read your paper, and you may be able to count on having a secondary audience of at least one: your mom.

Family notwithstanding, the primary and secondary audiences share common characteristics. Most of these readers are probably lawyers or lawyers-in-training; they are analytical, critical, and want to understand what you are saying. They are easily irritated by unclear thesis statements or a failure to fully defend a well-crafted thesis; they are shocked by obvious flaws in analysis left unresolved. They are likely reading your paper for their own purposes—to determine your grade, to decide whether to publish your paper, to consider how to make a policy argument in a brief, or to get up to speed on a recent development in the law. They might be reading your paper as a springboard to something else, but they do not want to do any work to figure out what you are saying. We will return to talk more specifically about audience in several places where specific choices you must make as an author require consideration of your audience.

Planning Your Project

① topic Statement
② outline   ④ revised
③ 1st draft   ⑤ final
                     ⑥ polished

Planning for your scholarly project is essential to successful completion of your project, given the length of the paper and the amount of time you have to work on it. As soon as you can, find out when your final scholarly project is due and whether you have to submit any interim assignments. The standard set of benchmark assignments includes a topic statement, outline, first draft, revised draft, final draft, and polished paper (the paper you will submit for credit). Your supervisor may ask for all of these benchmark assignments, or none of them, save for the final paper. The interim assignments, in our experience, are essential to success because the size of your paper and the length of time available to work on the project can be overwhelming. Instead of thinking about your project at the broad level of having a 30-page paper due in eight months, breaking up the project into manageable pieces will help you stay committed to and excited about the project.

Once you have broken up your project into manageable pieces, you need to follow deadlines for each piece, whether self-imposed or set by your supervisor. If you are setting your own schedule, you might want to give yourself about a month for each interim assignment, with perhaps an extra few weeks in the beginning to develop a topic statement. You can get a sense of when you will need to plan for large blocks of time to work on your scholarly writing project if you set out the big picture deadlines in a way that helps you stay organized.

Ask your supervisor to help you set up a timeline if you do not have one built into the process (e.g. deadlines in the syllabus). Coordinating with your supervisor might also help make sure your supervisor is available to give you feedback at various benchmarks. And ask your supervisor to set a deadline for getting her feedback to you (if you are comfortable doing so).

After these deadlines are set, take the time to note them in your calendar. This will help you see where approaching deadlines conflict with other assignments or responsibilities (or other things like your sister's wedding or the Super Bowl). You should be rigid about following these deadlines, even if they are self-imposed or you are working with a supervisor who is generous with extensions. Remember that the initial relief at getting an extension just means you have a new deadline to meet, not that you no longer have to do the work. You can always move ahead if you make your deadlines in advance, but it can be hard (and stressful) to recover after you get behind.

Because your work on your scholarly paper will likely span at least an entire semester (or longer with final paper deadlines), you will be well served to spend time planning out the project and incorporating the deadlines into your calendar. This will make the entire project more manageable and less daunting. In planning your own project, consider the following sample week-by-week schedule of tasks. The table below offers suggestions of what to do each week, depending on whether you have a one- or two-semester course or project. The table also includes the types of interim deadlines you may have for your project. Your specific interim deadlines and goals for the scholarly project will determine what is most appropriate for you each week, but the suggestions below should help you figure out how to approach breaking down your project into manageable tasks. The table includes references to readings in the book where they will be most timely and helpful in the writing process.

Sample Week-by-Week Schedule of Tasks

One-Semester Course Deadlines	Weekly Tasks	Two-Semester Course Deadlines
Before the Semester Begins	If you have made your school's law review or a specialized journal, find out what subject matter areas are covered. For many journals, you can easily navigate to an online version of the latest issue through a quick Google search. You can also take a more traditional approach by looking up previously published articles on Lexis Advance, Westlaw, or other electronic databases. If you see a topic that interests you, highlight it now and keep track of developments in the field during the summer so you can enter the school year with a topic already in mind. If you are writing a paper for a seminar class, check out the course materials or textbooks to get familiar with what the course covers. *Read the Introduction to Scholarly Writing: Ideas, Examples, and Execution [hereinafter SWIEE], and consider reading or skimming one of the full-length student notes used in excerpts throughout the book.*	Before the Semester Begins
First Week	Start looking for an advisor; talk to your advisor or professor to find out the full scope of the possibilities for your project. If you already have a topic or area of law in mind, start thinking about how that topic will work within your parameters. *Read the entirety of SWIEE Chapter 1 to get a big picture sense of what it means to write a scholarly paper and to understand how this book can help you in that endeavor. See the section on Supervisory Resources for advice about how to find and choose an advisor.*	First or Second Week
Second or Third Week Topic Brainstorm or Topic List	Start zeroing in on a subject area. If you have a topic in mind, but it does not quite fit in with the subject matter of your journal or course, talk to your professor and brainstorm about whether you can make the topic work. If you are writing in a field that is not covered by the standard first-year curriculum, start developing your horizontal knowledge as you read more material on that subject. *Read SWIEE Chapter 2, Getting Started: Topic and Thesis, and Step One: Finding Your Topic.*	Third or Fourth Week Topic Brainstorm or Topic List

One-Semester Course Deadlines	Weekly Tasks	Two-Semester Course Deadlines
Second or Third Week	Continue background research in your topic area, with an eye toward developing your thesis. Keep track of all your sources—even though your thesis is in flux, you do not want to throw anything away yet. There is no perfect way to keep track of all these sources, but you will need to keep them organized along the lines of an annotated bibliography. *See SWIEE Chapter 3 for a discussion about organizing sources as you develop your horizontal and vertical knowledge, and advice on organizational techniques (e.g., using bullet points in Word, taking notes in a Google Doc, creating a research chart on Google Sheets, or saving authorities in Westlaw folders).* You should find a system that works for you, but keep in mind that in a few weeks you will want to be able to sort all these sources into sub-topics as you create your outline. *Read SWIEE Chapter 2, Initial Research and Pre-emption-Checking, and Chapter 3.*	Third or Fourth Week
Finding a Topic and Developing a Thesis		Finding a Topic and Developing a Thesis
Fourth or Fifth Week	Keep reading and taking notes. Set up alerts to stay current with new sources. *See SWIEE Chapter 3's text boxes with step-by-step instructions for setting alerts in Lexis Advance and Westlaw.* Your topic and initial thesis should be coming together at this point, at least enough to give you some direction for moving forward. *Read SWIEE Chapter 2, Step Two: Developing Your Thesis, and Examples: From Topic to Initial Thesis.*	Sixth Week
Topic and Initial Thesis; Initial Bibliography		Topic and Initial Thesis; Initial Bibliography
Sixth or Seventh Week	As you continue refining your thesis, start planning the other parts of your paper and put those plans into a detailed outline. Focus on broad ideas at this point; you will fill in the finer points as you move toward your first draft. *Reread SWIEE Chapter 3, especially Step Two for advice on how to shape your research into an outline.*	Tenth Week
Detailed Outline		Detailed Outline
Seventh and Eighth Weeks	Use the feedback you received on your Detailed Outline to plan how to move forward on your first draft. Do more research if that is what you need to do; focus on one particular section and dig deep, making sure you fully understand the research you are going to use to develop your arguments. Start filling in your detailed outline	Tenth and Eleventh Weeks
Works-in-Progress Meetings on Detailed Outlines		Works-in-Progress Meetings on Detailed Outlines

One-Semester Course Deadlines	Weekly Tasks	Two-Semester Course Deadlines
	with more bullets and complete sentences. Do not worry about what it looks like; just keep building your draft. When you need a break from drafting, spend an hour checking for proper citation format. This way you are still being productive, but can give your mind a break from the heavy-lifting of crafting a draft. *Consult SWIEE Chapter 4 for a discussion of transitioning to the first draft and advice for drafting the major and minor elements of your paper.*	
Ninth or Tenth Week First Draft	Continue working on your draft. Draft the Introduction and Conclusion; identify research or analytical gaps that need attention. When you need a break from writing, turn to doing additional research or thinking about how to fill these analytical gaps. *Review SWIEE Chapter 4's sections on Drafting the Introduction and Drafting the Conclusion.*	Third Week of Second Semester First Draft
Tenth and Eleventh Weeks Works-in-Progress Meetings on First Drafts	Keep working on your draft. Craft effective, substantive headings that will keep your reader on track. *Read SWIEE Chapter 4's section on Headings.* Keep track of questions and concerns you want to discuss during your works-in-progress meeting or other mechanism for seeking feedback on your draft.	Fourth and Fifth Weeks Works-in-Progress Meetings on First Drafts
Twelfth Week Second Draft	Incorporate all the feedback you received on your first draft into your second draft. Start thinking big picture about how your paper is coming together and develop a plan for moving forward based on the results of your evaluation. *Read SWIEE Chapter 5 for advice on how to evaluate your draft and directions for how to revise it. Also consult SWIEE Chapter 6 for a discussion about how to incorporate feedback, including how to apply feedback globally to your paper and what to do when you disagree with the feedback.*	Eighth or Ninth Week Second Draft
Thirteenth or Fourteenth Week Individual Conferences on Second Draft	Take a step back from your paper; take a break for at least a few days to give yourself the opportunity for a fresh perspective as you near the end of your scholarly writing project. If you have the energy now, start polishing by working through your paper for grammar and style	Ninth and Tenth Weeks Individual Conferences on Second Draft

One-Semester Course Deadlines	Weekly Tasks	Two-Semester Course Deadlines
	issues. *See SWIEE Chapter 7 for a list of 10 common errors and examples for how to fix them. Also consider doing a reverse outline of your paper, as described in SWIEE Chapter 5's section on Evaluating your Organizational Choices.*	
Exam Week Final Paper	Polish your paper, moving from the large to small scale. Revisit your Introduction and Conclusion to determine whether they fit with the final version of your paper, revising as needed. Review your footnotes, checking for accuracy and technical compliance. Confirm all cross-referencing is correct. *Reread SWIEE Chapter 4's sections on drafting introductions and conclusions.*	Exam Week Final Paper
Post-Final Paper Submission	Think about submitting your paper for publication or entering a writing competition. *Consult SWIEE Chapter 8 for a detailed discussion of how to get your paper published and a list of competitions to consider entering.*	Post-Final Paper Submission

---

You can also use technology to plan your project and keep yourself on track. Consider using Google calendar and sync the project milestones to your phone. You can customize the alerts to give yourself as many reminders as you need. Also consider blocking out days on your calendar as scholarly writing days. You can share your Google Calendar if there are other people you want to be aware of your commitments or schedule.

Setting Yourself Up for Success

Different students will have different standards for what constitutes a successful scholarly writing experience. As a new scholarly writer, you need to establish what success means for you and think about how your strengths and limitations as a writer will affect your ability to achieve it. Whether your goal for the paper is lofty or simply achievable, you will have to spend time and effort completing this project. This time and effort will be well-spent if you possess some self-awareness about your strengths and weaknesses as a writer. For example, if you know you write best in the morning, you can schedule your writing time on your calendar accordingly. If you know that you tend to procrastinate, you might set pre-deadlines for yourself, so you have an extra 2–3 day window before the actual deadline. Taking time for self-assessment is critical to a successful writing project because it can help you recognize potential issues in advance when you have time and energy to take action.

Think about the aspirations you have for your scholarly paper. Are you excited about the opportunity to write about a topic of your choosing? Are you already thinking about a journal in which you would like to be published? Do you intend to meet the minimum requirements to earn credit, but do nothing further? Success can mean anything from publishing in a top law review to fulfilling a graduation requirement to winning a prestigious writing competition. In order to set yourself up for success, you need to reflect upon your ultimate goal.

At this point, you should have a good sense of what it means to take on a scholarly writing project. Now, think about your personal goals for the project and what issues you can anticipate even at this early stage in the writing process.

Checklist: Getting Started

great potential discussion prompts

- What are my goals for the paper?
- What are my deadlines and interim assignments?
  - How much time do I have between deadlines?
  - Is there a major event on my calendar that I will have to work around?
- What about this process do I find most and least daunting?
- What can I learn from past writing projects?
  - In other writing projects, what part of the work do I most look forward to (editing, revising, getting something down on paper/computer)?
  - What part do I want to avoid (same list of options)?
  - Where do I get stuck (getting started, picking up after a break, footnotes, etc.)?
- What other issues and obstacles can I anticipate and address at this stage?
- What other people can I use as resources during the writing process (advisors, librarians, fellow students)?

This self-assessment can be an important first step toward making the scholarly writing process introduced below (and described in detail in the chapters that follow) work for you.

The Scholarly Writing Process

As we see it, there are five stages to the scholarly writing process:

1. Thinking
2. Preparing
3. Executing
4. Refining
5. Finishing

You will notice that the chapters in this book are organized around these stages. Even though we have identified these five stages as a broad framework for thinking about the writing process, these are not steps that you will move through, one-by-one, finishing one completely before you start the next. The scholarly writing process is recursive, and the stages give you a rough structural guide to your progress. You are probably in the Thinking stage now, and it is in many ways the most important stage. Good writing comes from good thinking, and it is worth spending due time during this stage because you want to come up with a topic and thesis that are interesting to you. You will work on this scholarly writing project for a long time, and writing on an undesirable topic will only make the experience more challenging. You may want to work on establishing relationships during this stage—with law librarians, supervising faculty, senior law students as appropriate, and other people you may want to rely on throughout your scholarly writing process. We will discuss this stage in more detail in Chapter 2.

The Preparing stage is a time to continue thinking about your topic and thesis, but here you will engage with your topic and thesis through in-depth research. During this stage, you will fully research your topic and thesis, with the ultimate goal of developing the requisite amount of expertise on your topic as described in Chapter 3.

The next two stages, Executing and Refining, are where you will do the bulk of your writing. During the Executing stage, covered in further detail in Chapter 4, you will plan and write your first draft and any accompanying interim assignments. This is the time to think about large scale organization and begin to put together the pieces of your paper. Your goal during this stage is to develop a good working draft that you can take to the next stage.

The Refining stage is a time for evaluation, where you will step back from your project and look at it with fresh eyes. You will use this stage to identify gaps in your writing, places where you need to more fully explain a point, or perhaps have written too much. During this stage, you will critically evaluate your thesis by asking whether it is clear, and revise your paper to more fully support your thesis. You may also decide to rework the organization of your paper after seeing it as a whole draft. In Chapter 5, we discuss specific guidance and strategies for you to use during the Refining stage. As discussed further in Chapter 6, the Refining stage is also a time for you to receive and incorporate feedback (including peer edits and faculty comments) to shape and reshape your arguments in support of your thesis, leading to an overall stronger paper.

The final stage, Finishing, is covered in the two final chapters of the book. This stage is where you will focus on proofreading and polishing your paper. This stage is intended to emphasize technical edits, and focus less on the substantive aspects of your paper, which should be in good shape by the time you get to Finishing. In Chapter 7, we identify common errors in scholarly writing and offer self-editing strategies for preparing your final paper. In Chapter 8, we discuss strategies and logistics for publishing your paper.

CHAPTER 2

THINKING:
FINDING YOUR TOPIC AND DEVELOPING YOUR THESIS

As you know from reading Chapter 1, writing a scholarly paper means finding a topic (a subject area or legal issue) and developing a thesis (a statement of your position or argument within that topic area). Scholarly writing may feel more liberating than some of the practical legal writing you have done because you are in control of your topic and thesis. There will be no canned fact pattern as a starting point to your scholarly writing project, and no fictitious jurisdiction in which you have to argue your points. As a more advanced law student and legal writer, you have earned the right to say what you want to say in your scholarly paper. Your subject area might be somewhat limited based on your seminar course, thesis program, or law journal. But within these subject area restrictions, you still have the chance to pursue what you want to write about.

Although this freedom from restraints is exciting, choosing a topic and developing a thesis can be the most challenging and time-consuming tasks of a scholarly writing project. Students consistently report to us that this is the hardest part of the process. We cannot wave a magic wand and help you find the perfect topic and thesis. We do, however, have guidance that can help you find a topic and develop a thesis. The more time and thought you can devote to this stage of the writing process, the more likely you are to come up with a topic and thesis that will satisfy your requirements and make for an enjoyable writing experience.

Before you start looking for a topic and drafting your thesis, find out what, if any, topic or thesis restrictions are on your paper. For example, if you are assigned to write a case comment, your topic and thesis must be linked to the case. Because of this narrow scope, you should read the case first before you even try to think about a topic and thesis. Similarly, if you are writing a paper for a seminar course, a thesis program, or a specialty journal, find out what specific limits are on your topic and thesis.

Also make sure to find out what, if anything, your supervisor wants to review with respect to your topic. Some professors will require you to submit a topic statement and short explanation of what you expect to write about in your paper. Your journal editor might require you to turn in three possible topics for your journal note, and then either choose one for you or help you choose the best one. Or you may be left to choose your own topic without any review.

In this chapter, we present the Thinking stage in two steps: finding your topic and developing your thesis. But before we discuss these two steps, we begin with an introduction to the differences between topics and theses, and explain what characteristics you should keep in mind when you work through the first step to find your topic.

Getting Started: Topic and Thesis

The starting point for your topic search is the broad area of the law in which you are situated. This may be dictated by the subject matter of your journal, the scope of your graduate program, or the syllabus of the seminar in which you are enrolled. If you are writing as a member of a general law review or doing an independent writing project, you may be free to choose any area of the law.

Even if you are in some way limited by the forum in which you are writing, most of these subject areas are fairly broad, and your first step is narrowing them to a topic within the subject area. You may be able to start with a fairly narrow topic, depending on the level of command you have of the subject or the amount of direction you receive from your seminar professor or journal editors. More often, though, student scholarly writers will start with a broad topic area and then, after some initial research or discussion with a supervisor, whittle the topic down to a more specific, narrower topic before developing a thesis. For example, if "immigration law" is your starting point, you can narrow it to a topic such as "the widow penalty in immigration law." Or if your starting topic is "art law" and you are writing for an international law journal, you will want to find a topic at the intersection of international law and art law. The topic-narrowing is an essential part of the process; the more you can narrow your topic from a general subject area, the easier developing a thesis will likely be for you because you will have some outer limits on where you can go with your thesis.

thesis →

Your thesis is what you decide to say about your topic: it is your position, argument, or solution; and defense of that position, argument, or solution. Remember, writing a scholarly paper is an opportunity for you to tell the world what you think, and why you are right! The thesis is also what gives you ownership of the topic. This is not just an opinion piece, of course—you will defend your thesis with authority and legal analysis—but the bottom line is you have to decide what to say. And you have to say it clearly and without hedging.

Finding a topic and developing a thesis may not always be two distinct steps, and students have many different starting points when it comes to finding a topic and a thesis. Some graduate students enroll in an LL.M. program with an idea for a thesis already in mind. Some journals provide new members with a short list of topics from which they can (or must) choose. Other student writers have some ideas based on their past educational, professional, or personal experiences. If you are in any of these, or other, fortunate situations, where you have a topic or thesis idea from the very beginning of the writing process, that is good news for you!

If, however, you have no idea what your topic will be, you are in good company. Most students arrive at the beginning of the scholarly writing process without a topic. You are probably anxious to choose a topic and get started; you might feel pressure to just pick something and get this decision over with. But do yourself a favor; do not rush this part! Choosing a topic without care and deliberation can leave you with a topic for which you cannot muster the energy and enthusiasm required for a project of this magnitude.

There are three basic characteristics of a "good" topic. A good topic is interesting to you and your audiences, manageable, and thesis-worthy. It is worth thinking about these characteristics before you start the process of finding your topic because you can use them as a foundation to help you get to a topic that works for you.

3 charac of good topic

1. Your topic must interest you and your audiences.

If you only get one thing out of this chapter, take this advice to heart: Pick a topic you are interested in because you have to spend a lot of time working with it. Think about it—if you choose a topic that you do not really care about, that you think is boring, or (worse!), a topic you do not understand, how hard will it be to motivate yourself to work on that paper month after month after month? Unlike other writing projects, this project will probably take at least one semester—possibly two—to complete, and if your paper is selected for publication, you may spend more than a year working on it. That means you have to be invested and interested in your topic.

At the same time, your paper cannot just be all about you—you want to consider your audiences and choose a topic that will interest or excite them. As we discussed in Chapter 1, your paper has both primary and secondary audiences. Pleasing these audiences will expand your chances for publication and earning a good grade. What do your primary audiences want you to write about? First, they want you to write about something within any parameters they have set for you: the subject matter of your journal, course, or graduate program. Second, they want you to produce a paper that will attract attention and generate interest, especially to publishers. This means making sure your topic is fresh and interesting. Third, they want your paper to avoid extremes. For example, if your journal note topic is too complex or too boring for the average law student journal editor to follow your argument or if your seminar paper topic is too simple, your paper will probably alienate or distract your audiences.

Remember your broader secondary audience, too. If you are able to write and publish in a field that will grab an employer's attention, you will get more out of your paper than just a bullet point on your resume. You may be able to use your paper to get interviews and improve your marketability by considering employers as part of your secondary audience. For example, perhaps you know you want to work for the Federal Trade Commission after law school. Choosing an antitrust topic or a topic related to consumer protection will give you the opportunity to demonstrate your interest in the type of work the FTC does. You may be able to use the ideas expressed in your paper to get an interview, and then impress the interviewer with your knowledge on an area of interest to the agency. In contrast, if you are considering writing about a controversial topic, addressing a particularly sensitive issue, or taking an incendiary position, some employers may decide against interviewing or hiring you based on your scholarly paper. Remember these topics might be interesting, but not something you want to pursue for this project.

2. Your topic must be manageable.

Unfortunately, interest alone is not enough when it comes to topic selection. One common problem students encounter when writing scholarly papers is choosing an overly broad topic. Think about whether you will be able to get a handle on your topic with enough understanding to write a scholarly paper within the time frame you have been given for the project. Choosing an overbroad topic is a surefire way to get in over your head; be open to the possibility that you will need to narrow your topic to make it manageable.

You may find it difficult to determine whether your topic is manageable; manageability can only be determined on a case-by-case basis. If you know nothing about a topic, you may need more time than your schedule allows to get the requisite background knowledge in the field. You might start with something unmanageable (for example, a comparison of the treatment of a copyright issue in two different countries) and then trim it down to something less burdensome (a challenge to the conventions in one of the two systems instead). Or you might come up with an idea that involves a fairly new area of the law about which little has been written. This scenario can cause a manageability issue because there may not be enough source material for you to rely on in writing your paper.

A topic can also be unmanageable because of the research support it would require. For example, your topic may require information that you do not have access to, such as classified documents. If you have a great idea, but it turns out the sources will not be available until 2090, that idea needs some rethinking. Or if you find a topic that requires you to work with a lot of international sources, you might have an issue because you will need to translate international cases. Or you might be able to handle the translation, but then you need to build in time for that added task.

You might be able to recognize manageability issues like these based on your initial research into a topic. But you should also consider asking for your supervisor's opinion on the manageability of your topic, especially if your supervisor does not require approval of a topic before moving forward. If your supervisor reviews and approves your topic, you can be relatively certain that the topic is manageable. If your professor suggests that you narrow your topic before moving on, take that advice because chances are your professor knows the area better than you do and can more easily spot manageability issues.

We mention manageability not to deter you from taking on a challenging scholarly project, but to encourage you to be realistic as you select your topic. You may decide that you are willing (and have the time) to learn about a topic area that most students would likely avoid, or you might be so excited about learning about a topic that you decide you do not care if you have to do more work than your peers. Taking on a project that borders on unmanageable may pay off for you, in terms of publication opportunities, your grade, impressing faculty and peers, and even potential employers. Just know what you are getting yourself into, and give yourself time to evaluate whether you want to (and can) do what you need to do to make a challenging topic manageable.

3. Your topic must be thesis-worthy.

A topic is thesis-worthy when it can yield many different sub-topics and, ultimately, thesis statements. To determine whether your topic is thesis-worthy, you may find it helpful to visualize the relationship between a topic and thesis.

(handwritten note: ⌐Draw a picture of connections)

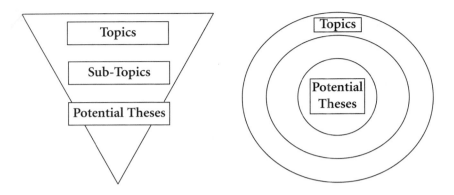

Remember how we described the relationship between a topic and thesis earlier in this chapter: your thesis is a sub-part of your topic. One way to think about the topic-thesis relationship is as an inverted pyramid; the wider area at the top is your topic, and the narrower part at the bottom is your thesis. There can be a number of sub-topics within the area in between the top and bottom leading to a variety of thesis statements.

You can also think about the topic-thesis relationship as a series of concentric circles. The outer-most ring is your topic area at its broadest point. Each successive circle moving toward the center represents a narrowing of your topic and as you get closer to the center, there can be multiple theses.

Aim to choose a topic that can yield many different thesis statements. You want to choose a topic that is narrow enough that it is manageable, but that is wide enough at this early stage that it can generate several thesis statements. Students often feel stuck if they start with a topic that is too narrow; this approach to finding a topic will help you avoid getting stuck because you will have a number of thesis options from the outset.

With these characteristics of a good topic in mind, you are ready to move forward to finding your topic.

Step One: Finding Your Topic

Student writers are often overwhelmed when they first consider what they want to write about because they begin by looking for a thesis. This instinct is natural—of course you want to determine what you want to say and get the writing process started. This approach does not work, however, because it jumps over an important first step; you must identify a topic before you can craft your thesis. Instead of this thesis-first approach, we teach students to start with an idea. You need only a small kernel or nugget of an idea to get yourself started on the road to finding a topic. From this idea, which need not be legal, you can do research to find legal topics implicated by your idea. This "idea-first" approach to finding a topic gives you the opportunity to start with something that you know interests you, even if you know very little about it.

To help you achieve this first step, finding your topic, we first explain the idea-first approach in more detail and then give you specific techniques to help you brainstorm for ideas. Finally, we explain how to use your ideas to find a topic.

Idea-First Approach

The idea-first approach begins with you thinking about all the things—legal issues, current events, that case you read for Con Law, an experience from college, that Instagram post—that are interesting to you right now. Be open-minded and cast a wide net to generate a list of ideas from which you can craft potential topics. Ideas can come from anywhere—something you like, something you dislike, something you are good at, something you are not good at, or a past experience.

Once you have some ideas, your goal is to find topics implicated by your ideas. Using the three characteristics of a good topic as your guide, think about how your idea might relate to a general area of the law. How this transition actually happens will vary based on your level of existing knowledge with the topic, how sophisticated your idea is, and what, if any, structural restraints you have on your topic. For example, if you came to your idea because of a past experience, you may have a high level of knowledge already. This may make your transition from idea to topic seamless because you automatically think about your idea within the topic area. If you do not have this background on your idea, you should jump ahead to do some initial research to help you make the transition from idea to topic.

For example, imagine you have been worrying that children who are living alone on the street are not properly fed or educated, and you think this is unacceptable. From there, you have an idea that poor children should be adopted so they can have homes, which will help solve the problem you have identified. You then take that idea and build on it to think about international adoption as your (very broad) topic. With that in mind, you do some initial research and ultimately narrow your topic by region (Latin America) and segment of the population (street children).[1]

---

1. One of our research assistants, Lindsey Welsford, used this idea to find her paper topic.

The idea-first approach works even if you have topic limitations. Students often feel that their initial idea needs to fit within a topic limitation; this is not the case. You can still start with your idea, unrestricted by specialty topic or anything else, and work with it to see how you can connect your idea to your assigned specialty topic area, general law review requirements (e.g., issue must be of national significance), or other limitations.

For example, imagine you are a student on an international law journal tasked with writing a scholarly note on an international law topic. You have not yet taken any classes on international law and are worried about finding a topic within this topic limitation. However, you studied racial profiling in an undergraduate class, and found it fascinating. That is enough of an idea to move forward on developing a topic, even though there is no obvious connection between racial profiling and international law. You might think about racial profiling in airports, and then do some initial research to find a topic about racial profiling in Europe and the United States. This way, you have found a way to write about your idea and also meet your international law topic requirement.[2]

You might also choose a topic based on something you want to learn more about. For example, Monica came to law school with an interest in art law and a background in Italian. Because there were no course offerings in art law, she wanted to pursue this topic through her international law journal note. She started by searching for news on art law, and eventually came across the case of Marion True, a former curator of the Getty in Los Angeles, California, who was on trial for receipt of stolen goods and participation in a conspiracy to traffic in stolen goods. After reading more about this case, Monica identified key words and then used those search terms in Lexis and Westlaw databases to find legal sources. While she was still developing her ideas, Monica organized a visit by an art law speaker as part of her role in the Art Law Society at her law school. She sought out two experts in the field and asked one whether he would be willing to talk to her about her topic. Armed with some broad ideas on what she wanted to write about, Monica talked to this practitioner and he helped guide her to crystallize her idea into a workable topic.

An idea could also come from an existing relationship you have with a professor or an area of law in which you have developed an interest. For example, Collin worked as a research assistant for a professor widely-recognized as an expert in the field of federal procurement law. Collin knew he wanted to write on something in the broad topic of federal procurement and originally thought his topic could be the Federal Corrupt Practices Act (FCPA), as an

---

2. Another of our research assistants, Joe Pollak, took this route to his paper.

easy transition from some of his work as a research assistant. But then a reporter called the professor to ask about contractor employees winning employment discrimination lawsuits against their government supervisors. The professor had not heard about this and he shared the issue with Collin, inspiring him to take this on as his topic for his law review note. This topic, though different from his original FCPA idea, still satisfied Collin's interest in writing on federal procurement, and came with the added benefit of cutting-edge timeliness.

These experiences are unique to these student authors, but that's the point—every student will take a unique path to finding her ultimate topic and thesis. The important thing is that you keep an open mind so that every potential path is open to you. Similarly, do not limit yourself by committing to a topic too early; it is perfectly acceptable to work with a few ideas before deciding which idea will be the focus of your paper. Then, after some initial research that helps familiarize you with the topics, you can choose your specific topic. For example, Collin knew he was interested in writing about the topic of personal services contracts, but started with multiple ways to approach his paper. He considered several angles: arguing for a change in the Title VII statutory definition of "employee," arguing in favor of the existing statutory definition of "federal employee" as sufficient to prevent one of the problems he identified with contractors benefiting from the Civil Service laws, or arguing that the distinction between civil servants and contractors is obsolete, thus making the prohibition on personal services contracts an impractical hurdle.

The caution here about committing to a topic goes both ways, however, because you also want to be careful not to drag out committing to a topic as a way to procrastinate working on your scholarly project. When you find a topic that meets the good topic characteristics and you think you can enjoy learning and writing about, commit to it! You can then move forward to the next step.

Tools for Brainstorming Ideas

You might feel like you have no ideas for your paper. We doubt that this is true, but if you are feeling that way, take the time to brainstorm for ideas. Keep in mind your brainstorming is about coming up with ideas that interest you; you are not yet looking for what you could say about the material.

Start with what you know, or at least what you know you are interested in. You might have some interests based on your summer work experience or classes you enjoyed. If you had a career before law school, draw on your professional and personal experiences that give you a different perspective than some other law students. Even though you are probably not yet an expert on any particular area of the law or legal issue, identifying things that interested you in the past may give you some ideas of what you might like to write about now.

Look around in your everyday life for things that just do not seem right or do not sit well with you for some reason. This could be anything from how you got a traffic ticket after following a misplaced Yield sign to a recent Supreme Court opinion on race-based preferences in employment practices. What sorts of things get you excited and engaged? Are there issues that you like to talk about and debate with friends? Think about things from classes that stuck out in your mind, issues that sparked your interest for whatever reason. Perhaps your professor discussed an unclear or inconsistent area of law, and you were interested in learning more. Your casebooks might also lead you to an idea. Many casebooks have notes and questions following the case excerpts. Often these notes ask questions about unsettled areas of law or issues the law does not address. Those questions present possible paths to a topic. Check out your library's collection of casebooks if you are interested in writing on something you have not yet studied in law school.

Take your brainstorming beyond your thoughts by talking to — and listening to — friends, family, peers, and even strangers. Your friends and family will probably not have a bank of ideas for you, but they will have things to talk about, and these things might give you an idea. Find out what they are talking about, what sorts of things are problematic for them in their work or personal lives. Are there things they do not understand or wish were different? Are they complaining about something that happened to them? Are they happy or excited about something? You do not necessarily need to start with a problem or something bad; you might be able to get an idea about something good when you ask how or why it turned out that way. You can also get ideas from overhearing strangers' conversations. We do not advocate that you spy on people, but if you are in line at the bookstore, and you hear two students you do not know talking about how they use a drug to help them study, you might get an idea from that conversation. Keep your eyes and ears open, and be open to anything that might spark an idea!

While brainstorming, consider keeping a journal or some form of notes to keep track of your ideas. You can return to this list to think about which ideas most interest you, and then work from one idea or several ideas to find a topic or possible topics. At this point, record anything and everything that interests you. Keep notes on why you think something would make a good topic, or what about the topic interests you. But do not stop there; also note why something seems like it might not work. If you do some preliminary research on one of your ideas and decide you would need an engineering education to be able to fully understand the issues and how to offer solutions, make a note of that. That will help you steer away from unmanageable topics.

As you are brainstorming, consider meeting with someone in your law school's writing center. You might not have anything written yet, but the writing center staff is often equipped to listen and ask questions to help you talk and think through your ideas. Plus you can benefit from establishing a relationship with someone early in the process when you are ready later to get some input on a draft.

If you are not getting any ideas based on people and experiences, consider news and information sources as useful brainstorming tools. These sources provide a wide coverage of topic areas, and they are easy to access from television, radio, or online. You can skim headlines or articles to see if something sparks an interest. You can listen to talk radio or podcasts to hear what other people are interested in or what issues are under debate. Consider blogs, social media, and special news programs, too, as fodder for ideas. You can read topical blogs on topic areas that interest you or are related to your specialty journal topic area (e.g., http://dunlapcodding.com/phosita/ (an intellectual property law blog) or http://www.governmentcontractslawblog.com/ (a government contracts blog)). Many law journals include accompanying online-only content. You might get some ideas from the commentary on current issues or questions raised in responses. For example, *Harvard Law Review* uses the online-only *Harvard Law Review Forum*, https://harvardlawreview.org/topics/forum/, to publish responses to articles and commentaries on current issues.

You never know what you will run across or what might lead to you to a topic; that is the point of reviewing these varied sources. For example, Emily got the idea for her note topic after she read a *New York Times* article about how hard it was to discharge student loan debt in bankruptcy.[3] She found the article compelling and thought it would also be of interest to student readers such as her journal editors.

Following Twitter hashtags in your areas of interest can keep an influx of ideas coming. For example, Jessie might have followed #CrimPro while she was working on her comment. You can also follow more general legal writing topics. Popular recent hashtags include #legalwriting #appellatetwitter and #legaltech.

---

3. Tara Siegel Bernard, *Judges Rebuke Limits on Wiping Out Student Loan Debt*, N.Y. TIMES, July 17, 2015, available at https://www.nytimes.com/2015/07/18/your-money/student-loans/judges-rebuke-limits-on-wiping-out-student-loan-debt.html.

One cautionary note about using news and current events as brainstorming fodder: Because the publication process means there will be at least a couple of months between you completing your paper and it appearing in print, be careful with ideas about hot topics that will have cooled by the time your paper is published. You can definitely use the news to get ideas, but try to find something that will stand the lapse of time to publication.

Your law school's library may also have some topic selection resources available to help you construct a productive brainstorming process.[4] For example, Georgetown Law Library has an online research guide for writing a scholarly paper, available at http://guides.ll.georgetown.edu/seminar_papers. Georgetown Law also has a number of topic-specific research guides including guides on international law, state specific research resources, and legal history. Many law libraries make these resources publicly available so you may want to reach outside your own library for a specific topic area. You may be surprised by what you can find in perusing a library's list of research guides. For example, Georgetown Law has an Ebola Research Guide and UCLA School of Law has a research guide on hate crimes. The Library of Congress also has an extensive list of legal research guides, available at https://www.loc.gov/law/help/how-find.php.

You should also consider using electronic research platforms (Lexis, Westlaw, and Bloomberg) to combine some of these news and information sources to possibly speed up your brainstorming process, or to find materials you would not think of on your own. These platforms provide hundreds of databases of materials, organized and searchable in ways that can help you develop some topic ideas. For example, rather than going to five individual news sources' websites, you can use the electronic databases to skim all the recent articles in those sources, and many more, at the same time, with one date-restricted search. Also, because the materials are organized by topics and sub-topics, you may find materials you never knew existed, and would not come across if you did your own website search for sources. Students often assume that a generic internet search is an equally good starting point to search for topic ideas, but Lexis, Westlaw, and Bloomberg contain news sources that are subscription-only (meaning they are not publicly available and will not show up with a Google search).

To help you get started, we have included a short list of specific tools available on these research platforms.[5] Keep in mind that Lexis, Westlaw, and Bloomberg are constantly trying to improve their platforms, which means that the most reliable (and current) instructions will always be those provided by

---

4. Thank you to Georgetown Law Reference Librarian Andy Lang for the helpful suggestions and tips included here.

5. All electronic research directions in the book were correct at the time of publication.

the platform itself. There are typically multiple pathways to access the same content on these platforms. We have selected some specific paths here to illustrate the various resources, but you should not consider these tips as an exclusive list. Also note that the electronic research platforms provide tutorials in addition to the standard "Help" link, and the tutorials are an additional tool available to help you think about a topic and get familiar with the tools to learn more about that topic.

Use Lexis Advance Resources

- *Browse Lexis Practice Centers.*
  1. Click the Practice Area or Industry tab.
  2. On the bottom left, click into the View Our Practice Centers link.
  3. Select a Practice Center. Most Practice Centers have a box for News & Analysis that pulls from multiple news sources in the Lexis platform. A box listing "Top Sources" will include significant secondary sources like treatises and journals.
- *Skim treatises, law reviews, and journals*
  1. Click the Practice Area or Industry tab and select a topic.
  2. Each topic landing page has a Secondary Materials category highlighting some of the more significant treatises or journals and a link allowing you to view the complete list.
  3. Clicking into a resource listed under the Treatises, Practice Guides & Jurisprudence category will take you to a table of contents for the source.
  4. Use the + signs to open up a more detailed view of the table of contents.
  5. Skim through the table of contents materials to find something that interests you or gives you an idea.
  6. Some titles have a "What's New" section at the beginning of the table of contents that allows you to see recent updates to the source.
- *Skim legal news.* Lexis has a robust collection of both legal and general news sources. You can browse the category or retrieve specific publications by typing the title into the search bar and selecting the publication from the dropdown menu.
  1. To browse legal news publications, select the Legal News content type.

2. Within Legal News you can narrow by publisher, jurisdiction, or subject.

3. By exploring the publisher categories you may find several sources of interest, such as ALM Media publications, Mealey's, and Law360.

4. If you select a specific publication, Lexis will take you to an Advanced Search template to search within that publication. To browse all articles rather than run a search, click the Actions button at the top of the screen and select "Get all documents for this source" from the dropdown menu. From here, you can apply filters to narrow the list by date, subject, practice area, etc.

5. To set up an email alert for a publication, click the bell icon next to the Source Results title.

6. Other good sources that are difficult to browse include the Emerging Issues series and Newstex Blogs. The easiest way to access these sources is to start typing them into the search bar without searching, then clicking the source from the suggestions that appear as a dropdown menu.

- *Skim general news sources.*
  1. Click on the News link under Content Type.
  2. There are a number of categories you can apply to search combinations of different publications. To change the scope, click the small "*i*" next to the category.
  3. You can also pick a title from the list of Top Publications.
  4. Similar to the process described above for Legal News, if you select a specific publication, Lexis will take you to an Advanced Search template to search within that source. To view the articles rather than running a search, click into the Actions button at the top of the screen and select "Get all documents for this source" from the dropdown. This will allow you to browse all articles or apply filters to narrow the list by date, subject, practice area, etc.
  5. If there is another publication that you want to see that is not featured on the News page, you may be able to find it by going to the Browse dropdown at the top of the screen, selecting Sources, then either searching the title with the "Find a source" bar or browsing by category for News. Then follow the same steps above to access the full list of articles for that publication.

- *Create alerts to retrieve information for you.*
  1. Any search you run can be set to automatically update and send new results via email. This is an easy way to stay on top of new developments.
  2. After you click Search, your search string will appear at the top of the screen; click the bell icon next to your search to create an alert. The pop-up will prompt you to select content to search, set the frequency, and set delivery times and format for the alert.

Use Westlaw Resources

- *Browse Practitioner Insights pages.*
  1. From the Westlaw research page, click into the Practice Areas tab.
  2. Practice areas that have a Practitioner Insights page are indicated with an asterisk (*).
  3. Practitioner Insights pages aggregate content from a range of sources, including news, legal news, and blogs to keep you up to date on developments in that practice area.
- *Browse practice area materials.*
  1. Not all practice areas have Practitioner Insights pages, however, you can still access a wide range of secondary source material by browsing through the Practice Areas tab.
  2. The landing page for a Practice Area has a combination of primary and secondary sources. In some instances there may be links to separate, jurisdiction-specific practice centers in the right-hand column.
  3. Under the Secondary Sources category, Westlaw will highlight some of the more significant titles and provide a link to see all secondary sources in your selected subject area.
- *Skim treatises, law reviews, and journals.*
  1. Click into Secondary Sources from the All Content tab.
  2. Apply filters to narrow your results by topic and publication type. It might be useful to limit your initial list to "Law Reviews

      & Journals," "Texts & Treatises," and "Legal Newspapers & Newsletters."

   3. Clicking into a Treatise takes you to the table of contents for that publication. Use the + signs to expand the table of contents, allowing you to skim the materials to find something that interests you or gives you an idea.

   4. Clicking into a journal, law review, or newsletter will usually provide a list of its 10 most recent articles, and you can use the search bar to search within that publication.

- *Skim news sources.*
  1. Click into News under the All Content tab. The News page collects trending headlines from a range of sources and allows more directed searching.
  2. From the News page, you can select certain kinds of News content to search such as Blogs; Journals, Magazines, & Newsletters; or Newspapers. You can also click into the News Index and browse to specific publications by title.
  3. Opening a specific source will provide a list of the 10 most recent articles, and you can use the search bar to search within that publication.

- *Skim the West Key Number Digest Outline.*
  1. Under Tools, click into the West Key Number System link.
  2. Skim through the West Key Number Digest Outline to find something that interests you or gives you an idea.
  3. Open up a more detailed view of each Key Number and specific issue by clicking on the links.
  4. You can search at any level. You can also specify which content you want to search by clicking the checkbox to "Specify Content to Search" at the top, checking boxes next to the appropriate content, and then entering your search terms.

- *Create WestClip search alerts.*
  1. To create new search alerts from scratch, click the Alerts button in the top right corner of the screen.
  2. Click the + Create Alert button. You will have choices to create alerts based on Dockets, Publications, KeyCite, and more, but to create an alert for a specific search, select "WestClip."
  3. It will first ask you to set a name for the alert.

4. Next, select content by type, jurisdiction, and practice area. You will have options to select either broad or narrow categories. Click "Add" next to a specific content type to set that as the material your search will look through. A running tally of the categories you select will be displayed on the right.
5. Then you will enter your search string. Use Boolean Terms & Connectors to achieve the best results.
6. Next, you can choose delivery settings, specifying how you would like to receive the results.
7. Finally, you will set the frequency for your alert.
8. Westlaw offers guidance on creating alerts through the help function.

Use Bloomberg Law Resources

• *Browse BNA Law Reports.*
1. From the Browse All Content menu in the top left corner of the landing page, open the News category, then select BNA Law Reports. BNA content is widely respected and frequently used by practitioners.
2. Browse the BNA Law Report subject areas. One particularly useful Report is the United States Law Week, which provides weekly coverage of general legal developments and monitors circuit splits.
3. If you find a Report in a relevant subject area, you can set email notifications that will push new issues of the Report directly to your email. To set an alert, click the Manage Email Notifications button in the top right of the screen.

Make an appointment to meet with your law school's Lexis, Westlaw, or Bloomberg Academic Account Representative to get one-on-one assistance with topic brainstorming.

Shortcuts

You might be wondering whether there are any shortcuts to finding a topic. Of course there are, but in this context a "shortcut" is really just a way to get someone else to choose a topic for you. In our experience, most students who run into problems with their scholarly papers can trace the problem back to a topic selection strategy that led them to a bad topic (or at least a bad topic for them). This is most often because they relied on someone else to choose a topic for them. This shortcut can cause you to struggle throughout your scholarly writing project, mostly because you are not truly invested in the topic as you would be if you started with your own idea.

We have seen students get someone else to pick a topic for them in several different ways. They have gone to a professor to solicit ideas for a topic. They have used databases that offer ideas for scholarly legal writing topics. They have decided to focus on a concept like a circuit split or a pending Supreme Court case. None of these are bad resources if they lead you to a topic you care about and can get invested in, but the right way to use these resources is to make them part of your topic selection strategy—use them to brainstorm your own ideas—not to wind up with a canned topic and thesis that someone else created.

For example, you should talk to professors about topics. In fact, we encourage you to seek out professor-experts in the area of law in which you plan to write and work closely with your supervisor on topic development. You should not, however, make an appointment with a professor you have never met before and try to elicit a canned topic from her. When you try to use a shortcut, you may find yourself choosing a topic you deem "bearable" or "something you can live with."

When you take these shortcuts, you skip over an entire part of the topic and thesis development process. The process of thinking about ideas and topics, and ultimately identifying your topic for your paper, is integral to your relationship with your paper. You may need to reach back at later stages in the paper to remind yourself of why you chose your topic. This reaching back to something that inspired you will be useful when you are deep in your paper, and are having trouble staying motivated to keep pushing through. If you have no ownership in the idea, you have no opportunity for this type of reflection.

We understand that shortcuts are sometimes attractive given your other responsibilities and commitments, and some students have been able to successfully write a paper using these strategies. But we also know many students have struggled throughout their writing process and that much of that struggle can be attributed to poor topic and thesis development. Instead of relying on someone else to give you an idea, give yourself the opportunity to come up with an idea. Chances are, taking that approach to finding your topic will lead you not only to a better paper, but to a better paper-writing experience on the whole.

To gauge where you are in Step One, take the following quiz. All of these questions are important parts of developing your topic. You may want to discuss some of these questions and your thoughts with your faculty advisor or a peer; we encourage you to do that (to the extent these discussions are allowed by your school's academic integrity code). Talking to other people about your thoughts and ideas may help you to better develop your ideas, and also get some early advice and constructive criticism which may save you time down the road.

Step One Quiz: Finding Your Topic

- What things interest me in everyday life?
  - If I go to read a newspaper or magazine, what articles am I likely to read, and which ones do I likely avoid?
  - Do I have any hobbies?
  - What are my personal skills and interests?
- Have I seen something on the news lately that bothers me or makes me uncomfortable?
  - Was there something I heard on talk radio or a podcast and just had to talk about with family, friends, or colleagues?
  - Was there something I read on an internet news source and had to keep reading to find out more information?
- Was there something in class that stood out in my mind as just not right?
  - Do I get into heated debates after class with friends? What do I like to debate?
- Did I work on something over the summer but did not like the outcome?
  - Did I try to argue for a different result only to be told there were no alternatives?
- Do I have subject area limitations?
- What are my limitations in time and ability to understand a new topic area?
- What requirements do I have for a topic?
  - Do I have to submit a list of topic ideas, or informally discuss topic ideas with a faculty advisor or peers?
  - Do I have to submit a topic statement?

Initial thesis — (handwritten)

Step Two: Developing Your Thesis

After you have committed to a topic, you are ready to develop your thesis. Your thesis at this point is what we call an "initial thesis" because you have only limited knowledge about the topic area. After you work through the in-depth research we discuss in Chapter 3, you will be able to refine your thesis to reflect a more sophisticated understanding of your topic. You will probably refine your thesis several times as you work toward your final paper. Thus, there is no pressure for you to develop the perfect thesis at this point. There is also no need for you to try to fully evaluate the soundness of your thesis at this early stage. In Chapter 5, we explain how and when to evaluate your thesis as part of the Refining stage.

Writing your initial thesis statement early in the writing process, during the Thinking stage, gives you direction for your transition into the Preparing stage, where you will do in-depth research and prepare to construct your scholarly paper. A common problem for students writing scholarly papers is that they do not develop a thesis early in the writing process; instead they just start writing with a vague idea about what they want to say. As you can imagine, most of those papers, although they probably receive credit, go unpublished. Instead of writing aimlessly, you will benefit from some direction before you delve deeper into the writing process. Drafting your initial thesis gives you that direction. Also, once you have an initial thesis, you can solicit feedback from supervisors, which can also direct your research as you move forward.

Characteristics of a Good Thesis

As with topic selection, you can use the characteristics of a good thesis to guide your thesis-development process. Ideally, you want your thesis to have three characteristics: it says something concrete, it is easily identifiable, and it is manageable. Keep in mind you are just beginning to formulate your thesis, and may not be able to meet all these characteristics with your first attempt at an initial thesis. As you are refining your thesis throughout your project, return to these considerations and check to see whether your thesis satisfies them. After discussing these thesis characteristics, we will look at examples of the process of starting with a topic and developing an initial thesis.

1. Your thesis must say something concrete.

Most importantly, your thesis must say something. That probably seems obvious; of course your thesis will say something, in the sense that words have meaning. But a thesis is more than stringing together words to make a sentence;

After ch 3 – refined thesis

it is a statement of your position, your argument, your idea, your suggestion, or your take on a topic. To really say something, your thesis should do more than report something or provide a summary of something. It should be a clear articulation of a concrete idea, in whatever form. Check to see whether your thesis says something by asking, "so what?" If you cannot come up with an answer, your thesis probably needs more work.

What your thesis says must have value to the reader. A thesis that is purely your personal opinion or stance on an issue likely has no use to any reader. You want to give the reader something he can use, but the possible uses are limitless. We could not even attempt to list all the possible uses your thesis could have for readers, but here are a few: you want to shed light on something that is generally accepted to get readers to start thinking critically about how an issue is handled; you want to draft legislation to fix a problem and give readers a head start toward making that happen by drafting the legislation yourself; you want readers to be aware of something that has gone unnoticed. A reader might use your paper as a source in her own scholarly work, or a practitioner might use your ideas to make a new argument in an appellate brief. Think about how a reader could use your thesis, and incorporate that use into crafting your initial thesis.

2. Your thesis must be easily identifiable.

If you have something to say, you want your reader to be able to quickly and easily identify what that is. Your thesis is not something to reveal only at the end of the paper, like the solution in a mystery novel. In your final paper, you will want a reader to be able to immediately know your thesis as soon as she reads it, and not have to search for it or try to cobble it together herself after reading through the entire paper.

Even though you have only an initial thesis at this point, and you know you will edit and refine your thesis as you move forward on your project, it is worthwhile to draft your initial thesis in a way that makes it easy for a reader to tell it is your thesis. This is true for two reasons: (1) drafting even your initial thesis in a clear, easy-to-find manner helps you to focus your idea because you have to write it in a way that a reader can understand; and (2) using clear language for your thesis from the outset will probably increase the level and quality of feedback you receive from supervisors. Because they will be able to easily identify your thesis, your supervisors can fully evaluate it and give you feedback to move forward on strengthening it. We discuss taking and incorporating this feedback in detail in Chapter 6.

Structurally, consider drafting your initial thesis as a sentence with a "should-clause" and a "because-clause." The should-clause lets you tell the reader what you want to happen—your proposal or position—and the because-clause gives the rationale for your proposal or position. This structure works well for most scholarly papers, especially when you have a thesis proposing a solution to a problem, or when you are explaining how a court's recent decision was right or wrong. Start by identifying the problem or issue and then write what should happen followed with the explanation of why that should happen. This sentence structure helps the reader identify your thesis. We will look at this structure in the examples below.

3. Your thesis must be manageable.

You already know you should choose a manageable topic, but manageability is relevant to your initial thesis development as well. Remember that you do not have to solve every problem or explain every detail of an issue in your paper. Craft your thesis in a way that will keep your paper manageable, giving you the ability to fully defend your thesis. If your thesis is long and complicated in sentence structure, you may wind up with a long and complicated paper. You might not be able to do everything you want to in one paper. If you are aware of the possibility of crafting an overbroad thesis in the beginning, you can work to narrow it as you learn more about your topic.

If you find yourself in the position of having too much you want to accomplish in a single paper, write a "scope" footnote early on that defines the narrow thesis you have selected for your project and explain how the paper fits in the broader context that is outside the scope for this paper. That way you can help guide yourself to stay on track, and also let the reader know you have thought about the bigger picture. You can also use the scope footnote as a jumping off point for your next scholarly project.

Initial Research, Research Consultations, and Preemption-Checking

Keeping these characteristics of a good thesis in mind will help you move from topic selection to thesis development. You cannot move from topic to thesis without conducting some research. During this initial research stage, your purposes are to develop a better understanding of your selected topic, get a general sense of what other authors have written on your topic, and start to develop a thesis on the topic. You should canvas the topic generally, especially if the topic is new to you, and look for sources that provide you with enough detailed background on your topic so that you can develop your thesis. This initial research is distinct from the more careful, in-depth research you will do after drafting your initial thesis. We discuss that intense research in Chapter 3.

As part of your initial research, consider meeting with a librarian at your law school's library.[6] Many academic law libraries provide research consultations for students working on scholarly writing projects. Setting up a meeting with a research librarian may have a formal procedure, such as completing a short form explaining your project, or it may be as simple as asking a reference librarian if you can set up a meeting. Although the specifics will vary by institution and your particular research needs, generally a research consultation meeting will give you the opportunity to talk with a legal research expert and ask questions about strategies, important sources, and research techniques. Law librarians can offer insightful advice about resources available through your school's library, including specialized databases, unique archival materials, and interlibrary loan.

These consultations can be valuable at any stage in the research process. Keep in mind, though, that law librarians cannot choose your topic for you and they cannot guess at your questions, so the more you have in mind about what you think your topic is, the more productive your research consultation is likely to be. Even so, do not hesitate to reach out to a law librarian when you think "I do not even know what to ask"—if you can articulate some sense of your topic area and initial thoughts, you can probably at least get some tips for finding sources to better understand and refine your topic. And then you can return for a fuller research consultation later.

Law librarians are adept at developing strategies to approach research questions, highly skilled in crafting effective search strings and navigating library catalogs, and knowledgeable about what resources are available at your institution. You can expect to leave a research consultation with new strategies, a greater understanding of the key sources for your project, and potentially a few relevant sources as well. While the librarians do not do your research for you, they will work with you to help you understand the tools and strategies for your research.

Some examples of techniques covered in research consultations at Georgetown Law Library include: locating obscure legislative history documents, obtaining court filings from dockets, accessing historical newspapers and pamphlets, using subject headings to quickly find related materials in the li-

Georgetown website tools!

---

6. Thank you to Andy Lang again for the information and guidance on research consultations.

brary's catalog, understanding foreign law and navigating its sources, finding regulatory history and monitoring proposed regulations, and retrieving municipal codes and ordinances.

Your initial research is also intended to help you check against preemption. Preemption is a legitimate concern, but students often misunderstand the scope of preemption, fearing that another author's paper on the same topic as the student's paper means the student was preempted. In fact, preemption only occurs when another author has published a paper putting forth the exact same thesis you intended to propose and defend in your paper, for the exact same reasons. Preemption can also happen when events change the premise on which your thesis is based.

Preemption does not happen when another author publishes a paper with a topic similar to yours; your topic cannot be preempted. Some overlap with other published pieces is fine; for example, papers on similar topic areas may have similar material covered in the background section. Monica feared the worst when she came across an article with background content and sources similar to her paper. After taking a deep breath, Monica read the rest of the article and discovered that the author took a completely different approach. That author discussed specifics about the Italian model, including detailed analysis on things Italy should and should not have done. Monica, however, used Italy as a model for other countries; though she recognized Italy's model as imperfect, her approach was generally supportive while the other paper was generally critical. Thus, even though there was significant overlap in the background sections of the two papers, Monica's thesis was not preempted.

Preemption can also occur when Congress takes legislative action or a court renders a new opinion, but usually these types of preemption can be overcome with some adjustment to your paper. True, you may end up doing some unanticipated work on your paper, working to refine your thesis based on the changed landscape, but that is much easier than starting over from scratch. For example, if you are writing a paper advocating legislative change, your paper could be preempted if Congress enacts that exact same legislative change while you are working on the paper. But even that scenario does not mean you must abandon your work; you can then slightly modify your topic and thesis to focus on how that change solves a problem, why that change has benefits beyond those intended, how that change is a model for legislative change in other areas, or any number of slightly altered approaches. If Congress took a different approach, even if it reaches the same result as your proposed solution, you can still write your paper, with the additional argument that Congress got it wrong and your way is better.

Similarly, a decision in a case is not a death-knell for your paper about that topic. Depending on the timing related to where you are in the writing process, you can adapt to this recent update. You could analyze the opinion, identifying weaknesses; you could argue that the opinion does not go far enough, or goes too far. In fact, even last-minute court decisions can usually be managed by taking a slightly different approach to your thesis or adding a section to acknowledge a recent event. For example, Natalie added an Epilogue section to her Note to deal with a Supreme Court grant of certiorari for review of the case she analyzed in her Note. In addition to acknowledging this recent event, which happened after she completed her paper and submitted it for publication, Natalie provided some analysis of how, even after oral arguments on the appeal, the issue at the core of her paper remained unresolved. By doing this, she avoided preemption and added one more piece of support for her thesis.

Many times in our own research, we have come across articles whose titles suggest that another author's work has preempted our idea. However, titles often do not convey the article's thesis, so it is important to read the piece to find out what the author's actual thesis is. Realistically, preemption is rare and unlikely to happen to you. In the rare event that your initial research yields an article that puts forth the same thesis that you planned to use, you must modify your thesis. However, even just a slight modification can be sufficient to avoid preemption. Having a topic that can give rise to many sub-topics or multiple theses is a useful guard against preemption. At this early stage, you can simply take a small step back and take your initial thesis in one of these other directions.

Examples: From Topic to Initial Thesis

By the end of the Thinking stage, you will have identified an idea that interests you, a legal topic that relates to that idea, and an initial thesis for your scholarly paper. Remember, you will revise your thesis several times throughout your writing project. In fact, many student writers do not fully understand their topic and develop their thesis until they conduct the in-depth research that we discuss in Chapter 3. These excerpts from student notes illustrate the process of transitioning from topic to initial thesis.

Shaina's Note

Topic Statement:

At the present time, more than eighty immigrant widows across the country face possible deportation because their citizen spouses died before the couple was able to file a joint application for permanent resident status. Administrative agencies and federal courts alike have construed current immigration law to invalidate spousal applications for permanent residency if the American citizen filing the petition for their immigrant spouse dies before the couple's two-year anniversary. This harsh interpretation of spouse-based legislation adversely affects foreign-born widows of American citizens by effectively punishing them for their spouses' misfortune and potentially separating them from their American-born children.

Initial Thesis:

> To resolve inconsistencies in judicial interpretation of immigration law, I will propose that Congress take legislative action to amend spouse-based immigration law.

Shaina's topic statement identifies a problem: inconsistent judicial interpretation. Her initial thesis proposes a solution: a legislative amendment that will resolve this inconsistency. After she learns more about the problem through in-depth research, she will refine this thesis to advocate for a specific legislative action, but this is sufficient as an initial thesis.

Chris's Note

Topic Statement:

> Under the current legal regime, fathers of aborted children have no right to termination but fathers who if given the choice would abort the child are required to pay child support upon birth. The Court should declare such a legal regime an unconstitutional infringement of the father's right to procreational autonomy that is protected by the Due Process Clause under the Fourteenth Amendment.

Initial Thesis:

> This note will propose that after balancing a father's right to procreational autonomy, the Court should develop a scheme that gives adequate weight to the father's right to procreational autonomy while subsequently protecting the mother's right to an abortion. Frankly, I am still struggling internally as to the proper solution because of the weight of public policy and the issues of proof involved in establishing a bona fide interest in not becoming a parent. The most obvious solution is to craft a narrow exception providing fathers that have expressed a pre-conception or pre-viability preference to not father

children, either generally or with that specific person, to exempt themselves from parental responsibilities.

Chris has committed to his topic at this point, but is honest about his concerns
and potential misgivings. He has identified an obvious solution but is open to
other theses that fit within this topic. This flexibility will serve him well as he
refines his initial thesis later in the process.

Natalie's Note

Topic Statement:

The Second Circuit rationalized its decision in *Pyett* solely by analyzing prior case law (one Second Circuit case and three Supreme
Court decisions). It did not give any policy reasons for its decision.
Yet, it seems like the Court is really affirming the District Court's decision for policy reasons (the opinion reads like an effort by the Court
to make the case law work in favor of the employee!). The case law
could easily be interpreted in the complete opposite way. In fact, the
defendant employer's interpretation of prior case law seems more
plausible.

Initial Thesis:

Despite the Court's unpersuasive reasoning in *Pyett*, there is a good
reason to hold that a union-negotiated arbitration provision that
waives an employee's right to a federal forum for statutory claims is
unenforceable (even though the Supreme Court has held that individual employees not represented by unions can waive that right).
Allowing unions to include such a waiver in a collective bargaining
agreement will create a catch-22 for minorities and other members
of the protected classes. They essentially have the option of either
waiving their right to a federal forum or foregoing the benefits of
union membership. It's a lose-lose situation that takes the whole
"take-it-or-leave-it" concept to a whole new level. The Court should
have emphasized this.

Here, Natalie has used a case as the basis for her scholarly paper, and must
find something to say about the case. She has a lot of initial ideas, which is
fine at this stage, but ultimately she will need to commit to one fully-developed
thesis. As she learns more about her topic, she can choose which of her ideas
is best.

Collin's Note

Topic Statement:

There is a longstanding rule in the Federal Acquisition Regulations (FAR) that forbids federal agencies from contracting for "personal services," which the FAR describes as positions that essentially create an employer-employee relationship between the federal government and contractor personnel. Despite this prohibition, federal agencies have become more reliant on contractor personnel to fulfill their missions—and thus more involved in their direct supervision.

As a result, an increased number of employment discrimination (Title VII) cases are being brought by contractor personnel directly against federal agencies (rather than against their contracting company, such as a staffing agency or temporary hiring firm) based on the concept of "joint employer liability." As applied by both the federal courts and the Equal Employment Opportunity Commission, joint employer liability allows individuals primarily employed by a contracting company and assigned to a federal agency to sue that agency for employment discrimination, claiming that the agency is a "joint employer."

This ultimately demonstrates that the prohibition on personal services contracts has failed to prevent the creation of employer-employee relationships between the federal government and contractor personnel. Furthermore, the fact that federal courts and the EEOC have developed legal precedent designed to provide Title VII protection for contractor personnel working in federal agencies demonstrates that other areas of the law are already starting to adapt to the reality that contractors and civil servants are beginning to blend into a (somewhat) unified federal workforce.

Initial Thesis:

While not all aspects of the contractor-civil servant distinction should be eliminated (i.e. contractors still should probably not be given the protection and benefits of the civil service laws), this note will argue that the prohibition on personal services contracts represents one distinction that no longer has any grounding in reality. As such, FAR 37.104 should be replaced with guidance for federal managers on how to properly and most efficiently supervise contractor personnel alongside civil servants.

Collin narrows in on a single rule of federal acquisition as the basis for his paper. Even with this narrow focus, there are a number of angles he could approach in his Note. Because he proposes a replacement for the regulation governing personal services contracts, he will likely need a solution that includes text for a modified or new regulation, along with an analysis of how that modified or new regulation will solve the problems he identifies with the current treatment of personal services contracts. For publishability, he knows that his paper must do more than evaluate the underlying policy implications of the status quo; he must also provide a legal solution. He will keep this in mind as he develops his thesis.

Monica's Note

Topic Statement:

The looting of art work is an age-old custom, one that is based in the reasoning "to the victor goes the spoils." As long as world peace evades humanity's grasp, looting of cultural artifacts will continue to present problems for the international community. The 1970 UNESCO Convention laid out ambitious plans and methods as models which countries should adapt in order to facilitate both efforts to reclaim art stolen from a certain country, as well as to facilitate the regulation of the art market and museum acquisition.

Italy does not only reclaim art, it also recognizes other countries' rights to art within its borders. For example, Italy has negotiated with Ecuador to maintain almost 200 artifacts on display in the Museum of Non-European Cultures in Rimini. Through the negotiations, Italy may keep the pieces for display, but they now include identification plaques stating "Property of Ecuador."

Italy has also created the Tutela Patrimonio Culturale (TPC), an arm of the Carabinieri, whose mission is the investigation and recla-mation of Italian cultural heritage. The TPC has 11 territorial teams throughout Italy, and is the leading team in Europe in the prevention and repossession of cultural heritage crime, working closely with EU-ROPOL. The strict criminal penalties for looting and conspiracy also serve as a deterrent to engagement with the black market. Currently, Marion True, the former curator of the Getty is on trial in Italy for looting and conspiracy.

Initial Thesis:

While Italy has made great strides, its model still is not perfect. Most of Italian art law focuses on antiquities, as opposed to art works lost during WWII. In criminal proceedings, the statute of limitations creates prosecutorial barriers. Furthermore, as a Schengen nation, border control must be tightened. Italy is a peninsula with numerable access points, but its border control must be much stricter in order to hinder the access to and transportation of stolen works of art.

In this note, I will argue that while the 1970 UNESCO Convention had excellent intentions, we are now 40 years past that date and the art world is still plagued with inefficient restitution and reclamation efforts. Instead, I will propose that Italy should be the paradigm off which other countries should model their efforts, eventually creating an international standard. In the absence of binding law, Italy has pressured museums such as the Getty and Princeton Art Museum into returning cultural objects by marshalling public opinion and voicing the legitimacy of its claims through the media. The Italian model is characterized by an activist government, as shown by Italy's MOU with the United States and the various settlements and litigation concerning art theft, looting, and conspiracy in recent years. The Ministry of Culture is very proactive, and bases its data and investigation systems on existing information on cultural heritage collected from museums and other institutions.

Monica has many broad ideas in her topic statement, and she will need to narrow the focus of her topic before she can refine her initial thesis as she continues to learn about her topic. She has the right idea in her initial thesis, focusing on using Italy as a specific model for other countries to develop their own art reclamation and restitution efforts. As she continues to master her topic, she can figure out how best to develop her Italy-as-model thesis.

Jessie's Comment

Topic Statement:

The goal of a deliberating jury is to reach a complete and unanimous verdict. If a complete and unanimous verdict cannot be reached, a mistrial is declared and the case is retried. However, in cases with multiple defendants, sometimes a jury is only able to reach a verdict on some of the defendants but not others. And in cases with one defendant charged with multiple counts, sometimes a jury is only able to reach a unanimous verdict on some of the counts rather than all of them. Rather than declare a mistrial on all counts and/or all defendants, the Federal Rules of Criminal Procedure proscribe that partial verdicts can be returned. This allows juries to return verdicts on the defendants and/or counts that they can agree on. This also ensures that all of the resources utilized in trying the case the first time around are not expended for naught.

Rule 31 of the Federal Rules of Criminal Procedure expressly states that a jury can return a partial verdict in a criminal trial as long as there are either multiple defendants or multiple counts. It explains that "[i]f there are multiple defendants, the jury may return a verdict at any time during its deliberations as to any defendant about whom it has agreed." And "[i]f the jury cannot agree on all counts as to any [one] defendant, the jury may return a verdict on those counts on which it has agreed." Like complete verdicts, the partial verdicts must be returned to the presiding judge in open court and must be unanimous. The allowance of partial verdicts, however, allows the jury to leave charges undecided. For as the rule states, "[i]f the jury cannot agree on a verdict on one or more counts, the court may declare a mistrial on those counts [and] [t]he government may retry any defendant on any count on which the jury could not agree."

Rule 31, however, is incomplete. Its plain text implies that a partial verdict can be received at any point, as long as there are multiple defendants and/or multiple counts. It fails to discuss many important details. The Rule is silent as to how a jury should be instructed in regards to giving a partial verdict. It fails to discuss if and when individual parties should be consulted. It also fails to describe whether trial judges are required to receive partial verdicts, simply stating that the jury "may" return a partial verdict. It fails to discuss how this plays in with the fact that juries are allowed to return inconsistent verdicts.

Initial Thesis:

Due to the incompleteness of the Rule itself, a trial judge is left trying to interpret confusing case law to determine whether a partial verdict is appropriate in a given situation. The purpose of this Comment is to summarize existing case law and offer a practical guide for Federal District Court judges as to when a partial verdict, and a partial verdict instruction, is appropriate. The basis for this comment is looking at Circuit cases either affirming or overturning partial verdict convictions.

Even early on, Jessie had a clear idea of where she was going in her paper. Her topic was narrowed to critiquing a single rule of criminal procedure. With her initial thesis, she has committed to developing a practical guide for judges based on her critique. In drafting this initial thesis, she has set out a clear plan for moving forward by identifying her comment's goals and the components of analysis needed to meet those goals. Though she will later refine her thesis to more concretely describe the practical guide, her initial plans to write a guide remain intact.

Armed with your initial thesis, you are almost ready to move forward and learn more about your topic and thesis. Delving deep into your topic area and doing careful analytical research will help you refine your thesis and prepare to write your paper. To get a sense of where you are in the process, and determine whether you are ready to focus on research, take the following quiz.

Step Two Quiz: Developing Your Thesis

- Have I committed to a clearly identifiable legal topic?
- Do I have something concrete to say?
  - What kind of reaction do I hope to get from my reader?
- Do I have a one-sentence statement of my initial thesis?
- Is my initial thesis manageable?
- Am I comfortable enough with my initial thesis that I am ready to move on to focus on research?
- If required, do I have approval on my chosen topic and thesis?

Only when you can answer "yes" to all of these questions should you move on to the next stage: developing the knowledge you need to construct the rest of the paper.

CHAPTER 3

PREPARING:
DEVELOPING HORIZONTAL AND
VERTICAL KNOWLEDGE

We are all familiar with the plight of a person who knows nothing but needs to get caught up on something quickly. We are used to seeing this in movie montages. Elle Woods buys a new laptop and studies on the elliptical machine in order to excel in her Harvard Law classes and get a coveted internship. Baby Houseman stops carrying watermelons and learns the intricate steps to the mambo so she can cover for Penny at the Sheldrake. After a year of enlisting stand-ins to do his schoolwork for him, Thornton Melon crams for his final oral examination.[1]

You may find yourself in a similar situation with your scholarly writing project. You, of course, have some law school experience behind you, but you must now create your own movie montage. You must learn everything you can about your topic and thesis so that you can get to the cinematic experience of writing your draft.

As we noted in Chapter 1, scholarly writing is both more freeing and more daunting than practical, professional legal writing. Practical legal writing is bound by the primary legal sources that define the rules you will apply to a given set of facts. All your conclusions, analogies, and distinctions must be tied to the law, unless you are making an argument that the law should create an exception or apply to a new set of facts. Still, you are tethered to precedent, and must work within the confines of stare decisis.

---

1. If these characters are unfamiliar to you, see "Legally Blonde," "Dirty Dancing," and "Back to School," respectively.

Your scholarly writing project has no such boundaries. Now you can write about whatever you want, and say whatever you want about it: The choice is yours. Of course, in order to do this, you must become an expert on your topic, so that you can state, advance, and support your thesis.

In order to do this, you must do in-depth research to develop both horizontal and vertical knowledge. "Horizontal knowledge" is basic background and introductory material about your topic—it covers a great deal of breadth, but not much depth on any one point in an area of the law. You probably developed horizontal knowledge in many of your first year doctrinal classes; these classes provide a broad introduction into the subject matter, and can often be followed with an upper-level class that considers some smaller sub-part of the field in depth. In these upper-level classes, you will develop what we call "vertical knowledge," where you become more knowledgeable about a narrower part of the field.

vertical knowledge: in-depth information about your thesis

horizontal knowledge: introductory and background information on your topic

In the scholarly writing context, you must develop vertical knowledge with an even finer point on it. Here, the horizontal knowledge is enough background for you to understand the area of law in which you are writing. The vertical knowledge is the thorough exploration of your thesis. In the end, you need to develop horizontal knowledge about your topic and vertical knowledge about your thesis. Only when you have this finely honed expertise will you be competent to complete your paper and defend your thesis.

You already started to develop your horizontal knowledge when you did the initial topic research we discussed in Chapter 2. Now that you have decided on your topic and have an initial thesis, you can begin to master the material by further developing your horizontal knowledge and beginning to acquire vertical knowledge as well. Students often want to rush through the research because they want to get started on the first draft. They feel like they have not started the project until they start writing. Remember that this is the Preparing stage; as you do your research, you are also thinking about what you are going

recursive

to say in your first draft. Thus, you should not think of research and writing as separate endeavors. Until you are in the late stages of drafting your paper, you will move among the first three phases of the writing process: Thinking, Preparing, and Executing. They are recursive.

This chapter will focus on the steps required to conduct and master the research materials on your topic and thesis and will take you to the point where you are ready to make the first move from Preparing to Executing. Ultimately, this shift will require you to answer two questions: Do I know enough about this topic to confirm what I want to say, and do I feel knowledgeable enough to move forward with my thesis?

There are two initial considerations at the outset of the Preparing stage. First, you should think about what you need to submit to your supervisor during this stage. There may be some interim assignments you need to complete for your journal editor or professor (or yourself), such as a citation list, research report, or annotated outline. These interim deadlines will necessarily affect how long you can and should spend doing your research and you should be aware of what they are before you get started. Note that one of your supervisors may request an interim document that is not something you would normally write. We have seen students struggle to meet this type of requirement, even going so far as to engineer an outline after they have already written a first draft. This will not be a fruitful endeavor if you are contriving to meet the requirements set by your supervisor. Thus, you should see if you can get your supervisor to be flexible about what you submit to him. Most advisors just want to make sure that you are on the right track and are not wedded to a particular form; they just think that by saying "outline" or "research plan" they are helping crystallize things for you. If they are not, ask them if you can submit something else.

Second, you should think about organization; part of working through this phase is getting organized. You are going to have to digest a large amount of material in a short time — material that you will want and need to refer back to later, as you get deeper and deeper into your writing. So, at this point, you need to consider how you want your research materials and notes to be organized when you start writing.

Various types of organizational systems can work for this type of project. Some front-end thinking about how you want to organize your research materials will help here. Ask yourself: What is going to work for me?

- A chart listing all your sources and research notes?
- A tabbed notebook of research materials?
- A Dropbox folder to save all of your source materials?

- A handwritten set of notes that you will transcribe?
- A stack of index cards for each of your sources?
- A Google Doc or Sheet that you can access on various devices?
- A thorough outline that you will transform into your first draft?

 Using cloud-based storage such as Dropbox or GoogleDocs lets you work on your project on multiple devices or at different locations.

You might also use research management software or apps as an organizational or notetaking system. For example, you might use Pocket (https://getpocket.com/) to keep track of online materials (by using the Pocket browser extension or app). Evernote (https://evernote.com/) lets you keep track of sources, annotate saved sources, and maintain research notes all on a single platform. Juris-M (https://juris-m.github.io/) is a tool you can use to collect, organize, and manage sources. Juris-M is an offshoot of Zotero (https://www.zotero.org/) and is designed for legal sources. Think about what apps and programs you use to take notes in other contexts (your class notes, for example) and whether one of them might be suitable for this project.

Lexis offers CaseMap (http://www.lexisnexis.com/casemap/casemap.aspx) as another option for organizing your research. CaseMap lets you organize resources by issue or sub-issue through linked spreadsheets that allow you to relate sources to each other. You have the ability to customize the spreadsheets when creating your research database. You can also keep track of your source citation information with CaseMap. Lexis and Westlaw also offer a research organization system through virtual folders, as described below.

Organizing Your Research Using Lexis Folders

- You can access your Folders through the "Folders" link under the "More" drop-down menu from any page or from the "Folders" pod on the Lexis Advance home page.
- To create a new folder, click "Create New Folder" from either the Folders pod, your search results page, or the Folders page; then name the folder and click "Create." You can select a specific location for your new folder as well.

- When viewing a document, you can save it to a folder by clicking the "Add to folder" icon at the top of the document. A list of options for saving the document appears.
- To save snippets of text to a folder, highlight the text in the document you are viewing. A shortcut menu that contains options for working with the selected text appears.
- To save a search, from the results list, select the Actions drop-down menu (near the top of the page) and select "Add search to folder." The Add to Folder dialog box appears. You can name your search and add notes about the search before saving it to the folder.
- To share the folder with other users, select the Share with Others tab and then enter the name or email address of the person you want to share with, then click "Add."

More information about Lexis folders is available at: https://help.lexis nexis.com/tabula-rasa/newlexis/gh_workfolders-topic?lbu=US&locale= en_US&audience=vsa.

Organizing Your Research Using Westlaw Folders

- Folders are available by clicking the "Folders" link at the top right of the screen.
- To create a new folder, after you click on the "Folders" link, click on the "New Folder" icon at the left of the screen. Select the location of your new folder, add a name to the folder, and click "OK."
- When viewing a document, you can save it to a folder by clicking and dragging the name of the document to the active folder at the top right. You can also save a document to your folder by clicking on the "Save to Folder" icon in the menu bar toward the top right. You can save an unlimited number of documents in your folders.
- To save snippets of text to your folder, highlight text in the document you are viewing. A window will pop up and the first option will be to "Save to [your folder]."
- To share folders with another user, such as your editor or advisor, click on "Options" at the left and then select "Share." Enter the name

of the person and the person's name will appear underneath. Click
on the name and then click "Continue."
- KeyCite information is automatically updated for documents that
are saved to folders.

More information about Westlaw folders is available at: http://store.
westlaw.com/documentation/westlaw/wlawdoc/web/wlnfoldr.pdf.

Your organizational system is your end goal; how you get there is the
research process that the rest of this chapter will cover. The five steps outlined
here are in approximate, but not fixed, order—how you approach them depends on your end goal. Ultimately you need to complete all five pre-writing
tasks so that you can make your initial move to the Executing stage. Those
tasks are:

1. Do the In-Depth Research
2. Develop Horizontal and Vertical Knowledge
3. Update Your Research
4. Revisit Your Initial Thesis
5. Approach the First Draft

Step 1: Do the In-Depth Research

This first step is the biggest one of the five: You need to do in-depth research on your topic and thesis. Your prior academic and practical
experiences have probably left you well-prepared to engage in sophisticated
legal research. Of course, those skills will directly translate to the scholarly
research context; however, in this endeavor, your research will likely involve
a more expansive list of sources than you generally use in practical legal writ-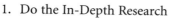
ing. You will use, but will likely need to go beyond, traditional case and
statute materials.

In fact, you may be wholly unfamiliar with the types of sources that are
available in the area of the law you have selected. This is why our first research
recommendation is that you leverage the human resources that are available
to you. A conversation with a journal editor, professor, or law librarian can

Jim —guest lecture?

get you up to speed and moving in the right direction much faster than random searches online or in the library stacks. Even if you have taken a course or worked in the field and have some general familiarity with your topic area, you may not be familiar with the scholarly resources and sources that are available to you as a legal researcher. Thus, a conversation with someone "in the know" can provide you with a good jumping off point for the rest of your research.

See if your library has a LibGuide on your topic or a closely-related field. Many libraries create LibGuides to compile subject-specific resources in a user-friendly format. For example, the Georgetown Law Library Guides are available at: http://guides.ll.georgetown.edu/home. If your library does not have a LibGuide on topic, search other law libraries. Many law libraries have publicly accessible research tools.

Authors of all types of legal research papers will need this jumping off point in order to develop the requisite horizontal knowledge in this area. If you are writing a case comment, of course, the case in question and all of the authorities it cites are also important pieces of foundational information. Beyond that, you may find useful information in one of these types of secondary sources, which you may have discussed in your first-year legal research and writing course:

- **Treatises** are collections of scholarly materials in a particular area of the law. In some fields, there are seminal treatises that are widely recognized as the premiere authority on that subject matter. They are comprehensive and often run in multi-volume sets. You will not likely need to read an entire treatise; rather, start with the table of contents or index to find the relevant sub-section(s) containing information on your topic area. Popular treatises include *Collier's on Bankruptcy* and *Wigmore on Evidence*.
- **Hornbooks** are similar to treatises, but they usually appear in one volume and are often directed at a student audience. Again, you can focus in on the chapter or sub-section that is relevant to your topic by using the table of contents or index.
- **Legal encyclopedias** contain comprehensive summaries on many different legal subjects. They can provide useful introductions to a particular area, but are not generally authoritative on a particular subject. Two common legal encyclopedias are *Corpus Juris Secundum* (or C.J.S.) and *American Jurisprudence 2d*. These are both available

in print or online. You can use an index to direct you to the specific entries that are pertinent to your paper.

Monographs are single-volume works, usually on a particular topic within a field. They are often interdisciplinary and historical in nature, and less focused on doctrine than treatises and hornbooks. They include volumes such as Andreas Lowenfeld's *International Economic Law* and Karl Llewellyn's *Common Law Tradition: Deciding Appeals.*

You can see which of these sources is available in your law school's library by searching the catalog, which is most likely online. Because your mileage may vary depending on the topic area you are working in, consider asking a person knowledgeable about the field to recommend the best option for you as you get started on your research. Any of these types of sources can be useful as you gather your initial information; they can provide background knowledge and information about other primary and secondary research sources in the field (even if you do not plan to cite them in your paper).

You may find it useful to delve into some other online research materials in your field as well. For example:

- The **Bureau of National Affairs** (www.bna.com) maintains a number of publications and collections in certain specialized fields. If your law library subscribes to this service, you can review background and current information in a variety of categories. BNA publications may be available through the BNA website, or through Bloomberg Law, depending on your school's coverage.
- **Mealey's Reports** provides legal news reports in over 50 subject areas. Mealey's is available on Lexis and all law students should be able to access the Reports with a valid Lexis ID.
- You may find a **Congressional Research Service** report helpful. The CRS (http://www.loc.gov/crsinfo/whatscrs.html) creates reports on many different legal and policy matters for members of Congress. Some of these reports are available to the public; you can access reports in the public domain through Open CRS (http://opencrs.com). Your law school may also have access to more CRS reports through subscription databases such as ProQuest Congressional. You can always ask a librarian to learn more about what resources are available.
- There may be an **online research guide** in your field that can get you started. The **Library of Congress** (http://www.loc.gov/rr/program/bib/bibhome.html) maintains an extensive list of research guides;

not all of them are law-related, but they can be helpful, especially if you are working on an interdisciplinary project. Many academic and government law libraries have also made legal research guides for particular fields available online. A quick internet search can turn up these types of resources, though you should make sure you are discerning in evaluating the source of such guides. Look for guides from major university law libraries or government-affiliated libraries such as a state law library. Depending on your research question, think about who might have an interest in helping you find the necessary materials. For example, while many law schools have great research guides for finding federal legislative history, typically the best guides to finding state-specific legislative history are managed by libraries *in that state.*

- You can also run a basic internet search using your favorite search engine, or something more targeted such as **Google Scholar**, which allows you to run a free online search of scholarly materials such as journal articles and books. Depending on the online availability of the materials you find in your search, you may need to gather the sources these searches retrieve using your library or one of the paid online legal research services.

  ○ No matter what search engine you use, an internet search will inevitably lead you to at least one **Wikipedia** entry. For the uninitiated: Wikipedia (http://en.wikipedia.org/wiki/Wikipedia) is a free, web-based encyclopedia project. Almost all of its articles can be edited by anyone who can access the Wikipedia website. Thus, it contains extremely up-to-date information that may or may not be reliable as a resource. In scholarly legal writing, the problem with Wikipedia is less about reliability and more about its very nature: Wikipedia is a secondary source, not a primary source, and your argument should be derived from primary legal research material. Thus, it is as useful as any other secondary source: It can get you to primary sources.

  ○ You might also consider using **Lexis Web** (http://www.lexisweb.com) as your search engine. Lexis Web allows you to search the internet for legal web sites that have been selected and validated by the LexisNexis editorial staff. You can run a search similar to one you would run on any search engine and then review the results; some of the results will be legal sources available on the web, and others will require you to sign on to Lexis to view them. You can also filter your results using Lexis-created classifications for different types of materials. You can view the User Reference Guide for Lexis Web at http://www.lexisweb.com/LexisWebBeta UserGuide.pdf.

When working with internet sources, be sure you have the correct URL for the website, and the date on which you last accessed the page. Remember that internet sources move around often, so you will want to follow up and verify these sources when you are putting the finishing touches on your paper. You may want to print or save the internet sources you use so that you know you will be able to find the information again later, even if the web address changes or the content is removed.

Permalinks (sometimes called "permanent" or "persistent" links) are URLs that you can create to help avoid "linkrot." One platform for turning an ordinary URL into a permalink is Perma.cc. This service is maintained by the Harvard Law School Library in collaboration with other academic law libraries and organizations. Anyone can create a free account that will allow the user to create up to ten permalinks per month, though many academic libraries and law journals have institutional accounts that will allow unlimited use. After creating an account, Perma.cc will use the source's URL to instantly create a permalink URL that will direct the reader to a snapshot of the cited webpage as it existed at the exact moment you created the permalink. More information is available at: http://perma.cc.

As a failsafe measure, it is also good practice to save copies of online sources locally (or, even better, to the cloud) so that you later have them to share with publishers and editors. This can be as simple as "printing" a webpage and, rather than sending it to a printer, selecting "save as pdf" instead.

Once you have some background information, you can start gathering more specific information about your topic and your thesis. Traditionally, new legal scholars worked with print indices such as the Current Law Index, the Index to Legal Periodicals, or the Current Index to Legal Periodicals. Now, because the information online is both easier to search and available almost instantly, a researcher need not look at the print indices to perform a thorough and successful search. However, the key to successful searching is how you craft your search terms.

- If you are searching for **journal articles,** you will want to use the full-text law review article databases on Westlaw and Lexis. The relevant databases are "Secondary Materials > Law Reviews & Journals" (on Lexis Advance) and "Secondary Sources" then selecting the "Publication Type" filter "Law Reviews & Journals" (on Westlaw). You can also narrow to this content type after running a search first, then applying the relevant filters for Secondary Sources and Publication/Content Type for Law Reviews and Journals.

- When doing online research for journal articles, you will probably want to transform your initial thesis statement into either a keyword or natural language search. You should consider "segment searching"—that is, limiting your search to a certain segment of the source materials.

  - For example, you can limit your search term to searches in the title or first paragraph. You can also run searches that have your key terms within close proximity to each other, such as in the same sentence, in the same paragraph, or within a certain number of words. These types of limitations will help narrow your search results, although you will want to be mindful not to be too limiting, especially when searching in titles.

  - To see the segment fields that are searchable, click the "Advanced Search" next to the Search bar in Lexis Advance or "Advanced" next to the Search bar in Westlaw. The searchable fields vary by content type so advanced searching options in Secondary Sources will let you search by article author, whereas advanced searching in Cases will let you search docket number or party name, among other fields.

- If your topic/thesis includes **statutory material**, you will want to see background materials such as committee reports and other legislative history. Legislative history research can be hard to find and tricky to navigate, especially for state statutes. As mentioned above, it is often good to seek background information about the legislative process in your jurisdiction (often by consulting a research guide maintained by a law library in that state) before seeking the specific documents. This ensures that you can understand how the legislative history documents fit together and which ones carry more authority.

  - On Lexis Advance, the easiest way to conduct legislative history research is to click into "Statute & Legislation > Legislative Histories." You can run searches in federal and state legislative sources, such as bills, committee reports, and the Congressional Record, from this page. For legislation passed by Congress in 1970 and after, consult the source "US—CIS/Index" for abstracts of Congressional documents and prepared legislative histories for all Public Laws. Legislative history compilations for major federal legislation passed before 1970 can be found by searching the CIS/Historical Index database.

- On Westlaw, you can select "Legislative History" from the home page to access databases of federal and state legislative history documents. Pay close attention to the scope notes for these databases (i.e. the little circled "i") to check the coverage dates. You can also often find related legislative history materials by first opening your statute sections, then clicking into the "History" tab at the top of the document display. This is a much easier way to see all of the documents associated with a particular statute, rather than searching for them individually.
    - The Washington, D.C., law firm of Arnold & Porter has compiled a comprehensive group of reports, hearings, congressional debates, and other documents for some major legislative acts such as the Americans with Disabilities Act and the Family and Medical Leave Act. Each of these compilations has its own Westlaw database. To access these from the Westlaw landing page, click "Legislative History," then in the "Tools & Resources" box on the right side of the screen, select "Arnold & Porter Legislative Histories."
- **Congress.gov** is a great free resource for finding federal legislative history documents as well as currently pending legislation. The coverage varies by specific document type, though most legislative history documents are available going back to 1995. The website provides authenticated pdfs of bill text, committee reports, the congressional record, and more.
- Your school's library may also have access to more sophisticated, legislative history-specific databases such as **ProQuest Congressional** or **ProQuest Legislative Insight**. These databases are extremely helpful for retrieving federal legislative history documents and are the most comprehensive in their coverage.
- You may also find information using **HeinOnline** or **SSRN**.
    - **HeinOnline** provides electronic, searchable access to articles from older law reviews, most of which are not available electronically elsewhere. If your library subscribes to this service, it will be most

useful to you if you are looking for journal articles that are outside the coverage of the electronic research services.

○ **SSRN** (http://papers.ssrn.com) provides a database of scholarly research in the social sciences and humanities. Many authors post a "preprinted" version of their articles that have been accepted for publication but are not yet in print. This can be a good resource as you gather preliminary information, however, be wary of self-published articles as a source for your own research paper.

Keep in mind that as you gather and review these sources, you should also be mining them for sources your searches did not uncover. For example, you should read the footnotes in a journal article carefully to see if there is any source material you should retrieve. Similarly, if you see a reference to a relevant committee report in the Congressional Record, you should pull the report in question. You can also use the electronic updating services—Shepard's (on Lexis) and KeyCite (on Westlaw)—to find related research sources (we provide step-by-step instructions for these services below).

When researching online, be careful not to stray too far from your initial research path by clicking through various links either within your search results or on the sidebars that pop up while you are researching. These links can take you to other relevant and useful sources, but can also take you far from your intended search. Make sure you backtrack to your initial search to make a comprehensive review of the results; do not let the wealth of information out there distract you from your original purpose. If you tend to wander from your original research path, try to plan ahead so that you can trace your steps back. You can keep track by opening new pages in new tabs or windows of your internet browser, or use your browser's history cache to track back to previously viewed pages. Both Lexis and Westlaw also allow you to view your recent research history. And, of course, you can keep a handwritten or electronic list of the searches you have run and the pages you have searched.

Beyond these basic research principles and resources is a wealth of information specific to your topic area. There are too many sources to list here, so our best advice is this: Again, talk to someone about research specific to your topic. Many libraries have subject specialists who are expert in your area of the law. Your school's vendor representative may also be able to refer you to relevant resources, as can the reference attorneys that work for the various research services.

> As you go deeper into your research, always keep preemption as a concern in the back of your mind. As we noted in Chapter 2, we do not want to overstate the risk of preemption, but as you move through the research phase and begin to read through the background material that will ultimately help you refine your thesis and build your arguments, stay alert for previous articulations of something similar to what you plan to argue.

The paid online research services have a wealth of topic-specific information that you probably did not use much during your first-year legal research and writing class. You can likely make use of one or more of these research tips on Lexis and Westlaw.

Lexis Advance Research Strategies

- *Search using the Lexis search box.*
  1. Describe your topic using a keyword or terms and connectors search in the red search box. Consider imposing pre-search Practice Area or Jurisdiction filters by using the tabs below the search box. Click "Search."
  2. Review results by selecting a source type along the top of the results list, and then narrowing via the filters on the left side pane.
- *Browse materials by Practice Area or Industry, then search treatises and other secondary legal and news sources.*
  1. From the Lexis Advance homepage, click into the Practice Area or Industry tab under "Explore Content."
  2. Depending on the practice area you select, you may see different options on the next page—look for the resources listed under "Secondary Materials." By selecting a content type, you can browse a list of all titles related to that practice area.
  3. Within a specific title, you can use the search bar to quickly look across sections in that source.
- *Locate a specific source whose name/title you know.*
  1. Click the Browse dropdown at the top of the Lexis Advance homepage.
  2. Type the source's name into the "Search for a source" bar and either select the source from the dropdown list of suggestions before searching, or run the search and select the source from the list of results.

---

  3. You can also do this from the main Lexis Advance search bar. Start typing in the name of your source, then click into the title from the suggestions list before running the search.

  4. To search within a single source, click directly on its name. This should take you to an advanced search page that will be limited to that specific publication or, if the work is a treatise, it may take you to a landing page with a search bar and the table of contents.

- *Choose a topic of interest from a list of possibilities suggested by Lexis Advance, then retrieve related materials via the Search by Topic or Headnote feature.*

  1. Click the "Browse" button at the top left of the screen, then click into "Topics."

  2. Identify your topic.

   A. Option 1: Describe your topic in the open field and click the magnifying glass.

   B. Option 2: Link into an area of law of your choice, then click the arrow to the right of a relevant topic to expand and reveal sub-topics.

  3. When you click into a sub-topic, you will have the option to "Get documents," "Add the topic as a search filter," or "Create a topic alert." Selecting "Get documents" will take you to a list of all documents (including both primary authority and secondary materials) that the database has identified as relating to that sub-topic. You can then apply filters or search within the results to narrow the scope for your research.

   A. The topics are used to organize cases in Lexis by headnote— each headnote is assigned to corresponding topics in this Topical Outline.

   B. If you find a case that is useful and want to find related materials you can use the case's headnotes to find other materials that have been sorted into the same topical categories by clicking into the topical outline that precedes each headnote's text.

- *Use Shepard's to validate your sources and search for related materials.*

  1. You can use Shepard's to validate a case, statute, agency regulation, law review article, or treatise section. Shepard's will also

help you find related materials, including cases that have cited the source, but also statutes, regulations, law review articles and other secondary sources, and court documents that have referenced the citation.

2. Anywhere you see a Shepard's symbol, clicking it will take you to the report for the corresponding document. Alternatively, click the "Shepardize this document" button to the right of the document.

3. Use the links in the top left to access citing references of a certain source or analysis type. The Shepard's report defaults to showing "Citing Decisions" first, but you can click into "Other Citing Sources" to see statutes, regulations, secondary sources, and other materials that cite to your document.

4. When viewing the "Citing Decisions," you will have the option to filter the cases by jurisdiction, court, depth of analysis, treatment of your case, date, and headnote. You can also run a search within the citing decisions.

5. You can also monitor your citations with Shepard's Alert. This service will update you when the Shepard's results for a particular source have changed. There are two ways to set up these alerts:
    ○ **Create an alert based on search results.** Click the bell icon above your results. The subsequent template will ask you the necessary questions to complete your Alert.
    ○ **Create a Shepard's Alert for the document you are viewing.** At the top of the Shepard's report, you should see the title of your document and a small bell icon to the right of it. Clicking the bell icon will allow you to create an alert for that document. The subsequent template will ask you a series of questions to complete the set up.

 You can track your research on Lexis.com via the History link in the upper-right corner, which stores searches for 30 days.

Westlaw Research Strategies

- *Search across a vast array of content with one search.*
  1. From the main screen, change your jurisdiction by clicking on the jurisdiction box next to the orange Search button. Select your jurisdiction and click "Save."
  2. Enter search terms in either Plain Language (WestSearch) or Terms & Connectors to search across different types of content including Cases, Statutes, Regulations, and Secondary Sources. The most relevant documents will be sorted at the top.
  3. Filter your results by clicking on a specific set of sources and then using filters at the left side of the screen.
- *Browse practice area materials.*
  1. From the Westlaw research page, click into the Practice Areas tab.
  2. The practice area materials pages go into varying degrees of depth; practice areas with Practitioner Insights pages (indicated with an "*") go into greater depth and collect content from a range of sources including news, legal news, secondary sources, and primary authority.
- *Search for a Key Number associated with your topic.*
  1. Click "Key Numbers" on the Westlaw home page.
  2. Type in terms that describe your topic in the "Search for Key Numbers" text box. Select the jurisdiction from which you want to retrieve case headnotes using the "Change jurisdiction" link under the Key Number search bar.
  3. Click "Search."
  4. In the displayed list, click a topic and Key Number to view a list of case headnotes classified under that topic and Key Number with links to the full text of the opinions.
- *Browse the West Key Number System to identify Key Numbers and terms related to your topic.*
  1. Click "Key Numbers" on the Westlaw home page.
  2. Browse the list of topics and subtopics.
  3. When you see a topic or subtopic related to your topic, you can click into it to see all headnotes tagged with that Key Number subtopic or you can search across multiple Key Numbers by checking the box next to each one you want to search, then

running your search terms through the search bar at the top of the screen.

4. If you click into a specific Key Number, you will have the ability to search within the results and filter by jurisdiction and date.

- *Use KeyCite to validate your sources and search for other authority.*

1. You can use KeyCite to view the history of a case, statute, administrative decision, or regulation to help determine whether it is good law and to retrieve citing references to find additional relevant information on your issue or topic.

2. From any document with a KeyCite signal flag, click on the signal flag itself to view subsequent negative treatment of the document.

3. Clicking on the "History" tab at the top of the screen will give you a graphical display of the history of the case. This tool can help you decipher complex case histories.

4. The Citing References tab will allow you to see other materials that have cited to your document, including cases, statutes, regulations, and secondary sources. There are filtering options, depending on the kind of content selected, that will allow you to limit by jurisdiction, date, publication title (for secondary sources), and headnote topic. You can also run a search within results using your specific search terms.

5. You can also monitor your citations with KeyCite Alert. This service will update you when the KeyCite results for a particular source have changed. There are two ways to set up these alerts:

   ○ **Use KeyCite Alert wizard.** Click "Alert Center" in the upper-right corner of any page. Click "Create Alert" at the top of the screen and select "KeyCite." Type the citation of the document you want to monitor. The form will ask you the necessary questions to complete your KeyCite Alert entry.

   ○ **Create a KeyCite Alert entry for the document you are viewing.** Click the small bell icon in the top right corner of the document display to create an alert. The wizard will ask you the necessary questions to complete your KeyCite Alert entry, which will notify you if the KeyCite information for that document changes.

Step 2: Develop Horizontal and Vertical Knowledge

Step 1 was about going beyond your initial research to explore your topic and thesis in depth. As you gather these research materials, of course, you need to analyze them. You first need to get familiar with your topic at a broad level. At this point, depending on how familiar you are with your topic, this can involve anything from a quick review of research materials to time spent reading whole monographs. This first pass through your research materials is where you will develop your horizontal knowledge.

This horizontal knowledge is the firm foundation on which you will build your vertical knowledge. Your vertical knowledge involves in-depth exploration of the legal concepts and analysis that relate to your thesis. For example, Shaina needed a general understanding of immigration and citizenship law before she could fully develop her thesis about the widow penalty. Similarly, Natalie needed to read and understand the *Pyett* case and the decisions that preceded it before she could confidently offer a critique of the court's analysis.

Once you feel comfortable with the amount of background information and horizontal knowledge you possess, you will review and analyze the sources you are likely to cite in your paper. This is the transition to developing vertical knowledge. This involves memorializing your thoughts and reactions to your research materials, such as whether you agree or disagree with the authors, how you plan to use the material in your paper, and whether the source indicates you will need to refine your thesis statement or do further research. These notes will be invaluable as you move through the Preparing stage, further develop your vertical knowledge, and begin to move into Executing. They will be particularly important because you will use them to incorporate sources into your first draft.

Both Lexis and Westlaw let you make notes in their documents. Your notes will show up whenever you look at the source again. You can color code your notes and highlight portions of a source's text to keep track of how you are planning to use a source or identify next steps that come to mind as you are reading a particular source.

As you review the research materials you retrieved in Step 1, you are probably going to identify gaps in and questions about your research. This can include everything from a list of sources you need to find to new search terms you should use to new jurisdictions and databases in which to run the searches you tried earlier. You should keep track of these areas for further research and, when you are ready, pursue them using the tools and techniques we discussed in Step 1.

Continue to move back and forth between Steps 1 and 2 until you feel confident in the amount of knowledge (and supporting material) you possess.

Because of the sheer volume of material you will amass as part of this project, you need to keep careful track of your research materials, and organize not only the materials themselves but your notes on them as well. This is where the organizational system you planned at the outset of this chapter will come into play. Use the chart/software/diagram that you selected to keep track of each source: what it is, what it says, and your reaction to it.

Consider how Shaina and Natalie organized their research in different ways. A chart for Shaina's research materials could look like this:

Authority	Law	My Notes
8 U.S.C. §1151(b)(2)(A)(i) (2000). 8 C.F.R. §204.2 (1999).	A foreign-born immigrant married to an American citizen for less than two years loses his or her right to permanent residence if the spouse expires.	
Immigration Marriage Fraud Amendments of 1986, Pub. L. No. 99-639, 100 Stat. 3537.	The original purpose of the two-year condition was to deter fraudulent marriages, arranged for the purpose of obtaining permanent residency, between immigrants and U.S. citizens. Back in 1986, when the requirement was passed, there was widespread concern about immigrants using sham marriages to obtain "green cards" for permanent residence.	
Immigration and Nationality Act was amended in 1990.	Includes widow or widowers of United States citizens as "immediate relatives" when certain conditions were met, and allows alien widows to self-petition for permanent residency upon the death of their citizen spouses, this provision was only extended to alien widows who had been married to their citizen spouse for over two years at the time of the spouse's death.	Hence, immigrant widows who lost their spouses prior to the couple's two-year anniversary were left to suffer the effects of the so-called "widow penalty" and to fend for themselves in deportation proceedings.

In contrast, Natalie used an outline format to keep track of the major cases and her reactions to them.

I. The Second Circuit rationalized its decision in *Pyett* solely by analyzing prior case law (one Second Circuit case and three Supreme Court decisions). It did not give any policy reasons for its decision. Yet, it seems like the Court is really affirming the District Court's decision for policy reasons (the opinion reads like an effort by the Court to make the case law work in favor of the employee!). The case law could easily be interpreted in the complete opposite way. In fact, the defendant employer's interpretation of prior case law seems more plausible.

   • *Alexander v. Gardner-Denver Company*: This case merely held that the arbitration of contract-based claims does not preclude the litigation of statutory claims in a judicial forum. This case was unlike the current case in that the arbitration provision involved in this case did not explicitly incorporate the statutory anti-discrimination requirements or specifically state that the parties agree to submit all federal causes of action to arbitration.

   • *Gilmer*: The Court held that an individual employee could be compelled to arbitrate. It did not reach the question of whether a union member could be compelled to arbitrate. However, the fact that an individual employee can now be compelled to arbitrate makes the holding in *Alexander* irrelevant to the issue presented before us because the Court's holding in *Alexander* applied to both individuals and union members. The public policy reasons the Court uses to support its holding would apply in the case of a union-negotiated arbitration clause as well. For example, the Court notes the "liberal federal policy favoring arbitration."

   • *Wright*: Here, the Court held that the general arbitration clause in a union-negotiated contract did not require a covered employee to arbitrate because it was clear that a waiver had not occurred. It stated that it would not address the question of whether a waiver was enforceable, but determined that any requirement to arbitrate in a CBA must be "clear and unmistakable." This suggests that the Supreme Court is not opposed to the idea of enforcing arbitration clauses in union-negotiated contracts. If it were opposed to such an idea, it would not have created a standard by which such arbitration clauses must be judged.

- *Rogers*: The Court here specifically stated that *Wright* "could be taken to suggest that, under certain circumstances, a union-negotiated waiver of an employee's statutory rights to a judicial forum might be enforceable." The Court then laid out the "clear and unmistakable" test, noting that such a "clear and unmistakable" waiver had not occurred.

Both of these are valid organizational structures, and there are many more ways you can organize your research. Just make sure you have a system that captures all of your vertical knowledge and, if necessary, fulfills an interim assignment requirement.

While you are working closely with the sources you are likely to cite in your paper, keep track of your citations. We know you are not going to follow this advice to the letter because such a task is tedious and time-consuming. We can hear you, out there. "Scholars don't write that way!" you scoff. "Is my professor sitting somewhere with a Bluebook at her side while she works on her latest law review article?" No, probably not, but professors have research assistants— maybe you!—to help gather that information together, and you do not, so keep the scoffing to a minimum.

So, it makes sense to invest some time in keeping track of your citations as you work through your research; at a minimum, you should be meticulous here if you are recording verbatim quotations that you think you will take forward into your draft. Type out full text quotes in your notes so you can transfer them directly to your draft. Beyond that, think about working on your citations at this early stage. Remember you are working with new citation rules and citation formats for sources you have not encountered before. Also, this is when you are most enthusiastic—think about how tedious a task this will be when you are close to being done and you have to put everything in proper citation form (or, worse, if you cannot find the original source material at all).

This approach worked for a former scholarly writing student, Ryan Talbott, who created a citation-tracking document during the researching/pre-writing stage. In it, he included all of the sources he expected to cite (akin to a bibliography) in proper Bluebook form. He even included short forms! That way, as he moved to drafting his note, he saved time by copying and pasting citations from his cite list instead of having to figure out citation form while he was writing. This also saved time because he resolved citation issues (such as what to do for sources not directly addressed by the Bluebook) consistently when he made his list, and did not have to backtrack to make sure he was consistent later on.

The electronic research services provide tools to simplify the citation process—these tools allow you to gather citation information directly from the sources you have accessed online. Be wary of shortcuts here: You should not cut and paste citation and quotation information from electronic sources into your research document or paper draft. First, this can bring assorted formatting problems and hyperlinked codes that can mess up your document. Second, the information in the sources—especially citation information—is often incorrect. Finally, this shortcut can hurt your "ownership" of the information—typing it out yourself forces you to really read it and be critical about its import.

As we said, though, we know you probably will not listen to this advice, and sometimes it makes sense to ignore it—if you are on a roll reading through articles, it might make less sense to take some time to work through the citation rules and we certainly do not want you to lose momentum. But, at a minimum, as you work through your sources, make sure you have all the information that you will need for the full citation—including dates and pin cites.

Of course, at the end of the writing process, you will go back and verify all of your quotes and citations, but this will go a lot quicker if you have been thorough and detailed throughout.

Step 3: Update Your Research

In the context of practical legal research, "updating" usually means case and statute verification: making sure the law you use is still good. Here, if your research involves cases and statutes, you of course want to do that, too. However, you also need to "update" your research by staying on top of developments in the law and newly published pieces on your topic.

Remember you will be working on your scholarly writing project for many months. Thus, you need to make sure your research is active even after you move out of the Preparing stage. This is important for both research and topic/thesis development (and, to some extent, preemption). This does not mean you have to run the same searches and revisit the same databases you have already reviewed. There are many tools you can use to keep your research active after you initially gather source materials. Consider the following, which will help you monitor your research results throughout the writing process:

- Search Alerts on Lexis Advance: This will allow you to track issues through term searches and receive updated search results via email.
  - Once you have run a search, click on the bell icon next to your search to create an alert.
  - Fill out the Alert form, which asks you to name the Alert, set the frequency for how often you wish to be updated, and choose delivery and notification options.
  - You can edit and delete your Alerts in the Alerts module on the Lexis Advance research home page or by clicking the "More" dropdown menu in the top right corner of the screen and selecting "Alerts."
- WestClip on Westlaw: This will run your Terms and Connectors searches on a regular basis and then deliver the results to you automatically or notify you that results are available.
  - Run a Terms and Connectors search. You must do this within a specific content type, such as "Cases," to be able to see the option to save your search. Once the Alert is set up, you can add other document categories to search.
  - Click the small bell icon at the top of the result list to create a WestClip Alert. The database identifier and your Terms and Connectors search are automatically entered for you, though you can alter them here if necessary
  - You can customize the delivery settings by choosing a delivery format, address, and layout.
  - The last step in the process allows you to schedule the alert, setting both the frequency and the delivery time.
  - Click Save Alert to save the entry in the WestClip Directory.
  - Alternatively, you can create a WestClip entry by clicking Alert Center at the top of any page. At the Alert Center Directory, click Create in the WestClip section. The WestClip: Create Entry page is displayed. Type a database identifier and Terms and Connectors search in the appropriate text boxes.
- Google Alerts: This will allow you to get email updates of the latest Google results from news sites, blogs, or the entire web.
  - Go to http://www.google.com/alerts.
  - Fill out the form indicating your search terms, the sources you wish to search, your desired frequency, and the email address to which you want your search results delivered.
- RSS feeds: If your research leads you to online news sites or blogs that you want to follow, you may want to set up an RSS ("Really Sim-

ple Syndication") feed to make it easier to stay on top of new information from these sources. Many news sites, blogs, and other websites syndicate the content on their sites so that users can read new posts and information through an RSS feeder. RSS feeders retrieve the feeds from various sites and allow you to read them in a single, aggregated location. This means you will not have to bookmark and view the individual pages to see when they are updated. Popular web-based RSS feeders include Feedly (http://feedly.com) and Digg (http://digg.com).

Because you want your final draft to be as complete and up-to-date as it can be, you must update your research as you work your way through the writing process. You do not want to compromise your credibility as an author by having stale information or missing one of the new developments in the field.

Step 4: Revisit Your Initial Thesis

By the time you reach this step, you have thoroughly researched and read all the relevant materials, have taken notes along the way, updated your research, and filled all the gaps you identified. Think back to the two types of knowledge you are gathering through this process: horizontal and vertical. At this point, you should possess a sufficient amount of both, and should have notes and reactions to all the sources you gathered and reviewed as you were developing this knowledge.

Once you reach this point, you should revisit your initial thesis to see if it needs any refinement. Some of you may have drafted an initial thesis that you knew was imperfect. Others may have felt confident enough to draft a more substantive initial thesis. Regardless, everyone should take a moment at the end of the Preparing stage to revisit, and possibly improve, their initial thesis. If your initial thesis involved a legislative action, but you were not sure what that legislation should look like, spend some time thinking about that now. If your initial thesis proposed legislation but your in-depth research uncovered the fact that something similar was already proposed in Congress and failed, modify your thesis to include a different approach. Think back to Shaina's initial thesis, which you saw in Chapter 2. Her topic was the problem of inconsistent judicial interpretation in spouse-based immigration law, and she drafted this initial thesis:

> To resolve inconsistencies in judicial interpretation of immigration law, I will propose that Congress take legislative action to amend spouse-based immigration law.

After completing her in-depth research, she was ready to refine her thesis to propose specific legislative action. Thus, her refined thesis was the following:

> To resolve inconsistencies in judicial interpretation of immigration law, Congress should take legislative action to amend spouse-based immigration law. First, Congress should enact an amendment to exempt foreign-born widows from the "two-year" marriage requirement for obtaining permanent residence status upon the death of their citizen spouses. [Second], [a]s a substitute for the two-year rule, I will propose that Congress should pass an amendment that would (1) allow immigrant widows to still be considered "immediate relatives" of U.S. citizens after the death of their citizen spouses and (2) permit widows to self-petition for permanent residency status, regardless of the length of their marriage to the U.S. citizens.

Shaina has now refined her initial thesis by including a "should clause" and making specific legislative recommendations. This added substance and specificity strengthen the initial thesis.

Like Shaina, Collin refined his initial thesis after working through his research and developing a mastery of the topic. His initial thesis was as follows:

> While not all aspects of the contractor-civil servant distinction should be eliminated (i.e. contractors still should probably not be given the protection and benefits of the civil service laws), this note will argue that the prohibition on personal services contracts represents one distinction that no longer has any grounding in reality. As such, FAR 37.104 should be replaced with guidance for federal managers on how to properly and most efficiently supervise contractor personnel alongside civil servants. This note will propose three recommendations:
> 1) Congress should direct the General Services Administration to delete section 37.104 from the Federal Acquisition Regulations, which prohibits federal agencies from contracting for personal services.
> 2) Regulations should be put in place (not sure yet by whom, but presumably Congress or the General Services Administration) that provide guidance to federal agencies on how to best manage their relationships with contractor personnel. These regulations will likely include recommendations and best practices on how to supervise contractor personnel, how to recognize those situations that are likely to create employment (and other) issues, and how to properly process a contractor's complaint.

3) Finally (and at the very least), both federal agencies and government contractors should be encouraged to institute training programs designed to help their personnel (i.e. federal managers and contractor employees) recognize potential problem situations. Above all, federal agencies and contractors need to realize how the application of joint employer liability to the federal government will impact their relationship with each other.

After thinking more about what he could accomplish in a single scholarly paper, Collin refined his thesis to the following:

The personal services prohibition represents an outdated and inefficient method of protecting the government's interest and should be abolished. Given the government's current reliance on service contractors, procurement officials should not be concerned with whether a contract creates an employment relationship with the government but with whether contractor personnel are being properly managed and supervised. Congress should thus explicitly abolish the personal services prohibition and apply government ethics laws to personal service contractors. This will reduce the ability of personal service contractors, who often perform discretionary functions on the government's behalf, to act in their own personal interest to the detriment of the government's mission.

Collin's refined thesis is narrowly focused on his specific proposal to abolish the personal services prohibition and to apply government ethics standards to personal service contractors. Though his analysis may still include some of the three recommendations he listed in his initial thesis, his revised thesis is crafted more succinctly. This revision is significant because Collin now has a more manageable thesis to defend compared to his original 3-part proposal, yet he has not lost any substantive value of his paper by narrowing it this way.

Through her in-depth research and understanding of partial verdicts, Jessie refined her initial thesis to more specifically describe her practical guide and highlight its utility. Jessie's initial thesis was:

Due to the incompleteness of the Rule itself, a trial judge is left trying to interpret confusing case law to determine whether a partial verdict is appropriate in a given situation. The purpose of this Comment is to summarize existing case law and offer a practical guide for Federal District Court judges as to when a partial verdict, and a partial verdict instruction, is appropriate. The basis for this Comment is looking at Circuit cases either affirming or overturning partial verdict convictions.

With a clearer sense of what her practical guide would offer to judges and a better understanding of the downsides of the existing partial verdict system, Jessie revised her thesis:

> By summarizing existing case law and offering a practical guide of best practices—in the form of *A Series of Practical Questions Answered*—this Comment seeks to advise district court judges on the appropriateness of issuing partial verdict instructions and receiving partial verdicts. This Comment in no way suggests that district court judges should not exercise discretion when determining whether to issue partial verdict instructions or receive partial verdicts; it merely strives to serve as a potential resource. The hope is that this guide will assist judges in making decisions—quickly—about whether to give a partial verdict instruction or receive a partial verdict in a particular case. Specifically, this guide assists a district court judge in (1) making fast, informed decisions; (2) avoiding a reversal on appeal, despite its unlikelihood; and (3) avoiding having their decision, although affirmed, labeled erroneous by a federal court of appeals.

Jessie's revised thesis is more substantive in giving the reader a full scope of what to expect in her paper; this reflects her deeper understanding of the challenges of partial verdicts. It also reflects a more deliberate purpose for the practical guide by directly connecting to concerns judges are likely to have in considering whether to change their approach to partial verdicts. Listing the three ways her guide will help judges also sets up a natural organization for her comment as she goes forward.

After you refine your initial thesis, you should start to think about your arguments. You may have had some sense of where you wanted your arguments to go even as you were drafting your initial thesis. You may only see the arguments come together after you have waded through the sea of research materials you have gathered. You may need to devote some time to this task specifically, because your arguments have not yet gelled. Now is the time to do this: through brainstorming, rough outlining, drawing issue trees or flowcharts—whatever helps you visualize where you want to go with your argument. The form does not matter; choose what works for you.

Then take these thoughts and return to your source material. You should start thinking about a hierarchy within these resources—what are the sources you will include in your paper? Did you start by reading a treatise to give you some background in this area of the law? This was probably a useful step for you, but you probably do not have to include this horizontal information in your paper. Have you read through numerous cases and deemed them unrelated to your case comment thesis? You can trim them from your research notes so that you have a clearer picture of the source material you will bring into your first draft. Is there one key article that you need to address in order to make your thesis sound? Make sure you have flagged or otherwise highlighted this article in your notes, so you know where it fits into your hierarchy of sources. Once you have done this, update your research chart, place your sources into piles, or make a list of which of your sources correspond to each of your draft arguments. This will help you get and stay organized as you move from the Preparing stage to the Executing stage.

This may seem like an unnecessary step to you—you may feel that you have been researching and reading for long enough and want to get started on the first draft. Earlier in this chapter, we warned you against rushing through the Preparing stage. You can get a false sense of progress if you open a Word document called "Paper First Draft" and just begin typing. You will serve yourself well if you are patient and allow yourself to revisit your thesis, think about your arguments, and analyze your research materials before you begin writing the first draft. As we said earlier, good writing comes from good thinking, and writing too soon can cut off some important thinking time. We will discuss more formal outlining and writing in the context of the first draft in Chapter 4. For now, your aspiration is to find some way to start linking your source material to your arguments, in whatever way works for you.

Step 5: Approach the First Draft

As you go through these steps, you are getting closer and closer to your first draft. This book is premised on the notion that writing is a process—one that is nonlinear, recursive, and made up of steps that flow into one another. Even so, there is a distinction between this organizing/research document and the actual, written first draft that is the subject of Chapter 4. Just as there is blurring between the steps in the process, there may be blurring between these concepts. You may have a research outline, an outline of the first draft, and then a fully-written first draft. You may start with a single document that evolves into the first draft as you move through the stages of the writing process. Regardless, there is a moment in which you shift from researcher to writer; you need to think about that mental shift as you move to the end of researching (even though you never really stop researching) and begin to focus on the product that is the draft.

Think about the phases of the writing process that we laid out in Chapter 1. This phase was about Preparing: doing in-depth research, reading and analyzing the research materials, and beginning to think about the organization of the paper. The next phase is Executing: putting fingers to keyboard and developing the points you plan to make in your paper. There is fluidity between these concepts: If, once you start writing, you decide that you need more information about what you originally thought was a minor point, then you must go all the way back to your research beginnings and retrieve the new source material. But there is a point after your initial research when you will move into writing the first draft, and you should be mindful of this shift.

When do you make this shift? Of course, it is not a permanent shift, so you cannot really make it at the wrong time. In general, think about finding the right time by asking yourself these five questions:

> **Is your research complete and updated?** You will, of course, keep re-searching your topic as you go through the writing process—to fill in gaps, explore new arguments, respond to feedback, even just to stay on top of your topic (this is especially important if you are working on something cutting edge or under consideration by Congress). But you need to get to the point where you have enough vertical knowledge to talk confidently about this area of the law, and are thus ready to lay the proper foundation for and begin to advance your argument. So, your research needs to be "complete" in the sense that you are the master of the information, and you feel competent enough to speak about it as an authority. As part of this, you will want to set up some of the tools you can use to stay on top of the research, as we discussed earlier in the chapter. However, what is key here is that *you* understand and have dissected the authority—you can bring in other supportive sources as you go, but you have to feel competent enough to begin. You need to feel confident, otherwise you may begin to doubt yourself later. You do not want a lax attitude in these early stages to affect your end product. To go back to the analogy that opened the chapter, you have to be Elle, Baby, or Thornton, post-montage.

> **Have you answered the questions you identified while analyzing the materials?** You may have been answering these questions as you went along—really this just feeds into your research being complete and updated. But you may have flagged non-research questions during this phase also—something you wanted to ask your professor, your journal advisor, or the attorney you worked for this summer. The answers to these questions may bear on the manageability of your topic

and the reasonableness of your thesis, so you want to get these answered before you move on as well.

Have you evaluated your topic and initial thesis statement? After you have immersed yourself in your research, you will revisit your starting point (remember, this is a recursive process). What were your original topic and thesis? How have they evolved (or must they evolve) based on what you learned while you were developing your horizontal and vertical knowledge? Can you explain your thesis to a new audience in a single sentence?

Have you culled your materials and organized them in a logical way? As we noted in Step 4, you need to take some time to get organized before you move on to writing the first draft. We cannot emphasize enough the importance of this—organized research materials are a necessary prerequisite to maintaining the integrity of your paper, from both a substantive and structural standpoint. Poor organization can lead to a lost argument, or a misattributed source, both of which are huge problems in the end. Take some time to get organized before you start writing, to prevent both of these types of problems at the outset.

Are you mentally ready to begin writing? A project of this size can be an overwhelming task, so make sure you are in the right frame of mind when you sit down to start writing—this is where you might really feel the occurrence of this shift. You can keep yourself busy running online searches and reading previously published articles, taking notes and outlining, and filling in a spreadsheet with good quotes, but at a certain point this is just busy work—the process is important, but only if it yields a product that meets the necessary requirements. Start on a day when you can get something done. Do not obsess over the first sentence. Start where it makes the most sense to start. We will discuss more drafting strategies in Chapter 4.

If you answered yes to all of these questions, you should feel comfortable moving on to start writing your first draft. Remember, however, that even once you feel you are ready to move on, and these steps have been completed, it does not mean that you permanently leave them behind. Starting your draft does not mean that you are done with your research. You might go all the way back to your thesis statement and change it once you begin writing. You may have to go back to research a point that you have promoted from a minor to a major one. Even after you have moved from

Preparing to Executing, you might need to revisit the Preparing stage as you work through your project.

The Preparing stage is all about you: making sure that you have the requisite knowledge to craft your scholarly paper. When you begin your first draft, you will need to address broader audience considerations. We will begin to discuss these considerations in Chapter 4.

CHAPTER 4

EXECUTING:
WRITING THE DRAFT

The scholarly writing process requires that you put together multiple "first" drafts. The Executing stage involves construction of your *first* first draft—getting all of your thoughts down on paper in a rough, unedited draft for your eyes only. Chapter 4 will guide you through the construction of this first draft, which we call the "non-public draft." This draft is "non-public" because it is something you will share only with an audience of one: yourself. Many students find it easier to move their scholarly writing projects forward after they have this first, rough draft written.

With a rough draft, you can move on to the Refining stage, discussed in Chapter 5. At the end of your first pass through the Refining stage, you will have constructed the first draft that you will share with an outside audience.

Before you start writing, make sure that you have considered everything that goes into the construction of this first public draft. How long does it have to be? When is it due? Who is going to read it? Is there anything post-research (but pre-draft) such as an annotated outline that your first audience wants to review? Answer these questions and plan accordingly. Careful planning will allow you to work efficiently, comply with deadlines, and save yourself some headaches later on in the writing process. Once you have a plan in place, you are ready to move on to actual construction of your non-public draft.

Major Elements of the Draft

Although you have probably read legal papers and articles in the past, you may not have considered the actual architecture of these documents. A legal research paper or article is actually quite simple in structure. It has four basic parts:

- an **Introduction** that offers a snapshot of the entire paper, including an articulation of your thesis statement and a roadmap of the sections that follow
- a **Background** section that provides information about your topic and lays the necessary foundation for your thesis
- the **Analysis** or **Discussion**, where you lay out the arguments in support of your thesis
- a short **Conclusion**, which allows you to wrap up the points you set forth in the paper

Now is a good time to look back to the model paper that we discussed in Chapter 1. Back then you used it to envision your final project and understand what it means to engage in scholarly writing. Now, giving it a more detailed look can help as you prepare to write your own draft. This is particularly helpful if you are writing for a specific context, such as a journal that has offered you a sample published note or a thesis that satisfied the requirements of your program. Through this review, you can get a sense of the finished product and how the elements discussed above work together for your specific scholarly project.

The Introduction and Conclusion are the bookends of your paper. They anchor the opening and closing and carry the weight of the arguments contained within the heart of your paper, which is comprised of the Background and Analysis/Discussion sections. Proportionally, the Background and Analysis/Discussion sections will comprise the bulk of your paper. We recommend drafting them first.

Drafting the Background and Analysis/Discussion Sections

Every scholarly paper needs to advance a thesis on a firm foundation of what has come before it. This is why we stressed the importance of developing horizontal and vertical knowledge in Chapter 3. Your goal in the Background and Analysis/Discussion sections is to use this knowledge to set forth the relevant and necessary background information, and then build upon that information with the arguments that support your thesis statement.

Think of your thesis statement as the nucleus of your paper: it is the solid core around which the rest of the paper will be built. Once you have this core in place, think next about how you want to proceed with the draft.

Remember the goals of the Background and Analysis/Discussion sections, which can vary based on what type of paper you are writing. In a case comment, the Background section will typically set forth the decision on which the comment is focused, including any procedural history and major precedents on which that decision relies. In a broader research paper, the Background section should explain any necessary foundational information, such as the history of the statute the paper will challenge or the nature of a particular problem the paper attempts to solve. Once this backdrop is established, you can begin your own analysis. In a case comment, you will offer your view of whether the case was decided correctly and why. Other papers need to offer analysis and arguments in support of their thesis statements. There may be some blurring between the two sections, and in fact you may move information from one section to the other as you proceed through the draft.

Legal authors generally approach the Executing stage in one of two ways: writing from the inside out, or writing from the outside in. Writing from the inside out means starting with the argument and building the rest of the paper around it, filling in the source material after the analysis/discussion is written. This could also be called "writing backwards."

A lot of academics write from the inside out. This is because they are established experts. If you came to your topic with some background knowledge, after doing some initial legal research you may have accumulated enough horizontal and vertical knowledge to be ready to "write backwards." However, this requires expertise on your topic and thesis, so this method might not work for you because you are likely cultivating your own expertise as you go through the writing process.

The alternative, of course, is to "write forwards" or from the outside in—to work with sources as you go. There are varying degrees of formality when it comes to this approach to writing. The most formal is starting with a detailed, annotated outline and transforming that outline into a draft. This could even start as early as the research phase. Your starting point is your research chart. Then you can reorganize the research chart so that the sources are organized around the major points you plan to make in your argument. You can then build an annotated outline, or a tiered outline laying out the substance of your argument. Then you can add shape to the outline, moving it from outline to draft.

You do not need to be rigid as you move from research material to outline to draft. You can certainly use a combination of these and other techniques to put the full draft together. But the idea is that you are working with source material from the beginning, as opposed to writing backwards, where you write a source-free draft and then fill in the authorities and other pieces after you draft the initial points. Ultimately, whichever method you choose, you wind up with the same work product—a well-sourced, argument-driven draft. Just be sure to choose the method that fits with your level of comfort. Most student scholarly writers are more comfortable with writing forwards, because this method is less reliant on expertise and allows for more development of vertical knowledge while you are writing.

Here, it may help to mentally separate drafting the two major parts of the paper—the Background and Analysis/Discussion sections. You may want to use a different drafting strategy for each—because the background section necessarily involves a logical progression among sources, it might make sense to be more linear there. Depending on how confident you are about your argument, you might write the Analysis/Discussion section differently.

During this first draft you may "overwrite" the background section— that is, you may find that you include more background than your ultimate audience requires. This is okay for now. Unless you are a true master of this material, drafting the Background section can be another way that you continue to learn about this area of the law. Ultimately, though, you may need to prune some of that background information because it will be too basic or detailed for the average member of your audience, or even the audience for your first public draft. We will discuss this further in Chapter 5.

Note that, ultimately, these two elements may encompass more than two sections of your paper. For example, in Shaina's Note, Sections I–IV set forth the necessary background for her proposed solution. Natalie includes some necessary background even in the section labeled "Personal Analysis," so that she can eventually get to her argument that there is a catch-22 and her proposed solutions to the problem. We will discuss the interoperation of these sections in Chapter 5, but for now, what they need to accomplish should be clear to you, as should the two ways you can approach the actual drafting of the body of the paper.

If you are overwhelmed about diving into these sections, or just want a smaller task to get your writing started, you could try one of the following strategies:

- **Draft the headings to the major sections and subsections of the paper.** This is really just another way of saying "make a bare-bones outline." Think about the major sections and sub-sections that your paper requires and write out these headings, then make sure they are arranged in the right order. Do not worry about adding in authority or nuance, or even the format of the headings themselves (we talk more about heading format below). Just try and outline the major points you want to make, in order to get the body of the paper organized.

- **Write an executive summary of the paper.** Rather than try and tackle the whole Analysis/Discussion section in detail, try and write a one- or two-page executive summary of all the points you plan to cover in the paper. Think of this as a "prose outline"—it covers everything you want to say in the paper but in narrative form. This exercise will help make your thoughts more concrete and allow you to manipulate what you have written so that you can organize your thoughts later. You can then use this summary as a touchstone when you move on to drafting the Analysis/Discussion section and building out all of your points.

- **Draw a diagram of the arguments you plan to make.** If you tend to conceptualize things visually, or are just having a hard time mapping out the organization of this particular paper, consider liberating yourself from outlines or sentences and sketch out an organizational framework in a diagram. If you have a general sense of your organization, you can do this with a flowchart. If you are still trying to figure out the interrelationship of your arguments, you can write them all down and add in the organizational structure after you have memorialized everything you want to say without regard for order. This strategy can free you from being overly structured during your attempt at early organization and allows you to take a bird's-eye view of the paper; this can help you see how the arguments are linked and should be organized. See, for example, the diagram of Chris's organizational structure on the next page.

Any of these techniques can help you get started and can make approaching these sections less daunting. Once you have used one of these devices to plan out your arguments, you can move to drafting using one of the strategies we laid out above.

Drafting the Introduction

The Introduction is the first thing the reader will read, but it is probably not the first thing you will write. Although it may seem logical to start writing

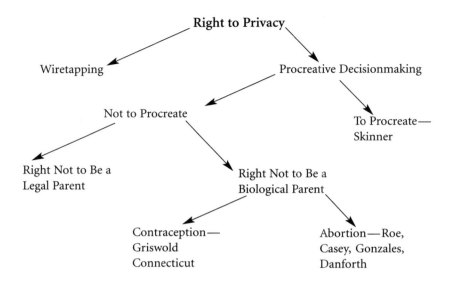

with the first element of the paper, think it over: Can you introduce something that does not yet exist? This is why we recommend you start by writing the Background and Analysis/Discussion sections of your draft first.

That said, you do not have to save the Introduction for last. At some point while you are writing, you may think of a great opening paragraph to your paper, or at least get an idea of how you would like to open the paper. For example, you might find a case with an interesting set of facts that you think would make for a compelling opening. If you are so inspired, get it down on paper! Know, though, that you will have to revisit your Introduction once your other sections are complete, so that you can properly set the table for your discussion and make the paper internally consistent.

The goal of the Introduction is, of course, to give the reader a snapshot of what your paper is about. A secondary aspiration is grabbing the reader's attention and making her want to keep reading. The Introduction should articulate the thesis statement clearly, and set up the context for it. You will also want to use the Introduction to roadmap the sections and arguments that follow (we discuss roadmaps further, below). Proportionally, you want to accomplish this in a few pages; the length will vary with the overall size of the project. For example, a master's thesis will probably have a longer Introduction than a case comment. Reviewing your model paper or other aspirational works can help you get a sense of the proportion here.

There are various ways to construct an effective Introduction. Some Introductions simply describe the topic and thesis to the reader. Some papers open with a "human interest" angle, using a story involving real people to illustrate the problem that the paper attempts to solve. Other papers open with a hypothetical situation that provides a similar type of illustration. Whether you use a real or hypothetical "story" as an opening depends on your topic and whether a good, real example exists; both of these are effective ways of placing your thesis statement in context. You can also use these anchors in the paper's Conclusion, as we discuss in the next section.

Consider, for example, the process Nathaniel used to think through his Introduction. In Nathaniel's first draft he jotted down some ideas and quotations that he wanted to include, starting with an anecdote about how Independence Hall had been allowed to fall into disrepair and leading up to an introduction to "historic preservation."

- Anecdote: 1991 and 1992 listing of Independence Hall on 11 most endangered places. In talking about this project, envisioned that the idea of expanding protections for historic structures would be for the benefit of more obscure vernacular, privately owned structures imperiled by over development, disuse, neglect. Take for granted that certain icon structures are "taken care of." How did a National Historic Landmark, a National Historic Site, a World Heritage Site, a unit of the National Park Service fall into disrepair ... in the 1990s!!!!
- National Trust article: Often called the "birthplace of the nation," Independence National Historical Park was created to showcase and preserve authentic structures, sites and historical objects that tell the story of the founding of the United States over 200 hundred years ago. Under the stewardship of the National Park Service, America's "most historic square-mile" attracts millions of national and international visitors annually. Yet while tourists experienced the unfolding drama of this landmark space, severe deterioration is occurring behind the scenes. Although the National Park Service puts on a brilliant façade, it does not have enough money for more than "quick-fix" maintenance and lacks adequate resources to repair leaky roofs, replace archaic plumbing, heating and air-conditioning systems or remove such potential hazards as asbestos and PCBs.
- What is historic preservation? "Preservation is the management of change and active use of remains for present and future purpose, not an inflexible reverence for a sacrosanct past." Crafting the built environment to reflect a conviction that the past is "inextricably

linked to the future" does not mean the latter must be a paralyzing burden on the former. Yet the tension as played out on the built landscape so often suggests otherwise. Ada Louise Huxtable: "That combination of civilized sentiment and historic sensibility that makes cities rich and real and nothing to do with real estate values that make cities rich and sterile."

Nathaniel returned to the Introduction later in the writing process to develop it more fully. In his next draft, he put a first-person spin on his opening paragraph, sharing his own conflict with the reader.

> For the past twenty years, the National Trust for Historic Preservation has published a list of the eleven "Most Endangered Historic Places" in an effort to "rais[e] awareness of the serious threats facing the nation's greatest treasures." It only takes a glance at the accompanying descriptions to understand why these places—even the ones we have not heard of—are worthy of our attention. The cynic in me thinks the list is really "Preservation for Dummies;" only a fool would consider losing places of such caliber to history. In the interest of not wanting to appear a hopeless ideologue, I try to counterbalance my frustration with a belief—or hope—that if these places are lost, it is because we as a people are making informed choices about what we hold as most important.

In a later version (the first draft that he submitted for editorial review) he began instead by introducing the article that was his inspiration for his paper. The article was written thirty years ago but still had relevance when Nathaniel wrote his paper. By doing so, Nathaniel could impress upon the reader that the problem he addressed was longstanding and needed a solution.

> Just over thirty years ago, environmental ethicist Christopher Stone responded to serious deficiencies in the nation's system of environmental protection with a novel proposal: give substantive rights to natural objects. Stone's approach essentially elevated the natural object above the uneven patchwork of protection afforded it by law to a common and higher standard; even in the absence or deficiency of environmental protection laws, natural objects would have a default right to exist free from damage—a right that must be rebutted by would-be exploiters. Through a guardian, they would have legal standing to bring an action on their own behalf. Further, any damage to them would, by right, be measured by their own injury and run to their

own benefit. Thus, for instance, if a forest was to be cut, the logger must "compensate" other forests by an amount commensurate with the value of the forest lost. Such a system recognizes the intrinsic value of the natural object, its worth to future generations, and, in so doing, forces a more thoughtful consideration of its use.

This version survived intact in his final paper.

Some papers open with a notable quotation from a case, a scholar, a philosopher, a movie, or any number of other sources. This can be an effective way to open your paper as well, but we have seen many students who think this is the only way to start an Introduction, and thus we offer a few words of caution here. Do not work hard to find a quotation to serve as your opening. As you now know, there are several creative ways to open your paper. You may, however, find a worthy quotation in the course of your research. A "worthy" quotation is one that is closely connected to your topic and thesis, is attributed to a credible source, and amounts to a good "sound bite." For example, a generic quote about the state of immigration law in the United States would not be an effective opening to Shaina's Note, but a quote from a prominent legal scholar about the widow penalty might be worthy of her opening sentence. If in the course of your research you come across a worthy quotation, you can use it but make sure it is clear to the reader why you chose it. Make a connection between the quotation and your topic and thesis within the first few sentences of your opening paragraph.

Ultimately, there are several angles you can take when writing the opening to your Introduction. As with Nathaniel's Introduction, described above, your opening paragraph is something that may change frequently through the drafting process, so be open-minded and try not to get wedded to a particular opening. And remember: several types of Introductions could be successful. Consider this human interest introduction to Natalie's paper:

> For fourteen years, Steven Pyett worked as a night watchman in a commercial office building owned by Pennsylvania Building Company (PBC). Thomas O'Connell and Michael Phillips also worked as night watchmen in the building for many years. However, in July of 2003, PBC transferred these three employees to "less desirable" positions. Pyett and O'Connell were reassigned as night porters, and Phillips was reassigned as a cleaner. The following month, PBC hired new security personnel, including night watchmen, from Spartan Security, a security services provider. The new employees were younger than Pyett, O'Connell, and Phillips, all of whom were more than fifty years of age at the time they were transferred.

This opening puts a human face on the *Pyett* case that Natalie is writing about. Now consider the more general opening paragraph she used in her final paper:

> Employees struggle for power in the workplace. Due mostly to the employment-at-will doctrine, the tilt in the balance of power tends to favor employers. As a result, many of the laws that regulate the employment relationship were designed to shift power toward employees in order to achieve some sense of equilibrium. For example, although employers could historically discharge employees for any reason whatsoever, Title VII of the Civil Rights Act of 1964 (Title VII) offered employees a cause of action against employers who discharged them on the basis of race, color, sex, religion, and national origin. Unfortunately, the rules that govern agreements to arbitrate employment discrimination claims—which employers now frequently include in both individual and union-negotiated employment contracts—fail to effectively balance the interests of employers and employees. Rather, the rule that applies to individual employees tips the scale too far in favor of arbitration agreements while the rule that applies to union employees tips the scale too far away from arbitration agreements, either way robbing the employee of meaningful forum choice.

Both versions do what good openings must: introduce the reader to the subject matter and get her to keep reading. They are both effective alternatives to open the paper. Your Introduction also needs to state your thesis overtly at some point, usually after you have set forth the relevant background information but before you roadmap the rest of the paper. Many papers use direct language when stating the thesis, such as "This note will establish...." or "The objective of this paper is...." For example, Natalie's paper states:

> This Note argues that, based solely on prior case law, particularly *Circuit City*, the *Pyett* court should have held that an arbitration clause is enforceable against an employee regardless of the employee's union status.

Shaina's thesis is less direct but still clearly stated:

> To rectify this legal wrong, Congress should enact legislation to abolish the widow penalty for all alien widows, regardless of whether the citizen spouse filed a petition prior to death or marriage length.

If you use this less direct approach, try to include signaling words that tell the reader this is the thesis you plan to advance, as Shaina did.

Most Introductions end with a roadmap of the major subsections of the paper; the "parts" highlighted here should correspond with the heading breaks in the body of the paper. For example, here is Shaina's roadmap:

> Part I of this Note describes the process of becoming a legal permanent resident through marriage to a U.S. citizen. Part II discusses how the modern-day widow penalty was formed and explains the rule's categorical exceptions. Part III explores the dueling interpretations of the two-year rule, advanced in relevant court cases by the government and petitioner-widows. Part IV analyzes pending legislation that seeks to alleviate the harsh effects of the widow penalty in some respects. Finally, Part V addresses the need to adopt legislation that allows all alien spouses to self-petition for LPR status upon the death of their citizen spouses, regardless of marriage length.

This type of roadmap tells the reader how the rest of your paper is organized. It takes the reader through the sections of the paper and establishes the goal of each. Note how overt it is—each sentence corresponds to each of the numbered sections of the analysis that follows the Introduction. This type of roadmap is quite common (and may be a convention of many journals), but it is also possible to have a softer roadmap as well.

Natalie's roadmap is less rigid. Her roadmap opens with her thesis statement and then lays out the arguments she will make in support of that thesis. These sentences roughly correlate with the sub-sections of her analysis section; at a minimum, they provide an overview of the Note as a whole. Here is Natalie's roadmap:

> This Note argues that, based solely on prior case law, particularly *Circuit City*, the *Pyett* court should have held that an arbitration clause is enforceable against an employee regardless of the employee's union status. Nonetheless, the *Pyett* court properly declined to apply the *Circuit City* rule to CBAs because the *Circuit City* rule results in a catch-22 for both union and non-union employees, one that disproportionately affects members of the classes protected by the antidiscrimination statutes. Rather than extend an intolerable rule, the *Pyett* court created a somewhat superior, but far-from-ideal, paradoxical standard whereby union workers with significant bargaining power can never be compelled to waive their statutory rights, but non-union workers with very little bargaining power can easily be compelled to do so. As this Note suggests, the law unfairly denies non-union employees the protective shield it

offers union workers. Additionally, the law unnecessarily denies union workers the capacity to agree in advance to arbitrate federal statutory claims, even if it is in their best interests to do so. Thus, lawmakers should develop standards that adequately and equally protect the rights and interests of all employees whether they are union or non-union workers.

This Note also proposes solutions to the problems associated with the contract-formation stage of the arbitral process. Any viable solution must enable employees to make informed choices regarding arbitration and, most importantly, must prevent employers from presenting arbitration clauses as conditions of employment. Anything less would deprive employees of meaningful choice and undermine the goals of the antidiscrimination statutes.

You have a lot of flexibility when it comes to writing Introductions, and both Shaina's and Natalie's are effective examples. As long as the Introduction articulates the paper's thesis, places it in proper context, and lays out the framework for the paper for the reader, it has accomplished what it needs to. You can read three complete Introductions, with annotations, in the Appendix.

Drafting the Conclusion

The Conclusion should include a brief restatement of your thesis and the major arguments that support it. By now, the reader has read through all of your arguments in detail, so your Conclusion can be short. The tone can be different, because you have already done the hard work of explaining your argument to your reader. You should not introduce anything new in your Conclusion. Consider Chris's Conclusion:

Although the Supreme Court has focused on protecting the procreative autonomy of women, the Court has not considered the right of procreative autonomy held by biological fathers. Although a woman's right to have an abortion gives her full autonomy over her procreative decisions, the impossibility for men to become pregnant has inhibited recognition of their similar decisionmaking rights. Although it is understandable that courts have construed the right to abortion as evolving from a right to bodily integrity, after reviewing the relevant Supreme Court case law, it becomes evident that the Court's focus was on the ability of an individual to make uniquely introspective decisions regarding personhood—what the *Casey* Court referred to as "choices central to personal dignity and autonomy." Such choices should include whether to be a father to a child, which is distinct from whether to produce a child. It is such a realm of decisional privacy that this Note advocates protecting. As this Note has shown, the father-child relationship comes with significant moral, legal, economic, and sociological consequences. *Gonzales v. Carhart* provides the final step toward judicial recognition of the right to decide not to be a legal father by permitting the consideration of such emotional harm in the constitutional calculus.

There are significant complications in the application of the right to decide not to be a legal father. While these difficulties present a compelling argument to give little if any weight to the paternal right to avoid legal parenthood, the recognition of such a right is necessary to clarify the jurisprudence of procreative autonomy. Neither Sharon Irons nor Lauren Wells deserved child support. Moreover, both Richard Phillips and Matthew Dubay had real and intimate interests in avoiding declarations of paternity. Therefore, notwithstanding any complications, the courts should have more seriously considered the biological fathers' constitutional interest in avoiding the psychological, physical, and emotional harms of being declared legal fathers.

Chris's Conclusion sums up the major points of his analysis, with a tone that conveys that the reader should be familiar with these points from the preceding sections. It also refers back to the examples he offered in his Introduction.

Collin's Conclusion also summarizes his analysis, and brings his Note full circle by referring back to the story about General McKissock's consulting work with Sapient he used in the Introduction. He also clearly identifies the solution to the problem that he identified at the outset of the paper.

> The solution proposed by this Note would eliminate the unbalanced ethical scheme between government employees and contractors and would reduce the need for federal agencies like the Army's CCE to separate its contractors from its government employees. Agencies would be able to directly supervise their contractor personnel, and both personal service contractors and federal employees would be subject to the same set of government ethics laws. Agencies would ultimately be able to more efficiently designate tasks according to which individual was best qualified, based on knowledge and experience, to handle that specific project.

This solution would apply to senior mentors employed under personal service contracts through the Pentagon's senior mentor program. This approach would not allow the Pentagon to avoid applying ethics laws to its senior mentors simply by hiring them under contract. These senior mentors would instead be subject to the same ethics rules as the regular Pentagon officials with which they work. As such, Gen. McKissock would have been considered a "federal employee" for government ethics purposes and would have been required to file a public financial disclosure form before he started consulting for the Marines. If he decided to remain as a director of Sapient, Gen. McKissock would be prohibited from working on any government project for which Sapient planned to compete, and he certainly would not be allowed to lobby the officers he advised. Most importantly, this approach would extend beyond the Department of Defense and apply to all executive agencies.

To be clear, this new approach does not completely abolish every distinction between contractors and government employees, nor would it be desirable to do so. Matters concerning hiring, firing, and compensation would still differ between these two categories, as the civil service laws would continue to apply only to employees formally appointed into the civil service. Nevertheless, abolishing the personal services prohibition and expanding the scope of government ethics laws to personal service contractors is a necessary step to properly managing the government's growing use of service contractors. Shifting the focus of policymakers toward ensuring proper oversight, management, and accountability of service contractors will help guarantee that contractors are being used appropriately in our government.

By reaching back to the narrative he introduced at the beginning of the paper, Collin's Conclusion concretely explains the benefits of his solution; he has "showed" the reader why he is right, rather than just "telling" him.

Minor Elements of the Draft

As your draft takes shape, you will want to be aware of the other minor organizational elements of the paper. These include headings, footnotes, small-scale roadmaps, and your title.

Headings

Each of the sections and subsections of your paper should have a substantive heading. These headings do not, however, have to be argumentative in stance. Each section should be numbered in a hierarchical form (what is and is not included in this hierarchy may vary based on publication standards) and should be roughly parallel in structure.

The headings will correlate with the roadmaps placed within your paper; taken together, they can give the reader a useful guide to the paper and the arguments contained within it. For example, the headings of Shaina's Note are as follows:

Introduction
I. Legal Residence in the United States Through a Spousal Relationship
    A. "Immediate Relatives": The Gateway to a Green Card
    B. Attaining Legal Permanent Residence: The Petitioning Process
II. The Formation of the Modern-Day Widow Penalty
    A. The *Pierno* Decision
    B. The *Varela* Interpretation
    C. Automatic Revocation Upon Death
    D. The Immigration Marriage Fraud Amendments of 1986
    E. The Immigration Act of 1990
    F. Exceptions to the Widow Penalty
III. Understanding the Widow Penalty Through Case Law
    A. The Board's Definition of "Spouse" and *Chevron* Deference
    B. Plain Language of the Statute and "Whole Act" Canons
    C. Practical and Humanitarian Reasoning
IV. Pending Solutions to the Widow Penalty
    A. Judicial Reform
    B. Private Bills
    C. Legislative Reform
V. Proposed Solutions to the Widow Penalty
    A. Amendments to the "Immediate Relatives" Definition
    B. Enactment of Amendment and Inherent Difficulties in Adoption
        1. Endorsement by Congress
        2. Elimination of the Widow Penalty in Its Totality
Conclusion

These examples use standard outline numbering, which is how most legal papers are organized and numbered. However, there is increasing support for the use of scientific numbering in legal research papers, because it provides the reader with more precise organizational information. Using scientific numbering, the first section of Shaina's paper would be renumbered as follows:

1. Legal Residence in the United States Through a Spousal Relationship
    1.1. "Immediate Relatives": The Gateway to a Green Card
    1.2. Attaining Legal Permanent Residence: The Petitioning Process

A case comment may have general headings for the major sections, with more specificity in the substantive sub-sections. Sometimes a particular journal has specific requirements for these major headings. Natalie's Note has the following headings:

Introduction
I.   Facts
II. Procedural History
III. Court's Analysis
IV. Personal Analysis
    A. The Path to *Pyett*
    B. Dismissal of the *Circuit City* Analysis
    C. Abandonment of the Clear and Unmistakable Test
    D. Catch-22
    E. Remaining Problems
V.   Solutions
Conclusion
Epilogue[1]

You might also consider whether your readers would benefit from a Table of Contents at the start of your paper. This can give the reader a sense of the whole of the paper at the outset and can communicate the organization of a particularly complicated analytical structure.

---

1. The Epilogue is not commonly included in a note or case comment, but was included here because of an update to the subsequent history of the *Pyett* case.

Footnotes

The concepts of citation and attribution should be familiar to anyone who has done research-based writing in the past. In scholarly legal writing, unlike in practical legal writing, most citation and attribution will take place in footnotes. Footnotes are important for three main reasons: (1) they credit the original source of the information you are discussing in the paper; (2) they provide information to the reader about where the original source material can be found; and (3) they ensure the reader that you are a credible authority on the topic.

Footnotes often present a lot of challenges for new scholarly writers. As a newcomer to the field in which you are writing, you may wonder: Is any idea—especially a law student's idea—original, or are all ideas a synthesis of other ideas, or at least an outgrowth of them? Other questions that have challenged new scholarly writers include the following:

How much authority do I need to cite?

What if someone, somewhere, came up with the same idea I did, but I don't know about it because I didn't find that particular source in my research?

What can I assume is general knowledge that does not require reference to a source?

What if a source is correct but has a bad reputation?

When should information be in the text of a paper and when can it be relegated to the footnotes?

These are important questions, the answers to which largely depend on the particular paper, argument, source, or information in question. Still, there are some broad principles you can use to guide you through the decision of how and when to cite authority in your paper. First, when in doubt, cite. Most of the time, the need to cite will be obvious because you are using language from an authority or attributing an idea you found in source. However, in the instances where you are not sure, use a citation—it is rarely, if ever, wrong to have an "extra" source cited. Second, if you have done the thorough vertical and horizontal research we discussed in Chapter 3, you should not worry too much that you are inadvertently "stealing" the idea of another author. Robust research should mitigate the fear that someone else has had the same exact idea that you did. Remember that you did a preemption check for that very thing!

When it comes to general knowledge and sources with bad reputations, you should use common sense. Monica comfortably relied on the fact that most people know what the Mona Lisa is, and did not offer attribution about it in the Introduction to her paper. Had she been referring to a more obscure work, she could have referred the reader to an online resource that explained the artwork and perhaps even had an image associated with it. For example, she might have wanted the reader to know about "Profile of the Bella Principessa," a lesser-known work by DaVinci. Googling the name of the painting might have taken her to the Wikipedia entry for the work. Knowing many legal readers are (still, and rightfully) skeptical of Wikipedia as a source, she could have used the Wikipedia article to find a more acceptable source on the subject, such as the newspaper articles cited in the footnotes of the Wikipedia entry.

Finally, when considering the difference between footnotes and body text, the important thing to remember is that scholarly writing is reader-based writing, as we discussed in Chapter 1 in the section on Primary and Secondary Audiences and in Chapter 2 when we noted that interest to the reader is critical to choosing a topic and thesis. Generally speaking, you should ask yourself, what does the reader need to know? What will give her an added boost without being too burdensome? What is the natural trajectory of the argument and what are the tangents/offshoots? Think about what is necessary to your argument versus what is helpful for the reader; the former belongs in the body text, and the latter probably is best located in a footnote. Ideally every reader will read every word of your paper, but you cannot guarantee this will happen, and you do not want to seem lazy, sloppy, or incompetent because your argument overlooks an obvious point in the body text but addresses it in an unread footnote. The more substantive information the footnote contains, the more likely it is that substance needs to be placed in the text of the paper itself.

It is useful at this point to think about different types of footnotes and the purposes they serve for both author and reader. Think of footnotes as serving one of two purposes: they either tell the reader what you are saying or they tell the reader what you are *not* saying. A footnote that tells the reader what you are saying can offer attribution, definitions, explanations, or tangential information. A footnote that explains what you are *not* saying may limit the scope of your analysis or identify related discussions in the field. These footnotes can show that you know a particular point or area of the law is implicated, but you determined it is not necessary to support your thesis. The following charts provide examples of the most common types of footnotes.

Footnotes That Tell the Reader What You Are Saying

Type of Footnote	Purpose	Example
Authority/Source of a Proposition	Attribute to the proper authority Allow the reader to access the source on her own Build credibility with the reader	**In-text Sentence:** The United Nations Educational, Scientific, and Cultural Organization held a convention in 1970 on the Means of Prohibiting and Preventing the Illicit Import, Export and Transfer of Ownership of Cultural Property (UNESCO Convention). **Footnote:** UNESCO Convention on the Means of Prohibiting and Preventing the Illicit Import, Export, and Transfer of Ownership of Cultural Property, Nov. 14, 1970, 823 U.N.T.S. 231 [hereinafter UNESCO Convention].
Several Related Authorities Cited for a General Proposition	Summarize background material with proper attribution	**In-text Sentence:** Although the UNESCO Convention is heavily endorsed with 120 signatories to date,[1] scholars note that the fatal flaws are (1) the lack of enforcement legislation in most of the signatory countries,[2] and (2) inconsistent interpretation of provisions.[3] **Footnotes:** [1] UNESCO.org, *supra* note 14. [2] Schwartz, *supra* note 14, at 230. [3] *See* O'Keefe, *supra* note 13, at 99.
Definition	Explain legal terms of art without interrupting the discussion in the body text	**In-text Sentence:** According to the Federal Acquisition Regulations ("FAR"), a personal service contract is a contract that creates an employer-employee relationship between the contractor and the federal government. **Footnote:** *See* FAR 2.101 (2010). FAR 2.101 defines a personal service contract as "a contract that, by its express terms or as administered, makes the contractor personnel appear to be, in effect, Government employees." *See id.* The FAR mandates that all personal services be obtained by direct hire. *See* FAR 37.104(a) (2010).

Type of Footnote	Purpose	Example
Tangential, but Interesting, Non-Legal Knowledge	Show the depth of your research on the topic Add context and color to the discussion	**In-text sentence:** The Mona Lisa was a national treasure for France, where the painting has resided for four centuries, gracing the halls of Versailles during the reign of Louis XIV and the walls of Napoleon's bedroom. **Footnote:** Howard Chua-Eoan, *The Top 25 Crimes of the Century*, TIME (last visited Apr. 4, 2011), http://www.time.com/time/2007/crimes/2.html. **In-text Sentence:** The portrait was returned to France, but Peruggia was hailed as a national hero and served less than a year in jail. **Footnote:** The time Peruggia spent in jail was not altogether unpleasant. Scotti explains that "his jail cell filled with admiring letters, gifts, cigarettes, and sweets." The famous poet and novelist Gabriele D'Annunzio wrote a public tribute to the "hero." R.A. SCOTTI, VANISHED SMILE: THE MYSTERIOUS THEFT OF THE MONA LISA 167, 187 (2009)

Footnotes That Tell the Reader What You Are Not Saying

Type of Footnote	Purpose	Example
Limiting the Scope of your Paper	Identify the scope of the topic and thesis Note awareness but purposeful exclusion of related material that does not impact the analysis	**In-text Sentence:** The shortcomings of the Hague Convention triggered the subsequent enactments of remedial treaties, primarily seen in the UNESCO Convention and the UNIDROIT Convention. **Footnote:** Other conventions, such as the 1972 UNESCO Convention for the Protection of the World Cultural and National Heritage and the 2001 Convention on the Protection of the Underwater Cultural Heritage will not be discussed in this Note.

Type of Footnote	Purpose	Example
Identifying Related Issues	Provides the reader with sources to related authority Adds to author credibility	**In-text Sentence:** Scholarly debate centers around the various conventions, with discussions concerning how they should be amended, or which issues should be addressed in yet another subsequent remedial convention. **Footnote:** *See, e.g.*, Warring, *supra* note 14; Nina R. Lenzner, *The Illicit International Trade in Cultural Property: Does the UNIDROIT Convention Provide an Effective Remedy for the Shortcomings of the UNESCO Convention?*, 15 U. Pa. J. Int'l Bus. L. 469 (1994); John P. Shinn, *A New World Order for Cultural Property: Addressing the Failure of International and Domestic Regulation of the International Art Market*, 34 Santa Clara L. Rev. 977 (1994).
Acknowledging Counterarguments	Identify alternative approaches without distracting from your topic and thesis	**In-text Sentence:** As Stephanie Doyal points out in evaluating the UNIDROIT Convention, the lack of a definition could lead to different interpretations across party nations, resulting in the exclusion of cases from the scope of the UNIDROIT Convention. **Footnote:** Doyal, *supra* note 10, at 671. Ms. Doyal does point out that the UNIDROIT Convention has a mechanism to remedy any ambiguities or unforeseen problems within the text of the UNIDROIT Convention: "Article 20 of the Convention grants the President of the International Institute for the Unification of Private Law the authority to convene a special committee to review the practical application of the Convention. The President may do so at regular intervals or at the request of five Contracting States."

Keep two other concepts in mind when writing your footnotes. First, do not forget our tip about keeping your footnotes in proper form, even in early drafts. This will save you some time in the later drafting stages. Second, it is likely that almost every sentence in your paper will be footnoted. Do not be overwhelmed by this—ultimately, a lot of these will be successive citations to the same authority for which you can use *"Id."* Still, we recommend that you keep your footnotes in full citation form until you reach the Finishing stage. You will likely make a lot of changes to the paper and if you cut and paste your sentences into a new order, early overuse of *"Id."* in the footnotes can be confusing or, worse, incorrect.

Roadmaps

You can create flow among the different sections of your paper by including roadmaps at various points throughout. Roadmaps provide helpful guidance to the reader who is navigating her way through your paper. They guide the reader through the organization of your paper, your arguments, or your sub-points, and give the reader enough information so that she can jump to a particular section if she is only interested in a smaller portion of the paper.

Roadmaps have specific purposes in scholarly pieces. As you know, the Introduction typically ends with a roadmap that tells the reader how the rest of the paper is organized. This both sets up the framework for the paper and tells the reader what each section of the paper will accomplish. You can use these roadmapping techniques within the body of the paper as well. Again, the purpose here is reader-focused—you can use them to guide the reader through multi-faceted or complex sub-points you are using to advance your thesis. For example, Section I of Chris's Note opens with this paragraph:

> *Roe, Griswold,* and the other cases involving contraception and abortion stand for the proposition that there is a constitutional right to make one's procreative decisions free from undue interference by the State. This right, which stems from the same cases that created the broad right to privacy, is actually a bundle of two rights: the right to procreate and the right not to procreate.

Similarly, Section IV of Shaina's paper begins this way:

> There are three types of solutions that have been proposed, and some employed, to minimize the harsh consequences of the modern-day widow penalty. These pending solutions include (1) judicial reform via litigation within the U.S. court system, (2) the enactment of private bills that exempt individual widows from the two-year requirement, and (3) the adoption of federal legislation that preserves the widow

penalty, but allows an exception for widows who meet a certain burden of proof.

Both of these roadmaps set up the sub-sections that follow in a way that is helpful to the reader.

Obviously, you cannot write your roadmaps until you have fully developed your draft. Roadmaps are something you add in at the end of the drafting process, and you will have to update them as you change the organization of your paper in the refining steps that follow the non-public draft. It is useful to include them in early drafts, even though they are subject to change, because they are so helpful for the reader. They can also help you, as the author, crystallize what it is that you want a section to accomplish and provide a useful check for you to make sure that this is what you have done.

Titles

You do not need to worry too much about the title during the early stages of drafting your paper. In fact, it may be difficult to draft a title if you are not yet sure what your paper is going to ultimately say. However, often an idea for a title pops into your mind as you are immersed in getting the non-public draft together, so we will talk about titles briefly here.

Titles can come in many different forms: some are straightforward, some have a two-layered title that blends wit and substance, others may employ case names, puns, or other witticisms. Do not let your desire to have a clever title handicap your ability to get started on the paper. Here are several examples of starting and final titles:

Chris's Note:

Starting title: A Right Not to Father: *Gonzales v. Carhart* and the Acceptance of Emotional Harm as a Constitutionally Protected Interest

Final title: A Right to Decide Not to Be a Legal Father: *Gonzales v. Carhart* and the Acceptance of Emotional Harm as a Constitutionally Protected Interest

Shaina's Note:

Starting title: A Fate Worse Than Death: The Deportation of Surviving Alien Spouses Under the "Widow Penalty"

Final title: From Bereavement to Banishment: The Deportation of Surviving Alien Spouses Under the "Widow Penalty"

Monica's Note:

Starting title: The Return of Antiquities: The Failure of International Conventions and an Unlikely Legal Paradigm

Final title: "Think you can steal our Caravaggio and get away with it? Think again." An Analysis of the Italian Cultural Property Model

Nathaniel's Note:

Starting title: Needs a Title

Final title: Putting History On A Stone Foundation: Toward Legal Rights For Historic Property

Jessie's Comment:

Starting title: A Practical Guide to Partial Verdict Instructions in Federal Criminal Trials

Final title: On the Subject of Partial Verdicts: A Series of Practical Questions Answered for District Court Judges

Emily's Comment:

Starting title: Student Loan Discharge Exception

Final title: Student Loans: Path to Success or Road to the Abyss? An Argument to Reform the Student Loan Discharge Exception

These examples show how a title can evolve through consecutive drafts of the paper. Note that Nathaniel did not even develop a title until he was close to his final draft.

Make sure you back up your work often while working on your draft. Rather than just saving your paper locally on your computer, use a cloud backup like Dropbox, OneDrive, iCloud, or Google Drive that you can access from any device. This will back up your work although you might want to consider another method of saving your work. You might also change your computer settings to back up more frequently, use an external drive, or email each new version of your draft to yourself so you will always be able to retrieve the most recent version. No matter what option you choose, make sure you back up your work!

Dealing with Writer's Block

At some point during the construction of a writing project of this size and significance, you are likely to deal with writer's block. Modern writer's block conjures up images of an author with a blank word processing document open on a laptop screen, the flashing cursor counting the seconds that pass by with no productivity.

Your writer's block could come in several forms while you are working on this project. You might start out feeling completely overwhelmed by having to pick a topic (though Chapter 2 will help you push past that initial obstacle). You might get stymied when trying to move from your topic to a thesis statement. (Chapter 2 will help you here also.) Or you might have trouble starting your draft. (The tips in this chapter are designed to help you get past that roadblock.)

To get past writer's block, you must first identify the cause. The cause might be related to your relationship with your paper. You may not be able to write because you may need to do more research or you may need to find a different starting point. You may have too broad or too narrow a thesis. Another common issue that elicits writer's block is fatigue, either personal fatigue (where you are generally tired) or writing fatigue (where you are tired of working on the project). Of course, you could also be dealing with both of these things at the same time.

Writer's block can also be the result of a poor writing environment. Perhaps you have been working at home, but keep getting tempted by Netflix recommendations for your next show. Maybe you have tried to work in the library, but keep getting interrupted when friends pass by on the way to class. You may also have trouble getting started because you cannot find enough time to do anything productive; toting around your research materials and getting organized can take up a lot of time at the start of each writing session.

Once you have determined the cause of your writer's block, you should go about trying to overcome it. If you are not yet ready to write (at all, or the particular section that has left you stymied), then take a step back: do more research, chart out your arguments, or work on a different part of the paper. If the cause is fatigue in any form, then give yourself some room to relax—get a good night's sleep and start up again the next day, get some exercise, or take a weekend-long break from thinking about the paper. If you are bored or distracted, think about a change of scenery; think about leaving the library, closing your laptop, silencing your phone, or sitting outside for a while. If you are unable to find large blocks of time to work on the paper, perhaps you should plan to work in a place where you can keep your research materials set up (your desk at home) so that you do not lose the set-up time each time you sit down to write.

Another potential solution no matter the source of your writer's block is to talk about the struggles you are facing. The opportunity to talk things out may be built into the writing process if your professor asks you to present your paper topic to the class, or you have to participate in a works-in-progress session with some of your colleagues. You can do this informally as well. Ask a friend to chat about your paper, and maybe take notes for you, so that you can do the talking and he can capture what you say. Visit your professor's office hours to get feedback on a specific argument. Or, if one is available, go see a writing tutor who can talk over the issues with you.

One key part of getting over writer's block is leaving yourself enough time to push past it. If you are pulling an all-nighter to meet a deadline, you will have less time to implement one of these suggestions. This is yet another reason why planning out the writing process is so important.

You will be able to move past this obstacle if you are prepared and have planned well. Some amount of writer's block is inevitable, and you should relax when you come upon it—remember, this project is a large undertaking, so give yourself a break every once in a while! This point in the writing process is actually a good time for you to take a break. You should have a good working first draft of your paper, but you need to evaluate and revise it before you pass it along to someone else for critique. Consider taking a break before you move to the Refining stage that we discuss in Chapters 5 and 6.

CHAPTER 5

REFINING: EVALUATING AND REVISING YOUR DRAFT

The best part about being at the Refining stage is that you are well on your way in the writing process. The task at hand—completing your scholarly paper—might still feel daunting, but you should be feeling better than you were when you had only a blank page (or computer screen). After working through the concepts we discussed in Chapter 4, you have constructed your non-public draft. Now you are going to transition from your non-public draft to prepare a completed draft ready for a reviewer's critique. To make this transition, you will evaluate and revise your paper, identifying areas that need to be fixed before you can comfortably share your paper with your supervisor. In Chapter 6, we discuss the other side of the Refining stage—taking and incorporating feedback from others.

Many writers find the Refining stage to be the most labor intensive, but it can also be the most enjoyable and productive part of the writing process as you see your thoughts come together. Getting excited about how your paper is shaping up not only helps motivate you to keep working, but also helps you to stay engaged with your paper and continue working through the process. As we noted at the end of Chapter 4, taking a break before you start on the refining process will give you a better perspective for evaluating your paper with fresh eyes and a critical mind. Try to give yourself at least a day or two between completing your non-public draft and beginning the refining process, and do the same for all of the drafts that follow.

Evaluating your paper is an opportunity to step back and read your paper with a bird's-eye view to see if it has accomplished everything you wanted. In evaluating your paper, you will do three things: critically evaluate your thesis, identify weaknesses in the substance of your paper, and confirm that your organizational choices work for your paper. We discuss each of these in detail below.

Based on the results of your evaluation, you will then revise your thesis, arguments, and organizational structure, and make the accompanying changes to your paper. Students will approach this revising in different ways; some students prefer to work from start to finish, revising as they go, and others prefer to make a list of the problems in the draft and then methodically work through fixing each problem (but not necessarily in the order the paper follows). For example, if you discover a research gap in a sub-section of your Analysis/Discussion section, you might decide to start with fixing that problem before you work on revising your roadmap in your Introduction.

Revising your paper moves your paper forward. With each successive draft, you will go through the Refining stage, working to take your paper as a whole to the next level. As you move forward to your final paper, the amount of work required to evaluate and revise will decrease because your paper will be stronger with each draft.

Critically Evaluate Your Thesis

At this point in the writing process, you need to revisit and evaluate your thesis. Recall that this process begins with an idea that evolves into an initial thesis. This initial thesis was the starting point for your draft, and now that the draft is written, you must evaluate the thesis statement to determine what it says and whether it is valid. You also want to determine whether the rest of the paper supports your thesis, but you need to do this thesis-focused evaluation before you can properly perform that comprehensive evaluation. After each revised draft, check your thesis statement to make sure that it remains valid.

Start by making sure your thesis is clearly articulated and easily identifiable. Focus on the wording and placement of your thesis statement. Remember from Chapter 2 that your goal is to articulate your thesis as a one-sentence statement of your position. This one-sentence model can help you force yourself to narrowly and specifically craft your thesis; the one-sentence model also helps the reader because then she does not have to piece together several sentences or paragraphs to determine what your thesis is. Find your thesis among the opening paragraphs of your draft.

Once you perform this initial check on your thesis, you are ready to move on to a substantive evaluation of your thesis statement. Think back to Chapter

2 where we discussed the characteristics of a good thesis. At this point, you want to make sure that the current version of your thesis meets these characteristics. You can now think critically about your thesis and your position to see whether they stand up to criticisms because you have horizontal and vertical knowledge as a foundation for your evaluation. Your goal here is to identify weaknesses and correct them before submitting a draft or final paper for review; you want to be sure that your thesis is valid and supportable before anyone else reads your paper.

To guide your evaluation, you will probably find it helpful to work through the questions listed below. Critically evaluating your thesis will help you to determine whether and how you need to refine your thesis to make it easier for the reader to identify it in your opening paragraphs, or how to make a slightly different point if you determine that your thesis does not work in its current form. You can use your answers to these questions to determine what you need to do to revise your thesis. You may not be able to make any immediate revisions, but you will be able to generate a list of things you need to do based on your critical evaluation. You can then work through that list to create your next draft.

Chapter 5 Quiz: Evaluating My Thesis

- Does my thesis say something? Did I pass the "so what" test?
  ○ Does it make sense?
  ○ Is it too simple or too complex?
  ○ Are there biases or assumptions at play in my thesis?
    ▪ Are they fair?
    ▪ Have I addressed them as biases or assumptions?
    ▪ Have I recognized the alternatives?
- Have I made interpretations of rules or policies?
  ○ Are those interpretations fair?
- Am I over- or under-stating things?
  ○ Are there other issues or topics implicated by my thesis? Have I addressed them?
- What kind of results does my thesis create?
  ○ Are the results positive and supportable, or are they problematic? Or both?
    ▪ Is there a trade-off worth making? How or why?
  ○ Are the results of my thesis related to the problem I identified?
    ▪ Related to other areas?
- Are there unexpected benefits in other areas or unanticipated results in other areas?

Of course, every thesis evaluation will be different because the evaluation is specific to your thesis (as demonstrated in the following examples). You can, however, use this pattern of questions as a starting point to make sure you are adequately evaluating your thesis. Be open to a fluid, personalized evaluation and do not restrict yourself to asking only the questions in this list.

Consider the following examples of the thesis evaluation process. Chris's evaluation of his thesis could look like this:

> Q: Does my thesis say something concrete?
>
> A: *I have an argument for why biological fathers should have a right to choose not to be legal fathers, but I am not sure that is enough. Even if I convinced courts to recognize this right, I need more to explain why and how this right should be enforced. Are there circumstances in which the right should not exist? Are there other issues or rights to balance against the father's rights?*
>
> Q: Are other areas of law or issues implicated by my thesis? What are the results of my thesis? Did I consider these results in developing my thesis and arguments?
>
> A: *There is probably an issue with economic support of children born even after a biological father has expressed his right to not be a legal father. What happens if a mother has the baby when the father's right to not be a legal father is enforced? Is that fair to the mother, the child? I need to think more about that and address it. Are there family law issues at play here?*

Shaina's thesis evaluation could look like this:

> **What my thesis says:** There is a need to change the widow penalty.
> **Question or concern when evaluating:** There are some pending changes to the rule already. Why are those rule changes insufficient? Why/how does my rule proposal do a better job at solving the problem?
>
> **How to deal with it? What action do I need to take?** Include discussion of how the pending changes are not likely to solve the problems faced by alien-widows. Need to think through the existing mechanisms for change and argue why they are inadequate, even though these mechanisms generally support my idea to change the existing framework. I want to make sure my solution stands out as the right/best answer rather than waiting to see if these other solutions pan out.

What my thesis says: The best/most appropriate mechanism for changing the rule is for Congress to adopt a legislative change to eliminate the widow penalty.

Question or concern when evaluating: Are there ways to abuse my proposed rule? Would people get away with undeserved benefits? How can my solution ensure that the Immigration Service changes its enforcement of the widow penalty?

How to deal with it? What action do I need to take? I need to think about how to specifically avoid abuse of my rule, perhaps by setting a standard of proof to confirm the marriage was not a sham. Think more about this.

What my thesis says: My proposal can work with a legislative amendment changing the definition of "immediate relatives."

Question or concern when evaluating: What needs to be amended?

How to deal with it? What action do I need to take? I think I should draft the amendment language for my note, that way I can explain how easy it would be for Congress to take definitive action on this issue.

And Monica's thesis evaluation could look like this:

Did I say something concrete? Answer "so what?" Yes, I say Italy should be the paradigm for other countries to look to as a model for their own art restitution and reclamation efforts, and I advocate for an eventual international standard. I may have failed the "so what?" test though because the need for successful art theft reclamation and restitution is something that seems obvious to me, but may not be to all readers. I need to think more about how to set up some context for why this matters.

Are there biases or assumptions in my thesis? I might be biased in favor of Italy's system because I am Italian and was most familiar with Italy's system before I started my paper. I need to carefully and objectively evaluate the model and be sure to address counterarguments to avoid analytical gaps due to bias. I also need to make sure to explain how I determined Italy was the best model so that it does not seem like I just picked Italy based on my knowledge and heritage. I might be making some assumptions, too—that art is important and deserves to be returned if stolen. I don't think this is an unfounded assumption, but perhaps I can be clearer about that as a starting point.

Am I overstating the success of Italy as a model for other countries?
Possibly, but I can manage that by identifying the limitations and argue
what steps Italy should take to establish a true model paradigm. I can
build that in as a separate sub-section in my proposal/solution section.
Plus this will answer counterarguments about flaws in Italy's cultural
property protection.

You can see from these examples that by pausing for reflection and asking
critical questions, Chris, Shaina, and Monica were able to evaluate their thesis
statements more substantively than if they had simply read through their
papers. They asked questions that took them to further questions. They also
identified work they needed to do before they could move forward revising
their papers. With these evaluation results as a guide, they did additional research and thought more about their thesis statements, and then incorporated
revisions to respond to the questions and concerns they identified during the
evaluation.

Remember that the *form* of this evaluation does not matter. For the purpose
of illustrating the process, we have put the reactions into complete sentences,
but you should not feel constricted by that form. The possibilities for recording
your evaluation are endless; you might use margin notes, handwritten notes
in a notebook, color-coded Post-It notes, a table or chart, a combination of
these, or any other method of your choice. As long as you perform the
evaluative analysis, the form or appearance does not matter. Do what works
best for you in terms of the actual execution of evaluating your thesis, using
the list of questions and general critical reading and thinking as your guides.
You may also want to keep a separate list or somehow mark specific items on
your evaluation for things you want to discuss the next time you meet with
your advisor. As we explain in Chapter 6, in the section called Reaching Out
for More Help, setting your own agenda for meeting with your advisor is an
effective strategy to ensure you get what you need out of the supervisory relationship. It also demonstrates your thoughtful preparation for the meeting,
which may make your advisor more willing to help you.

Another way to evaluate the results created by your thesis is to consider how
your thesis will operate in different factual situations.[1] Do not be afraid of the
results you will get by using this evaluation process; instead, use the results of
applying your thesis to the scenarios to help you determine how to strengthen
your thesis. Consider this method with Chris's Note:

---

1. This is what Professor Eugene Volokh calls "test-suites." Eugene Volokh, *Test Suites:
A Tool for Improving Student Articles*, 52 J. LEGAL EDUC. 440 (2002).

Chris's Thesis: There should be a right for biological fathers to not be legal fathers when there is an actual and reasonable expression of that philosophical desire to not be a father.

Hypothetical 1: man uses a condom, which he considers an expression of his desire to not be a father, but woman becomes pregnant

Hypothetical 2: woman says she is infertile; man accepts this information as true and relying on the information, does not use a condom, and woman gets pregnant

Hypothetical 3: woman takes advantage of a mentally-disabled man to get pregnant, telling man he will not have to take any responsibility if she becomes pregnant, which she does

Hypothetical 4: man tells woman he is impotent based on his belief that he is, but condom-less sex produces a pregnancy

Hypothetical 5: man and woman are inebriated when they have unprotected sex, and woman becomes pregnant

Hypothetical 6: man tells woman he does not want to have children until he is financially able to support them; woman wins the lottery and tells man he does not have to pay for children but she wants to get pregnant; man has unprotected sex with woman resulting in pregnancy on the assumption that woman's lottery winnings will pay for child

After thinking through his thesis in the context of these hypotheticals, Chris can determine whether he can support his thesis under each of these scenarios. If one of the scenarios leads to a result he cannot support or results he did not foresee when he crafted his initial thesis, he can modify his thesis to address these results; this ultimately strengthens his thesis and paper as a whole. You can do the same by running your thesis through a series of hypotheticals, and using the results to further refine your thesis.

After you have critically evaluated your thesis, you are ready to move on to an evaluation of the substance of your paper.

Critically Evaluate Your Paper

While working on your draft, you may not have had the time or energy to stop and read through your entire paper because you were focused on the individual sections as you drafted them. You may have written notes to self about places you needed more research, or just needed to reflect on how best to articulate your thoughts on a certain point. Now you need to evaluate the interoperation of the sections of your paper and whether they provide adequate support for your thesis. This process can take several forms, but it generally follows the same form as your thesis evaluation: You want to ask a series of questions while reading your paper to identify what steps you need to take in the form of revising to strengthen your paper.

Your first step here is to read through your entire draft without marking it up, taking notes, or making changes. Just read it. You need to get a sense of the paper as a whole, and you can only do that if you force yourself to read through the entire piece without doing anything else that will distract you from this task. After you read your entire paper through once, read it again—this time with pen in hand or fingers on keys. Your goal here is to evaluate your paper to see what types of revisions it requires. Ask yourself general questions about the substance of your paper to get a sense of the overall quality, and then ask questions to determine how your Analysis/Discussion section supports your thesis.

To get a sense of the overall quality of your paper, determine what you like most and least about your paper; identify the strongest parts of your paper and what makes them strong; recognize what concerns you most about your draft. As you are reading your draft, look for good arguments and places you have articulated your arguments well. Look for good transitions between arguments, and effective use of sources. Finding these strengths in your paper is a great way to recognize the good work you have been doing and may inspire or reenergize you to keep going on your project. It is also useful to identify these strong parts of your paper because you can comfortably leave those parts alone until you have your next draft. Positive notes in your paper not only make you feel good about your work, but allow you to return to these spots in your paper as examples of how to improve weak areas.

With these general impressions in mind, you are ready to take on the specific evaluation of how your Analysis/Discussion section supports your thesis. You might find it helpful to think of this evaluation as a process of asking questions to identify analytical gaps in your paper and opportunities to strengthen your analysis. Analytical gaps arise in a variety of forms related to counterarguments, practical or implementation issues, and limitations on the scope of your thesis. Opportunities to strengthen your paper include use of examples, placing your thesis in a broader context, and reinforcing your thesis. With each successive draft, you should ask this series of questions, and whatever other questions arise while you are reading your draft.

Identify Weaknesses in Your Paper

Keep in mind that evaluating your paper for analytical gaps is essential to strengthening your analysis and improving your paper as a whole, but your approach to evaluating your Analysis/Discussion section does not have to follow the order in which we present the analytical gaps below. The revisions in response to evaluating your Analysis/Discussion section also require tailoring to your individual paper. In the examples in the following sub-sections, you can see how our student authors revised their papers in response to their evaluations.

Have I Addressed Counterarguments?

Even when you have effectively articulated your arguments in support of your thesis, there may be gaps left open by counterarguments you have not addressed in your analysis. This happens in part because it can be difficult to anticipate counterarguments while you are drafting; you need to have something written to see where the counterarguments arise.

Counterarguments may attack the feasibility of your solution, the mechanism you have chosen for solving a problem, or simply question why a current regime is unsatisfactory. You can use counterarguments to build up your own analysis by facing them head on and incorporating analysis about how or why the counterarguments do not defeat your thesis. Think of this as your opportunity to engage with the reader by acknowledging and answering the questions that come to the reader's mind while she is reading your paper. By anticipating her challenges, you can impress her with your thoughtful analysis and sound thesis.

Think back to what you may have learned about counterarguments in practical legal writing. Incorporating answers to counterarguments within your primary argument makes for a smoother, and often stronger, analysis because you are forced to recognize your arguments' weaknesses and shore them up.

Take a look at an example from Chris's paper:

Counterargument:

If biological fathers are able to avoid legal responsibilities for biological children, children will be left financially unsupported.

Evaluation:

Recognize this is a concern, but argue that the public policy interest behind the system of child support is on the State's behalf acting in the interest of the child, not the mother's or father's behalf.

Revised paper:

While this Note argues that the harm that the father seeks to avoid is emotional, there is obviously an economic component underlying paternity. This Note, however, defends the recognition of the due process right to decide not to be a legal father on two grounds. First, such a judicial move may serve as an additional layer of deterrence against unprotected sex because a woman's heightened awareness that she may be solely financially responsible for a child will give her even more incentive to use safe sex practices. In turn, this could result in a decrease in the number of unsupported children that are born. Furthermore, once a pregnant woman is in a situation in which the father would not be required to pay child support, she may more readily choose abortion, and thus the possibility of an unsupported child disappears. The promotion of abortion certainly may not be a policy the State wishes to adopt; however, this argument militates towards a determination that other rights outweigh the due process right rather than a determination that no right should be recognized.

Second, the courts are fairly unified on the notion that the public policy interest behind child support payments is on behalf of the State in place of the child, not on behalf of the mother or father. For that reason, the equitable policy is to shift the burden onto the State to support its own interest. Such burden-shifting would serve two functions. First, the burden-shift would ensure that all children would be properly supported because the problem of collecting child support from the impoverished or evasive father would no longer exist; instead, the State would assist in supporting the child. Second, the burden-shift would require the population, through its legislators, to decide what level of support the State should provide. This would help put the children of all single mothers (and fathers) in a more equal position while simultaneously forcing a political debate.

After identifying the gap raised by the counterargument and thinking about how to address it, Chris revised his paper to incorporate a sub-section into his solution section. This new sub-section followed his detailed explanation of how his proposed affirmative defense would work in the context of legal fathers. This revision made his answer to the counterargument about financial responsibilities part of his primary argument so that he did not leave himself open to potential criticisms the reader might have while reading about Chris's proposed right and accompanying affirmative defense.

Consider an example of how Collin addressed a counterargument:

Counterargument:

There are already mechanisms in place to resolve issues that arise from contractors performing personal services under a government contract; those are working fine and there is no need for a large-scale overhaul in an already complex federal procurement system.

Evaluation:

Yes, I need to acknowledge there are mechanisms in place, specifically federal courts and the Equal Employment Opportunity Commission, but then explain how these are only partial solutions and they do nothing to stop the official government policy of prohibiting personal services.

Revised paper:

The Equal Employment Opportunity Commission ("EEOC") has also dealt with an increasing number of cases similar to *Harris* and applied the same "common law agency test" to determine if the contractor employee is a de facto employee of the federal government. According to a recent article in the Washington Post, the EEOC has decided more than 90 cases in the last decade in favor of the contractor because the federal agency had sufficient control and supervision over that individual's work.

This raises serious concerns about the continued necessity of the prohibition, which has been openly flouted. While the official policy of the federal government, as stated in FAR 37.104, is that agencies are prohibited from supervising their contractors like employees, this policy has become so ineffective at preventing the creation of employment relationships that federal courts and the EEOC have begun to adopt ad hoc policies to remedy the situation, even if solely in the employment discrimination context. In 1997, the EEOC adopted guidance specifically recognizing the possibility that a contract employee may be considered a de facto employee of a government agency if that agency "has the requisite control over that worker." This guidance, along with federal court precedent, explicitly recognizes the possibility of an employment relationship between contractors and the government and seeks to regulate—rather than merely prohibit—this relationship.

After thinking about how the reader may view the judicial process to be a sufficient solution, Collin revised his paper to include more details about how federal courts and the EEOC provide only a limited, ad hoc solution. By including this discussion of the counterargument in his sub-section on how the personal services prohibition no longer reflects the current reality of the federal workforce, he built up even further the analytical basis that supports his overarching solution to deal with the personal services prohibition.

Take a look at another counterargument Collin addressed in his paper:

Counterargument:

The government workforce should be expanded to avoid the government's need to hire contractors to perform personal services. This would be better than allowing contractors to perform personal services because it preserves the distinction between government and non-government employees.

Evaluation:

This counterargument comes up in almost any federal procurement issue, but it is just not a practical solution.

Revised Paper:

Critics will likely argue that an alternative to abolishing the personal services prohibition would be to undergo civil service reform to reduce the government's reliance on service contractors. However, numerous structural and political obstacles stand in the way of any meaningful reform in the near future. Past experience contains numerous examples that demonstrate the difficulties of insourcing tasks from private contractors to government agencies, the reluctance of elected officials to move beyond their political devotion to "small government," and the dogged determination of public unions to fight against any changes to their compensation scheme and benefits.

One of the best examples demonstrating the difficulties of expanding the government workforce is the controversial creation of the Transportation Security Administration ("TSA") not more than two months after September 11, 2001. After the events of September 11, the Senate immediately took steps to nationalize the administration of airport security throughout the country. President George W. Bush and House Republican lawmakers, however, were hesitant to expand the size of the federal government. Specifically, lawmakers were concerned about increasing the size of the federal workforce by as much as 27,000 employees, and the White House refused to provide these new employees with civil service protections. Eventually, a compromise was reached that federalized all airport screeners but allowed airport operators to opt out of the federal program by showing that private screeners were just as effective. Not more than three years after TSA's creation, some lawmakers began questioning the need for TSA at all, claiming that its creation was a knee-jerk response to the September 11 attacks. These lawmakers claimed that private screeners could do a more efficient job than a government agency.

This example demonstrates the tremendous difficulties with insourcing major functions. Despite a strong national imperative to reform airport security following September 11, it took a considerable amount of political haggling to successfully establish the TSA and justify the expansion of the federal government. It is arguable that in the absence of the September 11 attacks, establishing an agency like the TSA would have been politically impossible.

In fact, implementing broad-based civil service reforms and performance-driven pay scales would be even more politically difficult and would require dramatic changes in the government workforce's compensation scheme. In 2005, the GAO examined the possibility of implementing federal pay reform and concluded that these reforms, while possible, would require considerable effort on the part of each specific agency to ensure that any new scheme provides sufficient transparency and accountability. Furthermore, Professor Richard J. Pierce Jr. sees "no possibility that Congress will [increase] the upper end of the government to the point at which the government can hire enough people to perform all government functions with government employees." We will instead continue to see an "increase in the proportion of the federal workforce that consists of contractors' employees." This demonstrates the numerous obstacles and difficulties standing in the way of civil service reform.

This debate also implicates a broader dichotomy between those who believe that all major government functions should be staffed primarily by government employees and those who advocate for the efficiency benefits of relying on private sector contractors. While this is, at its core, an ideological debate over the proper role of government, the practical reality is that the federal government remains heavily reliant on contractors to fulfill its ever-growing mandate. Steven Schooner, Co-Director of the Government Procurement

Law Program at the George Washington University Law School, has repeatedly explained that "despite a generation of bipartisan efforts to portray a 'small government' to the public, government mandates continue to increase, leaving agencies no choice but to increasingly rely upon contractors to provide mission-critical services." While increasing the size of the federal workforce would undoubtedly reduce the government's reliance on contractors, the example of the TSA demonstrates that such an approach is probably not a feasible alternative, even in the face of a national crisis.

There are also numerous benefits to relying on private contractors to perform certain functions. These benefits include surge capacity, greater flexibility, and more competitive incentive schemes. According to Professor Schooner, "[u]sing outside contractors for surge capacity offers the government the ability to supplement limited governmental resources far more quickly, efficiently, and effectively than the existing federal personnel or acquisition regimes permit." The CCE example indicates that this has proved true in practice. It typically takes CCE several months to hire contract specialists through the federal personnel system. By contrast, CCE has the ability to "order and have a contractor employee in place within as little as a couple of weeks."

Private contractors are also subject to a more diverse range of incentive structures, including compensation schemes, advancement opportunities, and the risk of termination. By contrast, many aspects of the civil service system limit the ability of government agencies to employ these incentives. This is one of the many reasons why CCE is so heavily dependent on private sector contract specialists. Given the high demand for contract specialists in both the government and the private sector, CCE officials have often expressed difficulty in providing adequate incentives to retain in-house specialists and prevent them from moving to private-sector firms. Compounding these difficulties is President Obama's recent decision to impose a pay-freeze for civilian federal employees through the end of 2012.

This strongly suggests the government will not reduce its reliance on contractors in the short-term. As a result, necessary steps must be taken to ensure contractors are properly managed and regulated. Abolishing the personal services prohibition is a vital element in this strategy. The prohibition has not only failed to prevent the government's current reliance on service contractors but also legally constrains agencies from appropriately supervising their contractors. This forces many agencies to create elaborate legal fictions to avoid violating the prohibition, while others ignore the prohibition completely and risk being held liable for regulatory violations.

In this example, Collin faced head-on the counterargument about expanding the federal workforce as an alternative to his proposed statutory and regulatory reform in a separate sub-section, headed Enlarging the Government Workforce is Neither a Feasible Nor Efficient Alternative. Using the example of the Transportation Security Administration, Collin demonstrated how that oft-suggested approach, to just increase the government workforce itself, is, in his view, ultimately doomed to fail.

Another alternative is to use counterarguments as a lead-in for your proposed solution to demonstrate why your solution is justified. That approach worked well in Shaina's paper, where she discussed the existing remedies for the widow penalty, including how each of the existing remedies falls short. Following her analysis of these insufficient solutions, she offered her proposed solution, and relied on her answers to the counterarguments to show why her solution was better than the existing remedies.

Take a look at the following examples from Shaina's paper, where she argues that the widow penalty should be abolished. Shaina organized her counterarguments into a separate section in her paper, IV. Pending Solutions to the Widow Penalty, which was followed by her solution section, V. Proposed Solutions to the Widow Penalty. Choosing this organizational method allowed Shaina to use the counterarguments to build up support for change, and then offer her specific proposed change in response to that identified need.

Counterargument:

Private legislation is an existing method for solving the widow penalty, so why do we need an additional solution?

Responsive Analysis:

The private legislative solution is an option, and has proven successful for several individual widows. The problems of the widow penalty, however, are far-reaching, and this piecemeal approach cannot solve the problem like a comprehensive legislative act could. Some widows may not have the resources to seek private legislation, and that is an unfair result to have some widows protected by private legislation while others have no chance of that protection.

Counterargument:

If Congress knew it had created legislation that had an intended effect to unfairly penalize widows, it would have amended the legislation already. In other words, the fact that Congress has not amended the statute itself suggests that it intended for the widow penalty to exist.

Responsive Analysis:

It is not fair to assume that Congress was aware of the potential penalties to widows married less than two years before losing a spouse when it passed the Immigration Act of 1990 which included a change to the definition of "immediate relative." It is impossible for Congress to carefully track the application of every statute, and it is inappropriate to assume Congress's lack of action is a stamp of approval for the widow penalty.

Counterargument:

There would be fewer procedural safeguards with the proposed legislative change, and that may lead to more sham marriages.

Responsive Analysis:

Statistics show the risk of sham marriages is low and there are additional penalties for sham marriage participants including incarceration and fines. These fears, therefore, do not invalidate my proposal to eliminate the widow penalty.

Consider the second counterargument example from Shaina's paper where the counterargument suggests Congress would have already done this — eliminated the widow penalty — if it wanted to. That Congress could have acted to correct a legislative problem is likely a common counterargument for any paper that proposes legislative change as a solution. If you have such a solution, you will want to address why Congressional inaction is not a sign of acceptance or promotion. You may also want to make sure you have analyzed any actions Congress has taken so that you can identify the remaining weaknesses, and make a case for why your specific legislative proposal is better.

Like Shaina, Monica anticipated counterarguments to help shape her solution section, specifically identifying the limitations of her proposal that the Italian system serve as a model for the entire international community.

Counterargument:

Is Italy really the best model when it has ongoing cultural property theft issues?

Evaluation:

I need to acknowledge Italy's shortcomings here, but emphasize the strengths of it as a model for others even with its imperfections.

Revised paper:

a. An Imperfect Paradigm—Flaws of the Italian Model

Although Italy is regarded as being on the forefront of cultural property protection and restitution and is often looked to as the paradigmatic model, the country nonetheless has shortcomings of its own. Italy's admirable success in the international arena is juxtaposed with the reality that cultural property is still pilfered from the country at an alarming rate. Therefore, it seems "that Italy is compensating for its inability to regulate patrimony theft on its own soil by making demands and pursuing claims against organizations abroad." To truly become a model country, Italy must first (1) establish better protection at museums and archaeological sites to stop illicit trafficking at the source, (2) create tighter border control manned by knowledgeable officials, and (3) follow through with cultural property prosecutions swiftly and efficiently.

i. As a culturally rich source nation, Italy must better protect the cultural property still within its borders.

Source nations must protect the cultural property within their own borders to halt the influx of illicit items into the black market. As R.A. Scotti, an author on art theft, remarked, "[t]oday, a soaring art market and the continuing problem of museum security have made art theft the third most prevalent crime in the world, surpassed only by international smuggling and drug trafficking." Source nations must protect their cultural cache, stationing specially trained security guards at excavation sites, storage facilities, and museums.

Italy in particular suffers greatly from continual looting, due to the overabundance of cultural property in the country, some yet undiscovered. Art thieves have increasingly shifted their attention to Italy's 100,000 churches, vulnerable targets that house many artistic masterpieces and significant reliquary. Churches have been stripped clean of their paintings, sculptures, wall decorations, and anything else that was transportable (some things requiring imagination and ingenuity to become movable, such as altars). In 2005 alone, there were 1,785 reports of artwork stolen from places of worship, mainly in Italy, France, and Russia. Although the amount of officers comprising the TPC is impressive, without stopping the looting that is occurring right in the TPC's backyard, Italy is doomed to a vicious cycle of searching for more and more pieces of stolen cultural property and fighting international battles with countries where these pieces surface.

ii. Italy must enforce stricter border control staffed with knowledgeable officials.

Stopping the looting at existing archaeological sites and establishing better protection for museums and other repositories will help to reduce the flow of stolen cultural property. The looting of art is still a prevalent crime, and there are thousands, if not millions of works circulating on the black market. Thieves often take illegally acquired cultural property "to regions with lax or nonexistent anti-theft laws and anti-import laws," where export papers are forged to falsify the provenance of the object. These regions must counteract this practice by amplifying or in some cases creating stricter laws concerning theft and imports. Italy in particular must increase its border patrol, as it is part of the Schengen Area, an area of European Union countries that have adopted common rules of border control. The Schengen Agreement practically eviscerates the borders between EU Schengen territories, as the Schengen Border Code prohibits systematic customs and tax controls on internal border controls. Further, Italy has 7,600 kilometers of coastline which it must patrol strictly, both in terms of ingoing and outgoing people and merchandise to cut off access in and out of Europe.

This border patrol must be manned by knowledgeable officials who have been trained to recognize stolen cultural property and genuine articles disguised as fakes. Although it is unrealistic that every border official will have the substantial skill and trained eye to make such determinations amidst their other duties, at least one member of each border squad should be well versed enough so as to flag potential illicit objects and detain the carrier until a more thorough investigation can be conducted. With the TPC's ever-expanding database and the increasing viability of wireless internet, the Italian government has the capacity to outfit border officials with the means necessary to triage cultural property movement quickly and effectively.

iii. Italy must swiftly prosecute those dealing in illicit trafficking so as to create a deterrent effect.

Although Italy's legislation imposes civil and criminal penalties on those who deal in illicit trafficking of cultural property, the deterrent effect of such threats lacks bite. In the world of art theft, "[t]he risk is small, the potential gain is tremendous, and if the thief is caught, the punishment is still minimal." Vincenzo Peruggia, the thief who stole the Mona Lisa and hid it for two years served less than a year in jail. Nearly 100 years later, Marion True was indicted, leading to one of the biggest scandals in the history of the art world. In True's case, the trial endured for five years, never progressed to the point where the defense could produce any witnesses or argue for True's innocence, and eventually ended when the statute of limitations ran on the charges against her. To truly deter art theft and illicit trade in cultural property, Italy must follow through with its criminal prosecutions in a manner that will garner respect for the nation's laws, as opposed to the mere threat of "facing a drawn-out legal ordeal, and ... the hypothetical threat of incarceration in a foreign country."

Accordingly, although Italy is indeed a pioneer in the realm of repatriation and protection of cultural property, the nation still must overcome significant hurdles before it can truly be considered a paradigm. The looting that occurs within its own borders contributes substantially to the trafficking in illicit cultural property. Italy must reinforce and reevaluate its guardianship of both its beloved cultural property and its geographical boundaries. Moreover, Italy cannot engage in scare tactics as it attempts to prosecute those who deal in illicit cultural property, but instead must implement swift and meaningful prosecution to deter future illicit activity.

This approach, incorporating counterarguments into her solution, worked well for Monica because it gave her the opportunity to explain her proposed solution and address the accompanying practical concerns. She set forth the three main flaws of the Italian system, and then explained how Italy must address the flaws to become a true model. Relying on that analysis, she then identified the three things other countries should do in their own restitution and reclamation efforts, relying on her version of a strengthened Italian model.

Finally, just as in practical legal writing, in scholarly writing you must strike a balance so that you address the counterarguments without giving them too much weight. You can refute them as part of your primary argument or take them on directly. However, an approach that goes point by point to raise a counterargument and then answer it weakens your analysis by making those arguments superior to your own argument. This approach can also make your argument disjointed. Also keep in mind that if you have weaker or tangential counterarguments that you want to address, but you think an in-text discussion will detract from the quality and strength of your argument by distracting the reader, you can use footnotes to make the points.

Can My Solution Be Implemented?

You can strengthen your Analysis/Discussion section's support of your thesis by showing the reader you recognize the obvious questions of how or whether your proposal can work and how it would be implemented. This practical angle is also an effective way to take your idea and turn it into something useful to the reader. This is particularly important when your thesis is built around an idea to change a rule or way of doing things. Without incorporating this implementation analysis, your reader will likely be left wondering how your proposal would work in reality, and may even assume it will not work. Even if you have a great solution to a problem, if there is no way to implement it, the solution itself has little value.

In the example papers, the student authors effectively incorporated implementation analysis to strengthen their papers. Their decisions to include practical implementation strategies probably helped their papers stand out from their peers', and likely increased their chances for publication. Of course, each paper's practical angle is specific to the context of the particular thesis, and we include several examples here as a starting point for you to think about your solution's implementation analysis.

In her paper, Natalie argues that arbitration agreements should not be required as conditions of employment and she advocates for employer protections that would make arbitration agreements more likely to be enforced by courts. In addition to arguing in favor of these changes, Natalie provides practical implementation guidance in her Solutions section:

> To ensure that the employer does not present the arbitration agreement as a condition of employment, the law should require the employer to provide the employee with the separate arbitration agreement prior to the start of employment, but not require that the employee submit the form until after the employment relationship has commenced. For example, the employee could sign her employment contract before she starts work or even as part of the employment application process. The employer would provide the arbitration

agreement and the requisite informational materials at that time and then inform the employee that she must complete and return the form within thirty days of her start date. This approach would ensure that the employer did not base its decision to hire the employee on her willingness to sign an arbitration agreement. It would also give the employee time to make an informed decision.

An employer could take extra precautions to ensure that courts will enforce their arbitration agreements. For example, a large employer may allow employees to submit their forms directly to the Human Resources Department. Then, the individual responsible for the hiring decisions could not refuse to hire, discharge, or otherwise injure an employee who declines to sign the arbitration agreement. Alternatively, a small employer without a Human Resources Department could assign its employees identification numbers, which the employees could then use to submit their arbitration agreements anonymously.

If your scholarly paper involves legislative change, include the legislative language you would like to see enacted. If you are arguing for an amendment, include the amending language for which you are advocating. Shaina did this in her paper:

Congress should adopt a legislative amendment that completely eliminates the widow penalty. It can do so by adopting the amendment provided below:

In the case of an alien who was the spouse of a citizen of the United States <<stricken text>for at least two years<<stricken text> at the time of the citizen's death and was not legally separated from the citizen at the time of the citizen's death, the alien (and each child of the alien) shall be considered, for purposes of this subsection, to remain an immediate relative after the date of the citizen's death but only if the spouse files a petition under section 204(a)(1)(A)(ii) within 2 years after such date and only until the date the spouse remarries.

With the removal of just five words ("for at least two years") from the immediate relatives definition, the proposed amendment will abolish the two-year rule, provide the Immigration Service with no discretion to automatically revoke alien widows' approved I-130 petitions, and allow alien spouses of U.S. citizens to self-petition for LPR status, despite the death of the citizen spouse and regardless of the length of the underlying marriage.

Collin's paper involved both statutory and regulatory change. First, he proposed a new statute:

> Solely for government ethics purposes, all personal services contractors, as currently defined by FAR 2.101 and FAR 37.104, are to be deemed "federal employees" and treated as such when applying government ethics laws, including 18 U.S.C. §§ 201–219 and all regulations promulgated by the Office of Government Ethics. The FAR Council should promulgate applicable regulations within the FAR to this effect.

As a complement to the new statute, Collin proposed a new clause for inclusion in the Federal Acquisition Regulation:

> ETHICAL OBLIGATIONS OF PERSONAL SERVICES CONTRACTORS
>
> (a) Every individual assigned to this personal services contract shall, before starting work on that contract, file a public financial disclosure form as mandated by the Office of Government Ethics and its regulations, 5 C.F.R. §§ 2634.301–311.
>
> (b) If this contract lasts longer than one year, all individuals under this contract shall be required to file public financial disclosure forms pursuant to section (a) for each year under the contract.
>
> (c) Pursuant to [incorporated reference to above congressional statute], every individual assigned to this personal services contract hereby acknowledges and agrees that he/she is subject to all government ethics laws applicable to federal employees, including 18 U.S.C. §§ 201–219 and all regulations promulgated by the Office of Government Ethics.

After writing the actual text of the proposed new clause, Collin explained how the new clause would be fairly simple to implement given the existing law and regulations that govern federal procurement.

Chris recognized the complexity of his proposal requiring a determination of when a man should not have child support responsibilities for a biological child. He created a five-prong test for courts to use in making this determination. He described his test as an affirmative defense:

> A biological father should be permitted to disclaim legal fatherhood in a child support setting when the following elements are satisfied: (1) the biological father had expressed, before conception, a deep philosophical objection to being a father; (2) the biological mother

believed or had reason to believe at the time of conception that the father had a deep philosophical objection to becoming a father; (3) the biological father believed and had reason to believe at the time of the conceptive conduct that the mother would terminate a pregnancy or that a pregnancy was impossible; (4) upon birth of the child, the father maintained his deep philosophical objection to becoming a father; and (5) the father can demonstrate actual emotional, psychological, or physical harm because he was forced to be a father. Such a test would be an affirmative defense in a filiation proceeding.

Remember that your proposal could be implemented any number of ways. You have the horizontal and vertical knowledge on your topic and thesis to be able to define the implementation parameters; use this knowledge to strengthen your paper by incorporating analysis that explains how to implement your proposal.

Have I Explained the Limited Scope of My Paper?

Thus far, the questions we have presented are intended to help you identify analytical gaps, and then determine how to revise your paper to fill the gaps and strengthen your analysis to improve your paper as a whole. Not all gaps require filling, however. Some gaps are better left alone, after a brief acknowledgement that the issues presented by the gaps are outside the scope of your paper. Your paper cannot cover everything, and trying to fit every detail in your paper will likely overwhelm you and the reader. To the extent some information is not required to support your thesis, consider how you can leave it out of your paper. You may still want to recognize the issue, perhaps, but you can decide that the particular argument or facet of an issue is beyond the scope of your paper.

When you find a gap like this, consider using a footnote to show the reader how that issue is beyond the scope of your thesis and thus, does not require detailed analysis. You may want to refer back to Chapter 4 where we discussed how one of the functions of footnotes is to do just that. Including a footnote lets you acknowledge the gap, but leave it unfilled. This is acceptable, as long as you do not use this technique to avoid doing more work. In other words, do not choose to carve out something just because you do not want to go back to do more research, or because you do not want to think about another reason your proposal is worthy of consideration. Instead, use this technique sparingly when there is something that really does not merit inclusion in your paper, but you want to alert the reader to your awareness of it.

For example, Chris's paper engages with a sensitive subject: abortion. His note, however, does not take a position on abortion, but rather focuses on a father's rights and legal responsibilities, including the right to not be a parent. Rather than ignore potential questions about abortion, he revised his paper to add a footnote to acknowledge the sensitivity of abortion as an issue, and successfully places that issue outside the scope of his paper.

Excerpted sentence from Chris's Note:

Furthermore, once a pregnant woman is in a situation in which the father would not be required to pay child support, she may more readily choose an abortion, and thus the possibility of an unsupported child disappears.

Text of the footnote:

This Note neither advocates for abortion nor takes a position against it. Instead, this Note assumes a legal environment where abortion is permissible and an option that a woman may consider after learning of an unwanted pregnancy.

Thus, Chris successfully acknowledges the potential gap, but effectively avoids a detailed analysis on abortion, which would likely detract from the strength of his paper by distracting the reader.

In another example, Collin similarly uses a footnote to explain the limited scope of his paper.

Excerpted paragraph from Collin's Note:

Without the personal services prohibition, there would have been no need to implement these inefficient reforms designed solely to reduce CCE's control over its contractor employees and avoid the creation of a personal services contract. CCE would have instead been able to continue employing its contract specialists based on their individual skill and expertise irrespective of whether they were CACI employees or government employees.

Text of the footnote:

This is not meant to imply that the government contractor-employee distinction should be completely eliminated. The GAO report identified concerns that CCE contractors sometimes failed to be properly identified as such in meetings, telephone calls, and on contract documents. This issue is important because, in the acquisition support field, the authority to negotiate and approve the terms of a government contract ultimately resides with the government agency, and contractors have no direct authority to speak on behalf of the government. Of course, these issues, while important, are beyond the scope of this Note.

Here, Collin recognizes the potential implication of his analysis, but cuts it off by explicitly limiting the scope of his argument and pointing out that his Note does not analyze this important issue.

Identify Opportunities to Strengthen Your Paper

Another way to approach the revising is to look for opportunities to strengthen your paper by focusing on what you could do to make your paper even stronger rather than looking for analytical gaps as we described above. You might find some of these specific questions cross over between solving analytical gaps and identifying opportunities to strengthen your analysis. The goal here is to give you a strategy for approaching the substantive revision.

Can I Use Actual or Hypothetical Examples to Illustrate My Analysis?

Using actual or hypothetical examples can strengthen the analysis in your paper and give the reader an additional level of understanding. Using examples is also an effective way to demonstrate the practical value of your thesis by showing how your solution would be implemented or demonstrating how application of your solution would get the right result. You can use actual examples (such as the scenario that led you to develop your thesis in the first place), or you can make up believable hypotheticals in order to make these points. Which you choose, of course, depends on the specific needs in your paper. Several of our student authors effectively used actual examples in their Notes, but used them in different ways.

Consider Shaina's paper first; her Note opens with actual examples, a powerful description of three widows' true stories:

> The death of a spouse can be one of the most tragic events of a person's life. This was the case for Dahianna Heard, who lost her husband Jeffrey, a security company contractor, when he was shot during an ambush in Iraq. The newlyweds were only three months shy of their

two-year wedding anniversary and had recently had a child together. The same tragedy was endured by Charmaine van der Elst Kirtland, a former SeaWorld dolphin trainer, who met her husband John at an international animal training conference. A week before their first wedding anniversary, John was diagnosed with colon cancer and passed away six months later, leaving behind two young stepchildren. And twenty-six-year-old Maria Raquel Pascoal felt the same pain as well when her husband of almost two years died of sleep apnea at age thirty, leaving her to raise their three-month-old son by herself.

In these circumstances, Dahianna, Charmaine, and Maria struggled with feelings of grief, despair, and regret for not having had an opportunity to say goodbye to their husbands. But there was another emotion that they experienced as well: fear. After their husbands' tragic deaths, these alien widows faced deportation from the United States.

Shaina returns to the stories of these three women in her Conclusion:

Strict interpretation of spouse-based immigration law, especially for alien widows who have lost their American spouses, is a significant concern that deserves immediate attention. Hundreds of alien widows, like Dahianna, Charmaine, and Maria, are being deported, with or without their children, based on a tragic happenstance that is out of their control. Without any explicit approval by the legislature, the widow penalty has been adopted by Immigration Service interpretation and never formally recognized by Congress as applying to all alien widows. As such, it is understandable that the widow penalty has been deemed a "crack in the law" that does not rest on sound or logical legal principles.

It has been suggested that the widow penalty has remained intact because the group affected by its consequence, alien widows, lacks a strong political voice. Proposed legislation in Congress, however, along with current cases in the federal courts, indicate that the widow penalty is gaining national attention. With immigration reform at the top of America's political agenda, Congress should adopt the proposed amendment to abolish the two-year rule within a narrow bill and allow widows of U.S. citizens to self-petition for LPR status, regardless of the length of the underlying marriage.

Immigration officials recently notified Dahianna Heard, the alien widow who faced deportation after her citizen contractor husband was killed in Iraq, that they would grant her adjustment of status application and stop deportation procedures. Although the Immigration

Service did not exempt Dahianna under the USA Patriot Act exception to the widow penalty because her husband did not die during active military duty, the Immigration Service seemed to have a "change of heart" after reviewing her dead husband's past military service record. Her first act of freedom, she said, after almost two years of feeling like a prisoner, would be to go to the Department of Motor Vehicles and get her driver's license back.

The result in Dahianna's case, however, is an anomaly. Immigration officials did not have a "change of heart" in the cases of Charmaine and Maria, who are currently subject to deportation procedures. Without legislative reform, the widow penalty will continue to punish those undeserving of punishment. But the death of a spouse should be penalty enough.

Even though Shaina does not refer to the women's stories in between her Introduction and Conclusion, the powerful descriptions of the women's situations stick with the reader throughout the background and analytical sections of her paper. Then, by returning to their stories in the end, she effectively brings together her entire paper creating a sense of cohesiveness for the reader.

In his paper, Chris similarly uses actual examples to open his Note, but he also refers back to one of the examples in his solution section to show how his proposed affirmative defense would have played out in the context of that example. His Introduction has two examples of men who did not want to be fathers:

Since the fall of 2004, Matthew Dubay and Lauren Wells had been romantically involved. Before engaging in sexual intercourse, Dubay and Wells discussed their procreative intentions. After Dubay told Wells that he was opposed to being a father, she responded that she was infertile and that she would use contraception as a precaution. Shortly after the relationship dissolved, however, Wells informed Dubay that she had become pregnant with his child. Dubay reiterated his desire not to be a father, but Wells carried the child to term and gave birth in 2005. Wells commenced paternity proceedings against Dubay, which prompted Dubay to challenge the state parentage law as a violation of his rights under the Equal Protection Clause. The district court dismissed Dubay's case for failure to state a cognizable claim. Ultimately, the Sixth Circuit affirmed the district court's ruling.

On February 19 and March 19, 1999, Sharon Irons allegedly engaged in oral sex with Richard Phillips, a man with whom she had been in a relationship since January. These were the only sexual acts in which the couple had engaged. In May, Phillips and Irons ended their relationship after Irons revealed she was still married, not divorced as she had led Phillips to believe. Eighteen months later, Phillips discovered through a petition to establish paternity that he had unknowingly fathered a daughter, Serena, who was born on December 1, 1999. Phillips sued Irons and claimed she "intentionally engaged in oral sex with [him,] so that she could harvest [his] semen and artificially inseminate herself." Ultimately, the appellate court dismissed Phillips' claims of conversion of his semen and fraudulent misrepresentation, but it remanded the case to the trial court to allow him to proceed on a claim of intentional infliction of emotional distress ("IIED").

Like Shaina's use of the widows' stories, these examples of Dubay and Phillips give the reader context for Chris's argument in favor of a right not to be a legal father. Later in his paper, Chris returns to the Dubay example to illustrate how his affirmative defense would protect Dubay:

> The facts as presented in the Dubay petition provide an easy example to demonstrate how the affirmative defense presented by this Note could fix some of the inequity of the child support system. Under the current regime, Dubay is required to pay child support solely because he is the child's biological father. Taking the facts as described in Dubay's complaint as true, however, Dubay would likely be able to assert this new affirmative defense.
>
> First, Dubay expressed to Wells his clear sentiment "[b]efore, during and after their physical relationship" that he did not want to have a child because of his and Wells' ages and their status as students. Such a statement likely satisfies the first and second prongs of the test because it appears to be an actual and reasonable expression of Dubay's desire not to be a father and it appears adequate to create in Wells an actual belief, or reason to believe, that Dubay did not want to be a father. Second, as the District Attorney's brief concedes, Wells told Dubay that she was infertile, thus satisfying the third prong of the test—that Dubay actually and reasonably believed pregnancy would be impossible. Presumably, Dubay would also maintain his objection relating to the child, and he must do so in order to fulfill the fourth element. Finally, for Dubay to satisfy the last element of the affirmative defense, there would need to be greater inquiry to determine whether Dubay had suffered any actual harm because he was forced to be a father. Assuming he had suffered harm, Dubay would satisfy all of the

elements of the affirmative defense and thus could be relieved of his child support obligations.

Chris returns once again to the examples of Dubay and Phillips in his Conclusion. Here he recognizes the complications presented by his argument, but Dubay's and Phillips's stories bring the reader back to understanding why his solution is worth considering.

> There are significant complications in the application of the right to decide not to be a legal father. While these difficulties present a compelling argument to give little if any weight to the paternal right to avoid legal parenthood, the recognition of such a right is necessary to clarify the jurisprudence of procreative autonomy. Neither Sharon Irons nor Lauren Wells deserved child support. Moreover, both Richard Phillips and Matthew Dubay had real and intimate interests in avoiding declarations of paternity. Therefore, notwithstanding any complications, the courts should have more seriously considered the biological fathers' constitutional interest in avoiding the psychological, physical, and emotional harms of being declared legal fathers.

Collin successfully uses actual examples throughout his Note to illustrate the problems with the personal services prohibition and to explain how his proposal would avoid such problems. Like Chris and Shaina, Collin opens with an example of a recent event to illustrate the reality and exigency of his paper.

> When Marine General Gary McKissock retired, he joined the board of directors of Sapient, a defense contractor that has received almost $100 million in federal contracts since Fiscal Year 2000. Defense contractors often aggressively recruit generals and admirals because of their valuable knowledge, experience, and contacts within the Pentagon. While working at Sapient, however, Gen. McKissock also served as a consultant to the Marines, receiving twice the salary he originally earned while on active duty. Yet despite the apparent conflict of interest, nothing in Gen. McKissock's contract prevented him from promoting Sapient's products, lobbying the very officers he was charged with advising, or using information he obtained as a consultant to help Sapient obtain future military contracts.

Collin returns to the example of General McKissock in his Conclusion. Here he explains how his proposed solution, specifically to require the General to file a public financial disclosure form, would have prevented the conflicts of interest. This reminds the reader of the exigency and reality of these conflicts of interest, and establishes legitimacy for his proposed solution by demonstrating how his solution would work in practice.

> This solution would apply to senior mentors employed under personal service contracts through the Pentagon's senior mentor program. This approach would not allow the Pentagon to avoid applying ethics laws to its senior mentors simply by hiring them under contract. These senior mentors would instead be subject to the same ethics rules as the regular Pentagon officials with which they work. As such, Gen. McKissock would have been considered a "federal employee" for government ethics purposes and would have been required to file a public financial disclosure form before he started consulting for the Marines. If he decided to remain as a director of Sapient, Gen. McKissock would be prohibited from working on any government project for which Sapient planned to compete, and he certainly would not be allowed to lobby the officers he advised. Most importantly, this approach would extend beyond the Department of Defense and apply to all executive agencies.

Collin also uses an actual example to illustrate the complex and inefficient supervision schemes created as a result of the personal services prohibition, giving the reader a concrete idea of these inefficiencies:

> For example, the GAO examined the Army Contracting Center of Excellence's ("CCE") contract with CACI, a private business, for contract specialists that "perform a range of acquisition services in support of government contracting officers." CCE, as a division of the Army Contracting Command, provides contracting and acquisition support services to the Secretary of the Army and the Army Headquarters staff. The GAO found that CACI contractors represented about forty-two percent of CCE's total contract specialists, and that these contractors worked directly alongside their government counterparts on the same projects. According to GAO interviews with CCE staff, projects were "generally assigned based on knowledge and experience, not whether the specialist [was] a government or contractor employee." Conventional wisdom dictates that this is the most efficient assignment strategy, as it enables the employer to utilize each individual's knowledge and experience where it would be most effective. Unfortunately, the GAO informed CCE that this assignment strategy ran dangerously close to violating the personal services prohibition, and CCE was

forced to take steps to separate its contractors from their government counterparts. All contractors were placed onto a separate team and became supervised by CACI managers instead of government supervisors. CCE also planned to move all contracting personnel to a separate area.

Without the personal services prohibition, there would have been no need to implement these inefficient reforms designed solely to reduce CCE's control over its contractor employees and avoid the creation of a personal services contract. CCE would have instead been able to continue employing its contract specialists based on their individual skill and expertise irrespective of whether they were CACI employees or government employees.

Monica also used a real story to capture readers' attention in her Introduction; the story of the theft of the Mona Lisa is mysterious and fascinating. Almost any reader is familiar with the Mona Lisa, and the story of its theft, discovery, and return is the perfect way for Monica to illustrate the problem of stolen artwork and other cultural property.

On August 21, 1911, the Mona Lisa was stolen. An amateur painter was copying the Mona Lisa at the Louvre, and when he returned the next day to continue working, the enigmatic portrait had vanished. After a few hours of frantic searching, the most famous museum in the world was forced to admit that the most famous painting in the world had been stolen from within its own walls. The Mona Lisa was a national treasure for France, where the painting has resided for four centuries, gracing the halls of Versailles during the reign of Louis XIV and the walls of Napoleon's bedroom. It was one of Leonardo da Vinci's masterpieces—an object of pride for all Italians. But more than that, the Mona Lisa was a global icon, one of the crown jewels in the art collection of humanity.

After two dismal years of searching, the Mona Lisa's captor contacted the Uffizi Gallery in Florence, looking to sell. The curators of the Uffizi recognized the painting as the original, and the thief, Vincenzo Peruggia, was arrested. Peruggia had worked at the Louvre as a glazier, and believed that France had no rightful claim to the portrait. He wrote to the Uffizi, "[The Mona Lisa] seems to belong to Italy since its painter was an Italian. My dream is to give back this masterpiece to the land from which it came and to the country that inspired it." The portrait was returned to France, but Peruggia was hailed as a national hero and served less than a year in jail.

Monica also used other actual examples of cultural property theft to show how the problem reaches beyond Italy:

> Various arrests conducted or aided by the TPC have achieved international attention, thereby creating a deterrent effect by spreading the message of a crackdown on illicit trade in cultural property. In 1995, Swiss and Italian authorities conducted a raid at the Geneva warehouse of Italian art dealer Giacomo de Medici, where they discovered thousands of photographs depicting objects that had been recently excavated illegally and sold, as well as tens of thousands of documents and as many as 4,000 antiquities in part or in whole. Medici was charged with smuggling, handling stolen antiquities, and conspiracy by Italian courts. In 2004, Medici was sentenced to ten years in prison and a fine of roughly fourteen million dollars. The evidence collected during the Medici raid led to the subsequent indictments and trials of Robert Hecht, an American antiquities dealer and heir of the Hecht Company, and Marion True, a former curator of the Getty in Los Angeles, California.
>
> True was indicted in 2005 on charges of receipt of stolen goods and participation in a conspiracy to traffic in stolen goods. The trial continued until October of 2010, when the statute of limitations on her crimes ran out. Hecht remains on trial, but according to his lawyer, the statute of limitations on his charges will also expire in July of 2011. Although they did not serve prison time, their trials nonetheless demonstrate that this type of behavior will not be tolerated.

And finally, Monica returns to these examples in her sub-section on the need for swift prosecution, by using these real cases to illustrate how cultural property thieves receive minimal—or no—punishment.

> Although Italy's legislation imposes civil and criminal penalties on those who deal in illicit trafficking of cultural property, the deterrent effect of such threats lacks bite. In the world of art theft, "[t]he risk is small, the potential gain is tremendous, and if the thief is caught, the punishment is still minimal." Vincenzo Peruggia, the thief who stole the Mona Lisa and hid it for two years served less than a year in jail. Nearly 100 years later, Marion True was indicted, leading to one of the biggest scandals in the history of the art world. In True's case, the trial endured for five years, never progressed to the point where the defense could produce any witnesses or argue for True's innocence, and eventually ended when the statute of limitations ran on the

charges against her. To truly deter art theft and illicit trade in cultural property, Italy must follow through with its criminal prosecutions in a manner that will garner respect for the nation's laws, as opposed to the mere threat of "facing a drawn-out legal ordeal, and … the hypothetical threat of incarceration in a foreign country."

You may not always have actual examples to draw upon, or you may decide that real examples are not quite right for your analysis. When that is the case, you can use hypothetical examples to illustrate your argument and provide context for the reader. For example, in Natalie's paper, she explains how there is a catch-22 situation for employees of a protected class. After identifying the existence of the catch-22, Natalie uses a hypothetical example to illustrate how this catch-22 plays out:

> Imagine that employee Jennifer, a black sales clerk, applies for a position at a retail store. The retail store requires a prospective employee, as part of her employment application, to sign an agreement that waives her right to a judicial forum for potential federal statutory claims. If Jennifer refuses to sign the waiver, the retail store may not hire her for the position. Jennifer will be out of a job for merely asserting her rights. Now imagine that Jennifer signs the waiver as part of her employment application. The retail store later transfers Jennifer to a "less desirable" position and hires a white person to fill her former position. If Jennifer was transferred to a "less desirable" position due to her race, Jennifer can sue her employer under Title VII. However, because Jennifer signed the arbitration agreement, she will not get her day in court. She can arbitrate the matter, but if, as some suggest, the arbitral process favors "repeat players"—namely, the employers— Jennifer will probably not prevail in the arbitral forum. She will be out of a job—at least the one she applied for—because she did not assert her rights at the start of her employment relationship with the retail store.

Any hypothetical examples you develop should be believable, like Natalie's— even though she made up her example, it is easy to imagine this exact scenario happening. Using the hypothetical scenario is also particularly useful here because the idea of the catch-22 is somewhat abstract; the use of an example about a hypothetical employee, Jennifer, gives the reader a sense of how this catch-22 affects people.

Notice how including this hypothetical gives Natalie the ability to demonstrate the type of situation she seeks to avoid in her solution. Readers might imagine a less offensive scenario, but it is unlikely a reader would disagree that Jennifer's situation is unfair. Thus, using the hypothetical here likely does more than give readers a sense of how the catch-22 plays out; it also helps Natalie get the reader on her (or Jennifer's) side.

Look for opportunities to use examples, either hypothetical or real, to illustrate your analytical points. For example, in Emily's comment about student loan discharges, she has a section describing "the modern student borrower." In an early draft, this portion of the paper defined various types of institutions and discussed the differences between traditional and nontraditional students. The draft probably met the reader's needs in understanding the landscape, but the description was fairly dry because the draft did not include any examples of students. Seeing an opportunity to use examples to further illustrate her thesis's exigency, Emily revised her comment to include an example of a student at a for-profit institution:

> Take, for example, Shawn Brighenti, who pursued a degree through the University of Phoenix Online in order to better support his family. After Shawn graduated, he claims potential employers told him that they did not consider the University of Phoenix an accredited school. After four years of searching, Shawn remained jobless and drowning in student loan debt.

This example gives the reader a stronger sense of what kind of challenges students face after incurring a debt with no salary to repay it, and likely primes the reader to be more excited to read Emily's proposed solution.

In another substantive revision to her paper, Emily noticed that she provided a superficial explanation of the undue hardship standard. In an early draft, she identified and moderately criticized the judicial test for undue hardship, known as the "Brunner test." Again, her paper met the reader's expectations in explaining the undue hardship standard. Here is her draft of this section:

The Unduly Hard "Undue Hardship" Standard

> In order to understand the real impact of the 1998 elimination of the waiting period, it is necessary to understand the burden a debtor has to successfully prove that maintaining a student loan debt would constitute undue hardship. The phrase "undue hardship" was never defined in the Bankruptcy Code and, thus, the judiciary has been charged with crafting substantive undue hardship tests. The "Brunner Test," set forth in *Brunner v. New York State Higher Education Services Corp*, is the most commonly used undue hardship test for student loan discharge cases.

The Brunner Test requires a plaintiff seeking a discharge of student loans in bankruptcy to prove undue hardship by satisfying the following three elements:

(1) that the debtor cannot maintain, based on current income and expenses, a "minimal" standard of living for herself and her dependents if forced to repay the loans; (2) that additional circumstances exist indicating that this state of affairs is likely to persist for a significant portion of the repayment period of the student loans; and (3) that the debtor has made good faith efforts to repay the loans. For the reasons set forth in the district court's order, we adopt this analysis.

The examination of the debtor under each prong of the test calls for a fact-intensive inquiry into the debtor's particular circumstances. Under the first prong, the court examines the debtor's income and expenses. The second prong requires a two-step analysis: (1) whether it seems as though the debtor's financial situation will likely continue and (2) whether the duration of this financial hardship will last through most of the repayment period. Lastly, under the third prong, the court assesses whether the debtor has acted in good faith by attempting to repay the loan.

The application of the Brunner Test has been plagued by judicial subjectivity and speculation. The second prong is arguably the most controversial because it effectively requires a judge to predict the debtor's future financial situation. The level of judicial speculation that goes into making this determination creates a "certainty of hopelessness" for a debtor seeking discharge.

The test, besides its substantive shortfalls, is also criticized for its complicated procedural issues. Debtors seeking to prove undue hardship must institute an entire second round of adversarial litigation after the consumer bankruptcy filing. Thus, even after successfully proving bankruptcy, the debtor must devote time and resources to carry on an entirely new court case. Therefore, the 1998 Amendment eliminating the seven-year waiting period had serious negative ramifications for a debtor seeking a student loan discharge as evidenced by the substantive and procedural shortfalls of the undue hardship standard.

In her revision, Emily capitalized on an opportunity to strengthen her argument by using this discussion to further illustrate the Brunner test's shortcomings with two examples.

Take, for example, an application of the third prong—a good faith effort to repay. In *In re Stitt*, Judge Mannes concluded that Monica

Stitt lacked the requisite showing of a good faith effort to repay because she had not entered into an income-based repayment plan. The court drew this conclusion despite the fact that under such a plan, Ms. Stitt's monthly payment would have been zero dollars based on her income. In contrast, Judge Kilburg in *In re Limkemann* found that the debtor had acted in good faith and was entitled to a discharge of student loans despite never having entered into an income-based repayment plan. Even though Mr. Limkemann was eligible for the plan, Judge Kilburg reasoned that eligibility was irrelevant because the debtor did not have the financial resources to satisfy a minimal monthly payment. In both cases, the student loan debtors were eligible to enter income-based repayment plans despite insufficient income; however, only Ms. Stitt was found to have acted in bad faith and denied a discharge.

In her revision, Emily started with an example that picked up on her opening narrative about Monica Stitt and then used another example in contrast to show the inconsistent results as support for her argument against judicial subjectivity in this context. These examples create context and in this particular topic area, bring the narrative to life and more fully engage the reader who is then more likely to respond favorably to Emily's argument.

Can I Place My Thesis in a Broader Context?

Another way to strengthen your Analysis/Discussion section in support of your thesis is to bring in other disciplines or use legal rationales from other areas to show how your thesis is supported. You may want to do this because your solution or argument is broad-reaching, affecting areas of law beyond the narrow legal issue or issues covered in your paper. If, when evaluating your thesis, you determined that your solution would have unintended benefits, you can explain those in your analysis to widen the scope of your analysis. Even though your thesis does not depend on these tangential benefits, benefits in other areas provide further reasoning in support of your thesis. You may also want to do this because you want to show that your idea about how to change a law or enforce a policy has found success in other contexts.

For example, when Chris evaluated his paper, he was concerned that readers might question the basis of his idea to use an affirmative defense to establish a man's intentions of not becoming a father. Recognizing the challenges in establishing a philosophical desire to not be a father and thinking about how courts would be able to determine the legitimacy of a claim to have this belief, Chris argued that courts could model the test after the test for conscientious objector status. Thus, Chris effectively incorporated another area of law in making his argument for his proposal. Reaching out to another area of established law, Chris answered criticisms about the difficulty in determining these beliefs by arguing that even though it would be difficult for courts to make these determinations, the difficulty is not reason enough to abandon his solution. And given that the courts have been able to determine conscientious objector status in similar ways, there is a basis in existing law that supports Chris's solution. This effectively gives a broader perspective to Chris's Note, and at the same time, lends support to his proposed solution by demonstrating that the type of defense he proposed exists in another context.

Have I Reinforced My Thesis at Every Opportunity?

As you are revising, try to find places where you may have softened your position or even just avoided a straightforward argument. This can happen when the writer is still mastering the material, still developing the substantive ideas, or still understanding the power of a scholarly paper. The reader is looking for your paper to deliver a solution, and part of the revision process is checking to make sure you have met that expectation. Your commitment should show throughout the paper, from the introduction, to the headings, all the way through to the conclusion. Check to make sure your paper takes every opportunity to persuade the reader of the soundness of your analysis.

For example, when Emily revised her draft note about the student loan discharge exception, she noticed that her introduction did not take advantage of the narrative. Her draft introduction started with details about Jane Doe in the present:

> Meet Jane Doe. Jane is forty-five years old, lives by herself, and is permanently disabled. She has never held a steady job—let alone a job that pays above minimum wage—and the last time she was able to work was approximately eight years ago. Today, Jane barely gets by—she lives in subsidized housing, receives monthly social security disability payments, is on Medicaid, and qualifies for food stamps. It is fair to say that Jane has had a tough road.
>
> However, Jane was once just a young woman eager to invest in her future. In 1989, she applied for and was granted federal student loans in the amount of $13,250 to attend a four-year college. Unfortunately, Jane left school after one year and defaulted on the loans shortly thereafter. Despite attempts to make periodic repayments, the financial obligation became too much for Jane to bear. After years of being unable

to make payments, what started as Jane's $13,250 student loan in 1989 grew, with interest, to become a $37,431 student loan debt in 2014.

Emily's revised introduction put Jane Doe immediately into the context in which the comment focuses by rearranging the details of Jane Doe's story. By starting with Jane's investment in her future, Emily appeals to pathos to engage the reader with the hardworking, student-loan-taking student Jane instead of the current 45-year-old Jane facing student loan debt.

> Meet Jane Doe. In 1989, nineteen-year-old Jane decided to invest in her future and go to college. Jane, a hardworking student, enrolled in a four-year university. She knew a college education would not be cheap and applied for student loans. Jane was easily approved for a federal student loan, and, after dotting the i's and crossing the t's, she received her loan money and began taking classes. To finance her freshman year, Jane received four student loans amounting to $13,250.
>
> Unfortunately, life soon got in the way, and Jane had to leave school after only one year. With $13,250 in loans and no degree, Jane faced a tough road ahead. After withdrawing from school, Jane properly deferred her student loans to give herself time to find a job. Unfortunately, Jane's lack of a college degree, compounded with her crippling speech disability, made it nearly impossible for her to find, let alone keep, a job. Eventually, Jane ran out of money. Approximately ten years after embarking on her bright college future, she was struggling; Jane obtained Social Security disability benefits, food stamps, Medicaid, and Section 8 housing. Still, Jane tried to make the best of a bad situation and refused to shirk her financial obligations — with the little money she had, she made several modest payments on her student loan. Ultimately, she filed for bankruptcy twenty-two years after leaving school.

With the young Jane in mind, Jane's later challenges and debt are better framed to support Emily's argument in favor of reforming the student loan discharge exception. The reader now has a sense of how the status quo plays out and seeks to find out how Emily can solve this problem.

On a smaller scale, Emily revised her main roadmap to more clearly and concretely tell the reader what to expect. Given the multiple revisions your paper is likely to undergo, taking some time to focus on the main roadmap during the revision stage is another opportunity to fully commit to your thesis. Early roadmaps tend to be more general as the writer is still figuring out how to construct the various sections. One of Emily's early drafts had the following roadmap:

This Comment explores the history behind the student loan discharge exception and the ramifications it has on student loan debtors in bankruptcy. Part II provides a comprehensive overview of the student loan discharge exception and policy proposals in favor of its reform. Part III begins with an analysis of the current policy proposals and ends by setting forth a new proposal for discharge exception reform. The comment concludes in Part IV with a strong recommendation that the student loan discharge exception be reformed.

The final published comment had this roadmap:

This Comment explores the history behind the student loan discharge exception and its ramifications for student loan debtors in bankruptcy. Section II provides a comprehensive overview of the student loan discharge exception and policy proposals in favor of its reform. Section III analyzes the current policy proposals and ultimately sets forth a four-part proposal for reform of the discharge exception. This Comment concludes in Section IV that the student loan discharge exception should be reformed according to the author's four-part proposal.

The revised roadmap shows some confidence that was lacking in the initial roadmap. The writer now has a four-part proposal rather than a generic "new proposal," and rather than characterize her recommendation as strong, Emily shows the reader the strength of her argument by telling the reader "that the student loan discharge exception should be reformed according to [her] four-part proposal."

In arguing for a change to the loan discharge exception, Emily sought to balance the realities of federal government student loan practices and students' needs for loans in the context of the diversity of students and institutions. Specifically, she argued for a risk-rating based on "type of academic institution and the institution's post-graduation employment outcomes." In an early draft, her argument was fairly thin:

Re-working the statutory language of the student loan discharge exception is a big piece of the reform puzzle, but it does not address the current problems of non-traditional student borrowers investing in high-risk academic institutions. A comprehensive reform of the student loan discharge exception should attack the student loan debt problem from all sides—this includes addressing the increasingly diverse student borrower population and the institutions for which they borrow. The rise of for-profit academic institutions has contributed to an increase in outstanding student loan debt and higher rates of default. Despite these troubling facts, the federal government has continued to issue student loans without giving for-profit borrowers so much as a warning that they are about to incur a potentially risky debt.

Federal loans should be risk-rated by type of academic institution and the institution's post-graduation employment outcomes. This will ensure that, before incurring a penny of debt, student borrowers know what to expect out of their chosen educational program. Thus, if a student borrower, in spite of a poor risk-rate, still opts to take on a student loan obligation, it is justified that they be held to a higher standard when seeking a discharge in bankruptcy. Modestly risk-rating federal student loans has the dual effect of making the federal government accountable for its lending behavior and imposing personal responsibility on the borrower. The hope is that this would expose academic institutions that dupe students to take out loans for a career that may very well never come to be. Risk-rating federal student loans recognizes inherent changes in the world of higher education and should be included as part of a comprehensive reform of the student loan discharge exception.

In a later revision, Emily fully developed the argument to show the reader the strength of her thesis with a more compelling explanation of what risk-rating would do to the various players.

A comprehensive reform of the student loan discharge exception must attack the student loan debt problem from all sides; this includes addressing both the increasingly diverse student borrower population and the institutions they attend. The rise of for-profit institutions has contributed to an increase in outstanding student loan debt and higher rates of default. Despite this, the federal government has continued issuing student loans without warning for-profit borrowers that they are about to incur potentially risky debt.

Federal loans should be modestly risk-rated by taking into account both the type of academic institution and the borrowers' prospective ability to repay their student loans. This front-end protection will ensure that, before incurring even a penny of debt, student borrowers are given information on their financial outlook. This is a more just system because the risk-rated loans would signal to a student borrower the financial risk associated with their chosen educational program. Students would be able to attend any academic institution they desire; however, the loan they take out may be subject to, for example, higher interest rates, if their academic institution is plagued by poor employment outcomes and graduation statistics. Modestly risk-rating federal student loans makes the federal government accountable for its lending behavior and, at the same time, imposes personal responsibility on the borrower. Risk-rating will also shed light on academic institutions that seek to dupe students into taking out loans for a career that might never be realized. Risk-rating federal student loans recognizes that the world of higher education has changed significantly since 1958, when government-led student loan programs were first created. As such, risk-rating is an integral step in the comprehensive reform of the student loan discharge exception.

In addition to more fully explaining her argument, notice too how Emily has responded to a possible counterargument for more incremental or focused changes by calling for a "comprehensive reform." By deleting the first sentence from her earlier draft, the argument becomes more powerful because it opens with the need for a comprehensive reform. That original sentence about the "big piece" of the reform puzzle undermines the stronger statement about attacking student loan debt from all sides, and thus excising it strengthened the thesis. The challenges faced by non-traditional students and high-risk institutions are then built into the argument in the second paragraph so the substantive content is preserved.

Evaluate Your Organizational Choices

Another way to evaluate your paper is to think about your organizational choices and determine whether they make sense in the context of your paper as a whole. You may have already done some of this evaluating when you took a bird's-eye view of your paper by reading it in its entirety at the beginning of this round of refining. As you worked through your evaluation and subsequent revisions, you may have been bogged down in the details; now you can step back and look at how your paper is shaping up as a cohesive piece with the benefit of your latest round of revisions. In Chapter 4, we introduced the major and minor parts of your paper and encouraged you to write them into your draft. Now you are ready to make sure the major and minor parts are organized in a way that supports your thesis, and makes it easy for the reader to follow your analysis.

To help you get a sense of where everything is, and decide whether everything is in its proper place, consider making a reverse outline of your paper after your latest round of revisions. Developing a reverse outline will let you see how your revisions changed the course or design of your paper and may allow you to identify additional opportunities for improvement in organization or content. To create a reverse outline, start by listing each heading and sub-heading from your paper. You can create a more detailed reverse outline by inserting the thesis sentences of each paragraph as bullet points under the appropriate heading or sub-heading. You can do this in whatever way this works for you: abbreviated bullet points, complete sentences, or a hybrid. Consider the following example from a revised draft of Chris's paper:

Introduction
I. Right to Autonomous Procreative Decision Making
II. Declarations of Legal Paternity Infringe on a Father's Right to Procreational Autonomy
    A. Biological Parenthood and Legal Parenthood are Severable Concepts.
    B. The Asserted Interest is Decisional and Emotional in Nature, Not Economic, and Comes with Significant Psychological, Moral, and Sociological Implications.
        1. Scientific Support
        2. Precedential Support
    C. Application of the Right
        1. Expression of Philosophical Desire Not to Become a Father
        2. Reasonable or Actual Belief by Biological Mother
        3. Biological Father's Actual and Reasonable Belief that the Mother Would Terminate Pregnancy
        4. Post-Birth Maintenance of the Deep Philosophical Objection
        5. Actual Emotional, Psychological, or Physical Harm
III. Counterarguments
        1. Recognition of a Biological Father's Right Not to Be a Father Does Not Leave Children Unsupported.
        2. Recognizing a Biological Father's Right Not To Be a Father Does Not Place an Undue Burden on the Woman's Right to Choose.
        3. There is state action in the court's refusal to recognize the biological father's constitutional right to avoid legal paternity.
Conclusion

When you have completed your reverse outline, you can check to see whether your revisions moved your paper in the right direction and get a sense of how the pieces of your paper relate to each other. You may also notice areas you want to focus on during your next round of evaluating and revising.

Chris went through several drafts before completing his final, published Note, and you can see his large-scale organizational changes by comparing the reverse outline of one of his earlier drafts (above) with the final paper's reverse outline below. Consider how he reorganized his section about applying the right he proposed in his paper. In his draft, this part of his paper was organized as a final sub-section within his Background section. You can see how it is better placed as the solution section in the outline of his final paper. Also notice how in his earlier draft, Chris had an entire section of his paper dedicated to addressing counter-arguments, and organized this as a separate section after he discussed his proposed right. Then, in his final paper, he incorporated the counterarguments into the solution section, part III., by adding a sub-section. He also added a sub-section to demonstrate how the right would play out in one of his actual examples.

Introduction
I. The Right to Autonomous Procreative Decisionmaking
   A. Origins of the Right to Procreative Autonomy
   B. Why the *Roe* Progeny Is About Procreative Autonomy
II. How Declarations of Legal Paternity Infringe on a Father's Right to Procreational Autonomy
   A. Biological Parenthood and Legal Parenthood as Severable Concepts
   B. The Right Not to Procreate: A Right to Decide Not to Be a Legal Parent and a Right Not to be a Biological Parent
   C. How a Paternity Declaration May Cause Significant Psychological, Moral, and Sociological Consequences
     1. Factual Support
     2. Precedential Support
   D. The Final Step of Infringement: State Action
III. Application of the Right to Decide Not to Be a Legal Father
   A. One Possibility: An Affirmative Defense During a Paternity Proceeding
     1. Expression of a Philosophical Desire Not to Become a Father
     2. Actual or Reasonable Belief by Biological Mother of the Biological Father's Desire
     3. Biological Father's Actual and Reasonable Belief that the Mother Would Terminate Pregnancy or that Pregnancy was Impossible
     4. Post-Birth Maintenance of the Deep Philosophical Objection

5. Actual Emotional, Psychological, or Physical Harm Because the Male Was Forced to Conceive of Himself as a Father
   B. A Brief Application of the Affirmative Defense: The Dubay Case
   C. Why Recognition of a Biological Father's Right to Decide Not to Be a Legal Father Does Not Require Children to Be Left Financially Unsupported
   Conclusion

Consider another example from Monica's Note. Monica's second draft headings included all the main substantive points she wanted to make in her paper. However, after stepping back and evaluating the organization of those points, she found ways to streamline and strengthen her organization for the final paper. Here are the headings from Monica's second draft:

I.   Introduction
II. Background
     a. International Standards For Regulating Cultural Property and Illicit Trade
         i.   The 1954 Hague Convention
              1. Deficiencies in the Hague Convention
         ii. The 1970 UNESCO Convention
              1. Deficiencies in the UNESCO Convention
         iii. The 1995 UNIDROIT Convention
              1. The UNIDROIT Convention—Deficiencies
III. Italy—A Case Study
     a. Cultural Property as Heritage of the People
     b. International Agreements
         i.   Implementation
         ii. Negotiations for the Return of Art Works
         iii. Reciprocity
IV. Analysis
     a. Adopt the Italian Model
         i.   Abandon the Unrealistic International Treaties
         ii. Domestic Legislation
         iii. Government Enforcement
     b. An Imperfect Paradigm—Flaws of the Italian Model
         i.   Protection at the Source
         ii. Strict Border Control and Knowledgeable Officials
         iii. Swift Prosecution

    c. A Cultural Chasm Too Great?

V. Conclusion

The next set of headings reflects Monica's final paper organization:

I. Introduction

II. International Standards For Regulating Cultural Property and Illicit Trade

    a. The Hague Convention

    b. The 1970 UNESCO Convention

    c. The UNIDROIT Convention

    d. Deficiencies in the International Conventions

        i. Deficiencies in the Hague Convention

        ii. Deficiencies in the UNESCO Convention

        iii. Deficiencies in the UNIDROIT Convention

III. Italy—A Case Study

    a. Cultural Property as Heritage of the People

    b. International Agreements

    c. Implementation and Enforcement of Legislative Efforts

    d. Negotiations for the Return of Art Works

    e. Reciprocity

IV. The International Community Should Adopt the Italian Model to Facilitate Effective Reclamation and Restitution Efforts

    a. An Imperfect Paradigm—Flaws of the Italian Model

        i. As a culturally rich source nation, Italy must better protect the cultural property within its borders.

        ii. Italy must enforce stricter border control staffed with knowledgeable officials.

        iii. Italy must swiftly prosecute those dealing in illicit trafficking so as to create a deterrent effect.

    b. Despite its shortcomings, the international community should adopt the Italian model when conducting reclamation and restitution efforts.

        i. Countries should take a realistic approach to the international treaties.

        ii. Domestic legislation must be enacted to address cultural property issues within a nation's borders.

        iii. Relevant legislation must be thoroughly enforced by government officials.

V. Conclusion—A Cultural Chasm Too Great?

Monica noticed that in her second draft, her Background section included deficiencies on each of the international standards she described. Instead of using three separate sub-headings on deficiencies, one for each international standard, she synthesized this part of the Background section by placing the deficiencies into a single sub-heading, as reflected below in section II.d., Deficiencies in the International Conventions. This streamlined her paper's organization by eliminating two sub-headings, and also allowed her to highlight the deficiencies as a consistent problem among the international conventions. Look for similar organizational repetition in your headings and check for the common error of using only one sub-heading at any particular level. If you have only one sub-heading (at any level of the organizational hierarchy), try to combine that material into the broader heading, or use another sub-heading, if that is analytically appropriate. The lesson here is no A. without a B., and no 1. without a 2., and so on.

Also notice how Monica changed her organization in part IV. Her final note flipped the organization of part IV. so that she discussed the counterarguments about the imperfections of Italy's model before her argument that the international community should adopt the Italian model. She then ends with her analysis about why countries should follow the imperfect Italian model. This reorganization was another strategic choice that strengthened the substance of her argument. Instead of arguing that Italy's system should be a model and then recognizing its limitations, she instead directly addressed the weaknesses of her solution, and then built them into her argument.

If you feel overwhelmed at the idea of reorganizing your paper, remember that writing your scholarly paper is a process; going through several rounds of evaluating and revising is essential to completing your paper. Fortunately, reorganizing is relatively easy with cut-and-paste functions in word processing programs. Also, because this is a process, you can avoid feeling overwhelmed because you have several drafts to work through to get yourself to your final paper. With each successive draft, the amount of work required to revise will decrease and you will continue to see your drafts through to your final paper.

Save multiple drafts of your paper along the way instead of saving over the original file every time. This will help you see how you have progressed, and will allow you to review your original organization after you make some large-scale changes. Consider using date or draft number information in the file name to help you keep track of your files.

Part of evaluating your organizational choices includes checking for internal consistencies within your paper. Read your headings alone and make sure that they are similar in construction. This is easy to do after you have completed a reverse outline, but you can just as easily skim through your paper reading only the headings to perform this check. Another measure of internal consistency is the proportionate relationship of the parts of your paper. One common downfall for student scholarly writers is to include too much background and not enough analysis or argument. Now that you have revised and strengthened your paper, including your Analysis/Discussion section, review your Background section and check to see whether everything you have included there is appropriate or necessary. Does the reader need everything in the Background section to understand your thesis and arguments in support of your thesis? Does the reader need more to follow your line of argument? Finally, remember to evaluate your title. As you refine your thesis and arguments, check to make sure your title accurately captures the substance of your paper. Refer back to the discussion of titles in Chapter 4 for more information and examples.

This chapter has focused on you as the evaluator in the Refining stage. The next chapter covers how to refine your paper based on feedback from others, including your supervisor, journal editors, and student peers.

Checklist: Evaluating and Revising Your Draft

- Have I critically evaluated my thesis?
  - Can I locate the thesis in the opening paragraphs of the draft?
  - Does my thesis meet the characteristics of a good thesis identified in Chapter 2?
  - Is my thesis valid and supportable?
    - Have I asked critical questions about my thesis?
    - Have I considered how my thesis will operate in different factual situations?
- Have I identified weaknesses in my paper?
  - Have I addressed counterarguments?
  - Can my solution be implemented?
  - Have I explained the limited scope of my paper?
- Have I identified opportunities to strengthen my paper?
  - Can I use actual or hypothetical examples to illustrate my analysis?
  - Can I place my thesis in a broader content?
  - Have I reinforced my thesis at every opportunity?

- Have I evaluated my organizational choices?
  - Have I used the right large-scale organizational structure for my paper?
    - Did I make a reverse outline to evaluate my organization?
  - Is my paper internally consistent?
  - Are my headings similar in structure?
    - Are there at least two points at each level of the organizational structure? (That is, no A without a B?)
  - Are the sections of my paper in proper proportion?
  - Is my paper properly titled?

CHAPTER 6

REFINING:
TAKING AND INCORPORATING
FEEDBACK

Refining your scholarly project based on your own evaluation (as we discussed in Chapter 5) is only part of the refinement process. You must also take feedback from others and revise your paper with those comments in mind. You are still ultimately responsible for evaluating and making decisions about revisions, but now you are evaluating in the context of feedback on your paper from others. We begin here with a description of the different types of feedback you may receive, and then move on to discuss how you should evaluate this feedback, how to appropriately incorporate feedback, and what to do when you need more feedback.

Types and Means of Feedback

Feedback from others generally comes in two main types: summative and formative. Both types of feedback can be given orally, in writing, or in combination. After describing summative and formative feedback, we will explain how the oral and written feedback you are likely to receive may vary.

Summative feedback is probably the type of feedback you are used to; this feedback comes at the end of a project. Summative feedback often includes a grade or its numerical equivalent along with a few specific comments on the paper. The feedback is evaluative, and may include guidance that could help you with future projects, but because it is necessarily given at the end of the writing process, it cannot be used to strengthen the paper.

In contrast, formative feedback is intended to guide and help you as you work on a project. When giving formative feedback, the reader/evaluator asks questions, responds to the text as a reader (and not as an editor), and looks for opportunities to help you further strengthen your analysis or understand areas of weakness. Depending on your reader's familiarity with your paper topic, you may also receive suggestions for sources to consult. Formative feedback typically does not include a grade or overall assessment. This can be frustrating, but it is by design because formative feedback is given while the project is in progress. Think of formative feedback as an opportunity for growth. Indeed, it can be quite disappointing to ask for formative feedback and receive mere platitudes in response. Effective formative feedback probes your arguments, pushes back on your assumptions, shines a light on your project's weaknesses, and motivates you to reengage with the project.

The difference between summative and formative feedback can be a little murky when it comes to interim-stage documents written as part of a scholarly writing project. You may receive comments that evaluate the execution of the interim assignment ("This outline lacks sufficient detail.") and comments that provide forward-looking feedback that will help you with the larger project ("You will need more source material to make the arguments you need to support your thesis.") Ideal formative feedback will give you specific guidance through questions and comments directed toward revision. For example, when Jessie Shields received feedback on her third draft, her professor's feedback began with an overall summative note:

Big picture:
1. *I like the organization.*
2. *I think a bit more could be somewhere in the beginning about the history of the rule & the legislative notes—i.e., why was it passed, what was it intended to do, why permit so much discretion*
3. *Through the paper, a consistent theme is that the worry is "coercion" or "short-circuiting the deliberative process." Can you say more about what that means—some theory of how juries are supposed to deliberate, I guess, which is stopped when they don't get to make the entirety of the decision? Seems to me sort of confusing and you could add clarity to the caselaw by unpacking what coercion and the deliberative process mean to judges[.]*

Feedback can be given in writing or orally, or a combination. When given in writing, feedback ideally includes both summative and formative comments. Summative feedback on a draft should describe the reader's overall impression and may include several strengths and weaknesses identified in your paper as a whole. In addition to the summative comment, written feedback normally includes margin comments where the reader notes questions, reactions, or otherwise indicates there is work for you to do. Sometimes the written feedback may take the form of line-editing; this type of feedback is most useful when you can understand the basis for the line-edit, such as when the reviewer offers a line-edit to illustrate what she means in a margin comment.

Oral feedback, too, ideally has an overall assessment component, often in the context of introductory remarks where the reader can set the stage for her more specific comments and questions. Like written feedback, oral feedback should identify questions and concerns the reader had while reading your draft. You may want to transcribe this oral feedback so that you can remember the comments later while you are revising. You may also want to take notes on your reactions to the oral comments. Oral feedback can come in a variety of forms, including a class discussion after you present your work-in-progress to your seminar class or an informal meeting with your journal editor to discuss your progress. You might get some oral feedback during class when your professor discusses something related to your paper, and you may get more feedback when you talk to your professor after class about how you plan to treat that issue in your paper.

These two means of receiving feedback are not mutually exclusive, and in fact, it is likely that you will receive a combination of oral and written feedback from most reviewers. For example, you may submit your draft and then meet for a conference with your supervisor. Your supervisor will probably return a marked-up draft to you, which he may use as the guide for leading the discussion at your conference. Similarly, you might meet with your journal editor to discuss your draft, and then after you make revisions based on her comments, she might review your next draft and provide written comments to let you know whether you adequately addressed the issues raised during your discussion. The point here is to be aware that you may receive both summative and formative, and oral and written feedback, even from the same person.

Workshopping: Giving and Receiving Feedback

Writing workshops are a common way to get and receive formative feedback on a work-in-progress, usually from one of your peers. You may be required to participate in a workshop as part of your seminar or notes group, or you may be able to otherwise find an opportunity to workshop your project (see Bright Idea below).

What exactly is a writing workshop? A writing workshop is an opportunity to present and get feedback on your work. Usually, you will share a draft with readers and then engage in a conversation with them about your intentions as the writer and their questions as a reader. Participants in a writing workshop may also have ideas about how to address those same questions. A writing workshop could include written comments in advance or afterward, but most often consists of feedback in the form of a dialogue between writer and reader(s).

Your role as the writer in a workshop is to be open to the questions and ideas you get about your work, even though some may feel—and in fact be—critical. Remember that you are trying to produce a publishable piece; take the feedback as an opportunity to strategize about how to revise your paper. Engage with the commenter by asking questions and explaining where or how you think you've answered her questions. That dialogue can lead you to identify gaps in your analysis, or places where you'd been thinking you had explained something but fell short for various reasons. Also keep in mind that the feedback is offered as a helpful contribution and not to rip apart your ideas (even though some comments may sound harsh). Take notes and feel comfortable responding to some questions without answers. It is fine to not have all the answers, but noting the value of the question can be enough to keep the conversation going.

You also may legitimately disagree with some of the feedback. That's fine too! In that situation, you might want to add a footnote to respond to a question or point raised. Or you may want to take on directly a counterargument to show how your argument withstands that attack. Or you may realize that you need to do some additional research to better understand the criticism before you can decide what to do with it. Whatever the case, you'll likely leave the workshop with a list of notes and things to do—an effective way to help yourself move forward at this stage in the writing process.

Keep in mind you may be called upon to play multiple roles in a workshop. For example, in a peer review or writers' workshop, writers may exchange papers and give each other feedback. Your role as a reader is to ask probing questions, look for places you can help the writer solve a problem, or describe what you found compelling about the paper. Be as courteous to the writer as you hope your readers are to you by taking the feedback seriously. Don't hold back when you see weaknesses and be able to articulate the weaknesses in a way that does not target the writer as a person. For example, you might say, "I noticed the third argument lost its footing when it...." A less paper-focused way to say that would be: "You fell apart in the third argument." In focusing on the paper rather than the individual writer, your comments are more likely to be heard and considered. And hopefully your readers take the same approach. If they don't, just insert "the paper" every time you hear them say "you."

Also keep in mind that just as all your readers may not be experts on the topic area of your paper, you will probably not be as well-versed in your workshop partner's paper topic as you are in your own topic. Even for a workshop where all the papers are on the same colloquium or seminar topic, the specific thesis and arguments of any one paper will probably be at least somewhat new to you. That lack of familiarity is actually a strength in terms of giving feedback because you will not have the knowledge to fill in any gaps in the paper. Even though some of your questions may be easily answered or some of your comments quickly managed, you should not hesitate to engage with the draft even if you know very little about the paper's topic. You can acknowledge that and the writer will be able to assess whether your comment or question is something her target audience would share. Sometimes you will have a series of questions to ask in the context of giving feedback. Here is an example of a set of questions to guide your evaluation:

1. Does the thesis make sense to you? Why or why not? (You might not be familiar enough with the subject area to know whether the thesis is novel, useful, and sound, but you can evaluate its structural logic.)
2. Are you interested in reading the paper based on the thesis? Why or why not?
3. Does the thesis describe a problem?
4. Does the thesis prescribe a solution?
5. Does the thesis seem manageable for a scholarly note? Why or why not?
6. Does the thesis seem too narrow or too broad?
7. Does the thesis include any biases or assumptions that may be problematic if left unaddressed in the paper?
8. What would you expect to see in the paper based on the thesis? (E.g., background on the Clean Air Act, a proposed statutory section, etc.)

If your seminar class, journal, or thesis program does not have a mechanism for peer review, or if your advisor is not able to provide as much feedback as you would like, consider creating your own Work-In-Progress ("WIP") group to get feedback from peers. Ask 4 or 5 other students or friends from your class or journal to exchange drafts, read the drafts, make written comments, and prepare to provide oral comments in a group meeting. At the actual meeting, each student can offer comments on the set of papers, and discuss plans for moving forward. There are several variations on WIP meetings, including exchanging drafts and providing oral comments only, which might be more manageable for you and your peers; exchanging drafts and providing written comments only; or presentation-style where each student discusses her draft and then takes questions from the group. Make sure you verify this collaboration is allowed under your school's academic integrity policy.

Evaluating Feedback

You should not feel like you have to automatically incorporate every change or suggestion you receive. Instead, you should evaluate all feedback with a lens through which you question its value. Remember this is *your* scholarly project, and you have the ability to direct the revisions. There is, of course, a balance here between your preferences and pleasing your audience. You will want to be aware of the possible repercussions of deciding not to incorporate feedback. If you decide not to take the path suggested by your advisor, are you precluding yourself from earning a high grade? If you do not incorporate a change suggested by your journal editor, are you reducing your chances of publication?

The source of the feedback matters in your evaluation. Your professor is responsible for grading your paper, and is also likely an expert in the subject area. Be aware of the possibility that your professor's expertise will be reflected in her comments and may require you to do some additional research before you can fully evaluate her feedback. Your professor will also likely be looking to see how you incorporate her feedback, making it essential that you take the time to read or listen to her feedback, and think about how to incorporate it into your paper.

If your scholarly project is a journal note, your journal editor's feedback also should be carefully evaluated. Your journal editor is a fellow law student, and he may have some knowledge about your general topic area, but he is not an expert. He is likely an expert on the technical and format requirements of a journal note, however, which means you may want to pay close attention to comments that fall into those categories. Journal editors are familiar with what it takes to be published in your journal, and following their advice may be essential to receiving a publication offer.

If you have multiple sources of feedback (for example, your advisor and a journal editor or peer), you may notice some competing voices in the feedback you receive. When that happens, you should evaluate and reconcile the feedback before you determine how to incorporate the feedback. Some decisions will be easier than others; for example, you can take your professor's feedback on the substance of your argument as having more weight than a journal editor's comments on the quality of an argument, given the expertise your professor has compared to your journal editor. Your journal editor, however, might be worth listening to when she tells you to write more background and your advisor notes that the background seems fine. This makes sense because your journal editor is evaluating your note through the publication lens, and knows how much background should be included to be considered for publication. Your professor, on the other hand, probably knows enough of the background or has a general understanding of the legal area so that any inadequacies in the background do not stand out as much to him.

Consider asking your multiple reviewers to give you comments on a single document. This works well with electronic commenting in a word processing program, where one person can make changes and insert comments, and then the next reviewer can build on that feedback, including agreement or disagreement with the existing feedback. You could also use GoogleDocs (http://docs.google.com), a program that allows you to share your document with multiple people, and ask your reviewers to insert color-coded comments on the document. These methods of consolidating feedback may not avoid conflicts, but they will at least get everything on one document and make your reviewers aware of their inconsistent feedback.

Not all decisions about conflicting feedback will be easy to resolve, however. You can get some help making these decisions by requesting a meeting with the sources of conflicting feedback to discuss the inconsistencies and how you should incorporate their comments. You can also have a virtual meeting with an email discussion on particular areas in your paper where you are not sure how to handle the conflicting feedback. With a meeting, in person or over email, you can get your reviewers to help with the evaluation as they work with you to resolve inconsistent comments.

Incorporating Feedback

Incorporating feedback generally means being responsive to comments received from reviewers, whether your professor or a peer. But it also means thinking about the substance of the feedback on a global level and recognizing places to incorporate a reviewer's comment even if the reviewer did not mention it at that particular place. Showing the reviewer you understand his comments can lead to a better paper and a good grade. There are four strategies to keep in mind while incorporating feedback into your paper: use feedback to put yourself in the reader's shoes, use feedback on a global scale where appropriate, let your reviewer know if you disagree with or misunderstand feedback, and do not wait for feedback before continuing work on your paper.

Use Feedback to Read Your Work as a Reader Would

One of the best aspects about getting feedback is that your reader is able to do what you may be unable to do: read with fresh eyes and without emotional attachment. Often as writers, we fill in gaps in our own writing or become attached to what we've written. It can be challenging to excise chunks of text, but when we get feedback suggesting we do so, that input can make it easier to let go. For example, in Jessie's draft, her Introduction included the following paragraph.

> Rule 31 of the Federal Rules of Criminal Procedure states that a jury may return a partial verdict in a criminal trial as long as there are either multiple defendants or multiple counts. The issue of when it is appropriate to give a partial verdict instruction, though, is subject to much dispute. It is entirely dependent on case-specific circumstances and there is no fixed rule either requiring or not requiring a partial verdict instruction. **Rule 31, although it allows the return of partial verdicts, is silent as to how, when, and if a jury should be instructed about their option of doing so. Since most jurors are entirely unaware that they are even allowed to return a partial verdict, they remain unaware until the District Court Judge informs them otherwise. A District Judge is under no obligation to issue a partial verdict instruction. However, they can be appealed for exercising their discretion not to.**

In response to the bolded sentences in this paragraph, Jessie's professor commented: *I don't understand what these sentences are doing—they seem like they are summarizing the argument that comes later, but you can't learn much from them. Cut them—make the introduction something that draws the reader in.*

In writing the introduction, it is easy to write too much because you want to introduce your topic and thesis in a way that will give the reader enough context to understand your paper and where it is going. The insightful reader-based comment here gave Jessie the confidence to delete the sentences that were weighing down an otherwise engaging introduction.

Use Feedback on a Global Scale

Use feedback on a global scale where appropriate. Instead of going through the comments and making edits only where there is a comment, take the concept underlying the comment and apply it throughout your paper. This applies especially to smaller, technical comments focused on style, format, or grammar, but it also applies to more substantive comments.

For example, a comment to single-space a block quote where you have double-spaced a block quote should be applied throughout your paper. Your reviewer may assume you will do this, even if he does not say so, and will therefore not write the comment again later in the paper when you made the same mistake. You should safely assume the same for all technical errors; if you see a correction once but never again, your reviewer is assuming once is enough for you to correct the error paper-wide. Some reviewers will not repeat comments, but will be dismayed to find errors remaining after giving feedback, even when the comment was not noted on every instance of the mistake. It is also possible your reviewer will miss an error; if you find a spelling error or grammar mistake when reviewing your feedback but notice that your reviewer did not say anything about it, go ahead and fix it.

On a substantive level, it might be harder to figure out the global application of an individual comment, but with careful thinking about the comment and what it means, you can probably find ways to incorporate it beyond the passage or section that led to the comment. Consider some examples from our student papers.

In Shaina's second draft of her paper, she had a sub-section called, C. Practical and Humanitarian Reasoning. This sub-section was part of the larger section called, III. Challenges to the Widow Penalty. The draft of that section is printed here, followed by feedback on this section.

C. Practical and Humanitarian Reasoning

Many commentators have also made compelling arguments that for practical and humanitarian reasons, the widow penalty is illogical.

The government has taken the position that it is counterintuitive for a court to hold that a spousal relationship endures beyond the dissolution of the marital relationship. Under its common, ordinary meaning, the term "spouse," the government argues, is a married person and, as a matter of law, marriage ends upon the death of one spouse. Furthermore, because the overall purpose of the "immediate relative" category is to promote the unity of families of U.S. citizens, the government maintains that this goal can no longer be met where the citizen spouse is deceased. Opponents of the widow penalty, however, have attacked this point of view by advancing a number of persuasive arguments.

First, commentators argue that if the general purpose of the "immediate relative" category is to unite families, then the enforcement of the widow penalty hinders this goal by separating citizen children from their foreign-born parents. In many of the widow penalty cases, deported widows have given birth to children in the United States and must make a difficult choice between taking her American children to a foreign land or leaving the children with the citizen spouse's relatives in the United States. Forcing immigrant parents to make this kind of decision via the enforcement of the widow penalty thus sends the opposite message—that the United States does not value families.

Moreover, many alien spouses affected by the widow penalty have, without delay, filed to attain permanent residence in the United States, and fully complied with applicable regulations. Hence, some challengers argue, and a few courts have agreed, that the "fortuity of the citizen spouse's untimely death is too arbitrary and random a circumstance to serve as a basis for denying the petition." In addition, opponents of the widow penalty argue that it is unlikely that foreign-born spouses pose a threat to our national security. Immigrants affected by the widow penalty do not enter the United States illegally, but are admitted through visas or other forms of legal immigration. Therefore, by pursuing alien widow deportations, some commentators argue that the USCIS is simply wasting resources that could be more effectively used to secure the country's borders. Furthermore, the number of persons affected by the widow penalty each year in no way rivals the number of illegal immigrants who enter this country each day.

Lastly, it has also been contended that the conduct the benefit requires—marriage—is itself the best deterrent for marriage fraud purposes. The inherent difficulty in convincing persons to enter into a marriage with practical strangers acts in itself as a significant deterrent to the conduct. Moreover, under state law, persons who enter into a valid marriage owe each other a duty of support, upon separation or divorce, enforceable in most states. Hence, a citizen who enters into a fraudulent marriage to help the alien receive immigration benefits will put him or herself at considerable financial risk, as the couple will most likely have to comply with formal divorce procedures upon dissolution of the marriage.

While the government thus advances one central line of reasoning to support the widow penalty's soundness, commentators continue to raise persuasive responses that question the logic behind the rule.

Shaina received feedback on these paragraphs that looked something like this:

- *Confusing introduction to this sub-section, not clear how the paragraph about the government's position on the meaning of spouse relates to the practical and humanitarian reasoning this sub-section is supposed to cover.*
- *Try to reorganize the paragraphs in this sub-section to present the practical and humanitarian reasoning first, and perhaps follow that by the government's position. That may help the reader follow this section, and also give you a good transition to the next section of the paper where you discuss the pending solutions including actions the government has already taken.*

Incorporating this feedback, Shaina reorganized her paragraphs within this sub-section, and also looked for other places in her paper where she could improve organization. She refined this sub-section on practical and humanitarian reasoning to first make the arguments for why the widow penalty is illogical. She then discussed the government's response to these arguments, including how courts have followed the government position until recently when there was a noticeable shift in several court cases. This ending to the sub-section set up a smooth transition to the next section where she discusses the inadequacies of existing solutions as further support for her legislative proposal. Compare the final version of the sub-section to the draft above:

C. Practical and Humanitarian Reasoning

Many commentators have also made compelling arguments that, for practical and humanitarian reasons, the widow penalty is illogical.

First, the widow penalty seems at odds with the overall pro-family and pro-immigration emphasis of Immact, suggesting that Congress did not intend to place such a harsh penalty for alien widows in the statute. For instance, throughout the Immact hearings, members of Congress spoke to "promoting family immigration" and "[u]nifying families" as both a goal of the proposed legislation and a critical priority of the American immigration system as a whole. Furthermore, congressional representatives applauded Immact for providing "unrestricted admission of the immediate family of U.S. citizens" and "increas[ing] the visas available for the closest family members of citizens and residents of the United States."

The widow penalty is inconsistent with a law supporting family unification and legal immigration, as it makes possible the separation of alien widows from their citizen children and decreases the number of visas available to family members of U.S. citizens. Enactment of the widow penalty provision thus sends the opposite message of the one Immact was intended to send—that the United States does not value families. Based on this divergence, it is difficult to understand why Congress would pass the widow penalty within the Immact, without any explanation of its disharmonious nature, unless Congress did not intend to do so.

Moreover, some challengers argue, and a few courts have agreed, that the "fortuity of the citizen spouse's untimely death is too arbitrary and random a circumstance to serve as a basis for denying the petition." Many alien spouses affected by the widow penalty have, without delay, filed to attain permanent residence in the United States, and fully complied with applicable regulations, yet are subject to deportation based on chance.

In addition, opponents of the widow penalty contend that it is unlikely that alien spouses pose a threat to our national security. Aliens affected by the widow penalty do not enter the country illegally, but are admitted through visas or other forms of legal immigration. Therefore, by pursuing the deportation of alien widows, some commentators believe that the Immigration Service is simply wasting resources that could more effectively be used to secure the country's borders. Furthermore, the number of persons affected by the widow penalty each year in no way rivals the number of illegal aliens who enter this country each year.

Lastly, it has also been asserted that the conduct the benefit requires—marriage—is itself the best deterrent for marriage fraud purposes, rendering the widow penalty unnecessary. The inherent difficulty in convincing persons to enter into a marriage with practical strangers acts in itself as a significant deterrent to the conduct. Moreover, under state law, persons who enter into a valid marriage owe each other a duty of support, upon separation or divorce, and this duty is enforceable in most states. Thus, a citizen who enters into a fraudulent marriage to help the alien receive immigration benefits will put himself or herself at considerable financial risk, as the couple will most likely have to comply with formal divorce procedures upon dissolution of the marriage.

In response to these challenges to the widow penalty, the government has taken the position that it is counterintuitive for a court to hold that a spousal relationship endures beyond the dissolution of the marital relationship. Under its common, ordinary meaning, the term "spouse," the government argues, is a married person and, as a matter of law, marriage ends upon the death of one spouse. Furthermore, because the overall purpose of the immediate relatives category is to promote the unity of families of U.S. citizens, the government maintains that this goal can no longer be met where the citizen spouse is deceased.

In sum, within the past fifteen years, most of the older court decisions have adopted the government's rationale and upheld the "widow penalty" based on *Chevron* deference to the Board's statutory construction and the plain meaning of immigration statutes. However, within the past two years, there have been a number of victories for widow-petitioners, as the Ninth Circuit and several district courts have struck down the widow penalty based on the Board's disregard of clear congressional intent, statutory language, "whole act" interpretations of the statute, and humanitarian concerns.

While four judicial decisions may seem like a small wrinkle in the grand scheme of judicial decisionmaking, the anti-widow penalty cases of *Freeman, Robinson, Taing,* and *Lockhart* were all handed down in the past two years. These cases reflect a slow, but identifiable, judicial trend towards a less rigid interpretation of spouse-based immigration law.

In addition to revising the specific part of the paper her reviewer commented on, Shaina used this feedback to reorganize other sub-sections throughout her draft before finalizing her paper. For example, in her draft, she discussed the pending solutions in the following order:

* Private Bills
* Legislative Reform
* Judicial Reform

Shaina thus ended the section on pending solutions with a discussion of the unsatisfactory response of courts in deciding cases involving the widow penalty. Just as the organization in the section on practical and humanitarian reasoning required some reordering, the organization in this section had room for improvement. Most significantly in this section, Shaina applied the feedback about ordering her paragraphs to effectively transition to the next section. You can see this if you compare her draft and final paper.

Shaina's draft, last paragraph before her proposed legislative solution:

> Furthermore, not every foreigner affected by the widow penalty has the legal ability or financial resources to bring suit in a court of law. Some alien widows may not understand domestic law, speak English, or have monetary funds to hire a private lawyer to sue the government in federal court. Furthermore, the implementation of deportation policies by means of discretionary, case-by-case determinations has potential repercussions for litigants, since Congress has acted to exclude many discretionary determinations from the ambit of judicial review.

The same section in final form gives Shaina a smooth transition to her own legislative solution by calling attention to the inadequacies of existing legislative solutions:

> In sum, these pending legislative solutions to the widow penalty seem to produce more arbitrary lines than effective change to the widow penalty. For instance, with a lack of guidelines for administration, how will the "preponderance of evidence" standard be administered in practice? One can imagine a heightened burden of proof imposed by government agencies that are prone to rigidity with regard to spouse-based immigration law. Further, why must alien widows prove that their marriages were bona fide when alien widows of military personnel killed during active duty are not required to make such a showing? The manner of the citizen spouse's death cannot confirm that the underlying marriage was valid. Lastly, is it fair to base an alien widow's opportunity to attain LPR status on the timing of the adjustment of status application filing, without engaging in an individual review of the facts? Some aliens and citizens have been in a serious relationship with each other for a number of years, but for various reasons do not marry until many years later. If the alien never has an adjustment of status application filed prior to the spouse's death, however, is it fair to automatically deny adjustment of status if the couple has been together for over twenty years, but the citizen dies within two years of marriage?
>
> Creating gaping holes in widow penalty jurisprudence, the proposed exemptions thus are unlikely to resolve the basic problems at the heart of widow penalty enforcement.

Shaina's draft had a gap in the transition between the end of the discussion on Judicial Reform and her discussion of her own legislative proposal. The last paragraph about Judicial Reform in the pending solutions section was followed by a new section detailing her legislative solution, but there was no apparent connection between that last paragraph and the new section. Then, in her final Note, Shaina's reorganization of the pending solutions ends with the discussion about legislative reform, which is a perfect transition to her own legislative solution.

Collin also successfully incorporated feedback to strengthen his final Note. In Collin's first draft of his Note, he had a sub-section about contractors being unable to use the civil service laws for employment protection. The draft of that section follows:

> c. Eliminating the Personal Services Prohibition Will Not Enable Contractors to Take Advantage of Civil Service Laws
>
> One of the major justifications provided by the FAR for the personal services prohibition is that the prohibition prevents agencies from conferring federal employee status to contractors without going through the procedures outlined in the civil service laws. While case law has demonstrated that it is possible for contractors to become de facto employees under employment discrimination laws, a contractor's de facto employee status does not automatically enable him or her to take advantage of federal employment benefits under the civil service laws. According to 5 U.S.C. § 2105(a) (2006), which defines the term "employee" under the civil service laws, an individual must be formally appointed into the civil service before he or she is considered a federal employee. Without this formal appointment, an individual would not be able to take advantage of the civil service's equal pay requirements, attendance and leave provisions, workman's compensation, retirement benefits, unemployment compensation, and other federal benefits.
>
> This was the Acquisition Advisory Panel's ("AAP") main justification for recommending the abolition of the personal services prohibition. The AAP argued that the statutory appointment requirement of federal employees demonstrates that the personal services prohibition "is unnecessary to achieve its intended purpose," which the AAP claims was "to assure that the supervision of contract personnel by federal employees does not confer federal employment status upon such personnel." Of course, the case law establishing that contractors may be deemed de facto federal employees for employment discrimination purposes contradicts the AAP's ultimate conclusion

that personal services contracts do not create any federal employment relationships. Nevertheless, the AAP's conclusion that personal services contracts would not confer civil service benefits on contractors is grounded in strong legal precedent.

In forming its conclusion, the AAP relied heavily on the legal precedent of the U.S. Supreme Court, which has repeatedly held that an individual "is not entitled to the benefit of a [government] position until he has been duly appointed to it." In one specific example, two Air Force trial attorneys sued the government after the Air Force and the Civil Service Commission denied their petitions for reclassification to a higher civil service pay grade. The Court rejected the attorneys' suit on the grounds that the Court does not have the power to grant the benefits of a federal position to a civil service employee in the absence of an appointment.

Additionally, the AAP relied on precedent from the Court of Federal Claims, which has explicitly stated that "[i]f [an individual] did not have a federal appointment, it will not be necessary to consider" the level of government supervision and the nature of that individual's job function. The court applied this rule in *Costner v. United States*, in which James R. Costner sued the government for civil service annuity benefits from 1949 to 1963. While Costner worked during that period as a contractor employee of RCA Service Company ("RCA"), which provided technical service personnel to the Air Force, Costner claims that he was nevertheless a federal employee because he was directly supervised by a military officer and he performed functions that would otherwise have been performed by federal employees. The court explicitly rejected Costner's argument, holding that "an abundance of federal function and supervision will not make up for the lack of an appointment" to the civil service.

These cases demonstrate that eliminating the personal services prohibition would not entitle contractor employees to civil service benefits based solely on the argument that they are de facto federal employees. As a result, any fear that formally allowing agencies to use personal services contracts would undermine the civil service is unfounded.

Collin received several comments on this section, including:

- *How does this relate to why you want to repeal the prohibition? Contractors would still not be federal employees and there just would be no prohibition.*
- *I'm not sure I see the point of this section.*

- *Is the point about civil service benefits an actual concern? It doesn't seem like it would be.*

After receiving perhaps the most unnerving comment to see on a paper, "I'm not sure I see the point of this," Collin set out to make it clear to the reader why he was writing about the Acquisition Advisory Panel's findings and how this content fit into his paper. Specifically, Collin reorganized his paper and included the AAP report earlier in the paper, as part of the overview on the personal services prohibition, rather than waiting to introduce the report until the second half of his paper. By moving the content and placing it within the greater context of the personal services prohibition, Collin successfully responded to the feedback. He also responded to the comment about civil service benefits by deleting the point about contractors remaining ineligible for civil service benefits from his next draft. Deleting that point was an easy fix that did not detract from the substance of Collin's paper.

Collin also used his professor's feedback on his draft conclusion. The first draft of Collin's conclusion was as follows:

VI. Conclusion

Under the approach proposed by this Note, agencies like the Army's Contracting Center of Excellence ("CCE") would not be required to separate its contractors from its government employees. CCE would be able to directly supervise its contracted contractor specialists, and both sets of specialists would be subject to the same set of government ethics laws. CCE would ultimately be able to more efficiently designate tasks based on which specialist was best qualified, based on knowledge and experience, to handle that specific project.

To be sure, this new approach would not completely abolish every distinction between contractors and government employees. Matters concerning hiring, firing, and compensation would still differ between these two categories, as the civil service laws would only be applied to CCE's government-employed specialists. Additionally, contractors would still probably have to identify themselves as contractors to avoid confusion about the contractor's status. The GAO found that CCE contractors often failed to identify themselves as contractors, which sometimes created the "impression that the contractor [was] speaking or acting for the government" beyond what was authorized in the contract.

This Note is also not advocating for the increased use of contractors. On the contrary, this Note seeks to level the playing field between contractors and government employees, two groups that are increasingly performing similar tasks. It could even be argued that by encouraging greater contractor oversight and a more effective application of government ethics laws, agencies will be less tempted to continue relying on contractors to such a dramatic extent, a reliance that has been created, in large part, out of convenience. This approach would not allow the Pentagon to avoid applying ethics laws to its senior mentors simply by hiring them under contract. These senior mentors would instead be subject to the same ethics rules as the regular Pentagon officials with which they often work. And this approach would extend beyond the Department of Defense and apply to all executive agencies.

Of course, this is not an attempt to solve all plights currently affecting the federal government's use of personal services contractors. Expansion of ethics laws, in some form, beyond personal services contractors might be necessary to better protect the government's interest. Agencies will still probably be required to determine the proper balance between contractors and government employees and the roles of each set of personnel in support of their missions. Accurate reporting and documentation of service contractors remains a daunting task, as indicated by the current problems facing the Defense Department's Inventory of Service Contractors. Nevertheless, abolishing the personal services prohibition and shifting the focus of policymakers towards ensuring proper oversight, management, and accountability of service contractors will help guarantee that contractors are being used appropriately in our government.

He received several comments from his professor, including:

- *You already defined the Army's Contracting Center for Excellence as CCE.*
- *Would it be desirable to completely abolish every distinction between contractors and government employees?*
- *Weak thesis sentence to start third paragraph.*
- *Condense your conclusion. You try to do too much in it. I think it'd be sufficient to revisit your opening hypo to show how your reforms would affect it. Don't overload caveats into your conclusion—disperse those elsewhere (sometimes in footnotes).*

Collin worked to incorporate this feedback into his next draft in a number of ways. The comment about not needing to reintroduce the acronym, CCE, was an easy fix. Collin also did a final polish on his paper looking for other places he may have reintroduced acronyms. Another easy fix was adding text to underscore his agreement with his advisor's comment about how abolishing every distinction would not be desirable. (See the sentence in bold at the start of the third paragraph below.)

In addition to streamlining and reorganizing his conclusion into three paragraphs instead of four, Collin revised the topic sentences of all three paragraphs, taking the feedback on the former third paragraph and applying it globally to all three paragraphs. Finally, Collin returned to the opening narrative about General McKissock to show the reader how his proposed solution would remedy the problem presented by McKissock's situation. He also moved the caveats to his proposal to other parts of the paper, building them in as potential roadblocks, but not in a way that undermines his argument.

Take a look at Collin's revised Conclusion, incorporating this feedback:

IV. Conclusion

The solution proposed by this Note would eliminate the unbalanced ethical scheme between government employees and contractors and would reduce the need for federal agencies like the Army's CCE to separate its contractors from its government employees. Agencies would be able to directly supervise their contractor personnel, and both personal services contractors and federal employees would be subject to the same set of government ethics laws. Agencies would ultimately be able to more efficiently designate tasks according to which individual was best qualified, based on knowledge and experience, to handle that specific project.

This solution would apply to senior mentors employed under personal services contracts through the Pentagon's senior mentor program. This approach would not allow the Pentagon to avoid applying ethics laws to its senior mentors simply by hiring them under contract. These senior mentors would instead be subject to the same ethics rules as the regular Pentagon officials with which they work. As such, Gen. McKissock would have been considered a "federal employee" for government ethics purposes and would have been required to file a public financial disclosure form before he started consulting for the Marines. If he decided to remain as a director of Sapient, Gen. McKissock would be prohibited from working on any government project for which Sapient planned to compete, and he certainly would not be allowed to lobby the officers he advised. Most importantly, this approach would extend beyond the Department of Defense and apply to all executive agencies.

To be clear, this new approach does not completely abolish every distinction between contractors and government employees, nor would it be desirable to do so. Matters concerning hiring, firing, and compensation would still differ between these two categories, as the civil service laws would continue to apply only to employees formally appointed into the civil service. Nevertheless, abolishing the personal services prohibition and expanding the scope of government ethics laws to personal services contractors is a necessary step to properly managing the government's growing use of service contractors. Shifting the focus of policymakers toward ensuring proper oversight, management, and accountability of service contractors will help guarantee that contractors are being used appropriately in our government.

Jessie received a list of big picture comments as well as margin comments on her draft paper. The big picture comment included this:

> *3. Through the paper, a consistent theme is that the worry is "coercion" or "shortcircuiting the deliberative process." Can you say more about what that means — some theory of how juries are supposed to deliberate, I guess, which is stopped when they don't get to make the entirety of the decision? Seems to me sort of confusing and you could add clarity to the caselaw by unpacking what coercion and the deliberative process mean to judges[.]*

To respond to this feedback, Jessie could have just added a section about coercion and the deliberative process to the Background section of her paper. That probably would have sufficed to begin building the case for why district court judges should care about her ideas and how they could use her practical guide to help them when faced with a partial verdict scenario. However, Jessie incorporated this feedback in a more substantive way by developing the role of coercion in her discussion of best practices for district court judges.

In the Background section, Jessie has a subsection with the heading, "The Purpose of a Jury in a Federal Criminal Trial," in which she explains the private nature of jury deliberations, the protections to ensure that a jury's decision is its own, and what happens when a jury is deadlocked. The ideas of coercion and the deliberative process come up here in the context of how juries are protected and the measures judges take to encourage juries to reach a unanimous verdict. She then added a new subsection within the best practices section to pick up on these themes by explaining what an appropriate partial verdict instruction entails specifically in the context of neutrality and non-coerciveness. Jessie used the case law to craft a sound summary of the characteristics of a neutral, non-coercive partial verdict instruction: A neutral, non-coercive partial verdict instruction simply informs a jury of its options, allowing it to deliberate autonomously and decide, for itself, whether a partial verdict is appropriate.

F. What does an Appropriate Partial Verdict Instruction Entail?

A partial verdict instruction should be neutral and non-coercive. Neutral in the sense that it should neither encourage nor discourage the return of a partial verdict instruction. Although Rule 31(b) allows a district court to receive a partial verdict, a jury should retain autonomy over its deliberative process. A non-coercive, neutral partial verdict instruction informs a jury of its option to return a partial verdict without suggesting that the jury should in fact do so. In *United States v. Speaks*, the Tenth Circuit found the partial verdict instruction issued by the district court to be non-coercive due to the fact that it informed the jury of its option to return a partial verdict without explicitly suggesting how or when the jury should do so. The court's specific instruction was:

> A verdict in this case is not necessarily a singular verdict. You may render a verdict on any count upon which you can agree. There may be some counts upon which you cannot agree; and in that event, you may not be able to render a verdict.

> Your reference here to being able to return a verdict suggests to me that you are thinking that you cannot return a verdict because you cannot agree on all of the counts. I urge you to go back and reconsider and see if there are any of the counts that you can agree on. And if there are counts that you can agree on, to render a verdict on those counts.

Although the district court urged the jury to continue its deliberations and to return any agreed upon counts, it did not specify when or how those partial verdicts should be returned.

In *United States v. Ruffin*, the Second Circuit, analogous to the Tenth Circuit in *Speaks*, found the district court's partial verdict instruction to be non-coercive. However, unlike in *Speaks* where the defendant argued broadly that the partial verdict instruction interfered with the jury's deliberative process, the defendant in *Ruffin* argued that the partial verdict instruction invited the jury to convict the defendant. The court's specific instruction was: "It is possible for juries to render a partial verdict, that is if the jury has reached a verdict on one count, it is permissible in the law for the Court to accept that verdict and ask the jury to continue to deliberate about other counts." The Second Circuit found the defendant's argument to be without merit due to the fact that the partial verdict instruction merely informed the jury of its options in a neutral manner, and therefore was not coercive.

A neutral, non-coercive partial verdict instruction also refrains from pressuring individual jurors to reconsider their views. In *United States v. McKinney*, the Tenth Circuit rejected the defendant's argument that the partial verdict instruction was coercive. At trial, the district judge's partial verdict instruction:

> advised the jury that if it had not unanimously agreed on a verdict on all counts by 2:30 p.m., he proposed to receive any unanimous verdict it might have reached on any one, or possibly more, of the counts, and that the jury would then resume deliberation on the remaining counts.

Here, the district judge, distinguishable from *Speaks* and *Ruffin*, suggests when the jury should return its partial verdict. Nonetheless, the Tenth Circuit found the district court's instruction neutral and non-coercive due to the fact that none of the jurors were pressured to reconsider previously held views. *United States v. Fermin*, analogous to *McKinney*, found a partial verdict instruction non-coercive due to the fact that jurors were not pressured to surrender their personal views. Considering *Speaks* and *Ruffin*, together with *McKinney* and *Fermin*, suggests that a neutral, non-coercive partial verdict instruction must not pressure jurors to reconsider previously held views, and should not instruct jurors to return a partial verdict at a specific time. A neutral, non-coercive partial verdict instruction simply informs a jury of its options, allowing it to deliberate autonomously and decide, for itself, whether a partial verdict is appropriate.

Communicate Your Disagreement or Misunderstandings about Feedback

As you know, you may not agree with every piece of feedback you receive. When that happens, know that you do not necessarily have to make every suggested revision. Be careful here, of course, to avoid putting yourself in a bad situation. There is a difference between ignoring all of your supervisor's comments because you do not want to do more work to respond to them and evaluating your professor's comments and then deciding that a suggested direction is not where you want to take your paper. When something like the latter happens, talk to your supervisor. If you can explain why you do not want to incorporate a proposed change, you can at a minimum, let your supervisor know that you did not simply miss her comment when you revised your next or final draft. Similarly, if you do not understand a comment, either written or oral, ask for a clarification. You do not want to miss out on valuable insight, and at the same time, you do not want to give the misimpression that you are ignoring feedback when instead you just did not understand it.

Collin received detailed feedback from his professor, but did not always apply the feedback as suggested by the professor's comments. Even when he disagreed with the professor's direction, Collin managed to be responsive to the broader principle underlying the professor's feedback. Consider an excerpt from Collin's first draft in section VI:

> Given the increased reliance by the federal government on service and body shop contracts and the blurred distinction between contractor employees and civil servants in government offices, this Note argues that the personal services prohibition has outlived its usefulness and that Congress should explicitly repeal FAR 37.104. While there is no actual legislative statute prohibiting the use of personal services contracts, the GAO and the Comptroller General have consistently stated that personal services contracts are illegal absent statutory approval from Congress. Therefore, an act by Congress would be the strongest approach to repealing the personal services prohibition. This section outlines the justifications for abolishing the prohibition by arguing that it prevents agencies from adequately and efficiently supervising their service contractors and has failed to prevent the creation of employment relationships between contractors and the government.

This section included four sub-sections and this paragraph served as the umbrella paragraph to the sub-sections. Collin received the following feedback on this paragraph:

- *You need to foreshadow part V. and say how government ethics laws must be applied to them and this is the first step (abolishing the restriction).*
- *You need to make clear right away how abolishing the personal services prohibition will fix the problem identified.*

Collin revised the paragraph as follows:

Given the government's growing reliance on personal services contractors and the blurring distinctions between contractors and government employees, this Note argues that additional protections are needed to ensure personal service contractors act in the best interests of the government. Currently, contractor employees and civil servants are governed by two different legal regimes even though they perform similar work. Additionally, the personal services prohibition unnecessarily limits the ability of agencies to supervise their contractor employees, and thus creates a disincentive for the government to manage its contractors. Therefore, Congress should explicitly repeal FAR 37.104(b) through legislation and apply current government ethics laws to all personal services contractors employed by federal agencies. This will enable the government to better manage and supervise its contractor personnel and ensure that these personnel are free from damaging conflicts of interest.

While there is currently no statute prohibiting the use of personal services contracts, the FAR currently provides that personal services contracts are illegal absent statutory approval from Congress. An act by Congress would thus be the best approach to repealing the personal services prohibition. This section explains why the prohibition should be abolished: (1) the prohibition prevents agencies from adequately and efficiently supervising their service contractors; (2) the prohibition has become so ineffective at preventing employment relationships that officials outside of the procurement realm are beginning to implement ad hoc mechanisms to regulate these relationships; and (3) increasing the size of the civil service to meet the government's needs is neither politically feasible nor practically efficient.

Collin strengthened this paragraph by more explicitly stating his proposed solution and more fully introducing the sub-sections, including a detailed roadmap in the second paragraph. What Collin did not do is "make clear right away" that his proposal would solve the problem. Instead, that information is four sentences in, when he says, "Therefore, Congress should explicitly repeal FAR 37.104(b) through legislation and apply current government ethics laws to all personal services contractors employed by federal agencies." Contrasted to his earlier draft, the sentence is clearer and contains more information, but placement-wise, they are comparable. Even though Collin did not reorganize this first paragraph to directly respond to his professor's feedback, he did apply the underlying feedback to be clearer about how his solution would fix the problem. This worked because he gave some context for his proposal, introduced his proposal, and told the reader that his proposal would enable the government to better manage and supervise its contractor personnel and ensure that these personnel are free from damaging conflicts of interest. In other words, he identified how his solution would address the problem, just as his professor suggested in his feedback.

You may also encounter places where your professor's feedback could apply on a global scale (and, in fact, your professor may have intended his comments to apply on a global scale), but you disagree that each place merits revision. In that situation, you should have a discussion with your supervisor. For example, your professor may have a passionate dislike for the passive voice and automatically comment "no passive voice" when it pops up for the first time in any paper. You also generally dislike the passive voice, but are familiar with the few circumstances in which passive voice is appropriate. If you think you are using it where appropriate and therefore do not change every instance of it in response to your professor's comment, at least mention that to your professor before turning in your next or final draft.

Consider using the comment feature in your word processing program to respond to comments received electronically. This way, you can directly respond to a comment your supervisor made by asking for a clarification or explaining why you do not think the suggestion is the right thing to do. This helps your supervisor quickly identify what he was thinking when he made the comment because the comment is linked to the text. You can have an electronic discussion this way, or have the questions embedded in the next draft for a one-on-one conference using your questions as an agenda for the conference.

From the perspective of the person providing you with thoughtful feedback, there is nothing worse than giving feedback, then reviewing the next or final draft and finding the same mistakes or questions unanswered. This is true for both professor and peer feedback, and both audiences may react to your failure to incorporate their suggestions. A professor may include responsiveness to feedback as part of your grade calculation, and journal editors may use responsiveness as a criterion when deciding whether to select a paper for publication. Journal editors' comments may be related to the appropriate structure or format for a journal piece and ignoring those comments means more work for the journal editors if they select your paper for publication—or, worse, if they foresee this large amount of work, your paper may not get selected. Thus, if you evaluate feedback and decide not to incorporate it, make sure you communicate that decision to the person who gave you the feedback. This way, you can let the person know that you understood the feedback, but that you decided to take a different direction to support your argument or just disagree with a stylistic choice.

Keep Working on Your Paper

Keep in mind that you do not have to wait for feedback to refine your paper. For example, if you turn in a second draft to your professor and your professor expects to meet with you for a conference in two weeks, you do not have to wait idly during those two weeks. Instead, continue refining your paper. You may be able to respond to some of your professor's concerns and questions by continuing to work on your paper, and may even be able to impress your professor with your work. Sure, you will probably make some changes during this waiting period that will raise new concerns after you meet with your professor and get her comments. But you may also be able to talk through these new concerns while meeting with her, which can be an effective way to figure out how to handle refining your paper.

Or you might make some refinements that match your professor's comments, putting yourself ahead of the game in terms of incorporating feedback. You can then use some of your conference to discuss how you think you answered your professor's feedback and get immediate confirmation that you are on the right track, or perhaps your professor will modify her feedback based on your current draft. Depending on your professor's availability and the schedule for your next meeting, you might be able to get him to look at a later draft, one that reflects his comments on your earlier draft or changes that you made based on your own evaluation. Ask him when he plans to read your paper to prepare for your conference and if you can have a revised draft ready by then, ask him if he is willing to read that updated draft instead. This way, you can get feedback that is more useful because it is on a current version of your paper. This saves time and effort for both you and your professor.

While you are waiting for feedback from supervisors, you might also want to go back and review sample notes with an eye toward refining your paper. Now that you have your paper in draft form, you can compare your paper to the sample notes to check to see whether you incorporated the things you identified as strong when you reviewed the samples as an introduction to your scholarly writing process. Looking at sample notes at this stage in your writing process might also illustrate some of the comments you received from supervisors, and give you a model to use in making your revisions.

Reaching Out for More Help

As we mentioned in Chapter 1, you may want more hands-on help from your advisor than your advisor is inclined to give. If you find yourself in that position, think about what you can do to get more help from your supervisor. For example, create an agenda or list of questions you would like to discuss with your advisor and arrange for a meeting. You can show your advisor that you have done the background work and are not just looking for her to do the work for you. Creating your own agenda for a meeting with your advisor also helps ensure you get what you want from the advisor and shows your advisor you are engaged in the writing process. Consider sharing your agenda or list of questions in advance, or even sending your advisor a draft of your paper with comments and questions embedded next to the related passages in your paper.

In addition to the feedback you receive from your professor or peers, you may want to reach out to other faculty, practitioners, or subject-matter experts for more feedback. Your supervisor will likely have some familiarity with your general topic area, but may not be an expert on your narrow thesis. To make sure you receive feedback on the substantive aspects of your argument, consider asking for help from other sources. Other faculty at your school may be a good place to start. A professor is most likely to help you if you can identify specific questions or concerns that you would like to discuss, rather than just asking a faculty member to read your paper and let you know what he thinks. You will probably also get more out of the experience by having an in-person meeting to discuss your concerns because you can use the professor's expertise to help you work through issues.

Depending on your paper topic, a practitioner may also be a good resource to consult. For example, if you are writing about a practical issue, getting in touch with someone who would ultimately implement your proposal to discuss his reactions to your proposal will probably give you insights different from those received from your supervisor and peers. A practitioner is likely to have experience and information that you would not find through normal research avenues. A practitioner may even be a source for you to include in your paper, perhaps identifying a counterargument and answering it, or making a statement in support of your proposed solution.

Consider contacting authors of the sources you most heavily rely on in your paper. These authors may also have unique insights and may be especially interested in helping you when they find out you intend to cite their works in your paper. Again, consider narrowing the conversation to specific questions or concerns, rather than just sending a copy of your paper and asking for feedback. You may want to initiate a conversation by writing a professional email with details about your thesis and how helpful you found the author's material in certain areas of your paper. The more specific you can be about what you would like to discuss with the author, the more likely you will get a positive response.

Reaching out for more substantive help at this point in your scholarly project, in contrast to reaching out to experts in your early topic and thesis development stages, may be particularly effective because of your mastery of the vertical and horizontal knowledge on your topic. You may have been hesitant to consult an expert when you had just an initial thesis, but now that you are invested in your thesis and have a solid, refined paper, you will probably be more confident in discussing your paper. Your increased comfort level and ability to discuss concepts and arguments with the experts will probably also make the experts more likely to be responsive to you, even if attempts to get their input at your topic development stage went unanswered.

At this point, your paper is shaping up after multiple refinements and rounds of feedback. This isn't necessarily the last feedback you will receive: you will get summative feedback from your professor when the final paper is submitted, and if the paper is accepted for publication, you may be working with editors who have feedback of their own (we discuss editorial feedback in Chapter 8).

When the Refining stage is complete, your paper will be close to final form. All you have left to do is polish your paper, which is covered in the next chapter.

CHAPTER 7

FINISHING:
POLISHING THE FINAL
PRODUCT

Finishing is a separate step in the writing process. It follows Preparing, Executing, and Refining; the thinking is done, and now you are focused purely on mechanics. Presumably you have not completely ignored grammar and syntax throughout the writing process, but now you need to give them special attention. As we discussed in Chapter 5, throughout the refining and finishing processes, your perspective as you review the paper will move from a wide-scale bird's-eye view to a narrower review of the paper. Now, as you prepare to finish up the project, you must critically review the entire document and polish your paper so that it is technically and cosmetically perfect. You should plan for several close readings of your paper as you near completion.

This close reading is important for several reasons. First, dense and unclear writing can obscure good arguments. You want your paper, and the arguments within it, to be clear and readable. Second, polishing errors can compromise your credibility with all of your audiences. This, in turn, can affect the decisions your audience will make about your paper—specifically, publication decisions and grade assignments. Finally, polishing is a safety net that can be useful when you come to the final stages of a project you have been working on for a long time. It gives you a chance to double-check that you have properly attributed all of your sources, and you can make sure you filled all the holes you left for "later."

This stage will run smoothly if you finish your paper in an orderly fashion, moving from the large-scale to small-scale issues. You have already looked at some of the issues at the largest-scale, as we discussed in Chapters 4 and 5: overall organization, logical order, flow between sections, construction of headings, and proportion. Now you want to look at matters on a smaller scale, including paragraphing, sentence structure, grammar, spelling, punctuation, and citation.

You probably have some tools available to help you here; most word processing programs have grammar and spell-checking features that you can use as a first step. However, these tools will not catch every typo or every instance of an error. With this in mind, we have compiled a list of the ten most common small-scale errors we have seen in student scholarly writing. They are organized along the lines we suggest you critique your writing: from errors at the largest-scale to those at the smallest.

(1) One common error involves **poor paragraphing**. In general, each paragraph in your piece should put forth and defend one idea. One problem to look for is long paragraphs that have many ideas that can be broken out into separate paragraphs (each with a strong topic sentence, as we will discuss below). Consider this paragraph from an early draft of Chris's paper:

> When asked to imagine a father, most people picture a combination of three different types of "father." These constructions occur at different points in a child's life. He becomes a biological father when the child is born. A male is a child's father because he is the male-gamete provider, but that does not mean he has any idea that the child exists. He acts as a father under a social definition when he meets the expectations that have been "institutionalized within family, religion, law, and culture." This involves a "patterned set of parenting behaviors [that] reflect a society's ideals about the rights and obligations of men in families." This includes activities such as teaching his child to ride a bike or attending his child's concert at school. And he becomes a legal father when the law imposes the obligations and duties of fatherhood upon him. Some fathers are identified through court proceedings, or whatever the law says.

Now consider the rewrite:

> When asked to imagine a father, most people picture an amalgamation of three different types of "father": biological, social, and legal. It is at different points in a child's life, however, that a male becomes each of these constructions.
>
> First, and perhaps most intuitively, a male becomes a child's biological father at the moment when the child is born. Here, a male is a child's father because he is the male-gamete provider. To say that a male is a child's biological father does not say much of their interac-

tions, however, because the male may not know of the child's existence or, in the case of sperm donors, even have met the mother.

Second, under a social definition, a person fathers a child when he acts according to a "patterned set of parenting behaviors [that] reflects a society's ideals about the rights and obligations of men in families." Such a set of values and expectations has been "institutionalized within family, religion, law, and culture." For example, a man fathers when he teaches his daughter to ride a bicycle, attends his son's school band concert, or sends his teenager to bed as a disciplinary act.

Finally, a male is a father when he takes on the legal obligations, duties, privileges, and responsibilities of fatherhood. Although many children have a legal father as the result of a declaration on their birth certificates, others have fathers as the result of filiation hearings, where a court issues a ruling that a particular male is a given child's father. Thus, legal parenthood is distinguishable from biological and social parenthood because it does not have a correlation with a person's actions; a man is a legal father if the law says he is.

The original paragraph covers the "three types of father" that Chris uses as part of the foundation for his thesis, but because he has packed all this information into one paragraph, it is long and unwieldy. In the final version, he has unpacked these ideas into separate paragraphs, with attention and care given to each point. He has also used a roadmap and sequencing language to guide the reader through his points.

Long paragraphs can obscure important points that have not been given a place of emphasis. Early in the Background section of Jessie's paper, she introduces a hypothetical example of an inconsistent verdict—an important piece of background information for her readers, but one that is lost amidst other introductory information about the role of the jury:

The goal of a deliberating criminal jury is to reach a complete and unanimous verdict. Jury deliberations are a private affair. They are shielded from outside influence. In certain cases, jurors can even be sequestered. The thought process of a jury cannot be inquired into until after the trial has ended and all jurors have been discharged. Jurors are also entitled to return logically inconsistent verdicts. This is allowed based on the recognition that "jury deliberations necessarily involve negotiation and compromise," and the belief that "[j]ury unanimity, not consistency of theory, is the touchstone of a valid verdict." An inconsistent verdict will only be a reversible error if it is both "extremely contradictory and irreconcilable." The following hypothetical is an example of an inconsistent verdict: Defendant is charged with possession of marijuana with intent to distribute, and as well as with using a phone to commit that offense. The jury finds the defendant guilty of using a phone to commit the offense, but acquits the defendant of possession of marijuana with intent to distribute. Although this finding is logically inconsistent, it is characterized as "jury error," and would be affirmed on appeal.

In a revision, Jessie broke this long, complex paragraph into two: one that describes the role of the jury and one that introduces the reader to the idea of an inconsistent verdict, with her hypothetical procedural scenario as an example.

> Juries play an extremely important role in federal criminal trials and the justice system therefore affords them considerable protections. Their task is to reach a complete and unanimous verdict. Their deliberations are a private affair. Courts explicitly shield juries from outside influence, and occasionally go so far as sequestering them. These protections help ensure that the ultimate decision is that of the jury— and the jury alone.

> Jurors may return logically inconsistent verdicts. This allowance recognizes that "jury deliberations necessarily involve negotiation and compromise," and reflects the belief that "[j]ury unanimity, not consistency of theory, is the touchstone of a valid verdict." An inconsistent verdict constitutes reversible error only when it is both "extremely contradictory and irreconcilable." The following hypothetical is an example of an inconsistent verdict: a defendant is charged with possession of marijuana with intent to distribute, and with using a phone to commit that offense. The jury finds the defendant guilty of using a phone to commit the offense but acquits the defendant of possession of marijuana with intent to distribute. Although this finding is logically inconsistent, an appellate court would likely characterize it as mere "jury error" and affirm the conviction.

Another paragraphing problem involves the relationship between sentences within a paragraph. Effective paragraphs have sentences within them that build on each other. This makes it easier for the reader to follow your point, and is particularly effective in legal writing, when you are building an argument based on legal authorities or concepts. For example, consider this paragraph from Shaina's Note:

Congress has provided **two different processes** for alien spouses to attain LPR status, such that one or the other applies in the petitioning process. Upon marriage to an alien, a U.S. citizen, either by birth or through naturalization, **may file a Form I-130 petition on his spouse's behalf,** claiming that the spouse is entitled to classification as an "immediate relative." The term "**immediate relative**," as applicable to the U.S. citizen's petition, is set forth in the first sentence of 8 U.S.C. § 1151(b)(2)(A)(i) as the "children, spouses, and parents of a citizen of the United States, except that, in the case of parents, such citizens shall be at least 21 years of age." **For aliens whose citizen spouses have not filed an I-130 petition on their behalf,** the INS provides a separate self-petitioning right, permitting an alien spouse to file a petition on her own behalf on a Form I-360 self-petition. Supporting documentation to **prove bona fide marriage,** such as a marriage certificate, must be filed by the petitioning spouse with the Form I-130 or Form I-360. Generally, however, the Immigration Service will recognize the validity of the marriage as long as **the marriage is lawful in the place where the marriage took place.**

This paragraph is effective because it is focused on one concept: the two processes by which alien spouses can attain LPR status. The purpose of the paragraph is made clear by the topic sentence. The paragraph goes on to discuss each one of these processes in turn. Shaina highlights the difference between the two processes—a filing by the citizen-spouse and a self-petition—by using language that contrasts the two factual situations. Within the discussion of the two processes, she carefully lays out the information the reader needs about each. In the first, she notes the Form and the standard—one must be an "immediate relative"—and then uses the next sentence to define the term. When discussing the second process, she does something similar, in establishing how one proves a bona fide marriage. These relationships are marked in bold.

When polishing your paper, look at each paragraph in isolation to make sure it contains one main idea that is presented in a logical, methodical manner.

(2) Another common paragraphing problem is **weak topic sentences.** You can easily overlook topic sentences as you edit and move text around within the body of your paper. Each paragraph of your final paper should have a strong topic sentence that concisely states the main idea of each paragraph and introduces the information that follows. You can then use this strong foundational sentence to construct a well-built paragraph, as we discussed above. Furthermore, you should be able to read only the topic sentences to get a sense of the writer's thesis, supporting arguments, and authority.

For example, take a look at these three paragraphs from Natalie's final paper:

Though the *Pyett* court correctly declined to extend an intolerable rule, the law regarding arbitration clauses in a post-*Pyett* world is not ideal and may even be considered inequitable. First, the law is under-protective because it safeguards union workers, but not non-union workers, even though non-union workers have less bargaining power than union workers. Second, the rules offer protection to a class of people less likely to require the protections of Title VII compared to the class of people to which the rules do not offer protection. Finally, the law is also over-protective because it invalidates all arbitration clauses in CBAs, some of which are freely entered into by informed parties on equal footing.

When read together, the rules in *Circuit City* and *Pyett* establish a legal system that protects the powerful, but not the powerless. Under *Circuit City*, a non-union employee can easily be compelled to waive her federal forum right despite the fact that she has very little bargaining power compared to her employer. After *Pyett*, a union employee with comparatively more bargaining power, however, can never be compelled to arbitrate employment discrimination claims and, thus, almost always has a choice of forum. While union employees often enjoy more benefits or privileges than non-union employees, neither group should enjoy a preferred status when it comes to statutory rights.

The *Circuit City* decision is unfair because it shifts power away from the powerless employee and toward the powerful employer. The decision also arbitrarily allows transportation workers, but not non-transportation workers, to retain a certain degree of power. Thus, a bus driver cannot be compelled to arbitrate an employment discrimination claim, but a sales clerk at a bus station ticket window can be compelled to do so. The *Pyett* decision then divides non-transportation workers into union workers and non-union workers. Thus, after *Pyett*, the sales clerk at the bus station ticket window can be compelled to arbitrate only if she is a non-union employee.

Reading through these topic sentences, the reader can glean Natalie's thesis and the points she uses to support her analysis. When you are in the Finishing stage, review your own topic sentences and think about the relationship between consecutive topic sentences. Where appropriate, edit the topic sentences so that they clearly and concisely articulate the main idea of each paragraph.

Even subtle changes to topic sentences can add to the overall strength of your paper. Consider the topic sentences (marked in bold) from an early draft version of part of Emily's paper.

> **Student loans are common today, but the history of student loan programs in the United States is relatively new.** After World War II, young adults began to seek out higher education in greater numbers. Colleges raised tuition prices in order to accommodate their growing student populations and, in exchange, colleges themselves would loan money to students in need. Families grew more comfortable with the idea of going into debt in exchange for a college education because the media advertised that advanced degrees would likely result in greater income. Although colleges and individual states attempted to offer potential students financial assistance, this assistance could not keep up with the increased cost of tuition and demand for higher education.
>
> **The Cold War and the 1957 launch of the Soviet satellite, Sputnik instigated federal involvement with student lending.** The United States, in an effort to remain competitive in the Cold War, sought to establish a growing population of scientists and engineers to rival its Russian counterparts. The National Defense of Education Act (NDEA) of 1958 created the first student loan program; these loans were given out to needy undergraduate students pursuing teaching careers or technical careers in science, math, or engineering. The loans were issued directly by the federal government, but were primarily available to selective institutions. The NDEA boosted the amount of money available to student borrowers.
>
> **The Higher Education Act (HEA) of 1965, signed by President Lyndon B. Johnson, greatly expanded the federal student loan program.** Instead of issuing loans directly from the federal government's purse strings, the loans were made by private bankers, but insured by the government. This financial structure made issuing student loans a more attractive option for private lenders. This structure also made student loans less burdensome for the federal government because the government was only financially responsible for paying the interest on the loan while the student was in school.
>
> **Because Congress was responsible for interest payments, every time interest rates rose Congress had to "quickly pass legislation authorizing higher payments."** This problem, coupled with the fact that private lenders disliked issuing these loans because they had to wait for the borrower to finish school before receiving repayment, led Pres-

ident Richard Nixon to create a secondary market for student loans: Nixon established the Student Loan Marketing Association (Sallie Mae). The HEA has been reauthorized several times since it was first enacted, but the original Act "permanently established a philosophy of higher education as an issue of national interest."

These four paragraphs provide background on federal student loan programs, but they can do a bit more than that by setting the stage for Emily's later argument. By subtly revising the topic sentences to frame this background, Emily demonstrates how there have been problems since the early days of federal student loan lending.

In her final published comment, the topic sentences (also marked in bold) are stronger, offering more than a guide to the paragraph's topic by also supporting the underlying themes of the comment.

> **Student loans are practically a rite of passage for anyone seeking a higher education in today's society, but student loan programs in the United States are a relatively recent development.** Following World War II, a greater number of young adults sought higher education. Colleges raised tuition prices to accommodate this growing student population and offered loans to needy students. Over time, families became more comfortable with the idea of taking on debt for a college education. Although colleges, and even some states, offered students financial assistance, such assistance could not keep pace with rising tuition prices and student demand.

> **The Cold War and the 1957 launch of the Soviet satellite, Sputnik, prompted federal government involvement with student lending.** The United States, in an effort to remain competitive in the Cold War, sought to establish a growing population of scientists and engineers to rival Russian counterparts. The National Defense of Education Act of 1958 (NDEA) created the first federal student loan program, which distributed loans to low-income undergraduate students and specifically focused on "expanding the labor pool of scientists and engineers while simultaneously increasing the quantity and quality of scientific research." The federal government issued loans directly to borrowers and funding was predominately available to select institutions. The NDEA increased the amount of money available to student borrowers.

> **The Higher Education Act of 1965 (HEA), signed into law by President Lyndon B. Johnson, significantly expanded federal student loan programs.** Instead of issuing loans directly to colleges (like under the

NDEA), the HEA allowed the federal government to insure loans issued by private banks. Both attractive because private lenders had assurance that their loans would be repaid, and the federal government only had to cover the borrower's interest payments for the time the borrower was in school. The HEA has been reauthorized several times since 1965, but it was the original Act that "permanently established a philosophy of higher education as an issue of national interest."

The HEA significantly expanded federal student lending, but it was not without shortcomings. Every time interest rates rose, the federal government's financial obligations increased, requiring Congress to "quickly pass legislation authorizing higher payments." Additionally, private lenders became frustrated since, in order to receive repayment on the principal amount of the loan, they had to wait for the borrower to finish school. These issues led President Richard Nixon to create a secondary market for student loans—the Student Loan Marketing Association (Sallie Mae).

(3) Between sentences you may encounter the problem of **overuse of generic transitions.** Transitions can be generic or substantive, and generally you should expect to use both in your scholarly project. Generic transitions are connector words that provide merely a technical connection, guiding the reader to the next step or second argument, for example. Commonly overused generic transitions are "Furthermore ..." and "Moreover...." In contrast, substantive transitions are phrases that provide a link back to the previous idea in the same sentence as the new idea is introduced. Generic transitions are easier to include, but substantive transitions usually lead to clearer writing. Consider the following example of two paragraphs from Natalie's Note.

> **Naturally,** the *Gardner-Denver* rule would also benefit non-union employees whose employment contracts contain both nondiscrimination provisions and arbitration agreements. **However, under the *Gardner-Denver* approach,** employers may not offer their employees additional causes of action unless the employees specifically bargained for such additional protections. **Because most employees lack bargaining power individually,** most employees would not reap all of the benefits of a return to the *Gardner-Denver* rule. **However, the rule would at least ensure that** individual employees could continue to litigate statutory claims despite the efforts of employers to deny them that right.
>
> **Though a return to the *Gardner-Denver* rule would benefit employees** and serve as a significant deterrent to employment discrimi-

nation, such a solution would probably not satisfy employers. **Alternatively, the EEOC has proposed a rule** under which employees could elect binding arbitration after a dispute has arisen rather than before. **Such a rule** would help balance the interests of the employer and the employee. **The employer could** avoid the costs of litigation in cases where the employee chooses arbitration, **and the employee could** realize the benefits of arbitration where it is in her best interest at the time of the dispute.

Notice how Natalie smoothly transitions from paragraph to paragraph and from sentence to sentence by including a mix of generic transition words and substantive transition phrases (marked in bold). These transitions help the reader follow the argument Natalie makes in her Solutions section because she does not overuse generic transitions.

Transitions can also help make the move from one section to another. For example, in Emily's Comment, she includes a brief transitional paragraph between Section II, the background, and Section III, where she discusses her proposal for changing the student loan discharge exception. The substantive transition wraps up the background and makes a clear connection to the following section. The transition also gives Emily an opportunity to reinforce her argument in the first sentence in Section III, the Discussion, by noting that the change she is advocating for is not one of the existing policy proposals she just described in the background section.

> The policy proposals listed above represent the most popular and recent ideas to modify the student loan discharge exception. While they differ in many crucial respects, they share a common theme: the discharge exception, as it stands now, should change.

III. Discussion

> A comprehensive reform of the student loan discharge exception requires more than adopting an existing policy proposal.

Substantive transitions can also be helpful in concluding a specific subsection of a paper. Section II of Jessie's Comment addresses a series of questions that district court judges might have about partial verdicts. The section addresses six separate questions, each with its own subheading, and Jessie transitions to the conclusion of each section with a substantive transition that calls back to the question posed. For example, one subsection addresses this question:

If No Partial Verdict Instruction is Given, Does There Need to Be a Signal from a Jury in Order for a Court to Give The Instruction During Deliberations?

And the closing of the section, which uses cases as specific examples of when this question arises, offers this conclusion, with the transitions marked in bold:

A signal from a jury indicating it has reached a partial verdict is also sufficient to prompt a partial verdict instruction from the court, even if it has not explicitly asked to render such a verdict. **In *United States v. Heriot*,** the jury signal came in the form of a question. **The jury asked:** "If we cannot reach a unanimous verdict on one of the five counts, what is the effect on the overall outcome of the trial?" **The court gave** a partial verdict instruction immediately after the jury asked this question, despite noting to counsel that "it was 'disinclined to accept partial verdicts.'" **In *United States v. Patterson*,** the partial verdict instruction came after the jury indicated that it had reached a partial verdict, but, **unlike in *Heriot*,** the court did not give the instruction immediately. **When the jury stated that** "it had agreed on verdicts for two of the three counts," the court initially responded by instructing the jury to continue deliberating. **Later, the court, unprompted by the jury,** issued a partial verdict instruction. **On appeal,** the defendant argued that "the partial verdict instruction given sua sponte several hours later pressured the jurors to abandon further deliberations." **The Tenth Circuit disagreed. Acknowledging that** "[w]hen issuing a supplemental sua sponte instruction, the court must be especially careful that the jury does not interpret the very issuance of the instruction as an indication that its deliberations are taking too long," the court ultimately held that there was no undue pressure placed on the jury. **The court observed** that "the instruction came shortly after a question asking whether deliberations should continue." *Patterson* **and** *Heriot* **demonstrate a district court judge's wide discretion when determining whether to provide partial verdict instructions—at least in situations where the court has received some signal of jury deadlock.**

(4) Many new scholarly writers find themselves writing sentences with **overly complex subjects.** It makes sense that this would happen; you are working with complicated, nuanced concepts and want your sentences to reflect that. However, if you have a sentence with a complicated subject, you may have organized the sentence improperly. This problem can usually be remedied if you flip the

sentence around, and make the subject the object. Consider for example, this sentence from Shaina's Note:

> A legislative amendment that completely eliminates the widow penalty is a necessary solution to this ongoing problem.

An improved version of this sentence, and one that appears in the final version of her Note, is this:

> Congress should adopt a legislative amendment that completely eliminates the widow penalty.

The rewrite takes the complex subject and makes it the object. Similarly, look at this example from Natalie's Note:

> An individual employee's right to a judicial forum for an employment discrimination claim can be waived by signing an employment application that contains an arbitration clause.

Again, the sentence is focused on the wrong concept, as evidenced by the complicated subject. This is corrected in the rewrite:

> It is now well-settled that an individual employee may waive his or her right to a judicial forum for an employment discrimination claim merely by signing an employment application that contains an arbitration clause.

Occasionally, you will find that you will have to use a complex subject in order to get your point across. If you do so, keep the rest of the sentence tight, so that the sentence itself does not become overly complex. Keep the subject close to the verb; this can substantially increase clarity. Also, be economical with the words you use to construct the rest of your sentence. Shaina does this well in this sentence from her final Note:

> Judicial reform by means of litigation within the U.S. court system is one vehicle utilized by individual petitioners to alleviate the hardship caused by the widow penalty.

Keeping subjects simple can substantially increase the clarity and readability of your sentences. Read these carefully; at this point, you may have read these subjects so many times that they no longer seem complex to you. Consider reading the sentences aloud or counting the number of words the subject comprises to determine whether your subject is unnecessarily complex.

(5) Another common writing hiccup is **subject-verb agreement.** Many students write sentences using subjects and verbs that are not in agreement, in one of two ways. First, they may have a subject engaging in an activity in which it does not or cannot usually participate. Second, they have a singular subject and a verb in the plural, or vice versa. Take, for example, this sentence from Natalie's paper:

> Though the *Pyett* court correctly felt it could not extend an intolerable rule, the law regarding arbitration clauses in a post-*Pyett* world are not ideal and may even be considered inequitable.

This sentence needs to be corrected in two ways. First, courts do not "feel" things; the verb needs to be more concrete. Second, the subject of the second part of the sentence does not match the verb. So, correctly rewritten, the sentence becomes:

> Though the *Pyett* court correctly declined to extend an intolerable rule, the law regarding arbitration clauses in a post-*Pyett* world is not ideal and may even be considered inequitable.

You can avoid both of these types of errors by reading through your paper and checking just the subjects and the verbs. Ask yourself whether each sentence has a verb appropriate for the subject with which it is associated and whether the subject and verb are both in the singular or the plural.

(6) Another common problem involves **over-quoting.** This problem can arise when using any type of source—a case, a statute, or some type of secondary source. The tendency to over-quote is understandable, particularly in earlier drafts, when you are still trying to make sure that you understand the legal concepts you are writing about. Eventually, however, you want to make sure you limit your discussion to the relevant parts of the authorities you are citing, and that you strike a balance between quoting the language and paraphrasing where appropriate. This will make your paper more readable and ensure that you have focused on the relevant portions of the law.

It is particularly important that you do not use a verbatim quote as the entire opening sentence of a paragraph; this can be confusing to the reader, and probably means that you do not have the strong topic sentences we recommended above. If you have not stated the topic sentence in your own words, you probably have not told the reader the purpose of the paragraph. Readers sometimes skim through quoted passages, so minimizing quoted language can improve the readability of your paper.

Consider this paragraph from Shaina's Note:

> Another provision subject to much debate in this regard is 8 U.S.C. § 1154(b), which provides in pertinent part that "[a]fter an investigation of the facts in each case ... the Attorney General shall, if he determines that the facts stated in the petition are true and that the alien on behalf of whom the petition is made is an immediate relative specified in section 1151(b) ... approve the petition...." While the government has relied on Congress's use of the present tense in the provision to justify its dismissal of alien widows' petitions, as widows are no longer "spouses" in the present tense after the death of their citizen spouses, the court in *Robinson v. Chertoff* rejected this contention as contrary to the unambiguous intent of Congress. Believing the statute's use of the present tense to be insignificant, the *Robinson* court declined "to stretch the language of § 1154(b) to the point where agency inaction may disqualify an applicant simply because the passage of time renders obsolete information that was true and accurate at the time the I-130 petition was filed." Rather, the court explained, under the clear command of the statute, if the Attorney General determines that the information in the petition is correct and that the alien spouse is an immediate relative, he should approve the adjustment of status application, regardless of the subsequent death of the citizen spouse.

This paragraph strikes the right balance between quoting and paraphrasing. It quotes the statutory language in relevant part and offers both quoted language and paraphrasing from the case law. The quoted language is readable and the paragraph is not so laden with quotes that it is difficult for a reader to follow.

When considering quotes, use the actual language of the law as a starting point but be judicious in choosing how much of the law you need to include. Do not be afraid to paraphrase supporting points and secondary authorities or to limit the amount of language you quote by using ellipses. Finally, make sure you have properly substantiated all of your quoted or paraphrased language with the appropriate citation(s).

(7) Another common problem involves **overemphasis** or **unneeded modifiers.** Too often, student writing contains words like "clearly" and "obviously" or phrases such as "It is clear that...." or "It is obvious that...." Do not tell the

reader something is clear or obvious—show her. If you do not do the work for the reader, these words and phrases will not do it for you. The same is true for adverbs such as "very" or "only." Be thoughtful when using these; consider whether they are necessary or can be edited out.

Similarly, avoid overly dramatic adjectives such as "terrible" or "outrageous," which can seem alarmist and unsubstantiated. Lay out the case and let the reader conclude that something is terrible—show it to her, do not just tell it to her.

Consider, for example, this excerpt from Nathaniel's paper, where he discusses how the National Park Service allowed Independence Hall in Philadelphia to fall into serious disrepair:

> Sixteen years after Stone introduced his proposal, the National Trust for Historic Preservation ("Trust") began publishing a list of the eleven "Most Endangered Historic Places" in an effort to "raise awareness of the serious threats facing the nation's greatest treasures." For two consecutive years in the 1990s, Independence Hall, the centerpiece of the "most historic square mile" in the nation, found a sad place on the Trust's list. Though the cash-strapped National Park Service (NPS) had managed to keep up appearances for years, Independence Hall had been quietly, but dangerously, deteriorating behind the scenes. A deferred maintenance policy of undertaking only small, provisional repairs allowed a leaky roof to severely weaken the structure, and the sprinkler system, according to the Park Service, was in such disrepair that a fire in the building could have leveled the place in under a half-hour.
>
> Despite the fact that Congress had charged the NPS with the preservation of National Landmarks like Independence Hall—and despite the fact that the NPS itself had created the definitive standards for the care and treatment of such property—nearly every Congress and administration, Republican and Democrat alike, failed to provide political and financial support sufficient for the task. Consequently, one year's operational deficits and deferred maintenance became the succeeding year's backlog. As of 2007, the Park Service's maintenance backlog was estimated to be between $4.1 and $6.8 billion—more than double its annual operating budget. While Congress finally approved a major overhaul for Independence Hall in the 1990s, a secure source of funding for future maintenance is still lacking.

It would have been easy for Nathaniel to use (and overuse) dramatic modifiers in laying out this story. Instead, he mostly lets the facts speak for themselves. For example, instead of saying that Congress "clearly" failed or acted "outrageously," he notes Congressional inaction across several decades, and the accompanying financial consequences of that inaction. When he does use adjectives and modifiers, they are subtle, like the reference to the landmark's "sad place" on the list of endangered places. These paragraphs show the reader what the problem is; they do not just tell her that there is a problem.

(8) Conventional wisdom in legal writing is that you can use the **passive voice** if you are trying to obscure the actor or emphasize the object, but should otherwise strive to use the **active voice**. Active voice is clearer and often more concise than passive voice. Consider this example from an early draft of Jessie's paper, about a seminal district court case:

> Language from *DiLapi* is cited often, both within and outside the Second Circuit.

Here, there is no need to obscure the actor (the Second Circuit and other courts), so a rewritten version of this sentence might look like this:

> Courts both within and outside the Second Circuit often cite *DiLapi*'s analysis.

The rewritten sentence is only one word shorter than the original. However, when making this edit, Jessie saw an opportunity to provide a little more detail about why *DiLapi* is so often cited. This is the sentence that appeared in the final version of her paper:

> Courts both within and outside the Second Circuit often cite *DiLapi*'s analysis, which underscores that a district court is under no obligation to either accept a partial verdict or issue a partial verdict instruction absent an express request from a jury.

Adding this information to the original version of the sentence would have resulted in an overly-complex subject (as discussed above). The final version provides important information to the reader in an active and clear way.

In scholarly writing, there will be few instances where you should need the passive voice to obscure an action; if you find yourself trying to obscure a point, it is likely an issue that you need to address in your paper. However, you may want to use the passive voice to emphasize the object of an action, rather than the actor.

Take a look at these examples from Natalie's paper. In this two-sentence passage, she identifies the actor (PBC) in the first sentence and uses the active voice to establish what the actor did (transferred [the] three employees). She then uses the passive voice in the second sentence because she has already established who the actor is, and the employees (the object) are more important than the actor in the second sentence.

> However, in July of 2003, PBC transferred these three employees to "less prestigious" and "more physically demanding" positions. Pyett and O'Connell were reassigned as night porters, and Phillips was reassigned as a cleaner.

The sentence would be less effective if phrased in the active voice:

> PBC reassigned Pyett and O'Connell as night porters, and reassigned Phillips as a cleaner.

Compare the context above, with that of this sentence, which also uses the passive voice:

> Nearly twenty years after *Gardner-Denver* was decided, the arbitration clause issue was reexamined in *Gilmer*.

Here, the actor is important, and is missing from the sentence as phrased. Presumably, Natalie wanted the reader to know which court decided these cases. So, the final version of the sentence was as follows:

> Nearly twenty years after the Supreme Court decided *Gardner-Denver*, the Court reexamined the arbitration clause issue in *Gilmer*.

This edit made the actor clearer and the writing crisper. Look for similar opportunities for clarity and crispness in your writing during this finishing stage.

(9) Student scholarly writing is often very **wordy**, perhaps because many students have authentic voices in their writing—increasingly, we write like we talk, and when we talk we are not particularly concerned with an economy of words. Look for places this may have occurred in your writing, and edit these phrases for simplicity. For example:

- "because of the fact that" should just be "because"
- "the reason is because" should be "the reason is"

Look also for opportunities to eliminate noun phrases that can be replaced with an active verb. Again, this could be a function of "writing as we talk." Take this example from Shaina's Note:

> In widow penalty cases, the government has made an invocation of the "*Chevron* doctrine" and argued that courts are required to give deference to the Board's permissible interpretation of immigration law.

This sentence has two phrases—"made an invocation" and "to give deference"—that could be replaced by verbs. So, the rewritten sentence becomes the following:

> In widow penalty cases, the government has successfully invoked the "*Chevron* doctrine" and argued that courts are required to defer to the Board's permissible interpretation of immigration law.

These edits will make your paper more readable, and can also be useful to students who are trying to trim sections of their papers to comply with strict maximum word requirements.

(10) Your final check should also include a review for **internal consistency and correctness among repeated references.** As your paper evolves through multiple drafts and many revisions, it can be hard to monitor these changes. Common errors here include the following:

- **Serial references that are incomplete or out of sequence.** Make sure your sentences are properly labeled "First…," "Second…," and so on. Make sure that every "First" has a "Second" point that follows it.
- **Mismatched headings and subheadings.** You should have more than one heading on a given level of a hierarchy. If one of your subsections has only a first-level heading ("A" or "1" for example), you should merge it into the larger section.
- **Inconsistent use of acronyms or other shorthand references.** If you use standard acronyms or create shorthand references for your paper, make sure you define them and use them consistently. Upon first reference, state the full name and the acronym or abbreviation you will use in the rest of the paper. Then use the shortened version for all future references. Remember that the default settings on most standard spell-check programs will not pick up mistakes in capitalized abbreviations, so you will need to proofread these carefully.
- **Mistaken or incomplete cross-references in footnotes.** A properly sourced and cited paper will have cross-references within and among the footnotes so that you can refer the reader to other parts of the document or previously cited sources. Over the course of the writing process, these cross-references may need to be updated if you move text around or add references that change the numbering of the footnotes. If you have created these cross-references manually, you should make sure they are accurate. You may, however, want to format your footnotes so that internal cross-references are updated au-

tomatically. The chart below explains how to do this using various word processing programs.

Word for Office 365	To create the cross-reference, put your cursor where you want the cross-reference to be. Then click References > Cross-reference. Click Footnote in the "Reference type" pulldown. Click Footnote number in the "Insert Reference to" pulldown. Click Insert to close the dialog box. To update the cross-references, right-click the reference and click Update Field.
Word 2016 **Word 2013** **Word 2010** **Word 2007**	To create the cross-reference, click Insert > Links > Cross-reference > Footnote. Then choose the footnote number and click > Insert > Close. To update the cross-references, put your cursor in the footnotes area, and click Ctrl-A (to select all footnotes) > F9.
Word 2016 for Mac **Word for Mac 2011**	To create the cross-reference: (1) Click View > Print Layout. (2) Click where you want the cross-reference to appear. Then click Insert > Cross-reference > Footnote. (3) Click the footnote number you want the cross-reference to refer to, then click Insert > Close.
Word 2008 for Mac	To create the cross-reference, click Insert > Cross-reference > Footnote. Then choose the footnote number. To update the cross-references, click Word > Preferences > Print > Update Fields > OK. This will update the cross-references even if you do not actually print the paper.
WordPerfect	To create the cross reference: (1) Go to the existing footnote you wish to reference and click Tools > Reference > Cross Reference. In the dialog box choose the Reference Type (Footnote) and create a shorthand name for the reference (such as "footnote 2") in the Select Target box. Then click the Mark Target button. (2) Move the cursor to where you want the cross-reference to appear. Then, in the same dialog box you used in Step (1), click Mark, then Generate. To update the cross-references, return to the same dialog box and click Generate.
Google Docs	To create cross-references in Google Docs, you will need to download an add-on. See, for example, https://github.com/davidrthorn/cross_reference/blob/master/README.md.

These ten items are the most common and most complicated errors we have seen in student writing, but the list is obviously not exhaustive. You must consider all concepts related to grammar, syntax, and punctuation and correct any errors in your final paper. Think about past writing endeavors. Do you habitually overuse commas? Do you always forget whether to include other punctuation marks inside quotation marks? Take a critical look at your paper to make sure you have resolved these issues. If you tend to struggle with matters of language generally, use a grammar or style manual to perfect your paper. Also, make sure you have complied with any specific (and potentially quirky) requirements that your journal imposes.

Finally, although we have mentioned it before, **citations** are also a problem in many student papers. Too many students plan to deal with citations at the end of the writing process but do not leave themselves enough time to perfect them. In Chapter 3, we advised that you keep track of your citations throughout the writing process, but recognized that you were likely to fall at least slightly short of our aspirations for you. Now, make sure that you not only have the proper citation format for all of your authorities, but that you also have correctly quoted passages and that you have the right pinpoint citation information for each piece of authority. If your paper is substantively complete, you can use short-form citations for subsequent citations to the same source. If you included short forms or "*Id.*" in your early drafts, make sure that the references in the final version are complete and correct.

We close this chapter with a few tips that can help you during this finishing phase. You *must* proofread your paper several times before you can consider it completed. Consider using one or more of these tips or tools when your paper is close to complete.

- **Proofread with a fresh pair of eyes.** Time-permitting, take a break from writing before you attempt to proofread your paper. At a minimum, let yourself have a night's sleep before you take this critical look at your paper; ideally, you will take a break of a day or more. At this point, you have read the paper so many times that you might not be able to trust your eyes anymore—you may not be able to read every word and see every error. Giving yourself time away from the paper can help remedy this problem. If time is of the essence, one of these techniques may help you with a thorough technical scrub of the paper:
  - **Read backwards.** Do not read the paper in order—start from the last paragraph and work your way backwards. This is a good way to check the purpose and execution of each paragraph individually. This will also prevent you from giving more attention

to the first part of your paper than you do to the last; the longer you read, the more likely you are to have "proofreading fatigue."

○ **Read in more than one proofreading session.** Another way to avoid fatigue is to break up your proofreading so you do not do it all at once. Even if you take only short breaks between sections, this will allow you to give equal attention to each part of your paper.

○ **Read aloud.** Reading your sentences aloud can also help you find errors that you will overlook if you are merely visually proofreading. Do not, however, do this in the library or any other place that is likely to bring you looks of confusion or derision.

• **Engage a proofreader.** The freshest pair of eyes will be one that has not looked at the paper at all before. See if there is someone who might be willing to proofread your paper for cosmetic errors. Before you do this, however, make sure that your school, journal, and professor allow this type of external assistance; you may be required to work entirely independently on the project, and you do not want to run afoul of plagiarism or academic integrity rules. If it is permissible to ask someone else to proofread your paper, you might be well-served to ask a non-legal audience; that person will be able to focus on the technical aspects of the paper without regard for the legal substance.

Subject to the rules governing your paper, you may be able to use a citation-checking service. These include Shepard's BriefCheck on Lexis Advance, West's Drafting Assistant, Juris-M (https://juris-m.github.io/) or non-law-specific programs like RefWorks (www.refworks.com) or Zotero (www.zotero.com). At a minimum, Westlaw and Lexis Advance allow you to copy citation information when viewing a source—a useful shortcut when you are taking notes on a source, but you should take the time to make sure the citation information is accurate and in proper form.

No matter which technique you choose, make sure you are thorough when you complete your final reviews of your paper. At this point, you probably have a lot of comments, suggestions, and line-edits to process. Make sure that you have made all the changes that you intended to make, whether based on external feedback or on your own notes. You may need to make a list the feedback you plan to input into your final draft, so that you can check off the comments as you incorporate them. And check to make sure you have followed the proper guidelines for submission—for example, are you supposed to submit two copies of the paper, one with your name on it and one without? Follow these rules carefully.

Finally, in this Finishing stage, make sure that you are vigilant about which version of your paper is current. After all of this work, you do not want to make the mistake of turning in the wrong version of many drafts. Jessie used a naming convention for each draft of her paper, which included both a draft number (ultimately she went through 8 versions of the paper) and a description of the status of the draft. Maintain the attention to detail that you have used throughout the writing process. You might find it difficult to maintain the enthusiasm and meticulousness that you had in the early stages of the writing process, but try your best to give an appropriate amount of time and attention to finishing your paper.

In addition to keeping track of drafts you have written, be vigilant about which draft you submit. Most word processing programs allow you to view a paper with tracked changes without actually accepting all of the changes, just so you can read a clean copy. However, if you submit the paper without accepting the changes, the reader will also be able to see tracked changes, comments, and other information you might not want them to see. Make sure you accept all changes before submitting your paper to a reader.

CHAPTER 8

FINISHING:
PUBLISHING YOUR PAPER

Congratulations! After many hours of planning, working, and sweating it out, you have finished your scholarly writing project. Take a moment to reflect on this accomplishment, and think about how far you have come since the first day you sat down and tried to think of an idea to get the process started. At times you probably wanted to give up, but it was worth it—finishing a scholarly piece as a law student is no small task, and you have now developed a great deal of vertical knowledge in an area of the law that interests you.

For many of you, this will be the end of the line—you have completed whatever requirement you set out to fulfill, and thus you have accomplished your goal. We encourage you to push past this finish line, however, and take your writing experience to the next level: Consider trying to get your paper published.

There are at least two good reasons why you should consider publication. First, you put a lot of effort into it and should try to get as much out of the experience as you can. Law schools have upper-level student writing requirements, in part, to encourage new thinking and good ideas from students. You have taken the time to put your ideas together and establish expertise. Why not share your fresh perspective with a wide audience? Putting your paper out for publication is largely an administrative task; this can be time well spent if there is a large payout. That is the second reason: the payout here is publication credit, which is a high-value commodity in the legal profession. Employers often view publications as an impressive resume line, particularly specialized employers such as judges hiring clerks and law schools hiring new professors. (It can also be a way of connecting with a potential employer during a job interview.) The value of a publication is truly unmatched in the legal world as a way to make your mark as a contributing member of the legal community.

This chapter aims to give you guidance on how to navigate the publication process, from planning a publication strategy to seeing your paper through the editorial process. The more effort you put into your submission strategy and presentation, the higher the probability that you will get published. Some of you will have an easier path to publication than others; if you are a journal staff member, you are likely eligible for a publication spot in your own journal. Still, if you wrote a paper for a seminar class, or if your paper was rejected for publication by your own journal, you should consider finding a publication outlet for your work.

The road to publication can be broken down into seven manageable steps. First, evaluate your publication prospects. Second, ensure that you have permission to publish your piece. Third, develop a submission strategy by researching the available publication outlets. Fourth, prepare your submission package, including a cover letter, abstract, and resume. Fifth, submit your piece to publishers. Sixth, negotiate your way through the offer process. Finally, guide your paper through the process of editing for publication.

If you wrote your paper as a journal staff member and your journal has agreed to publish your paper, your path to publication is a little more direct. You can jump from step one to the final step for our advice about the transition from working with a supervisor to working with an editor.

Step 1: Evaluate your publication prospects.

Your first step is to determine how "publishable" your paper is. This evaluation involves two concepts: how much revision your paper requires, and how your paper measures up to selection criteria used by many journals.

If you are going to submit your paper for publication, you will need to incorporate the last round of feedback you received from your supervisor. Depending on the quality of your final draft, this could mean your paper requires a significant amount of editing—or even more research and drafting—before it is suitable for publication. Make sure you have the time and energy required to engage in the steps we discussed in Chapters 5, 6, and 7 a few more times.

☀ If you are thinking about publication before you submit your final draft, you may want to mention that to your professor, and ask that she keep it in mind as she reviews your final paper. This can lead to more substantive feedback because she knows you plan to revise the paper again, and can also elicit a frank evaluation of whether your professor thinks it is publication-worthy.

If you decide that the required pre-submission revisions are manageable, you should evaluate your paper in light of common selection criteria for legal journals. When we surveyed law review and journal editors, we asked them about their priorities when they are reviewing a submission. This advice probably applies to any type of submission, whether it is to a legal journal or other publication. Below are the criteria, in order of importance, that many journals use to evaluate submissions—you should think about these criteria, and how your paper satisfies them, as you consider whether and where to submit your paper for publication.

1. Strength of argument or proposal: Journals place a great deal of emphasis on the author's ability to advance a persuasive thesis using thought-provoking analysis. As you know from our discussion of topic selection, most journals are not looking for the author to summarize existing law or regurgitate legal theories without providing any additional analysis.

2. Novelty of the topic: Journals want authors to bring a fresh and creative perspective to their topics. Fresh and creative, though, does not mean "fringe" or "radical"—usually only well-known authors can get away with making outrageous arguments.

3. Organization: A well-organized submission can stand out from other submissions because evaluators have to quickly get the gist of hundreds of submissions. An editor can review a submission quickly if it is well-organized and uses carefully crafted headings and sub-headings.

4. Execution of the article: Editors who are swamped with hundreds of journal submissions often do not follow the old adage about not judging books by their covers. They look for work that is complete and presented professionally. If the submission looks like a work-in-progress with incomplete sections or margin notes, they will be unimpressed.

5. Attribution to sources: If an evaluator notices a lack of attribution in a paper, she will worry that these arguments may have no basis in fact or law or that even if they are substantiated somewhere, it will be a lot of work to edit the piece and obtain the sources. Most journals will not take this risk, especially on a student writer.

6. Timeliness of the topic: Journals like timely topics because publishing these types of pieces shows that the journals are relevant and responsive. However, they still realize that by the time your paper is published, your topic may have disappeared from the front page.

In order to address timely topics without the constraints of the full publication process, some journals have created online companion websites or online symposia to address hot topics. These provide additional, less formal, publication opportunities.

---

7. Audience: Journals are always thinking about audience, especially specialty law journals that often have a subscription-based practitioner audience. These editors will look for articles that relate to the topic of the journal and will draw in a large audience.

8. Style and voice: Once you get past basic spelling and grammar rules, authors bring their own style and voice to their submissions. Some styles capture a reader's attention better than others.

9. Reputation of the author: Some journals will investigate how many times an author has been cited or published to gauge whether they should extend an offer. Others take into account the pedigree of the author's education. As a student author, you probably do not have much of a reputation on which you can rely, but this is a relatively less important factor in the journals' decision-making process.

10. Citations: Although editors ranked this factor the lowest, a well-cited submission will probably get some brownie points from evaluators because it shows that the author is dedicated, serious, and professional about her work. In addition, if selected for publication, it creates a lot less work for journal editors down the road.

Once you have evaluated how much effort you can and will expend in revising your paper once more, and considered how your paper stands up to common criteria used in publication decisions, you can move on to the process of developing and executing a submission strategy.

Step 2: Secure permission to publish.

Before you invest any time in a publication strategy, make sure that you have permission to publish your paper. If you wrote your paper for a course or seminar, or through an independent study, you should have free rein to submit your paper for publication or to enter writing competitions. If you have any hint that this might not be the case at your law school, ask your professor for clarification or for guidance through the process.

However, if you are a staff member on a law school journal seeking to publish elsewhere, you may need to secure permission because most law school journals have a right of first refusal on the work product of their staff members. In other words, your journal has the option to accept and publish your piece until it officially tells you that it will not publish your piece.

The submission process for journal members is fairly simple: most journals accept the required notes, comments, and essays from their members and review all of them for potential publication. Only a small percentage of these, however, will get offers for publication. Many journal editorial boards let students know early on in the writing process when they will make their publication decisions—this is generally built into their publication timeline. Thus, journal staff members should know the date by which they will know if they have received an offer for publication. If you get such an offer, of course, you should take it, and permission is a non-issue.

If your journal has informed you that your piece has not been selected for publication, then you have most likely been given the green light to start marketing your paper elsewhere. Do not take the journal's decision as a referendum on the quality of your paper. There are many reasons why your paper could be of publishable quality but will not be published in this particular journal— perhaps it does not fit with the available space for the next issue or the journal made a last-minute decision to include several notes with variations on a similar theme. We know several students whose journals rejected their pieces, but then found a publication home at other law reviews and journals. The key question here is permission; if you are unsure whether you have permission to publish, talk to your journal editors.

Step 3: Decide where you want to submit.

If you take some time to research, plan ahead, and organize your publication strategy, you will conserve a lot of time and energy, and submit higher quality and more professionally presented work product to journals. As an initial matter, you should ask around and see if anyone else at your school has published a paper in a law journal or entered or won a writing competition. This word of mouth can be invaluable, and get you the best information in the most efficient manner—for example, maybe a fellow student who took your seminar course last year entered and won a subject-specific writing competition that you might enter this year. You might also consider asking a faculty member about potential publication resources—she may know of a particular specialty journal that often accepts student submissions, or a writing competition sponsored by a professional organization to which she belongs. Your law school's student affairs office or student government might also know about other student publication successes.

As you learn more about potential publication outlets, keep track of certain things using an organizational device such as a list, chart, or spreadsheet. These include:

- name of the publication
- contact information
- submission deadline
- submission requirements
  - abstract
  - cover letter
  - resume/curriculum vitae
- substantive requirements
  - citation format
  - page length

What you include in your list will vary based on the journal's submission requirements. For example, you may not need to include the journals' physical addresses if you are planning to submit your paper electronically.

A publication spreadsheet might look something like this:

Journal	Contact Info	Requirements	Submission Deadline	Notes
Temple Journal of Baseball and the Law	P.O. Box 1627 Philadelphia, PA 19122 tjblaw@law.temple.edu	Cover letter Resume	April 1	50 page limit for student articles
Georgetown Sports Law Journal	600 New Jersey Avenue Washington, DC 20001 gusportlawj@ georgetown.edu	Cover letter Abstract	April 15	
Temple Baseball Review	P.O. Box 5555 Philadelphia, PA 19122 tubaseballjourn@ law.temple.edu	Cover Letter	April 1	Prof. Murray recommended submitting here

A second variation:

Journal Info	Deadline	Cov Let?	Abst?	CV?	Notes
Temple Journal of Baseball and the Law P.O. Box 1627 Philadelphia, PA 19122 tjblaw@law.temple.edu	April 1	Y	N	Y	50 page limit for student articles
Temple Baseball Review P.O. Box 5555 Philadelphia, PA 19122 tubaseballjourn@law.temple.edu	April 1	Y	N	N	Prof. Murray recommended submitting here
Georgetown Sports Law Journal 600 New Jersey Avenue Washington, DC 20001 gusportlawj@georgetown.edu	April 15	Y	Y	N	

Take a broad approach here. If you find a legal journal or publishing platform that interests you, write it down. We recommend that you put your selected publishing platforms in order of your preference with your first choice at the top and your last choice at the bottom. That way, when journals start to respond to your submissions, you can react quickly to decide whether you should accept or wait to see if a more preferred journal offers to publish your piece. For example, if you get an offer from a lower-ranked journal, you may want to ask several higher-ranked journals for an expedited review. (Expedited review is discussed further in Step 6.) Another way to organize is by deadline, to ensure timely compliance with all of the deadlines. You may avoid this, however, by simultaneous submission to multiple publications, which is generally a good strategy.

Once you decide how you will keep track of your options, consider the different avenues of publication. There are three main categories: traditional print law journals, internet-based publications, and law student writing competitions.

Paper-Based Law Reviews and Legal Journals

For the aspiring student writer, paper-based law reviews and legal journals are the gold standard for publication. Thus, your highest aspiration should be publication in a traditional law review or journal. Although law reviews and legal journals have been criticized for their stubbornness to embrace the modern age and their student-review process, they are still highly regarded in the legal community as a mark of scholarly distinction. Journals maintain this respect because journals set a high bar for publication and will only publish papers that demonstrate intellectual rigor and thought-provoking analysis. Also, because paper-based journals take painstaking measures to only publish high quality work product, every premise asserted by an author must be attributed to a source. As a result, readers can trust that what they are reading is factually correct.

When generating the list of traditional law journals you want to submit to, you may find it helpful to separate this task into two different phases—one search for general law reviews and one search for specialty legal journals. First, you can generate a list of all general law reviews that are both willing to accept non-member student submissions and desirable publication outlets for your paper. General law reviews are usually the flagship journal for a given school and generally do not limit themselves to specific topics.

Do not be confused if a general law review does not have the words "law review" in its title. Usually any legal journal that does not indicate coverage of a special area of the law is a general law review. For example, the *Georgetown Law Journal* is a general law review.

Thus, if there are 200 ABA-approved law schools in the United States and at least one general law review at each law school, then you have an abundant number of submission options. Do not be overwhelmed by these numbers! Washington & Lee School of Law maintains a searchable electronic database that can connect student authors to general law reviews; you will not have to search 200 individual websites to get the submission information you need. You can access the Washington & Lee database at http://lawlib.wlu.edu/LJ/.

Deans Allen Rostron and Nancy Levit have also compiled submission information for general law review submissions in an online guide, available at https://papers.ssrn.com/sol3/papers.cfm?abstract_id=1019029. The guide is updated approximately every six months.

After you review the general law reviews, you can add specialty law journals that are germane to your topic to your publication list. There are over 1,000 specialty law journals for you to choose from because law schools typically have several specialty law journals. Because specialty law journals cover a narrow subject matter, they usually receive fewer paper submissions which, in turn, means you may have a better chance of getting your piece published. Some specialty law journals publish less frequently than general law reviews, which can mean they have less space for student submissions. Nevertheless, you should make specialty journals part of your publication strategy because student writers often have better success with specialty law journals than general law reviews. The Washington & Lee data base has information about specialty law journals.

When searching for specialty law journals, avoid a narrow scope. For example, do not rely too heavily on the title of the specialty journal. If you searched only for journal titles that had the words "health care," you might miss the *Yale Journal on Regulation*, which might also be interested in publishing a paper on a health care topic. Go back to your initial canvassing here as well; your professors and fellow students may be able to suggest some specialty journals for you. A quick Google search might also lead to a list of subject-specific journals that someone else has already compiled.

At the end of this process, you may also want to seek out journals that are not contained in the Washington & Lee databases. There are several other journal databases to review to finalize your list or chart of potential publication options. For example, Journal Seek (http://journalseek.net/) has the largest category-driven journal information on the internet, with information about more than 40,000 journals (click on "Law" in the category browser). Lexis provides a directory of general student-edited law reviews, special focus student-edited law journals, non student-edited peer review and trade journals, and university presses (https://www.lexisnexis.com/ap/academic/form_legal_reviews.asp).

Some of the source-finding resources you looked at in Chapter 3 may be useful here as well; now that you have done research in this field, you may be aware of industry-specific journals and publication outlets that might be interested in publishing your piece. Practitioner journals are also often willing to accept student submissions. In fact, one of our research assistants published a piece in BNA's "Computer and Internet Lawyer."[1] You could also run a quick internet search to catch any other outliers that may not be reflected in these other databases. You may also want to consider the possibility of submitting to non-legal journals if your paper represents an intersection of two fields.

Internet-Based Publication Platforms

Although traditional law journals will probably be your top publication choice, they are not without their disadvantages. For example, it takes a lot of

---

1. Jonathan Band & Ben Grillot, *The Hobgoblin Argument: An Inconsistent Approach to Intellectual Property Damages,* THE COMPUTER & INTERNET LAW. (Nov. 2008).

time to churn out an issue of a published journal—by the time your article appears in print, its utility could be lessened or its validity could be preempted. Also, as we noted above, there is a high barrier to entry. The supply of journal submissions always outstrips demand—there are thousands of submissions for only about 2,000 7-inch by 10-inch pages in the average law review volume. That means that journals make tough decisions and reject many submissions.

Internet-based publications have become a viable alternative to paper-based journal publications. They have several attractive qualities. First, because the publication process occurs at a much faster pace than their paper-based counterparts, you will most likely not have to worry about sacrificing timeliness or risking preemption. Second, because internet-based publications are not really limited by page space, it may be easier to get your work published without major editing to decrease the length of your paper. Third, internet-based publication options may have lower barriers to entry. For example, they may be willing to publish a variety of pieces on the same topic as part of an online symposium. The main disadvantage is that these vehicles may be considered less prestigious than traditional published journals, but do not let that weigh too heavily on your decision about whether to pursue these publishing options.

Some journals have expanded their traditional paper-based operations to include additional publishing opportunities on the web. Other publications, such as *The Columbia Science and Technology Law Review* and *Stanford Technology Law Review*, have gone completely internet-based. Internet-based publishing vehicles are gaining increased acceptance within the legal community. Some of these online-only components have special restrictions, such as a requirement that they be in response to an article published in their paper-based companions, so it would be wise to go to their websites and consult the specified requirements.

Legal Writing Competitions and Contests

In our experience, too few law students take advantage of legal writing competitions and contests. These competitions are a great way to earn recognition and prize money. In addition, there are a wide range of opportunities for participation. There is a writing competition for almost every legal topic imaginable, from rare books to American Indian law.[2]

Writing competitions usually come with two possible primary benefits: prize money and publication. Some offer both! The winners are often given prize

---

2. *See* http://www.aallnet.org/sis/lhrb/cohen.html; http://adams.law.ou.edu/ailr/competition.cfm.

money (usually ranging from $500 to $5,000 for first place), and some also offer a paid trip to an annual conference where you will receive your prize and meet leaders in that legal field. Competitions that are associated with a publication, or an organization with a publishing arm, may also offer to publish the winner's piece.

Finding a writing competition is pretty easy. Law schools advertise them to try to bring well-deserved recognition to their student body. One of the offices or departments at your law school may maintain a website dedicated to listing writing competitions. If your school does not, you can most likely access another school's website by running an internet search for "legal writing competitions." Some popular annual competitions include the following, which are listed along with the subject matter of the contest and the 2010–11 top prize:[3]

- ABA Section of Business Law Mendes-Hershman Student Writing Contest (business law): $2,500 for first place
- ABA Criminal Justice Section William W. Greenhalgh Student Writing Competition (American criminal constitutional procedure): $2,500 and possible publication in *Criminal Justice* magazine
- Constance Baker Motley National Student Writing Competition (all papers furthering and promoting a progressive vision of the Constitution, law, and public policy): $3,000 and possible publication in the *University of Pennsylvania Journal of Constitutional Law*
- American Inns of Court, Warren E. Burger Prize (issues of legal excellence, civility, ethics and professionalism): $5,000 and publication in the *South Carolina Law Review*
- GRAMMY Foundation Entertainment Law Initiative Writing Competition (entertainment law): $10,000 and an all-expense paid trip to the Grammy Awards
- Jones Day, William E. Swope Antitrust Writing Competition (antitrust law): $10,000
- Judge John R. Brown Award for Excellence in Legal Writing (no topic restriction): $10,000 for first place, $5,000 for second place, $3,000 for third place, $1,000 for two finalists
- Tannenwald Writing Competition (tax): $5,000 for first place, $2,500 for second place, $1,500 for third place

---

3. Many of these also include a trip to an annual conference or meeting where an official award is presented. We have included only monetary prizes and publication opportunities in this list.

Note that some of these competitions welcome all student submissions, whereas others only allow one entry from each law school. If you are interested in one of the latter type of competitions, you will need to investigate how your school determines which student's paper to submit. You might have to "win" an internal competition, or you could be the default competitor if no one else is interested.

It can be hard to keep track of writing competitions and contests—new contests appear each year, and sometimes it is hard to track down current information on annual contests that do not have updated submission information. Your school may have an internal list of writing competitions. For example, Georgetown's office of J.D. Academic Services maintains an online list of writing competitions at https://www.law.georgetown.edu/students/writing-competitions. cfm. The American Bar Association also sponsors a number of annual writing contests. You can find the ABA Writing Contest Site at https://abaforlawstudents. com/events/law-student-competitions/writing-competitions/.

One unique legal writing competition is the Burton Awards, which honors legal writing that uses plain, clear, and concise language and avoids archaic, stilted legalese. Law school deans or their designees can nominate a student whose work was published the previous year for one of the law student writing awards. Zachary Mason, a recent Georgetown Law graduate, won one of the 2017 awards for his note, "Online Loans Across State Lines: Protecting Peer-to-Peer Lending Through the Exportation Doctrine," which was published in the *Georgetown Law Journal*. You can read the full article at 105 Geo. L.J. 217 (2016). Nathaniel Guest, whose paper is featured throughout this book, won a 2010 prize. You can check out the Burton Awards website at http://www.burtonawards.com/awards-student.html.

We encourage you to consider all viable publication outlets as part of your publication strategy. Use the following checklist to make sure you have all the necessary information before you move on to the next step:

Checklist: Is my submission strategy complete?

- Complete your paper.
  - Revisit the concepts we discussed in Chapters 5, 6, and 7, incorporating any feedback you received on your final paper. Make sure the paper is finished and polished with no missing information or citations.
- Make a detailed spreadsheet or list of all the publication options that you have chosen, including:

- ◦ Paper-based legal journals and law reviews
- ◦ Internet-based publications
- ◦ Writing competitions and contests
- Rank this list in order of your preferences, from top to bottom.
- Supplement the spreadsheet with important information about the publication.
  - ◦ General or specialty law journal
    - If it is a specialty law journal, what is the topic? It is a good idea to check the website because the relevant topics are often more expansive than what the title of the journal suggests.
  - ◦ Status of submission (submitted, unsubmitted, accepted, rejected)
  - ◦ The journal's preferred submission dates
  - ◦ The journal's discouraged submission dates (usually around summer or winter breaks)
  - ◦ Formatting nuances

Step 4: Prepare your submission.

This step takes a chronological approach to the various things you should do to prepare your paper for submission.

Check your calendar to time your submission appropriately.

First, you must decide when you want to submit your paper. Usually the answer is immediately after you are finished writing it, but there are a few cases in which you may want to postpone your submission. For example, if you finish writing your paper in December, it may be in your best interest to wait until February to submit your paper to publishers.

For paper-based journals, there are two ideal submission periods:

- Late February to Early May: This is usually the best time to submit a paper because this is when the new editors have just started their positions on the journal editorial board and they are seeking articles to fill the next volume. This will likely also fit with your timeline if you are a journal staff member looking to publish outside the journal, or a student who wrote a paper for a fall semester course.
- Late August to Early November: This is usually the second best time to submit a paper because journal editors are coming back to

campus, again looking to populate the next volume. This submission cycle will give you more time with your paper if you finished it in the spring, either as part of your coursework or as a journal staff member.

There are two time periods to avoid:

- December and January: Journal editors are either studying for final exams or they are away for the winter break.
- June and July: Journal editors may not be around campus, and, if they are, are less focused on reviewing submissions than they are at other times in the year.

In any case, many journals deviate from this anecdotal advice. Some journals will advertise preferred submission time frames on their websites. If not, consider making a brief phone call to determine the preferred submission time frame.

If you are entering your paper in a writing competition, make sure you note the deadline for submission (and whether the deadline means the paper must be postmarked or received by that date).

Write an abstract.

When it comes to abstracts, there is a wide expectation gap between most authors and journal editors. Authors often ignore them or write them as a last-minute afterthought, assuming that a catchy introduction or a well-written cover letter is enough to persuade editors to publish their work. The majority of journal editors, however, think that abstracts are important components to any submission.[4] Abstracts help persuade editors to publish your piece and give the impression to editors that they are working with a professional who cares about the quality and presentation of his work. Some journal editors, due to time constraints, may only have time to read an abstract, so if your paper does not have one you will be disadvantaged in the selection process. Therefore, you should give serious thought to submitting an abstract with your paper.

---

4. Leah M. Christensen & Julie A. Oseid, *Navigating the Law Review Article Selection Process: An Empirical Study of Those with All the Power—Student Editors*, 59 S.C. L. Rev. 175, 199 (2007) (finding that 100% of the top 50 law journals read abstracts and 92% of specialty journals read abstracts).

Crafting an effective abstract can be challenging. An abstract is a condensed version of your paper in about 250 to 400 words. You should attempt to answer the following questions when drafting your abstract:[5] What are the topic and thesis of your paper? What arguments does your paper put forth in support of your thesis? What are the implications of your thesis and supporting arguments? Why should the journal be interested in publishing your paper?

In crafting your abstract, you can draw from the Introduction and Conclusion sections of your paper, as in this abstract of Shaina's paper:

The death of a spouse can be one of the most tragic events of a person's life. This event is even more tragic for the hundreds of alien widows and widowers who face automatic deportation from the United States because of the so-called "widow penalty." The widow penalty affects widows and widowers whose American citizen spouses died before the couples celebrated their two-year wedding anniversaries. Under the Immigration Service's current interpretation of immigration law, if the citizen spouse dies before the second anniversary of the marriage, the alien spouse is no longer considered a "spouse" for immigration purposes, and the Immigration Service will automatically deny, with no individual review of the facts, the alien spouse's application to adjust status to legal permanent residence ("LPR"), or a green card. This is likely a "crack in the law" not intended by Congress, and should be remedied.

This paper argues that Congress should act to rectify this legal wrong, by enacting legislation to abolish the widow penalty for all alien widows, regardless of whether the citizen spouse filed a petition prior to death or marriage length. By exempting alien widows from the two-year marriage requirement for obtaining LPR status, and allowing them to self-petition for LPR status upon the death of their citizen spouses, Congress could put an end to the Immigration Service's automatic deportation of grieving widows and its subsequent separation of families. With immigration reform dominating congressional dockets in recent years, legislative reform of the two-year rule is feasible at this time if the Immigration Service's unjust application of the widow penalty can be highlighted.

---

5. For more advice about writing abstracts, see the blog discussion at http://legalhistory
blog.blogspot.com/2007/10/how-not-to-write-abstract.html.

If you would like to see some other examples of legal abstracts before you start your own, go online to review some samples. SSRN (http://papers.ssrn.com) requires that authors submit abstracts with their papers; many law professors have posted their papers to SSRN, so you can see many abstracts of varying styles and substance.

Write a cover letter.

Not all journals require cover letters, but almost all have said that it does not hurt to include one with your submission. Therefore, the default should be to include a cover letter, unless you are explicitly told not to include one. It is good form and also shows that you care about your submission. Plus, it is yet another opportunity to grab an editor's attention and explain why your paper is well-suited for publication.

An effective and persuasive cover letter includes the following elements:

- **Letterhead:** Ask for your school's permission to use law school letterhead. It makes your submission look more official and increases the chances that your submission will be noticed.
- **Heading:** Include your name, address, phone number, and email address in the top right corner of the page. Address the letter to the Articles Department or Articles Office, and use the journal name and address. Use the date that you are planning to send your submission.
- **Salutation:** You have two main options here. You could use a generic opening to your letter (e.g., Dear Editorial Board) or personalize the letter by addressing it to the highest ranking articles editor. The highest ranking articles editor is usually easy to determine by reading the masthead of the journal.
- **Body:** Tell the journal about your article and why the journal should publish it. Be persuasive.
    - Consider using a hook to get the editors' attention by opening with a startling fact or statement. Then, once you have his attention, explain why he should publish your paper.
    - Keep it short and sweet. Say what your paper is about, and why readers will care about your paper. State this clearly and succinctly.
    - There is no reason to emphasize your status as a student. Avoid starting your letter with a phrase like, "As a third-year law student at...." Of course, if the editors ask if you are a student, you should not misrepresent your student status. But avoid highlighting your

student status in your cover letter by focusing on telling the editor about your paper.

- ○ Consider including some data about your article, such as the word count and number of footnotes. Editors are often working within a limited page count for each volume and this data can help them determine whether and how your article will fit.
- ○ Editors may balk at accepting an article with lots of hard-to-find sources because that will mean lots of work for the editorial staff. If you have cited source material that may be difficult to access (e.g., books or legislative history), offer to provide copies of the source material to the editors. This can be easily managed through a shared Dropbox or other file sharing service to which you can upload PDFs of your sources.
- **Sign-off and Signature:** Stick to something safe like "Regards" or "Sincerely." We would shy away from more casual phrases such as "Kind regards," "Sincerely yours," or "Cheers." You will have lots of opportunities to show the editor your style and voice, but this is not one of them.
- **Proofreading:** Make sure that there are no spelling or grammar mistakes in your cover letter. This just gives the editors an excuse to send your paper straight to the trash bin.

It is also a good idea to have a generic cover letter on hand because some electronic submission services only allow you to attach a single cover letter.

A cover letter is more likely read if it is put directly in front of the reader. Therefore, if you are emailing the submission to the journal publication, rather than attaching a formal cover letter to the message, write a short cover letter and abstract in the body of your email. This ensures that editors will at least glance over your cover letter and avoids the problem of sending a bland email message stating "see everything attached to this email."

Update your resume.

Many journals like to see a resume, biography, or curriculum vitae attached to your submission because the editors want to get to know the person behind the submission: who you are, where you go to school, where you have been published, and how often you have been cited.

You probably already have a resume on hand. Before you use it as part of your submission packet, you should revisit your resume and make sure it is up-to-date. Think about the audience here, which might be different from the audience for your job or clerkship search. If you have published before, make sure that information is featured prominently on the resume. Also, you may want to stress the academic and legal scholarship portions on your resume. For example, you may want to elaborate on any research assistantships or legal writing awards that you have received.

Make sure your resume is polished and perfect. You do not want your article to make it to the "no" pile because your resume said that you attend "Tempel University School of Law."

Revisit the formatting of your paper.

Publication outlets may have specific formatting requirements with which you must comply when submitting a paper. You should familiarize yourself with the formatting requirements of each journal or other publication platform and follow them. Some will have exacting requirements, while others will offer specific but not all-encompassing advice. For example, many journals require that submissions comply with the latest edition of the Bluebook and advise authors to use good judgment for everything else. Some journals will be silent on the issue.

To help you properly format your paper in the absence of any specific advice, we have put together a few default format rules that you should generally follow.

- **Alignment:** Left-aligned justification is preferable to full justification.
- **Citations:** Footnotes are usually better than endnotes. Unless told otherwise, citations should always comply with the latest edition of the Bluebook. The citation font is usually Times New Roman or another serif typeface, size 10.
- **Text font:** The text font should be in Times New Roman or another serif typeface, size 12. A monospaced typeface such as Courier or Courier New is usually not encouraged.
- **Spacing:** Double-space, unless specifically told to single-space.
- **Headings:** Headings are usually formatted as follows:
  - Level 1: Uppercase Roman Numerals (I., II., III.), Small caps, Size 12, Centered
  - Level 2: Uppercase Letters (A., B., C.), Italics (no small caps), Size 12, Centered
  - Level 3: Numbers (1., 2., 3.), Regular font, Size 12, Left-aligned
  - Level 4: Lowercase Letters (a., b., c.), Regular font, Size 12, Left-aligned

    ◦ Level 5: Lowercase Roman Numerals (i., ii., iii.), Regular font, Size 11, Left-aligned

One final note for those of you who are planning to enter a writing contest or competition but not to submit to journals generally: You may have to take a few of these steps as well. For example, some contests want entrants to send an updated resume along with the paper. You may also have to fill out an application form or cover sheet. Follow the competition rules carefully as you prepare your submission.

Consider the following short checklist before you move on to the mechanics of submitting your paper:

Checklist: Am I ready to submit my paper?

- Do I have permission to publish?
- Did I research the various types of publication outlets and decide where I would like to submit my paper?
  - ◦ Did I consider all available publication opportunities, including traditional paper-based legal journals, internet and other publishing platforms, practitioner publications, and writing competitions and contests?
  - ◦ Have I made a list prioritizing the various publication outlets that interest me?
- Did I keep track of the various submission methods for the journals?
- Is my paper ready for submission?
  - ◦ Have I reviewed the proper timing for submission?
  - ◦ Did I prepare other parts of my submission, including an abstract, cover letter, and resume?

Step 5: Submit the paper.

There are various mechanisms you can use to submit your paper for consideration for publication to traditional paper law reviews and journals. If you are pursuing one of the other publication platforms, follow the submission guidelines that they provide; the processes there are too varied to generalize here.

Not too long ago, the article submission process was much slower and more time-consuming than it is now. Imagine the labor needed to type several manuscripts, send them through the mail, and wait months for a publication decision. Legal journals function at a much brisker pace today and the submission process is relatively easy.

Even just a few years ago, direct mail submission was an option some authors used to submit their manuscripts. Today, absent a few journals,[6] student-edited law reviews welcome electronic submission either by direct submission to an institutional email address or by using one of the major article submission services.

Several legal writing competitions and contests are "old school" and ask that entrants send their submissions via direct mail with multiple copies. If you are submitting to a writing competition, make sure you follow their instructions to the letter. For example, if they ask for multiple copies, they probably need those copies to send out to competition judges, and if you do not send the requisite amount, your entry may be disqualified.

The two major submission platforms are ExpressO (http://law.bepress.com/expresso/) and Scholastica (https://scholasticahq.com/law-reviews). These are fee-based submission platforms that allow you to create an account, submit manuscripts, track offers, withdraw offers, and accept an offer. ExpressO gives students one free submission. Some law reviews accept submissions using both services, others may prefer one particular service, and still others might allow (or require) direct submission.[7]

You may end up using a variety of these submission methods depending on your choices of where to seek publication, and any specific guidance provided by these publishers. Because your goal is publication — and any publication is better than no publication — we recommend that you send in all of your submissions at the same time. Rather than game the system at the outset, cast a wide net and see what comes back. Although in some disciplines, authors must submit their article to one journal at a time and await a decision before they

---

6. For example, the *Stanford Law Review* only accepts submissions through its website (https://www.stanfordlawreview.org/submissions/). Other journals may require peer review or exclusive submission — or both — and have accompanying special requirements for either direct mail or electronic submission (the *Journal of Legal Education* (https://jle.aals.org/home/submissions.html) has such requirements).

7. You may also wish to consult the student-focused journal submission guidance from Deans Rostrum and Levit and two co-authors, available at https://papers.ssrn.com/sol3/papers.cfm?abstract_id=1656395. This guide was published in 2016. If you are considering a submission to an online law review supplement, consider Professor Colin Miller's guide, available at https://papers.ssrn.com/sol3/papers.cfm?abstract_id=1410093.

can submit it to the next, law authors can and do submit to multiple (often many) journals at a time.

After you get everything submitted, take a deep breath, and wait.

Step 6: Evaluate your publication offers.

You might not have to wait for long. Steel yourself for this truth: you are probably going to get multiple rejections in a very short time. Try not to take this personally; rejection can happen for a host of reasons that have very little to do with you and the substance of your paper (in fact, the faster the rejection, the less likely it is that anyone looked at your paper at all). Most of your professors have suffered this indignity as well, so you can feel comfortable knowing rejection is often part of the process to getting published.

If you do not hear anything right away, try to relax. We know waiting for a decision from a journal can be excruciating, but try not to pester the editors about a decision. An offer of publication is likely to come from one of the current editors, by phone call or email. Before you start calling your family to tell them the news, though, you should ask the offering journal for some basic information about the offer. First, find out when the offer expires and get this date in writing, just to ensure that there is no possibility of miscommunication and both sides are clear on the terms. Second, ask how they are planning to publish the piece, and in what issue. (Refer back to Chapter 1 for a discussion of the varied nomenclature journals use for different types of published pieces.) Finally, see if there are any major changes planned for the paper. For example, do you have to cut 2,000 words? Change to a different citation format? And who is responsible for the planned changes—you, or the journal editors and staff members? Find out as much as you can about the offer so you know its explicit terms.

You should also find out the protocol for accepting (or rejecting) the offer, because you should not accept the offer on the spot. Instead, ask these five questions before you commit to an offer of publication.

Am I comfortable with the terms of the offer? Consider the offer the journal gave you. Do the terms seem reasonable? Are they asking anything that makes you uncomfortable, such as a quick turn-around time or a thirty percent page reduction? What are the policies on copyright when publishing with the journal? Do they require an exclusive license, or can you negotiate something less? Make sure that, taken alone, this is an offer you are willing to accept.

Most authors publish a draft article to SSRN once it has been accepted
for publication (with a note that publication in a particular publication
is forthcoming). Before you do this, make sure you secure permission from
the journal editors and check with your law school to see if there is a stan-
dardized format for SSRN postings.

*How does this offer compare to the other places to which I have submitted but
not yet heard?* Take out your spreadsheet or list of publishers and see where this
publication fits within your personal rankings. Check your notes to see and review which publications have rejected your piece. Think about whether your
top choice is still an option, or whether this publisher is your best option given
the others that have rejected your paper. It might be hard to decide when comparing journals to each other after you get an offer from a lower-ranked journal.
Think about what you can gain by taking this offer. Is there a monetary award
or presentation included? Does this publisher intend to publish your paper
within the next two months, or will it be a year or more before your paper appears in print? Are you going to be looking for a job in another city after graduation, and this publisher is located in that city? In short, how an offer compares
to your other potential publishers depends on you and your preferences. Also
consider asking professors for advice on what to do, if you have time.

Should I try and trade up? From here, you must decide whether you should
accept this offer or use this offer to try to get a "better" publication offer. As
we discussed above, a "better" offer could be one from a more "prestigious"
journal or one that is for some reason a more attractive publication opportunity
to you. Instead of accepting on the spot, you will most likely want to see if you
can use the offer from one journal to influence other journals to give you an
offer. As long as you have not accepted the first offer, you are completely justified, if not expected, to engage in this practice. Pull out your spreadsheet and
see where the offering journal ranks among the other journals that you submitted your paper to, but have not yet heard from. Then, consider whether
you would take an offer from any of these over the one you have in hand. If
so, then check the journal's website for instructions on how to request a
response from that journal. Some ask you to send an email to a special "expedited review" inbox, while others tell you to pick up the phone or email the
senior articles editor. Then, contact the journal to let the editors know you
have an offer but would prefer to publish in their journal. Because the journal
already knows that your paper is publishable in one journal, they will put your
paper on top of the "papers to read" pile and they will try to have a decision
within a few days. You may feel some loyalty to the journal that has already

given you an offer, but this type of "article-shopping" is completely acceptable under the current system.

Can I try and trade up? Know, however, that if your offer expires in under 48 hours, you will probably not have enough time to request an expedited review from your higher-ranked journals and have a decision before the offer expires. Most expedited reviews take at least a few days and may take up to a week. You could call the offering journal and ask for more time to give your decision; most journals are flexible and willing to work with authors. A short extension of a week might be enough time to request expedited reviews from higher-ranked journals. If the journal cannot give you any more time to consider its offer, and it is an offer you are comfortable accepting, we urge you to seriously consider the offer and lean towards accepting the offer rather than letting it expire in the hope that better journals will offer you a slot.

Am I ready to accept the offer? After you have taken these initial steps, take another minute to reflect. This inquiry process could take place within an hour or within several days if you shop the article. If you are comfortable with the offer and can see no reason to wait, pick up the phone or send an email to accept the offer. Now you can call your family.

Step 7: Navigate the publication process.

Accepting the offer is the easiest part of this whole process. After you accept the offer, be sure to get the offer confirmed in writing. Ultimately, you will sign a publication agreement that will include details about things like copyright permissions and the number of print copies the journal will provide you.

Once you have received written confirmation from the journal that they will publish your paper, contact all of the other journals and respectfully withdraw your submission. Journals really appreciate it when you let them know that you are withdrawing, because it saves them time and effort later. If you are rejecting a journal's offer, give particular care when you tell them that you decided to publish with another journal. Be open, honest, and polite. Tell them how much you appreciate the offer and how great you think their publication is.

Next, turn your eye toward publication by getting familiar with the journal's publishing schedule. Who edits your paper first? When do you get to accept or decline the edits? If the journal editors do not tell you, you should feel comfortable asking. It will save all of you time in the future. Some good general advice to keep in mind throughout the publishing process is to be humble and easy to work with—meet deadlines and be responsive.

A normal publication schedule works like this: The journal takes your accepted piece to do what journals do—edit, edit, edit. If you are a journal member yourself, this process will be familiar. That usually means that, at a minimum, the editors are going to collect every source that you cited in your paper and check to make sure that your source says what you claim it says. Editors will also check your spelling, grammar, and citation formats.

Journals may differ in the amount of other feedback and proposed changes they offer you prior to publication. Some publications will start by offering some big picture feedback and suggested edits and then, once those are incorporated, begin a technical line edit involving sources, citation, and punctuation and grammar. You might also have multiple editors assigned to your piece through each of these rounds. Other publications might accept your work as-is and immediately begin a technical edit.

Make sure you understand the timeline and process for these rounds of feedback. No matter how this process proceeds, you should insist that the journal editors do all their work in tracked changes because you need to make sure the editors are not twisting your words or tweaking your argument. As an author, you have a right to see what changes they have made, and have final say on whether to accept those changes. You may want to reject some edits if you think they would materially sacrifice your writing style and voice, or undercut the strength of your arguments, but you do not want to quibble with minor changes. Do not, at any point, be arrogant or rude to journal editors. Engage in conversation with them if they suggest something with which you disagree. Explain why you disagree rather than just reject or ignore their input. Also let them know when you appreciate their suggestions or error-catching.

If at the end of this process you have tried these routes without success, but still want a way to get your ideas out there, we have a few other suggestions. If your article identifies a problem and proffers a solution, consider distilling your main ideas down to a short op-ed piece. This will get your name in print, publicize your ideas, and give your mom something to tack up on the fridge. You might also consider other, smaller publication outlets such as newsletters or online magazines. Think tanks, interest groups, and other policy organizations often have these types of publication outlets and might take submissions from students.

We recognize that not all of you will find yourselves with an offer in hand at the end of this process. Here, take a big picture perspective on your experience. Although your paper may not be published, your hard work was not wasted. Focus on the personal enrichment that you received from the scholarly writing process. Not only did you become an expert on your topic, you learned countless lessons about the research and writing process. You may want to take these lessons and move your paper forward again. You could use this round of rejections as an indicator that your paper needs a few more rounds of revision or a restructuring of the argument section. If you did not do so before, consider asking a professor for a few helpful suggestions. You may be able to find a place to publish after another round of revisions, or you may decide to move on to a new project using what you've learned. If you truly want to publish, be flexible and look for opportunities to do so throughout your academic and legal careers.

APPENDIX

This Appendix includes three annotated full-length student notes: two traditional law review notes and one case note. The two unpublished papers and published note are annotated to illustrate how the student authors executed the concepts we have discussed throughout the book.

Our notes are embedded in the papers. They appear in italics to set them off from the rest of the text. We have also included annotations to a selection of footnotes. Our notes in the footnotes appear in italics and bold text.

Jordan Schwartz's unpublished traditional law review note is first, followed by Katy Ho's published note, and then by Peter Smyth's unpublished case note.

Jordan Schwartz's Note

Jordan's Paper in Brief:
- *15,038 words including footnotes*
- *38 pages double-spaced using Times New Roman 12 point font for text and Times New Roman 10 point font for footnotes*
- *4 basic parts: Introduction, Background, Proposed Solution, and Conclusion*
  - *Introduction: approx. 3 pages (approx. 8%)*
  - *Background: approx. 25 pages (approx. 66%)*
  - *Proposed Solution: approx. 10 pages (approx. 26%)*
  - *Conclusion: approx. 1/2 page (approx. 1%)*
- *202 footnotes*
  - *Introduction: 5 footnotes (approx. 2%)*
  - *Background: 165 footnotes (approx. 82%)*
  - *Proposed Solution: 32 footnotes (approx. 16%)*
  - *Conclusion: 0 footnotes (0%)*

State Executive Emergency Powers and the Second Amendment: A Call for Judicial Courage During a State of Emergency

*This title contains two parts, as do many scholarly legal paper titles. Both of the parts here are descriptive and, taken together, effectively tell the reader what the paper is about. Look back to **Chapter 4** for more advice on constructing your title.*

By Jordan Schwartz

Introduction

Imagine that you are stranded in your home city in the wake of one of the world's worst natural disasters. The flooded city has deteriorated into a state of violence and lawlessness characterized by unfettered looting, robberies, and other criminal acts. In this period of unprecedented chaos, your only real hope and sense of security are rooted in your lawful ownership of a firearm. Now, envision the police knocking down your door, forcing you onto the ground, and ultimately, confiscating your firearm.

"No one will be armed. Guns will be taken. Only law enforcement will be allowed to have guns."[1] This dramatic proclamation by former New Orleans Police Superintendent Eddie Compass, made in the immediate aftermath of Hurricane Katrina, must be characterized as one of the most anti-American statements made by a state or local official in the context of firearm ownership and possession. It reflects the danger posed by an unchecked executive branch during a period of crisis. As horrific as Hurricane Katrina was, it should not have given rise to such flagrant disregard of the people's Bill of Rights.

Hurricane Katrina represented one of the most tumultuous disasters in the history of the United States. When most people discuss the horrors of that great natural disaster, they have visions of the destruction of the levees and the drowning of Ward Nine.[2] What most people fail to recognize is that, in addition to the enormous destruction and suffering caused by the natural disaster, many law-abiding citizens were denied one of their fundamental constitutional rights: the right to keep and bear arms.

---

1. *See* John R. Lott, *Defenseless Decision: Why Were Guns Taken from Law-Abiding Citizens in New Orleans?*, NATIONAL REVIEW ONLINE, Mar. 21, 2006, http://www.nationalreview.com/script/printpage.p?ref=/comment/lott200603210744.asp.

2. GORDON HUTCHINSON & TODD MASSON, THE GREAT NEW ORLEANS GUN GRAB (Louisiana Publishing Co. 2007) (offering vivid description of the enormity of Hurricane Katrina, including the destruction of the levees, mass human suffering, and subsequent state of lawlessness throughout the city).

Here is an attributing footnote. Most of Jordan's footnotes are used simply to attribute to sources.

*Jordan does a nice job of opening his note with a hypothetical example placing the reader in context. (See **Chapters 4 and 5** for a discussion of using hypothetical examples in your introduction and throughout your paper.) This scenario grabs the reader's attention and makes the reader interested to keep reading to find out what happens after the police knock on the door. In the next paragraph, Jordan effectively uses a quote that flows from the hypothetical and to effectively transition to the real events of New Orleans post-Hurricane Katrina. These introductory paragraphs give some context to Jordan's note by emphasizing some of the lesser-known damages of Hurricane Katrina and preparing the reader for a paper about state action to confiscate firearms.*

This Note addresses the use of state and local executive emergency power and its impact on the Second Amendment. As demonstrated in the aftermath of Hurricane Katrina, the use of state and local executive emergency power to interfere with individual rights is a distinct possibility. What is most dismaying about the specific events in New Orleans, as they relate to the possession of firearms, is that the state of lawlessness and danger meant that privately owned firearms were the only real protection available.[3] Ignoring the principle that the U.S. Constitution applies equally during times of crisis and normalcy,[4] city officials exercised executive authority in such a way as to trample on individual rights under the misguided attempt to promote law and order. That city officials may have lacked effective control over the population of New Orleans should not have translated into the forcible confiscation of firearms—an overbroad interference with fundamental constitutional rights.

In this paragraph, Jordan identifies his topic (the use of state and local executive emergency power and its impact on the Second Amendment) as he builds up to his thesis. He gives enough context and introductory material here to let the reader know what his thesis is based on—in fact, this is the idea that led him to his topic, and subsequently, his thesis. His thesis is the next sentence (marked in bold).

The use of state executive emergency power during times of crisis, when impinging upon individual constitutional rights, including the Second Amendment, should be subject to a heightened level of judicial review. This Note

---

3. *See* NRA: The Untold Story of Gun Confiscation After Katrina, http://www.youtube.com/watch?v=-taU9d26wT4 (providing firsthand accounts of forcible gun confiscation from law-abiding citizens).

4. *See* Ex Parte Milligan, 71 U.S. 2, 76 (1866).

calls for greater judicial assessment of executive actions that occurred during times of emergency, including actions brought to the attention of the judiciary during an exigency. This heightened standard of review would be a palpable departure from the traditional presumptions and deferential standards that have characterized the judiciary throughout American history.[5]

In addition to a clear statement of his thesis, Jordan includes some of his rationale in this paragraph to give the reader a preview to his proposed solution section and some context before the background section. Notice how his thesis sentence uses a "should clause," clearly identifying Jordan's position. You can also see that Jordan uses the third person to describe his paper in this paragraph (and in the roadmap below)—this is a convention of the journal he is writing for. Not all audiences will require this convention.

Part I of this Note describes the forcible confiscation of firearms in New Orleans in the aftermath of Hurricane Katrina to highlight the urgency of adopting a heightened standard of judicial review of emergency powers exercised during crisis. Part II sets out the premise that the Second Amendment confers an individual, fundamental right on the people. Part III of the Note details the historical background underlying judicial review of state and federal executive assertion of emergency power. This background highlights a jurisprudence that has sanctioned judicial unwillingness to check the power of the political branches at both the state and federal level when they have undertaken emergency actions that violate individual rights.

Against this backdrop, Part IV sets forth a novel framework for judicial review of state executive emergency power when those powers interfere with individual constitutional rights. Under this new structure, the judiciary would play a more active role in ensuring that fundamental constitutional rights are not discarded during crises. This framework requires state or local executive officials to demonstrate that 1) the executive had the legal authority to act, 2) the challenged action was in furtherance of a compelling government interest, and 3) the executive considered the action alongside other means. In assessing the second and third prongs of this test, courts should consider the number of available, less restrictive alternatives to the challenged action. The application of this standard reveals the unconstitutionality of the confiscation policy un-

---

5. *See* Michael Cook, *Get Out Now or Risk Being Taken Out by Force: Judicial Review of State Government Emergency Power Following a Natural Disaster*, 57 Case W. Res. L. Rev. 265, 270 (2006).

dertaken in New Orleans following Katrina and the potential for greater protection of individual rights during future disasters.

*A two-paragraph roadmap nicely shows the reader what to expect in the rest of
the paper. (See* **Chapter 4** *for a discussion on roadmaps and additional examples.)
As you can see from the roadmap, the Background section is comprised of Parts
I–III of Jordan's paper, and the Analysis/Discussion section is Part IV. Immediately
following this Introduction, the Background section begins. Adding a transition
phrase between the end of the roadmap and the first heading would add to the
readability here.*

I. The Forcible, and often Violent, Confiscation of Firearms by New Orleans Law Enforcement.

On September 8, 2005, approximately one week after Hurricane Katrina
pummeled the great city of New Orleans, Eddie Compass, former police superintendent of the city, declared that the people would not be allowed to possess firearms.[6] What followed was the systematic and forcible confiscation of
weapons from law-abiding citizens, as they were instructed to evacuate the
flooded city.[7] Although both Compass and New Orleans Mayor Ray Nagin have
repeatedly denied any order to seize firearms,[8] newspapers throughout the
country referenced Compass's bold declaration and Nagin's support of the policy.[9] On March 16, 2006, the New Orleans Police Department actually acknowledged it possessed approximately 1,500 firearms seized from private citizens
during the aftermath of Katrina.[10] Overall, the National Rifle Association
("NRA") found between thirty and forty cases of individuals whose firearms
had been seized by law enforcement.[11]

---

6. *See* Lott, *supra* note 1; *see also* Greg Langley, *Local Author Helps Document New Or-
leans Gun Confiscation Scandal,* THE ADVOCATE, July 29, 2007 at E3; Bill Walsh, *Police
Ordered to Stop Disarming Residents: Post-Storm Confiscations off Target, Judge Says,* NEW
ORLEANS TIMES PICAYUNE, Sept. 24, 2005, at A3 (recounting quote by Compass that only
law enforcement would be permitted to possess firearms and quote by Deputy Chief Warren
Riley that "We are going to take all the weapons.").
7. *See* Mary Foster, *Katrina Survivors Want Police to Give Guns Back,* CHARLESTON
GAZETTE, Apr. 18, 2006, at 2C.
8. *See* NRA v. Nagin, No. Civ. A. 05-20,000, 2005 WL 2428840, at *2 (E.D. La. 2005)
(noting that the defendants had denied any formal seizure of firearms).
9. *See* Langley, *supra* note 6.
10. Bryan Hendricks, *Arkansas Sportsman Authorities Went on Gun-Grabbing Spree after
Katrina,* ARKANSAS DEMOCRAT-GAZETTE, Sept. 7, 2006.
11. *See* Langley, *supra* note 6.

In this paragraph, the reader gets the basic story of firearms confiscation in New Orleans. The facts here suggest a controversy, which is likely to engage readers. This paragraph and background section could be strengthened by adding a roadmap of Part I at the end of the paragraph before transitioning to the first sub-section. Look back to **Chapter 4** *for a discussion of how to construct these types of roadmaps.*

A. The State of Lawlessness and Lack of Protection Accentuated the Need for the People to Possess their Lawfully Owned Firearms.

A state of lawlessness characterized New Orleans in the early part of September, 2005. During the emergency, there were extensive reports of looting throughout the city.[12] According to Wayne LaPierre, president of the NRA, the gun confiscation occurred "[a]t a time of complete collapse of the government's ability to protect people and they were trying to protect themselves."[13] The police confiscated New Orleans resident, John C. Guidos's shotgun and pistol, for example, and robbers subsequently looted his tavern.[14] Gordon Hutchinson and Todd Masson, authors of the recent book, THE GREAT NEW ORLEANS GUN GRAB, described the state of lawlessness throughout the city: "Also moving toward them was a great wave of looters, a malevolent horde of locusts destroying everything in their path."[15] These authors recounted the pervasive level of looting, including one instance in which looters ran up to a van and demanded that the occupants leave their vehicle.[16] Fortunately, the possession of a rifle by one of the occupants thwarted the success of the looters' illegal endeavor.[17]

---

12. *See* Lott, *supra* note 1. Lott recounts a mother's feeling of vulnerability when she and her two young children saw a homicide in the city after Katrina. *Id.*; *see also* John Hartzell, *NRA Asks Leaders for Gun Pledge Second Amendment: The Lobbying Group Wants Police Chiefs and Mayors to Promise not to Take Guns away from Law-Abiding Citizens; Police Say They Don't Have the Time, Resources or Desire To Do So*, DULUTH NEWS TRIBUNE, May 19, 2006 (describing the lawlessness in the storm's aftermath).

13. Walsh, *supra* note 6, at A3.

14. Lott, *supra* note 1. According to Guidos, the only time he saw police was when they forcibly confiscated his firearms. *Id.*

15. HUTCHINSON & MASSON, *supra* note 2, at 24.

16. *Id.*

17. *Id.* at 25. Nervously, the looter asked: "Is that a real gun?" *Id.* The woman in the back of the van retorted, "You bet your ass it's a real gun!" *Id.* This episode is one of countless examples of firearm protection in the aftermath of Katrina. Residents described the necessity of firearm protection: "We couldn't expect help from the cops. Thank God we had a gun." *Id.*

In this footnote, after attributing the source for the sentence, Jordan uses source material that may be distracting to a reader if placed in the text of the Note. The quoted material, however, is particularly effective as an example of interactions between looters and gun-toting citizens.

Similarly, sixty-two-year-old attorney LeRoy Hartley fought off armed looters by brandishing his firearm.[18]

Notice how the sentences in this paragraph support the thesis sentence; each sentence is used to demonstrate the extreme looting. Jordan also gives some support to his thesis by noting where firearms were used to prevent this problem. Notice, too, the effective use of quoted material in this paragraph. The quotes are synthesized into the paragraph and there is a good balance of quoted material and paraphrased material here. When a source has a particularly effective way of making a point, directly quote it. Look back to **Chapter 7** *for a discussion of appropriate use of quotations and the problem of over-quoting.*

B. The Forcible Seizure of Firearms by New Orleans Officials.

In the aftermath of Katrina, Governor Kathleen Blanco declared a state of emergency and issued emergency power orders under the state's Homeland Security and Emergency Assistance and Disaster Act.[19] Subsequent to the governor's action, which was not directed at firearm seizures, the city's police chief issued his infamous declaration: "No one will be armed. Guns will be taken. Only law enforcement will be allowed to have guns."[20] This eerie warning to law-abiding gun owners became reality by the state's law enforcement authorities, as well as members of state National Guard Units, the California Highway Patrol, the New Mexico State Police, and the Federal Bureau of Alcohol, Tobacco and Firearms.[21] The confiscation of firearms accompanied Mayor Nagin's mandatory evacuation order, which forcibly removed law-abiding citizens, who refused to evacuate, and then confiscated their guns.[22]

---

18. *Id.*

19. *See* LA. REV. STAT. ANN. § 29:724(D)(6) (2007); Proclamation No. 48 KBB 2005; *see also* La. REV. STAT. ANN. § 29:766(D)(8)(2007); Hendricks, *supra* note 10. Under the state's emergency power law, a declaration of emergency by the governor gives rise to the power to regulate firearms. *See* LA. REV. STAT. ANN. § 29:724(D)(6) ("suspend or limit the sale, dispensing, or transportation of alcoholic beverages, *firearms*, explosives, and combustibles") (emphasis added).

20. *See* Lott, *supra* note 1 (referencing the police chief's declaration and support by Mayor Nagin).

21. Hendricks, *supra* note 10.

22. *See* Walsh, *supra* note 6, at A3. In addition to the forcible confiscation of firearms, law enforcement unreasonably arrested and detained law-abiding citizens without cause, including Ashton O'Dwyer. *See* HUTCHINSON & MASSON, *supra* note 2, at 43. O'Dwyer, who was sitting on his lawn around midnight, was suddenly surrounded by members of the Louisiana State Police. *Id.* After demanding that the police leave O'Dwyer's property, the officers "cuffed him and threw him face first into the shrubbery lining his driveway." *Id.*

The city's confiscation policy was carried out with force and intimidation.[23] According to Todd Masson, "[t]here were countless instances of people minding their own business, doing nothing but defying authority by staying in their houses."[24] One of the earliest instances of the policy's execution was the assault on Patricia Konie and the forcible confiscation of her firearm.[25] Konie told the officers that she did not want to evacuate and that she had a pistol to protect herself.[26] The officers then proceeded to knock down Konie's door, tackle her, smash her face into a cabinet causing her teeth to become dislodged from her mouth, and then drag Konie outside of her home after confiscating her pistol.[27] On video, Konie described the pain of her injuries and showed extensive black and blue marks across her arms and face.[28]

While detaining O'Dwyer at the Union Passenger Terminal, O'Dwyer continuously asked if he was being arrested. *Id.* at 44. Ignoring O'Dwyer's requests to make a phone call, an officer pepper sprayed O'Dwyer three times. *Id.* Another officer charged at O'Dwyer and slapped him on the side of his face. *Id.* Ultimately, O'Dwyer was released at approximately 5 p.m. the next day. *Id.* at 48. A medical examination conducted the next day uncovered internal bleeding within O'Dwyer's thighs. *Id.* O'Dwyer filed a complaint with the FBI that is still pending. *Id.*

Here is an example of an explanatory footnote. Jordan explains in detail the somewhat tangential story of O'Dwyer. Including this long, complicated story in the text may have distracted the reader. For careful readers, however, the context included in the footnote will provide an additional example of the consequences of unfettered state action.

23. *See* Hendricks, *supra* note 10.

24. *See id.* Todd Masson, native resident of Louisiana and editor of Louisiana Sportsman, is one of the authors of the book, The Great New Orleans Gun Grab, which documents specific instances in which residents of New Orleans were deprived of their lawfully possessed firearms.

25. *See id.* A San Francisco television station, KTVU, filmed the incident in which members of the California Highway Patrol assaulted the woman of fifty seven years. *Id.*

26. *Id.*

27. *Id.*

28. *See* NRA: The Untold Story of Gun Confiscation After Katrina, http://www.youtube.com/watch?v=-taU9d26wT4 (video recounting the physical assault and confiscation of Konie's pistol). The forcible confiscation was not limited to Patricia Konie. Percy Taplet, 73, claimed that the state police confiscated his shotgun from his home when they evacuated him. Foster, *supra* note 7, at 2C. Taplet asserted, "I won't ever see that gun again believe me.... [I]t's gone like everything else in that storm." *Id.* Marie Galatis, an African American Baptist minister, described the widespread looting throughout the city and characterized her bible and firearm as important possessions in the midst of pervasive looting and vulnerability within New Orleans. *See* NRA: The Untold Story of Gun Confiscation After Katrina, http://www.youtube.com/watch?v=-taU9d26wT4. Unfortunately, for Galatis, the

Robert Zas and Buell Teel were also subject to the city's confiscation policy at gunpoint.[29] For Robert Zas, the experience was particularly disturbing in that the officers went so far as to smash a pearl gun given to Zas's wife by her father.[30] When Buell Teel asked how he could retrieve his rifles and whether the officers could write him a receipt, the officers told him to get a lawyer if he wanted his weapons back.[31]

These real examples both establish the background for Jordan's paper and also engage the reader. Even if a reader agreed with the policy to confiscate firearms, these stories are alarming. Remember, you want to draw thought and reaction from your reader; no doubt readers react to these stories. That helps Jordan get readers on his side, or at least interested in knowing what Jordan proposes to resolve this situation.

Infuriated by the city's action during one of the nation's most dreadful natural disasters, the NRA, the Second Amendment Foundation, and private citizen Buell Teel filed suit against Mayor Nagin and other city officials in federal district court, alleging that the officials violated the residents' constitutional rights and seeking an injunction to preclude any further confiscations and to require the return of lawfully owned firearms.[32] Notwithstanding the affirmative denials by Nagin and Compass that no firearm seizures had been ordered,[33] District Court Judge Jay C. Zainey issued a preliminary injunction on September 23, 2005, barring the confiscation of lawfully possessed firearms and requiring the return of any and all firearms that had been confiscated by city officials.[34]

Despite the judge's order, the city continued to confiscate lawfully possessed firearms.[35] On March 1, 2006, the NRA filed a motion to find Nagin and

---

police deprived her of her gun, denying Galatis the type of protection that the city could not guarantee in the aftermath of Katrina. *See id.*

29. *See id.*

30. *See id.*

31. *See id.*

32. *See* NRA v. Nagin, No. Civ. A. 05-20,000, 2005 WL 2428840, at *2 (E.D. La. 2005); Walsh, *supra* note 6; *Nagin, New Orleans Still Violate Gun Rights*, NEWSMAX.COM, Mar. 1, 2006, http://archive.newsmax.com/archives/ic/2006/3/1/171852.shtml.

33. *See* NRA v. Nagin, No. Civ. A. 05-20,000, 2005 WL 2428840, at *1–2 (E.D. La. 2005). According to the district court order, Nagin denied having issued any order or directive to seize lawfully possessed firearms. *See id.* Further, both Nagin and the police superintendent denied that confiscation of lawfully possessed firearms occurred and that the city possessed such weapons. *See id.*

34. *See id.*

35. *See* Langley, *supra* note 6, at E3 (noting that city authorities made no attempts to comply with the judge's consent order and return firearms seized by police); *see also* Nagin, 2005 WL 2428840, at *1–2.

Warren Riley, who succeeded Compass, in contempt of court for failing to comply with the September order barring the seizures and mandating the return of lawfully possessed firearms.[36] Finally, on March 16, 2006, the police department acknowledged the seizure of firearms and disclosed that the city possessed approximately 1,500 such weapons.[37] In April, the city permitted the NRA to examine the cache of weapons in custody of the police department[38] and began to return some of these weapons.[39] According to the Second Amendment Foundation, as of December 2007, the New Orleans police department has returned approximately 100 of the confiscated firearms.[40] The federal lawsuit filed by the NRA and the Second Amendment Foundation, alleging that the firearm seizure was unconstitutional, was slated to go to trial on February 19, 2008,[41] but has since been delayed to allow the NRA more time to find individuals whose firearms were seized in the wake of Hurricane Katrina.[42]

Jordan continues with the background material, explaining how people tried to take legal action to stop the confiscation program. The reader understands how the judicial route did not solve the problem. This sets up a nice transition to the next heading about legislative responses.

C. Legislative Responses to the Confiscation Policy.

The firearm confiscations of 2005 have flabbergasted state and federal lawmakers across the nation. The actions undertaken by Mayor Nagin and Superintendent Compass have led many lawmakers to propose, and ultimately enact, amendments to state and federal emergency laws to explicitly prohibit the confiscation of lawfully possessed firearms during a state of emergency.[43]

---

36. *See* Langley, *supra* note 6; Hendricks, *supra* note 10.

37. *See* Hendricks, *supra* note 10.

38. *See* Langley, *supra* note 6.

39. Hartzell, *supra* note 12.

40. *See* Michael Kunzelman, *Gun Seized After Katrina? NRA Wants You*, Yahoo News, Dec. 26, 2007, http://news.yahoo.com/s/ap/20071226/ap_on_re_us/katrina_confiscated_guns.

41. *See id.*

42. *Gun Seizure Lawsuit Against New Orleans on Hold*, Jan. 14, 2008, http://www.ksla.com/Global/story.asp?S=7567544&nav=menu50_2.

43. *See* Jeremy Redmon, *Legislature 2007: Katrina-Inspired Bill Could Stop Gun Seizures*, The Atlanta Journal-Constitution, Jan. 30, 2007, at 4D; Mary Jo Pitzl, *Bill Would Protect Right to Keep Weapons During an Emergency; Measure Inspired by Confiscations After Katrina*, The Arizona Republic, Feb. 28, 2007, at 4; David Kopel, *Congress Outlaws Gun Confiscation During Disasters or Emergencies*, The Volokh Conspiracy, Oct. 2, 2006, http://volokh.com/posts/1159809369.

Congress passed the Disaster Recovery Personal Protection Act of 2006, which specifically prohibits the confiscation of lawfully possessed firearms by any individual operating under the color of federal law during an emergency or natural disaster.[44]

In June of 2006, Louisiana became one of the first states to expressly prohibit the confiscation of firearms during a state of emergency.[45] Signed into law by Governor Blanco, the Emergency Powers Protection Act makes it unlawful for state authorities to confiscate or seize lawfully possessed firearms, weapons, or ammunition.[46] The fact that the Louisiana state legislature and governor amended the state's emergency power law may lend credence to the viewpoint that there were constitutional problems inherent in the gun confiscations of 2005.

In addition to the reform of Louisiana's emergency power law, several other states have similarly made it illegal for state and local officials to confiscate lawfully possessed firearms during periods of emergency.[47] The experience of law-abiding citizens in New Orleans will likely continue to drive lawmakers to propose and support measures that explicitly bar the government from seizing lawfully possessed firearms using emergency powers.[48]

Now the reader knows how Louisiana reacted to the confiscation, and has a sense of how this issue has been addressed on a state and federal level. Before the next

---

44. 42 U.S.C.A. §5207(a)(1)–(5) (2006).

45. *See* Hendricks, *supra* note 10; *Rights Restored* (June 15, 2006), http://www.NRAILA.org//News/Read/NewsReleases.aspx?ID=9550.

46. La. Rev. Stat. Ann. §29:738 (2007).

47. *See* Fla. Stat. §252.36(2)(h) (2007) (Florida law expressly barring the confiscation or seizure of lawfully possessed firearms, unless the person is engaged in criminal act); Ky. Rev. Stat. Ann. §39A.100(c) (2007) (Kentucky law excluding firearms and ammunition from list of property that can be seized or condemned by the governor); Mich. Comp. Laws §10.31(3) (2007) (Michigan law barring state and local officials from seizing lawfully possessed firearms).

48. Although several states and the federal government have explicitly precluded the confiscation of firearms from law-abiding citizens during crises, there remains a real and serious potential for executive abuses by law enforcement. As recently as March, 2009, the D.C. police department instituted a program in which officers summarily engage in consent-based searches of homes in pursuit of illegal firearms. *See* Allison Klein, *D.C. Seeks Consent To Search for Guns: Amnesty Offered for Access to Homes*, Washington Post, Mar. 13, 2008, at B01. Although the district's program is starkly distinguishable from New Orleans's forcible confiscation policy, the recent program reminds the American people of the potential for law enforcement conduct that tests the limits of the U.S. Constitution. *See* United States v. Rivas, 99 F.3d 170 (5th Cir. 2004) (holding that the defendant's statement, "You've got the badge, I guess you can," did not constitute valid consent).

section of background, which is a generic discussion of the Second Amendment, a transition showing the relationship between the New Orleans-specific material included in Part I and the generic Second Amendment material in Part II would help guide the reader. As written, this shift is somewhat abrupt.

II. The Second Amendment Guarantees a Fundamental, Individual Right of the People to "Keep and Bear Arms."

The Second Amendment states: "A well regulated militia, being necessary for the security of a free state, the right of the people to keep and bear Arms shall not be infringed."[49] There is serious dispute as to the appropriate interpretation of this constitutional guarantee. The current debate over the Second Amendment is largely characterized by two disparate camps: the individualists and the collective rights theorists.[50] Under the individualist approach, the Second Amendment confers a right on individuals to keep and bear arms.[51] The collective rights approach dictates that the amendment merely protects the states' right to regulate and arm their militias.[52] This Note espouses and is premised upon an individualist approach to the Second Amendment. This conclusion is based upon a textual interpretation of the Second Amendment, the history underlying the ratification of the amendment, and the original intent of the framers, particularly James Madison. The Supreme Court's recent decision in *District of Columbia v. Heller*[53] supports this conclusion and may signal the death knell of the collective rights approach to the Second Amendment.

---

49. U.S. Const. amend 2.

50. *See* William C. Plouffe, Jr., *A Federal Court Holds the Second Amendment Is an Individual Right: Jeffersonian Utopia or Apocalypse Now?*, 30 U. Mem. L. Rev. 55, 103 (1999) (asserting that the Second Amendment confers an individual and fundamental right on the people). *But see* Kenneth Lasson, *Blunderbuss Scholarship: Perverting the Original Intent and Plain Meaning of the Second Amendment*, 32 U. Balt. L. Rev. 127, 130 (2003) (criticizing the individualist interpretation of the amendment and writing that the Second Amendment confers a collective right that may only be invoked by the states). It should be noted that a third camp, the sophisticated collective rights theorists, also exists, but is virtually in line with those who subscribe to the collective rights theory. *See* United States v. Emerson, 270 F.3d 203, 219 (5th Cir. 2001) (noting that the sophisticated collective rights theorists recognize an individual right to keep and bear arms, but only when one is a member and engaged in militia service).

51. *See* Roger Roots, *The Approaching Death of the Collective Right Theory of the Second Amendment*, 39 Duq. L. Rev. 71, 71–72 (2000) (comparing and contrasting the distinct individualist and collective rights models for interpreting the amendment).

52. *See* Lasson, *supra* note 50, at 131 (highlighting the belief that the framers were primarily concerned with providing states with sufficient control over the militia).

53. District of Columbia v. Heller, No. 07-290, slip op. (U.S. June 26, 2008).

*Here, Jordan acknowledges an existing debate over how to interpret the Second Amendment. This background material is essential to his paper because he wants the reader to understand the legal environment surrounding the Second Amendment. The topic sentence here is a quote of the constitutional language at issue. As discussed in **Chapter 7**, using a quotation as the opening sentence to a paragraph can be confusing to the reader because the reader may not understand the purpose of the paragraph. Quoting the constitutional language, however, was the right choice for presenting the Second Amendment because it is the actual language at issue. Here, switching the first and second sentences would create a more effective paragraph because this paragraph is not really about what the Second Amendment states; it is about the debate over the interpretation of this language. Finally, acknowledging the debate shows that Jordan is aware of the opposing view, which could be used as a counterargument to his position.*

In the most recent decision from the Court's 2007 term, the High Court explicitly ruled that the Second Amendment protects an *individual* right to keep and bear arms.[54] *Heller* involved an individual challenge to the District of Columbia's virtual prohibition on handgun possession in the home, among other firearm restrictions.[55] Relying on a textual and historical interpretation of the amendment, the Supreme Court declared that the District's prohibition of handgun possession in one's home contravened the Second Amendment's protection of law-abiding citizens' right to keep and bear arms.[56] The Court announced, in no uncertain terms,

> [t]he handgun ban amounts to a prohibition of an entire class of 'arms' that is overwhelmingly chosen by American society for [self-defense]. The prohibition extends, moreover, to the home, where the need for defense of self, family, and property is most acute. Under any standards of scrutiny that we have applied to enumerated constitutional rights, banning from the home 'the most preferred firearm in the nation to 'keep' and use for protection of one's home and family,' would fail constitutional muster.[57]

Here, Jordan is able to use a recent Supreme Court decision to show additional support for his choice to take the individualist approach. This certainly adds credence to his position, showing that this is not a personal interpretation, but some-

---

54. Heller, slip op. at 19.
55. *Id.*, slip op. at 1.
56. *Id.*, slip op. at 56–57.
57. *Id.*

*thing supported by the highest court in the United States. This paragraph and quotation from the case were added after Jordan completed his note, as he updated it before seeking outside publication. Refer to **Chapter 8** for a discussion of how to update your final paper before submitting it for publication. Also, notice how Jordan avoided any hint of preemption by the Court's ruling by incorporating the decision into his argument. That approach is similar to Natalie's use of an Epilogue after the Court granted certiorari on the case at issue in her paper. Had the Court's analysis supported the collective rights approach instead, Jordan would have had to distinguish the analysis in a way that allowed his position to stand.*

A. The Rights of Englishmen Help to Elucidate the Meaning of the Second Amendment.

The framers drafted the Second Amendment in the context of a longstanding English tradition of possessing arms. Dating back to 1181, Englishmen not only had a right, but a duty to protect the state.[58] The Assize of Arms of 1181 required all free men to privately possess arms and to participate in law enforcement and military defense.[59]

The armed citizenry was challenged by Charles II who, in 1662, passed a militia bill that sought to deprive commoners of all firearms.[60] Continuing this assault on universal possession of firearms, James II increased the size of the standing army and disarmed Protestants.[61] The actions undertaken by the Stuart monarchs to disarm the population ultimately culminated in the Glorious Revolution of 1688.[62] The peaceful installation of William and Mary helped to usher in a declaration of rights, often referred to as the English Bill of Rights, which included the precursor to the Second Amendment: "That the subjects which are Protestants may have Arms for their Defence [sic] suitable to their Condition, and as are allowed by Law."[63] Although the English Bill of

---

58. *See* STEPHEN P. HALBROOK, THAT EVERY MAN BE ARMED: THE EVOLUTION OF A CONSTITUTIONAL RIGHT 38 (Univ. of New Mexico Press) (1984).

59. Robert J. Cottrol & Raymond T. Diamond, *Public Safety and the Right to Bear Arms*, at 3 (2007). Free men were expected to pursue criminal suspects, as well as assist in military defense. *See id.* at 4. The concept of an armed citizenry continued even under the absolutism of King Henry VIII, who required that "every man ... do use and exercise shooting in long-bows, and also to have a bow and shooting...." Halbrook, *supra* note 58, at 41 (quoting An Act Concerning Shooting in Long Bowes, 3 Hen. VIII c. 3 (1511)).

60. *See* HALBROOK, *supra* note 53, at 43.

61. *See id.*

62. *See id.*

63. *Id.* at 45. (quoting An Act Declaring the Rights and Liberties of the Subject, 1 W. & M., Sess. 2, c.2 (1689)).

Rights specifically conferred the right to have arms on *Protestants*, the right was viewed as fundamental in English and colonial society.[64]

The concept of an armed citizenry similarly characterized colonial America.[65] Colonial laws required all free men to participate in regular military training with their *own* arms.[66] Under colonial militia laws, all able-bodied free white men between the ages of 16 and 60 were members of the militia.[67] King George III questioned the colonists' commitment to the right to keep and bear arms when he undertook efforts to disarm the colonists.[68] The colonists ultimately confronted these efforts, as well as other efforts of subjugation, by waging a revolution that was won largely with individually owned arms.[69]

After taking the reader through a brief history of arms possession, Jordan explains why the Second Amendment should be viewed within the context in which it was framed.

B. The Framing of the Second Amendment Should Give Rise to an Individualist Interpretation.

The Second Amendment should be viewed within the context of the overall Bill of Rights. Those, who opposed the original Constitution, were concerned with 1) the protection of individual rights, 2) the fear that the federal government would undermine the militia, and 3) the fear of standing armies in relation to the strength of state militias.[70] Although the federalists, those supporting the original Constitution, did not believe a list of individual guarantees was necessary, they ultimately acceded to the demands of the anti-federalists

---

64. *See* Cottrol & Diamond, *supra* note 54, at 5.

65. Robert H. Churchill, *Gun Regulation, the Police Power, and the Right to Keep Arms in Early America: The Legal Context of the Second Amendment*, 25 LAW & HIST. REV. 139, 141–42 (2007)

66. *See id.* ("keeping" arms was incumbent upon every individual).

67. *See id.* at 145.

68. *See* Plouffe, *supra* note 50, at 70 (noting that the English monarch banned all imports of arms and ammunition into the colonies).

69. *See id.* at 71.

70. *See* United States v. Emerson, 270 F.3d 203, 237–39 (5th Cir. 2001) (referring to the history underlying the Second Amendment in interpreting the amendment). State conventions proposed a series of constitutional amendments, including the affirmation of state authority over the militia, and the right of the people to keep and bear arms, among other proposals. *See id.* at 241–45. The New Hampshire convention specifically recommended the following amendment: "Congress shall never disarm any Citizen unless such as are or have been in Actual Rebellion." JAMES MADISON, THE DEBATES IN THE FEDERAL CONVENTION OF 1787 WHICH FRAMED THE CONSTITUTION OF THE UNITED STATES OF AMERICA 658 (Gaillard Hunt and James Brown Scott ed., Oxford Univ. Press 1920) (1787).

by supporting a Bill of Rights.[71] James Madison, author of the Second Amendment, relied heavily on proposals from state constitutional conventions in writing the amendment.[72] In FEDERALIST NO. 46, Madison lauded the American characteristic of being armed, without mentioning the prerequisite of military service,[73] which helps to underscore his individualist interpretation of the Second Amendment.

Although the amendment went through several drafts,[74] anti-federalists and federalists, including Madison, Hamilton, and Jefferson, all viewed the substantive guarantee as an individual right.[75] Members of the First Congress interpreted Madison's proposed amendment as conferring an individual right.[76] Tench Coxe, one of the preeminent American thinkers and contemporaries of the framers, construed the amendment as guaranteeing the right to keep and bear *private* arms.[77] Madison's implicit support of Coxe's characterization of the Second Amendment further illustrates the widespread belief that the right to keep and bear arms was meant to be private in nature.[78]

In addition to the framers' strong individualist approach to the Second Amendment, subsequent scholarship by some of America's leading legal thinkers, including some contemporaries of the framers, also lends credence to an individualist interpretation. One of the earliest American legal commentaries on the amendment was offered by St. George Tucker, a leading legal scholar, who distinguished the Second Amendment from the gun rights of Englishmen.[79] According to Tucker, unlike the English Bill of Rights, the Second

---

71. *See* Emerson, 270 F.3d at 245.

72. *See* Plouffe, *supra* note 50, at 80 (writing that the most common proposal by state conventions was the right to keep and bear arms).

73. THE FEDERALIST No. 46 (James Madison) ("Besides the advantage of being armed, which the Americans possess over the people of almost every other nation...").

74. *See* HALBROOK, *supra* note 53, at 76–77.

75. *See id.* (referring to Madison's characterization of Bill of Rights provisions as private rights). *See id.* In a letter from Thomas Jefferson to George Washington, Jefferson articulated his love for the possession of arms, further demonstrating the founders' reverence for the individual right to keep and bear arms. *See* THOMAS JEFFERSON, THE WRITINGS OF THOMAS JEFFERSON 341 (Andrew A. Lipscomb ed., The Thomas Jefferson Memorial Ass'n 1904) (2001).

76. *See* HALBROOK, *supra* note 53, at 76–77.

77. *See id.*

78. *See id.* (noting that Madison favorably responded to Coxe's article characterizing the proposed amendment as applying to "private arms"). In response to the article and letter by Coxe, Madison responded by writing that the ratification of the amendment is "indebted to the co-operation of your pen." *Id.* at 77.

79. *See* Randy E. Barnett & Don B. Kates, *Under Fire: The New Consensus on the Second Amendment*, 45 EMORY L.J. 1139, 1219 (1996).

Amendment guaranteed "Americans ... this right 'without any qualifications as to their condition and degree.' "[80] Following the spirit of Tucker, William Rawle, also a leading legal scholar of the nineteenth century, similarly put forth a distinctly individualist interpretation of the amendment.[81] Rawle understood the amendment to protect self defense and hunting, strongly reflecting a view that the amendment extends to individuals and not merely the militia.[82] The legal commentary put forth by such preeminent scholars of the eighteenth century as St. Tucker, Thomas Cooley, and William Rawle offers persuasive bases for finding that the Second Amendment is a right that protects individuals and not simply the militia. The aforementioned commentaries were referenced in *Heller*,[83] which illustrates their significance to an accurate interpretation of the Second Amendment.

In sub-section B, Jordan carefully tracks the history of the right to bear arms, and brings the history up to the present day with the last sentence about how the Supreme Court referenced the same commentaries Jordan provided here as context in support of the Second Amendment as an individual right. Only with this history as background can the reader understand the basis for Jordan's thesis. This section also effectively uses topic sentences and the paragraphing techniques we discussed in **Chapter 7**. *Reading only the topic sentences, the reader can follow the main points of this section. Within each paragraph, the sentences are structured so that each builds on the one that precedes it.*

C. The Text of the Amendment Guarantees a Right of the People.

"A well regulated militia, being necessary for the security of a free state, the right of the people to keep and bear arms shall not be infringed."[84] Much of the debate surrounding the Second Amendment centers on two competing textualist interpretations. The amendment is divided into two phrases: the first

---

80. *Id.* at 1219 (citing St.George Tucker, Blackstone's Commentaries with Notes of Reference to the Constitution and Law of the Federal Government 144 (1803)). Similar to Tucker, Thomas Cooley, another leading American jurist of the nineteenth century, also shed light on the meaning of the Second Amendment. *See* Thomas Cooley, The General Principles of Constitutional Law in the United States of America 298 (Andrew C. McLaughlin ed. 1898). Cooley specifically reasoned that the Second Amendment confers an individual right primarily because the right is general in nature and rejected a reading of the amendment that solely protects the militia. *Id.*

81. *See* Barnett & Kates, *supra* note 77, at 1221.

82. *See id.* (citing William Rawle, A View of the Constitution of the United States of America 122 (2d ed. 1825)).

83. District of Columbia v. Heller, No. 07-290, slip op. at 33–34 (U.S. June 26, 2008).

84. U.S. Const. amend 2.

is a prefatory clause (the amendment's preamble), and the second is the operative clause.[85] According to the collective rights theorists, the operative clause should be construed as being limited by the amendment's preamble.[86] According to the individualists, the interpretation of the amendment should be based primarily on the plain meaning of the operative clause.[87] The debate surrounding the relevant interpretive importance of the two clauses was recently resolved in *Heller*, in which the Court announced that the operative clause of the amendment necessitates an individual right that is unconditioned on military service.[88]

The phrase "the people" appears throughout the United States Constitution,[89] and the notion that the framers intended different meanings for the use of the same word in one document is illogical.[90] The Supreme Court has embraced the view that the phrase "the people" is a term of art, suggesting a uniform definition.[91] The phrase "the people" in the Second Amendment demonstrates that the amendment's constitutional guarantee does not attach to the states, but rather inures to individuals. The assertion that the Second Amendment merely protects a state's right to regulate its militia is fundamentally inconsistent with the structure of the Constitution. As illustrated in *District of Columbia v. Heller*,[92] the Constitution vests people with certain

---

85. *See* U.S. CONST. amend. 2; Parker v. District of Columbia, 478 F.3d 370, 378 (D.C. Cir. 2007) (referring to the textual layout of the Second Amendment), *aff'd*, District of Columbia v. Heller, No. 07-290, slip op. at 64 (U.S. June 26, 2008) (No. 07-290); *see also* Sanford Levinson, *The Embarrassing Second Amendment*, 99 YALE L.J. 637, 644 (1989).

86. *See* Jack N. Rakove, *The Second Amendment: The Highest Stage of Originalism*, 76 CHI.-KENT L. REV. 103, 109–10 (2000).

87. *See* United States v. Emerson, 270 F.3d 203, 233 (5th Cir. 2001).

88. District of Columbia v. Heller, No. 07-290, slip op. at 3, 19 (U.S. June 26, 2008) (holding that the prefatory clause merely states a purpose and concluding that the amendment protects an individual right).

89. *See* U.S. CONST. amend. 1 ("Congress shall make no law ... or abridging ... or the right of the *people* peaceably to assemble....") (emphasis added); U.S. CONST. amend. 4 ("The right of the *people* to be secure....") (emphasis added); U.S. CONST. amend. 9; U.S. CONST. amend. 10.

90. *See* Emerson, 270 F.3d at 227.

91. *See* United States v. Verdugo-Urqidez, 494 U.S. 259, 265 (1990). "The Preamble declares that the Constitution is ordained and established by 'the People of the United States.' The Second Amendment protects 'the right of the people to keep and bear Arms,....'" *Id.* Distinguishing "people" from "militia," the Court cited to *Verdugo-Urqidez* in finding an individual right to keep and bear arms in its recent *Heller* decision. Heller, slip op. at 6–7.

92. District of Columbia v. Heller, No. 07-290, slip op. at 6 (U.S. June 26, 2008) (writing that "[n]owhere else in the Constitution does a 'right' attributed to 'the people' refer to anything other than an individual right"); *see also* Emerson, 270 F.3d at 203.

rights, whereas the states and federal government are granted powers.[93] To find that the Second Amendment amounts to a right held by the states would mark a distinct departure from the Constitution's structural delineation of rights and powers.

Another structural justification for interpreting the Second Amendment as providing for an individual right is the placement of the amendment within the Bill of Rights.[94] James Madison, author of the Second Amendment, declared that the provisions of the Bill of Rights "relate 1st to private rights[,]" and thus, do not alter the structure of government.[95] The broad consensus among members of the First Congress that the Bill of Rights would guarantee personal rights is consistent with Madison's characterization of the amendments and supports the contention that the Second Amendment secures an individual right.[96]

Here, Jordan uses statutory interpretation and the Court's recent decision to support his background position. In the sub-sections that follow, he goes through the text of the Second Amendment phrase by phrase to illustrate how the words of the amendment support his explanation in this background material.

i. A Textual Interpretation of the Phrase "To Keep and Bear Arms" Supports an Individual Interpretation of the Second Amendment.

The phrase "to keep and bear arms" itself connotes an individual right, particularly when the phrase is coupled with the words "the people." Although

---

93. Emerson, 270 F.3d at 228 n.24 (citing constitutional provisions to illustrate the principle that the Constitution does not confer rights on states); Gerard E. Faber, Jr., *Silveira v. Lockyer: The Ninth Circuit Ignores the Relevance and Importance of the Second Amendment in Post-September 11th America*, 21 T.M. COOLEY L. REV. 75, 103 (2004). Similar to the Second Amendment, other provisions within the U.S. Constitution confer rights on the people, while other provisions enumerate powers for the federal government. *See, e.g.*, U.S. CONST. amend. 1; U.S. CONST. art. I, §9. For example, the Constitution guarantees to the people the right of habeas corpus, while providing Congress with the power to regulate interstate commerce. U.S. CONST. art. I, §9, cl. 2; U.S. Const. art. I, §8, cl. 3.

94. *See* Parker v. District of Columbia, 478 F.3d 370, 381 (D.C. Cir. 2007) (noting that the Bill of Rights primarily confers individual rights), *aff'd*, District of Columbia v. Heller, No. 07-290 (U.S. June 26, 2008); RONALD D. ROTUNDA AND JOHN E. NOWAK, TREATISE ON CONSTITUTIONAL LAW §18.39 (3d ed. 1999).

95. *See* Roots, *supra* note 51, at 102 (quoting Madison).

96. *See id.* at 101 (citing Letter from Rep. William L. Smith to Edward Rutledge (Aug. 9, 1789)). Even in the infamous decision in *Dred Scott v. Sanford*, 60 U.S. 393, 417 (1856), the Supreme Court, in dicta, reinforced Madison's characterization by recognizing that the Second Amendment, like other provisions of the Bill of Rights, protects an individual right. The Court reasoned that if Blacks were citizens, they would have the right to possess arms. *Id.*

some scholars have interpreted the words "bear arms" to mean only those weapons carried by one engaged in military service,[97] there is strong evidence that the phrase is not limited to military service.[98] When America declared its independence in 1776, four of the eight independent states explicitly recognized a right to bear arms in their respective state constitutions.[99] The interpretation of the phrase "to bear arms" protected use of weapons both for military service and civilian self defense.[100] In addition, state bills drafted by the framers employed the word "bear" to protect individual hunting rights.[101] Finally, the 1828 edition of Webster's American Dictionary of the English Language similarly defined the word without regard to military service.[102]

Even if the phrase "to bear" is viewed as imposing a military limitation on the use of weapons, the inclusion of the phrase "to keep" in the amendment reinforces the principle that the Second Amendment is not solely restricted to military service. Moreover, the Supreme Court has likely resolved the debate surrounding the meaning of the phrase when it recently concluded that "to keep and bear arms" is not restricted to military use.[103]

---

97. *See* Aymette v. State, 21 Tenn. 154, 156 (1840) (finding that bowtie knife had no military purpose, and thus, was not covered under the state constitutional provision). However, unlike the Tennessee Constitution which, at the time, conditioned the phrase, to keep and bear arms, on the "common defense," the Second Amendment does not contain such a qualification. *See* U.S. CONST. amend. II.

98. *See* United States v. Emerson, 270 F.3d 203, 230 (5th Cir. 2001) (recognizing that early state constitutional provisions gave people the right to keep and bear arms for self defense and the common defense, illustrating that such provisions did not preclude use of weapons outside of military service).

99. STEPHEN P. HALBROOK, A RIGHT TO BEAR ARMS: STATE AND FEDERAL BILLS OF RIGHTS AND CONSTITUTIONAL GUARANTEES 21 (Greenwood Press) (1989). Pennsylvania, North Carolina, Vermont, and Massachusetts protected a right to keep and bear arms. *Id.*

100. *See id.* at 22. The declaration of rights of Pennsylvania, North Carolina, Vermont, and Massachusetts did not limit the right to bear arms solely to military service. *See id.* at 21–48; *see also* Ala. CONST. art. 1, § 23 (1819) ("That every citizen has a right to bear arms in defense of himself and the state"); Conn. CONST. art. I, § 17 (1818). The broad interpretation of state constitutional provisions that feature the phrase "to bear arms" reinforces the individualist nature of the Second Amendment.

101. *See* Emerson, 270 F.3d at 231 (citing 2 THE PAPERS OF THOMAS JEFFERSON 443–44 (J.P. Boyd, ed. 1950)).

102. *See id.* ("[t]o wear; to bear as a mark of authority or distinction, as, to bear a sword, a badge, a name; to bear arms in a coat.").

103. District of Columbia v. Heller, No. 07-290, slip op. at 16, 19 (U.S. June 26, 2008); *see also* Muscarello v. United States, 524 U.S. 125, 141 (1998) (Ginsburg, J., dissenting) (defining "carrying" by citing the Second Amendment and highlighting the phrase "to keep and bear arms").

ii. The Second Amendment's "Well Regulated Militia" Clause Does Not Eviscerate the Operative Clause.

The preamble of the Second Amendment should be read as consistent with the substantive guarantee contained in the operative clause. However, proponents of the collective rights theory insist that the "well regulated militia" language severely limits the scope of the substantive guarantee.[104] In the second most recent ruling by the Supreme Court on the Second Amendment,[105] the Court upheld an indictment under the National Firearms Act charging defendants with knowingly transporting a double barrel shotgun having less than eighteen inches in length.[106] Although the Supreme Court's decision in *United States v. Miller*[107] seems to adopt a view that the substantive guarantee must bear some relationship to the prefatory clause of the amendment, the holding does not reject an individualist interpretation of the Second Amendment.[108] Specifically, the Court held:

> In the absence of any evidence tending to show that possession or use of a 'shotgun having a barrel of less than eighteen inches in length' at this time has some reasonable relationship to the preservation or efficiency of a well regulated militia, we cannot say that the Second Amendment guarantees the right to keep and bear such instrument. Certainly it is not within judicial notice that this weapon is any part of the ordinary military equipment or that its use could contribute to the common defense.[109]

Thus, the Court adopted a test that focuses on the relationship between a regulated firearm and the overall preservation or efficiency of a well regulated militia.[110] If the regulated firearm is part of the ordinary military equipment

---

104. *See* Lasson, *supra* note 50, at 134 (writing that "militia" encompasses the collective body of the people, and does not cover individuals).

105. The most recent Supreme Court decision on the Second Amendment was announced on June 26, 2008, in which the high court declared that the amendment guarantees and individual right and struck down the District of Columbia's virtual prohibition on handguns in the home. *See* District of Columbia v. Heller, No. 07-290, slip op. (U.S. June 26, 2008), *aff'g* Parker v. District of Columbia, 478 F.3d 370 (D.C. Cir. 2007).

106. *See* United States v. Miller, 307 U.S. 174, 175, 178 (1939).

107. United States v. Miller, 307 U.S. 174 (1939).

108. *See* Miller, 307 U.S. at 178.

109. *Id.*

110. *Id.* This construction of *Miller* is consistent with the Supreme Court's decision in *District of Columbia v. Heller*, No. 07-290, slip op. at 49–50 (U.S. June 26, 2008).

or contributes to the common defense, the firearm falls within the protection guaranteed by the Second Amendment.[111]

Although federal and state courts have misrepresented the holding of *Miller*, the Court's central holding represents a test that does not eviscerate an individual right to keep and bear arms.[112] The notion that a relationship between a certain kind of shotgun and the preservation or efficiency of a well regulated militia is not within judicial notice does not diminish the merits of the individualist approach to the Second Amendment. In fact, in *Heller*, the Supreme Court construed the holding in *Miller* as consistent with an individual right, determining that law-abiding individuals have the right to possess arms that "have some reasonable relationship to the preservation or efficiency of a well regulated militia."[113] Had the defendants in *Miller* actually proffered some evidence to demonstrate a reasonable relationship between the firearm and its suitability for military use, the ruling may have come out differently, perhaps resulting in an invalidation of the federal statute and more easily laying the foundation for an individualist interpretation of the Second Amendment.[114]

You can see how the sub-sections of the Background section build on each other. Jordan takes the reader through the thought process that led him to develop a thesis about the Second Amendment and individual rights. After carefully establishing the relationship between the Second Amendment and the Bill of Rights, Jordan next explains how the Second Amendment is a fundamental right, another key part of the background supporting his proposed solution.

---

111. *Id.*

112. Despite the tendency of most state and federal courts to narrowly interpret the Second Amendment as merely conferring a right on the states, state courts, similar to the Supreme Court and recent federal appellate courts in the Fifth Circuit and D.C. Circuit, have employed an individualist interpretation of the amendment. *See* State v. Williams, 148 P.3d 993, 998 (Wash. 2006); Rohrbaugh v. State, 607 S.E.2d 404, 412 (W. Va. 2004); Hilberg v. F.W. Woolworth Co., 761 P.2d 236, 240 (Colo. Ct. App. 1988); State v. Nickerson, 247 P.2d 188, 192 (Mont. 1952).

113. District of Columbia v. Heller, No. 07-290, slip op. at 50 (U.S. June 26, 2008).

114. *See* HALBROOK, *supra* note 53, at 165; *see also* District of Columbia v. Heller, No. 07-290, slip op. at 51 (U.S. June 26, 2008) (emphasizing that the respondent, in *Miller*, did not appear before the Court). The judiciary's increasing recognition of an individual right to keep and bear arms has ultimately culminated in the Supreme Court's most recent decision from the 2007 term, in which the Court declared that the Second Amendment guarantees an individual right that is not conditioned on military service. District of Columbia v. Heller, No. 07-290, slip op. at 22 (U.S. June 26, 2008).

D. The Second Amendment Is a Fundamental Right which the States May Not Infringe.

As was the case with other provisions of the Bill of Rights, many federal and state courts did not find that the Second Amendment applied to the states during the nineteenth century.[115] However, with the passage of the Fourteenth Amendment,[116] the Bill of Rights became binding on the states.[117] Recognizing the Supreme Court's early unwillingness to apply the Bill of Rights to the states,[118] Congressman John Bingham proposed an amendment, which ultimately culminated in the adoption of the Fourteenth Amendment, that pro-

---

115. *See* Presser v. Illinois, 116 U.S. 252, 265 (1886) (concluding that the Second Amendment is a restriction on the national government, but does not bind the states); United States v. Cruikshank, 92 U.S. 542, 552 (1875) (holding that the Second Amendment, *like the other provisions of the Bill of Rights*, is not a restriction against the states) (emphasis added). Even before the inception of the incorporation doctrine, at least one state supreme court found that the Second Amendment was broad enough to apply to the states. *See* Nunn v. State, 1 Ga. 243, 251 (Ga. 1846). "The language of the *second* amendment is broad enough to embrace both Federal and State governments...." *Id.* (emphasis in original).

116. U.S. CONST. amend. XIV.

117. Congressman John Bingham, who ultimately wrote the Fourteenth Amendment, clearly and cogently supported the doctrine of full incorporation in which all of the provisions of the Bill of Rights became binding on the states. *See* MICHAEL KENT CURTIS, NO STATE SHALL ABRIDGE: THE FOURTEENTH AMENDMENT AND THE BILL OF RIGHTS 61 (Duke Univ. Press, 1986) (1986). Bingham's constitutional theory was that the privileges or immunities of citizens of the United States, which include the provisions in the Bill of Rights, may not be infringed upon by the states. *See id.* at 61; *see also* ROTUNDA & NOWAK, *supra* note 92, at § 18.39-40 (writing that most of the provisions of the Bill of Rights have been declared fundamental, and thus, have been incorporated as binding on the states).

It is important to recognize that the Supreme Court did not directly address the issue of incorporation in *District of Columbia v. Heller*, No. 07-290, slip op. (U.S. June 26, 2008) and, thus, litigation will almost assuredly ensue to determine whether the individual guarantee of the right to keep and bear arms is a restriction against the states. Although the question of incorporation of the Second Amendment has not been resolved by the Court, Justice Scalia may have hinted at the Court's willingness to incorporate in the future by citing the right to keep and bear arms as a driving force behind the ratification of the Fourteenth Amendment. *See Heller*, slip op. at 43–44. On June 27, 2008, the NRA filed lawsuits challenging city handgun bans in San Francisco, Chicago, and nearby Chicago suburbs. *NRA Files Second Amendment Lawsuits in Illinois and California Following Supreme Court Ruling*, June 27, 2008, http://www.nraila.org/Legislation/Federal/Read.aspx?id=4053.

118. *See, e.g.*, Barron v. Baltimore, 32 U.S. 243, 250–51 (1833) (holding that the Fifth Amendment is not binding on the states).

scribed state infringement on the privileges or immunities of U.S. citizens.[119] Bingham's intent, which paralleled that of many other supporters of the amendment,[120] demonstrates that the privileges or immunities clause of the amendment should be interpreted as prohibiting state abridgement of constitutional provisions contained in the Bill of Rights.[121] If the people's right to keep and bear arms is a privilege of U.S. citizenship, it should be protected from infringement by both the state and federal governments.

Even if one rejects the merits of full incorporation—that is, that each provision of the Bill of Rights applies to both the states and the federal government—there is nevertheless strong support for classifying the right preserved in the Second Amendment as a fundamental right. The U.S. Supreme Court has devised three evolving methods for determining whether a right is fundamental.[122] These tests include 1) the natural rights test, 2) the American scheme of justice test, and 3) the penumbra of the Bill of Rights test.[123]

Note how counterarguments can be addressed in a background section. Here, Jordan recognizes that his reader might not agree with full incorporation, and then provides an explanation of how the right is at least a fundamental right. This is another basis on which Jordan can justify his proposed solution.

Under the first test, the natural rights test, certain natural rights have been deemed fundamental, including the right to property.[124] Under the natural rights test, the right to keep and bear arms should be considered a fundamental right. Sir William Blackstone identified three universal, natural rights that inure to individuals: personal security, personal liberty, and private property.[125] That Blackstone heralded the right of having arms as an auxiliary right necessary

---

119. *See* U.S. CONST. amend. XIV, § 1; CURTIS, *supra* note 118, at 69. For those, who opposed the Fourteenth Amendment, the principal attack on Bingham's proposal was that the amendment was not necessary to make the Bill of Rights binding on the states. *See id.* at 69.

120. CURTIS, *supra* note 118 at 62.

121. *See id.* at 91. Representative Bingham and Senator Howard, who managed the amendment in the Joint Committee in the Senate, stated that the amendment would require states to obey the Bill of Rights. *Id.* No member of Congress contradicted them. *Id.* One of the most ardent supporters of the proposed amendment was Representative Thaddeus Stevens, who similarly viewed the amendment as incorporating the Bill of Rights to the states. *See id.* at 86.

122. *See* Plouffe, *supra* note 50, at 95–98. *Id.*

123. *See id.*

124. *See* Calder v. Bull, 3 U.S. 386, 394 (1798); Plouffe, *supra* note 50, at 96.

125. SIR WILLIAM BLACKSTONE, COMMENTARIES ON THE LAWS OF ENGLAND 144 (Garland Publishing, Inc. 1978).

for security, liberty, and property,[126] strongly supports the view that the Second Amendment is a fundamental, natural right.

Under the second test announced by the Court, the American scheme of justice test, a right is fundamental if it is based on "fundamental principles of liberty and justice which lie at the base of all our civil and political institutions"[127] and if it is "basic in our system of jurisprudence."[128] Under this test, the right to keep and bear arms should also qualify as a fundamental, individual right. Specifically, Justice Joseph Story wrote: "The right of the citizens to keep and bear arms has justly been considered, *as the palladium of the liberties of a republic....*"[129] There is perhaps no more succinct classification of the Second Amendment as a fundamental right than this declaration by the former Supreme Court Justice. This illustrative characterization of the Second Amendment helps to resolve any dispute as to whether the right to keep and bear arms is fundamental to American liberty and the nation's scheme of justice.[130]

Finally, under the third test of fundamental rights, a right is fundamental if it is within the penumbra of rights inherent in the Bill of Rights.[131] In *Griswold v. Connecticut,* the Court declared that the penumbra of Bill of Rights includes those rights which give "life and substance" to the enumerated rights.[132] Given Blackstone's classification of the right to have arms as an auxiliary right necessary to the realization of natural rights, and the fact that the Second Amendment is an explicit guarantee contained in the Bill of Rights, the right to keep and bear arms most definitely gives "life and substance" to the enumerated rights in the Constitution.

---

126. *See id.*

127. Duncan v. Louisiana, 391 U.S. 145, 148 (quoting Powell v. Alabama, 287 U.S. 45, 67 (1932)).

128. *Id.* at 149 (quoting In re Oliver, 333 U.S. 257, 273 (1948)).

129. JOSEPH STORY, COMMENTARIES ON THE CONSTITUTION OF THE UNITED STATES; WITH A PRELIMINARY REVIEW OF THE CONSTITUTIONAL HISTORY OF THE COLONIES AND STATES, BEFORE THE ADOPTION OF THE CONSTITUTION 746 (Hilliard, Gray, and Co. 1833) (emphasis added).

130. It is worth noting that the right to keep and bear arms was essential to the colonists' gaining independence from Britain. *See* supra Part II.A (discussing the role of private arms in the War for Independence).

131. *See* Griswold v. Connecticut, 381 U.S. 479, 484–85 (1965).

132. *Id.*

III. The Traditional Standard of Judicial Review of Executive
    Emergency Power.

*In this final background section, Jordan focuses on the standard of judicial review.
Notice how there is no text between the heading for III and the first sub-heading
for A. Instead of two headings in a row, an introductory paragraph here (between
III and A) to connect the background material in Part II would have been an effective guide for the reader.*

    A. Judicial Review of Federal Emergency Power.

The judicial standard of review of federal executive emergency powers exercised during times of crisis has traditionally been extremely deferential to
the executive, particularly on the question of reasonableness of emergency
powers.[133] Currently, a court assesses both the process and reasonableness of
an executive decision exercised during an emergency when evaluating its constitutionality.[134] Under the process prong of this test, the sole question is
whether the executive has emergency powers, as manifested in the form of legislation enacted by the legislature and signed into law by the executive.[135] Under
the reasonableness prong, a court assesses whether there is a factual basis for
using emergency power and whether the promulgated policy or statute is
related to protecting the interest of society.[136]

*This paragraph suggests that the following subsections will be organized by prong,
but instead they are organized by time/event. This paragraph could be
strengthened if it communicated more about the planned organization to the
reader.*

    i. Judicial deference during World War II.[137]

Judicial review of executive actions exercised during World War II was highly
deferential and represented a commitment to the traditional process-reason-

---

133. *See* Cook, *supra* note 5, at 270.
134. *See* Korematsu v. United States, 323 U.S. 214, 223–34 (1944); Cook, *supra* note 5,
at 281.
135. *See* Korematsu, 323 U.S. at 223–34; Cook, *supra* note 5, at 281.
136. *See* Cook, *supra* note 5, at 281.
137. The highly deferential posture taken by the federal judiciary in assessing challenges
to federal emergency powers that implicate individual rights was not limited to the period
of World War II. Specifically, during the Red Scare and McCarthy eras—arguably states of
exigency—the Supreme Court upheld federal statutes implicating fundamental First Amendment rights by articulating the clear and present danger doctrine. *See, e.g.,* Dennis v. United
States, 341 U.S. 494 (1951); Schenck v. United States, 249 U.S. 49 (1919).

ableness test. In *Ex Parte Quirin*,[138] the Supreme Court upheld the presidential creation of military tribunals for individuals, including at least one U.S. citizen, largely based upon the process prong.[139] The Court focused on Congress's authorization for the use of military tribunals rather than the individual rights of a U.S. citizen. The Court wrote, "[b]y the Articles of War, Congress has explicitly provided, so far as it may constitutionally do so, that military tribunals shall have jurisdiction to try offenders ... against the law of war...."[140]

The Court's decision in *Korematsu v. United States* similarly illustrates this deferential standard of review.[141] The Court upheld the executive's internment of Japanese Americans largely because Congress implicitly authorized the executive action and there was evidence of disloyalty on the part of some Americans.[142] The Court's focus on congressional ratification of the President's initial executive order manifested a commitment to the process prong of the test. Further, the attention to evidence of possible disloyalty on the part of Japanese-Americans reflected the Court's commitment to the reasonableness prong of the test.

ii. Judicial deference during the War on Terror?

Although some of the Supreme Court's decisions during the War on Terror have departed from the tradition of judicial deference by striking down executive actions, such as President George W. Bush's unilateral creation of a military commission system,[143] the Court's jurisprudence during this unconventional war still recognizes the primacy of process—that is, the authorization of executive action by Congress. In *Hamdi v. Rumsfeld*,[144] the Court upheld

---

138. Ex Parte Quirin, 317 U.S. 1 (1942).

139. *Id.* at 27

140. *Id.* The Court specifically determined that U.S. citizenship does not render one immune from military detention and trial. *Id.*

141. *See* Korematsu v. United States, 323 U.S. 214 (1944). During World War II, President Roosevelt promulgated Executive Order No. 9066, which declared that "the successful prosecution of the war requires every possible protection against espionage and against sabotage...." *Id.* at 217. After Congress ratified the President's executive order, President Roosevelt promulgated Exclusion Order No. 34, thereby mandating the exclusion of individuals of Japanese ancestry from the West Coast war area. *Id.* at 218.

142. *See id.* at 223–34. Interestingly, the Court did recognize that forcible exclusion and internment are far greater deprivations than is a government-imposed curfew, which was upheld in *Hirabayashi v. United States*, 320 U.S. 81, 104–05 (1943). *See* Korematsu, 323 U.S. at 218.

143. *See* Hamdan v. Rumsfeld, 126 S. Ct. 2749, 2808 (2006).

144. Hamdi v. Rumsfeld, 542 U.S. 507 (2004).

the military detention of a U.S. citizen captured in Afghanistan, largely based upon congressional authorization.[145] However, the Court determined that due process afforded Hamdi the opportunity to challenge his classification as an unlawful enemy combatant before an impartial decisionmaker.[146] Despite the imposition of certain procedural checks on the executive, the Court's decision did not meaningfully address the question of individual rights.[147]

The tendency of the judiciary to focus on process rather than individual rights was also manifested in the Court's decision in *Rumsfeld v. Padilla*,[148] where the Court reversed the Second Circuit's invalidation of military detention of a U.S. citizen.[149] *Padilla* involved a U.S. citizen captured on American soil and subsequently deemed an unlawful enemy combatant by President Bush.[150] That the Court chose to reverse the Second Circuit,[151] which struck down the detention of Jose Padilla, based upon jurisdictional grounds indicates the Court's continued deference to the political branches and overall preference for process over individual rights.

With some background on these cases, the reader can see how the Court has used the process and reasonableness prongs in deciding cases of federal acts.

---

145. *See id.* at 507.

146. *See id.* at 519.

147. *See id.* at 554 (Scalia, J., dissenting) ("The very core of liberty secured by our Anglo-Saxon system of separated powers has been freedom from indefinite imprisonment at the will of the Executive."); *see also* Hamdan, 126 S. Ct. at 2808 (striking down the President's military tribunals based upon separation of powers principles). Whereas *Hamdi* involved specific constitutional questions about individual due process requirements, *Hamdan* was silent on individual constitutional guarantees. The standard proposed in this Note is triggered when individual rights are implicated.

148. Rumsfeld v. Padilla, 542 U.S. 426 (2004).

149. *Id.* Dissenting from the Court's reversal on jurisdictional grounds, Justice Stevens concluded that jurisdiction was supported by established habeas exceptions. *Id.* at 460 (Stevens, J., dissenting).

150. Padilla v. Rumsfeld, 352 F.3d 695, 700, 716 (2d Cir. 2003).

151. *Id.* Although the Second Circuit's decision constituted a check on the executive during the current war on terrorism, similar to *Hamdan*, the decision focused primarily on separation of powers principles and not individual constitutional guarantees. *See id.* The Fourth Circuit's decision in *Padilla v. Hanft*, 423 F.3d 386 (4th Cir. 2005) is another illustration of judicial deference to the executive. Focusing on the process prong of the traditional test, the Court upheld the detention of Padilla by finding congressional authorization in the form of the Authorization for the Use of Military Force, Pub. L. No. 107-40. *Id.* at 391.

B. Judicial Review of State Executive Action During Crisis.

Similar to the judiciary's approach to federal executive actions exercised during emergencies, courts have also afforded great deference to the executive and legislative branches of the states. Under the Robert T. Stafford Disaster Relief and Emergency Assistance Act,[152] states and local governments have the primary responsibility to manage crises.[153] Under many state constitutions and statutes, the governor has broad emergency powers, including authority to declare a state of emergency.[154] However, these same constitutions and statutes often condition executive branch emergency powers upon legislative authorization.[155] Thus, in assessing state executive police power, courts continue to focus on 1) process: whether an executive has the authority to declare an emergency or to make a particular emergency decision and 2) reasonableness: whether the decision was reasonable.[156]

In *Home Building & Loan Ass'n v. Blaisdell*,[157] the U.S. Supreme Court demonstrated its commitment to this deferential standard by upholding a state statute ordering the postponement of foreclosures on mortgagees, who were unable to make payments as a result of the Depression.[158] Because the policy was enacted in the form of a statute rather than an executive proclamation, the Court was able to dismiss any challenge based upon process because the legislature authorized the executive's action.[159] Further, the Court found that the reasonableness prong of the test had been satisfied because there was an undisputed state of economic emergency.[160]

---

152. 42 U.S.C. § 5121 (2006).

153. *See* 42 U.S.C. § 5121 (2006); Jim Rossi, *State Executive Lawmaking in Crisis*, 56 DUKE L.J. 237, 241 (2006) (noting that the Stafford Act, which authorizes the President to declare emergencies, views federal resources as supplementing state resources).

154. *See* Rossi, *supra* note 154, at 242 (referring to Louisiana's constitution, which vests great emergency power in the governor). *See* LA. CONST. art. IV, § 5; *see also* LA. REV. STAT. ANN. § 29:724 (2006).

155. *See* Rossi, *supra* note 154, at 241.

156. *See, e.g.*, Home Bldg. & Loan Ass'n v. Blaisdell, 290 U.S. 398, 444–48 (1934); Cook, *supra* note 5, at 281.

157. Home Bldg. & Loan Ass'n v. Blaisdell, 290 U.S. 398 (1934).

158. *Id.* at 439–40 (1934). The Court found that an emergency existed and the legislation was aimed at protecting the interest of society, and thus, held that the state law did not violate the contract clause, due process clause, or equal protection clause of the U.S. Constitution. *Id.* at 444–48.

159. Cook, *supra* note 5, at 281 (citing Blaisdell, 290 U.S. at 398 (1934)).

160. *See* Blaisdell, 290 U.S. at 444. "An emergency existed in Minnesota which furnished a proper occasion for the exercise of the reserved power of the state to protect the vital interests of the community." *Id.* Further, as highlighted by Michael Cook, the Court also

C. Judicial Review of State Executive Emergency Powers Exercised During Natural Disasters Continues to Follow the Traditional and Deferential Process-Reasonableness Test.

Consistent with the tradition of judicial deference during emergencies, the judiciary has routinely upheld state executive actions in the wake of natural disasters based on the process-reasonableness test.[161] Judicial review of state executive action during Hurricane Andrew underscores this principle.[162] Prior to Andrew's making landfall, the Governor of Florida declared a state of emergency in portions of the state and authorized local officials to impose curfews.[163] Joaquin Avino, Dade County Manager, imposed a citywide curfew pursuant to the governor's order.[164] Residents of the county filed suit in federal court, claiming that the curfew violated their rights under the U.S. Constitution.[165] The Court determined that Avino, even though acting consistent with the governor's authorization, had independent authority based upon Florida law that provided local officials with power to impose curfews.[166] Because the manager acted according to state law, representing the agreement between the executive and legislative branches, the action satisfied the process prong of the emergency powers test.[167] In assessing the reasonableness of the curfew,

---

focused on the underlying motivation of the legislators and governor and ultimately concluded that these individuals did not act with bad-faith or pretext. *See* Cook, *supra* note 5, at 282. This may suggest that courts, in assessing reasonableness, should determine whether the use of emergency power was based on pretext or legitimate, good-faith reasons.

161. Although natural disasters and terrorist attacks are equally atrocious, there is a palpable distinction between the two contexts. The proposal for heightened judicial review of executive actions undertaken during emergencies is limited to state executive action. The more far-reaching question of whether this same standard should apply to federal executive actions in the wake of a terrorist attack is not resolved in this Note.

This is an example of a limiting footnote. Jordan has recognized an issue, or a question that may come to a reader's mind, and has put the issue outside the scope of his Note.

162. For another example of judicial deference in the wake of natural disasters, see *Moorhead v. Farrelly*, 727 F. Supp. 1109 (D.V.I. 1989). On September 17–18, 1989, Hurricane Hugo made landfall on the Virgin Islands, causing severe damage to St. Croix. *Id.* at 1110. After declaring a state of emergency, Governor Farrelly instituted the nocturnal curfew. *Id.* at 1113 (upholding the constitutionality of a nocturnal curfew between the hours of 6 p.m. and 6 a.m. by Governor Alexander Farrelly in the aftermath of Hurricane Hugo).

163. Smith v. Avino, 866 F. Supp. 1399, 1401 (S.D. Fla. 1994).

164. *Id.* at 1402.

165. *Id.*

166. *Id.* at 1403.

167. *See* Cook, *supra* note 5, at 284–85 (referring to *Avino*, 866 F. Supp. at 1403).

the district court and court of appeals focused on two factors: 1) whether the executive acted in good faith, and 2) whether there was a rational basis for determining that the curfew was necessary to maintain order.[168] The sole issue of dispute was whether the curfew was unreasonable, as the curfew made no exceptions for necessary activities.[169] Relying on *Korematsu*, the court of appeals deferred to the state political branches and held that the curfew was reasonable.[170]

The reader is now fully aware of the background that sets the stage for Jordan's proposal. This final example of the Florida curfew illustrates the need for a better standard because the court deferred to the state political branches, even when there were no exceptions to the curfew. This was an effective place to end the background because it highlights the strong judicial deference in these cases.

IV. A Proposal for Greater Judicial Courage During Crisis.

The lack of text between the heading and sub-heading is a gap. To make sure the reader follows what is happening in this section, an introductory paragraph or two to bring together the sub-parts that follow would present the reader with a cohesive understanding of Jordan's proposal on a large scale. Then the reader could read the sub-sections with the big picture in mind, which can be particularly effective when explaining the parts of your solution. If the reader skips headings or just reads them too quickly, as many readers do, the shift from the last sentence about deference to state political branches in the Korematsu case to the next sentence (under A) about the dismissal of judicial review of executive emergency powers, the reader may be lost as to what has happened in between. Take these opportunities to use introductory paragraphs and substantive transitions to keep the reader on track.

A. Persuasive Criticisms of the Traditional Standard Underscore the Need for a Heightened Level of Judicial Review of Emergency Powers Exercised During Crises.

The dismissal of judicial review of executive emergency powers requires unjustified trust and confidence in the political branches at times when excessive

---

168. Smith v. Avino, 91 F.3d 105, 109 (11th Cir. 1996), *rev'd on other grounds*, Steel Co. v. Citizens for a Better Env't, 523 U.S. 83 (1998).

169. *Avino*, 91 F.3d at 109; *Avino*, 866 F. Supp. at 1405. The plaintiffs did not challenge the motivation of the executive and agreed that the county was in a state of emergency. *Avino*, 91 F.3d at 109.

170. *Avino*, 91 F.3d at 109 (citing Korematsu v. United States, 323 U.S. 214 (1944)).

actions are most likely.[171] Two of the primary justifications for judicial review are 1) the theory of representation reinforcement, whereby any individual has an opportunity to vindicate his legal rights, and 2) the judiciary's role as a protector of those rights.[172] These underlying justifications for judicial review are no less important during emergencies than they are during times of peace.[173] The importance of robust judicial review to protect legal rights and enable individuals to seek legal redress was exemplified by Chief Justice John Marshall when he declared: "The very essence of civil liberty certainly consists in the right of every individual to claim the protection of the laws, whenever he receives an injury."[174] Thus, the judiciary must not stand by idly as individuals bring bona fide claims invoking the Bill of Rights to challenge the exercise of emergency powers that violate constitutional rights. Deemphasizing the role of the judiciary during emergencies will only serve to render an equal branch of government powerless at times when individual rights matter most.

Although some legal scholars embrace the view that the judiciary should play a minimal role—that is, exhibit deference to the political branches—in reviewing executive actions and their impact on individual rights during emergencies,[175] the potential for severe violations of individual constitutional rights warrants more robust scrutiny by the judiciary. Some scholars, who recognize the potential for executive abuses, advocate legislative power rather than judicial power to impose checks on the executive during emergencies.[176] However, this argument is flawed in that the legislative branch may not be able to sufficiently

---

171. *See* David Cole, *Marbury in the Modern Era: Judging the Next Emergency: Judicial Review and Individual Rights in Times of Crisis*, 101 MICH. L. REV. 2565, 2590 (2003) (recognizing the tendency of the political branches to overreact during crises).

172. *See* Judge D. Brooks Smith, *Judicial Review in the United States*, 45 DUQ. L. REV. 379, 386 (2007).

173. *See* Ex Parte Milligan, 71 U.S. 2, 76 (1866); *see also* Skinner v. Ry. Labor Executives' Ass'n, 489 U.S. 602, 635 (1989) (Marshall, J., dissenting) (criticizing the Court's holding that the federal government's mandatory railroad drug testing policy, which subjected employees involved in an accident to urinalysis tests without reasonable suspicion or probable cause, did not violate the Fourth Amendment). Although railroad accidents give rise to exigencies, warrantless and suspicionless drug tests may constitute unjustified infringements on fundamental Fourth Amendment rights. *See id.* Justice Marshall's dissent highlights the principle that individual rights should not be forsaken during exigencies. *See id.*

174. Marbury v. Madison, 5 U.S. 137, 163 (1803) (finding that the law afforded Marbury, whose right had been violated, a remedy deliverable by a trial court).

175. *See* Oren Gross, *Chaos and Rules: Should Responses to Violent Crises Always Be Constitutional?*, 112 YALE L.J. 1011 (2003); Mark Tushnet, *Defending Korematsu? Reflections on Civil Liberties in Wartime*, 2003 WIS. L. REV. 273 (2003).

176. *See* Bruce Ackerman, *The Emergency Constitution*, 113 YALE L.J. 1029 (2004).

check excessive executive power.[177] Although this Note does not purport to charge anyone with distorting the threat to public safety during the disaster of Hurricane Katrina, the confiscation policy was excessive.[178]

Scholars, including Mark Tushnet, for example, reject the need for a robust judiciary during periods of emergency based upon the principle of social learning.[179] Under this principle, although the judiciary endorses executive actions undertaken during an emergency, the nation subsequently comes together to repudiate the action as unjustified by the facts that existed.[180] Even though the American people have ultimately recognized that certain executive actions during times of emergency were unjustified and unconstitutional, such as the exclusion and internment of Japanese-Americans during World War II, this social learning doctrine does not validate unfettered judicial deference to the political branches during an actual emergency. Although the social learning principle has some merit—neither the federal government nor any state government will likely ever repeat President Roosevelt's mistake largely based upon social learning—it merely helps governments to play "catch up" with new situations that arise and fails to recognize the seriousness of government infringement upon individual constitutional rights that occur during emergencies.

The contention that meaningful judicial review of emergency powers is impossible is flawed. American courts have, for example, utilized ordinary constitutional law to adjudicate individual First Amendment challenges to the political branches during the Cold War, a period in which the nation faced deadly threats and an overall precarious future.[181] Further, this criticism undercuts the spirit of *Ex Parte Milligan*,[182] where the Supreme Court invalidated

---

177. *See* Tushnet, *supra* note 176, at 288.

178. *See* text accompanying notes 6–31 (highlighting the distinctively restrictive nature of the city's confiscation of firearms without suspicion or probable cause).

179. *See* Tushnet, *supra* note 176, at 284.

180. *Id.* at 283. Tushnet goes on to justify his social learning principle by referring to the nation's subsequent reaction to President Lincoln's suspension of habeas corpus and the appointment of military tribunals for U.S. citizens, the prosecution of individuals engaged in seditious speech during the Red Scare, the internment of Japanese Americans, and the prosecution of members of the Communist Party during the Cold War. *Id.* at 284–87.

181. *See* Laurence H. Tribe & Patrick O. Gudridge, *The Anti-Emergency Constitution*, 113 YALE L.J. 1801, 1851–52 (2004). Chief Justice Warren wrote: "Implicit in the term 'national defense' is the notion of defending those values ... which set this Nation apart. For almost two centuries, our country has taken singular pride in the democratic ideals enshrined in its *Constitution*, and the most cherished of those ideals have found expression in the First Amendment." *Id.* at 1853–54 (quoting United States v. Robel, 389 U.S. 258, 264 (1967)).

182. Ex Parte Milligan, 71 U.S. 2 (1866).

a military tribunal of a U.S. citizen.[183] Justice Davis pronounced that "the Constitution of the United Stated is a law for rulers and people, equally in war and in peace, and covers with the shield of its protection all classes of men, at all times, and under all circumstances."[184]

The Court's decision in *Milligan* to declare the military tribunal of a U.S. citizen unconstitutional while the civilian courts were open[185] represented judicial courage, the likes of which have not been seen in some time.[186] Although *Milligan* is indicative of the potential for meaningful judicial review of executive actions during crises, an important caveat is that the Court rendered its decision after hostilities during the Civil War had ended.[187] As such, one may interpret the opinion as being more illustrative of judicial courage in the period following an emergency than during an actual emergency. Justice Davis's historic opinion, coupled with the fact that the U.S. Constitution does not contain an emergency provision, eschews the traditional and unyielding deference to state executive actions that interfere with fundamental, individual rights, including the Second Amendment.[188]

Deemphasizing judicial review of executive power and its influence on individual rights runs counter to the spirit of the Constitution. The judiciary

---

183. *Id.* at 82.

184. *Id.* at 76. This emphatic declaration by Justice Davis illustrates the flaws inherent in arguments for extraconstitutional measures. *See* Gross, *supra* note 176, at 1096–1102, for a discussion of the merits of a proposal for extraconstitutional measures during crises. As recently as June 12, 2008, the Supreme Court declared that "[t]he laws and Constitution are designed to survive, and remain in force, in extraordinary times. Liberty and security can be reconciled...." Boumediene v. Bush, No. 06-1195, slip op. at 70 (U.S. June 12, 2008). In *Boumediene*, the Court held that the individual right of habeas corpus applies to foreigners held at Guantanamo Bay, Cuba; territory that is under the *de facto* sovereignty of the United States. *Boumediene*, No. 06-1195, slip op. at 25, 49. Although the decision may reflect a greater judicial willingness to guarantee the sustenance of individual, constitutional rights, it should not be distorted. A significant caveat is that while the United States continues to fight the War on Terror, almost seven years have elapsed since 9/11 and, thus, the country's status would unlikely be characterized as an emergency.

185. *Id.* at 82. The Court held that a U.S. citizen, who is not a citizen of a state at war with the nation, cannot be subject to a military tribunal when the civilian courts are open. *Id.*

186. *See* Part III.A.

187. The Court rendered its decision in 1866, which succeeded the end of the Civil War in 1865. *See* Encyclopedia Britannica, http://wwww.britannica.com.

188. Although the U.S. Constitution does provide Congress with authority to suspend the writ of habeas corpus under certain circumstances, *see* U.S. CONST. art. I §9, the text of the Constitution does not enumerate specific emergency powers that may be utilized by the federal government or state governments.

should serve as a check on the political branches and not rubberstamp infringements of fundamental rights. That an executive action may be taken pursuant to an act of Congress or supported by the American people does not render the action constitutional. Although the courts must continue to assess separation of powers concerns, the analysis must extend beyond process and ultimately determine whether executive action has unduly interfered with a fundamental, individual right. This analysis will require the courts to assess the reasonableness of executive actions within a specific framework—one that rejects inexorable deference to the political branches and embraces independent constitutional adjudication by judges whose mandate it is to protect individual, constitutionally guaranteed rights.

*Although not expressly stated as a response to counterarguments, this first subsection of the Proposed Solution part of the paper recognizes and addresses several counterarguments. This technique works well to build up to a defense of Jordan's solution by illustrating how these opposing positions are erroneous or problematic. Look back to **Chapter 5** for more information about how thinking about counterarguments can strengthen your analysis.*

B. Heightened Scrutiny: A New Framework for Judicial Review of Executive Emergency Powers Exercised During a State of Emergency.

Judicial review of state executive action undertaken during times of crisis should be subject to a heightened standard when such action interferes with individuals' fundamental rights, including those protected by the Second Amendment. Heightened judicial review of state executive actions should apply whether the individual challenge is brought after or *during* an actual exigency, as fundamental rights should not be abrogated *during* exigencies.[189]

In this first paragraph in sub-section B, Jordan has effectively restated his thesis; this is effective because it reminds the reader of Jordan's thesis and provides an introduction to this sub-section where Jordan describes his proposed heightened scrutiny in detail.

---

189. *See* Skinner v. Ry. Labor Executives' Ass'n, 489 U.S. 602, 635 (Marshall, J., dissenting); Milligan, 71 U.S. at 76. Although the test outlined in this Note calls for heightened judicial review of state executive emergency actions whether a challenge is brought after or *during* an actual exigency, it is important to highlight that the burden is on an individual with standing to file suit to challenge an executive's action. Thus, this Note does not propose a requirement that the executive obtain a declaratory judgment from a court prior to implementing an emergency action.

Fundamental rights are generally reviewed under the Supreme Court's strict scrutiny test in which the judiciary adjudicates whether an action was aimed at furthering a compelling government interest and whether the government's action was the least restrictive means to accomplish that objective.[190] Recognizing the practical implications of strict scrutiny judicial review—namely, that state executive actions would likely be invalidated with great frequency,[191] however, courts should instead adopt a heightened standard of review in emergency powers cases that incorporates some of the basic elements of the strict scrutiny test. By incorporating some elements of strict scrutiny and modifying others, this heightened hybrid standard of review more appropriately balances pragmatism and independent judicial oversight during crises.

Specifically, when justifying executive action against an individual claim of constitutional infringement exercised during an emergency, a state government or actor should be required to demonstrate 1) that the entity implementing the action had the authority to act, a process prong, 2) that the executive action was aimed at furthering a compelling government interest, and 3) that the action was considered alongside other means to fulfill the government interest, a reasonableness/strict scrutiny hybrid prong. Although the framework closely resembles the strict scrutiny test, the third prong of the test advocated by this Note is slightly different from narrow tailoring, which is required under strict scrutiny. Unlike narrow tailoring, which requires that a challenged action be absolutely the least restrictive means available to fulfill a compelling government interest, the test outlined above embraces modified narrow tailoring. This new standard merely requires that the government demonstrate that the implemented action was considered alongside other measures and whether such alternatives would have been less restrictive.

---

190. *See* Bridges v. California, 314 U.S. 252 (1941) (First Amendment's freedom to petition government clause); Cantwell v. Connecticut, 310 U.S. 296 (1940) (First Amendment's free exercise clause); De Jonge v. Oregon, 299 U.S. 353 (1937) (First Amendment's freedom of assembly clause); Stromberg v. California, 283 U.S. 359 (1931) (First Amendment's freedom of speech clause); Near v. Minnesota, 283 U.S. 697 (1931) (First Amendment's freedom of press clause).

191. Regulations reviewed under the strict scrutiny test are likely to be invalidated. *See, e.g.*, Shapiro v. Thompson, 394 U.S. 618, 634 (1969); Loving v. Virginia, 388 U.S. 1, 11–12 (1967) (invalidating state law prohibiting interracial marriage under strict scrutiny test); Gerald Gunther, *The Supreme Court, 1971 Term—Foreword: In Search of Evolving Doctrine on a Changing Court: A Model for a Newer Equal Protection*, 86 HARV. L. REV. 1, 8 (1972) (writing that the test is "strict in theory, fatal in fact").

Here, Jordan has identified the standard he proposes, a three-pronged test, and has also made clear that his proposal is not an extreme departure from the existing standard, which may make it more palatable to the reader. This small departure from the existing standard is enough, however, to correct the problems Jordan identified.

Unlike the traditional process-reasonableness test, this new standard is much less deferential to the political branches and provides greater specificity for the courts in adjudicating challenges to executive actions exercised during emergencies. Even though this framework is novel within the context of emergency powers, it still retains the important process prong of the traditional test, which has governed most cases of state executive emergency power during crises. Further, the second and third elements of the heightened standard may be construed as providing specific guidelines for adjudicating reasonableness of state executive actions during emergencies.

Because maintaining order during a state of emergency is a compelling government interest, it is unlikely that executive actors, undertaking actions to ensure public safety, will have great difficulty satisfying the compelling government interest prong of the proposed test. It is the other two prongs, the process and modified narrow tailoring, that will require executives to think more carefully before implementing policies that may impinge upon fundamental constitutional rights, such as the Second Amendment. Specifically, absent state constitutional or statutory authority to act, such as authority to declare a state of emergency, and absent a showing that the executive considered the chosen policy alongside other potentially less restrictive means, the state executive action will likely be invalidated under the proposed test. In assessing modified narrow tailoring, required by the third element of the proposed standard, the availability of less restrictive means for achieving a compelling government interest will be a factor in determining whether the executive has acted constitutionally. The number and restrictive nature of alternatives are factors that will help courts to better assess the reasonableness of executive action exercised during emergencies. The greater the number of less restrictive means available to the executive, the more difficult it will be for the executive to satisfy the third prong of the test. Ultimately, this three prong test will help the courts to more effectively balance fundamental rights with practical flexibility of emergency powers during crises.

And in these two paragraphs, Jordan defends his new standard, explaining how it would avoid the problems he identified in the background of his paper. Then, in the next section, Jordan applies his proposed standard to New Orleans to illustrate how his standard would have created a different result.

C. Application of the Test to the Forcible Confiscation of Firearms in New Orleans.

i. The Process Prong.

The framework outlined above can easily be applied to the confiscation policy carried out by executive officials in New Orleans after Hurricane Katrina. Under the first prong, the process prong, the question is whether the executive official had the authority to act in an emergency situation without specific legislative authorization. Although Louisiana law, at the time of the confiscations, did not specifically authorize the seizure of firearms during an emergency, the governor had declared a state of emergency, which triggered the Emergency Health Powers Act.[192] Thus, the city officials would likely be able to satisfy the process prong of the test.

ii. The Compelling Government Interest Prong.

The next step requires that the city officials satisfy the second prong of the test, the compelling government interest prong. Under this prong, the question is whether the executive action furthered a compelling government interest. The city officials would likely be able to show that maintaining order was a compelling government interest in the wake of Hurricane Katrina. No one can reasonably dispute that Hurricane Katrina was a devastating natural disaster, and the consequent lawlessness threatened public safety in New Orleans.[193]

iii. The Less Restrictive Means Prong.

The final step requires that the city officials satisfy the third prong of the test, the less restrictive means prong. Under this prong, the executive must demonstrate that the chosen action was considered alongside other means that could have furthered the compelling government interest. There is no evidence that either Nagin or Compass, or any executive official for that matter, seriously considered any less restrictive alternatives to the outright forcible confiscation of lawfully possessed firearms. That there were less restrictive means of attaining law, order, and security is very likely.[194] For example, the actions undertaken by executive officials in both Dade County, Florida and the Virgin Islands in the wake of natural disasters[195] represent less restrictive alternatives to the confiscation of lawfully possessed firearms.

---

192. *See supra* note 19 and accompanying text.
193. *See* Part I.A.
194. *See* Part III.B.
195. *See id.*

The less restrictive alternatives to the forcible confiscation of firearms included the imposition of curfews for those individuals, who insisted on staying in the city;[196] the prohibition on carrying firearms outside of one's home during certain stated times; the prohibition on carrying concealed, lawfully possessed weapons outside of one's home;[197] and the prohibition of possession of firearms by felons,[198] among other alternatives. These measures, similar to those implemented by executive officials in other states in the wake of crises, would have likely furthered the compelling government interest of maintaining order. The overbroad nature of the confiscation policy, when compared with the available alternatives, reflects the view that city officials acted in the most restrictive manner in attempting to maintain order. Absent any evidence that the city considered such less restrictive alternatives and given that there were several alternatives, a court, employing this new test, would likely invalidate the executive decision to confiscate firearms as a violation of the Second Amendment.[199]

The city's confiscation policy went even further than the restrictive gun regulations codified in the District of Columbia, which were invalidated in *District of Columbia v. Heller*.[200] Specifically, the confiscation of lawfully owned firearms, which included *all* types of legal weapons, is significantly more intrusive than is a ban on handgun ownership or a requirement that lawfully owned firearms be inoperable in one's home, both of which regulations were struck down in *Heller*.[201] Thus, because the confiscation policy was even more restrictive than what the Supreme Court construed as unconstitutional under the Second Amendment, the constitutionality of the policy is highly questionable.

Taking the New Orleans example through the new three-prong test, Jordan demonstrates how his solution would have likely led to a different—and better—result.

---

196. *See* Smith v. Avino, 91 F.3d 105, 109 (11th Cir. 1996); Smith v. Avino, 866 F. Supp. 1399, 1405 (S.D. Fla. 1994).

197. *See, e.g.*, WIS. STAT. §941.23 (2005) (prohibiting the carrying of concealed weapons).

198. *See* Lewis v. United States, 445 U.S. 55, 66 (1980) (finding that felony conviction is a valid basis upon which to prohibit possession of firearms).

199. Even under the current reasonableness test, the confiscation policy may not pass constitutional muster. The imposition of a citywide curfew is starkly distinguishable from the forcible confiscation of firearms from law-abiding citizens. Unlike the curfew in *Avino*, which was temporary in nature, the confiscation in New Orleans was such that residents were deprived of their firearms for over a year. The temporal distinction between a curfew and the indefinite confiscation of firearms illuminates the unreasonableness of the confiscation policy.

200. District of Columbia v. Heller, No. 07-290, slip op. (U.S. June 26, 2008), *aff'g* Parker v. District of Columbia, 478 F.3d 370, 399–400 (D.C. Cir. 2007).

201. *See id.* at 64 (invalidating the District of Columbia's virtual ban on handgun possession in the home and the requirement that a registered firearm be kept unloaded and disassembled).

*This is an effective technique to use to support a thesis because the reader can see
the hypothetical results of your solution in action.*

Even though the initial seizure of firearms summarily in the wake of Hurricane
Katrina would be rendered unconstitutional under the framework proposed in
this Note, city officials' actions following the state of emergency exacerbated
what was already a constitutionally flawed policy. The overbroad nature of the
confiscation policy was further evidenced by the city's possession of the seized
firearms for a duration that far exceeded the immediate emergency.[202] The city's
prolonged control over the hundreds of impounded firearms could not serve
any compelling government interest after the initial period of emergency had
elapsed. Although public safety and the maintenance of order were compelling
government interests in the immediate wake of Hurricane Katrina, over two
years have elapsed since the disaster, and the city's sustained control over the
seized firearms has not continued to further these once compelling government
interests—a requirement under the test articulated in this Note and under regular
strict scrutiny. Even assuming that a trier of fact does not strike down the initial
seizure of firearms as violating the Second Amendment, it seems highly unlikely
that the city's actions over the past two years would be upheld, as these actions
could not satisfy each of the three prongs of the framework outlined by this Note.

*In this last paragraph of the solution section, Jordan concedes that the initial
firearms seizure in New Orleans may have been upheld under his proposed three-
prong test, but then protects his position by concluding that the later acts would
not pass review under the test and would have been struck down.*

Conclusion

Unfettered use of state executive emergency powers can cause widespread
violations of individual constitutional rights. As illustrated by the forcible confiscation of lawfully owned firearms in the aftermath of Hurricane Katrina,
state and local government officials may transform periods of emergency into
periods of constitutional chaos by employing policies 1) they may not be authorized to implement, 2) that fail to serve compelling government interests,
or 3) that are distinctively excessive. The current test employed by the courts
in assessing the exercise of state executive emergency powers is improperly deferential, and as a result, courts should embrace the new three prong test proposed in this Note. By providing greater specificity and guidance than the
traditional process-reasonableness test, the proposed test would help the courts
ensure a proper balance between safeguarding fundamental, individual con-

202. *See supra* notes 35–40 and accompanying text.

stitutional rights and furthering compelling government interests, such as maintaining public safety, during emergencies.

Here, Jordan succinctly summarizes his Note and leaves the reader with a sense of urgency about the need for control over state executive emergency powers.

Katy Ho's Note

Katy's Paper in Brief:
- *8,808 words including footnotes*
- *25 pages double-spaced using Times New Roman 12 point font for text and Times New Roman 10 point font for footnotes*
- *4 basic parts: Introduction, Background, Proposed Solution, and Conclusion*
  - *Introduction: approx. 3 pages (approx. 12%)*
  - *Background.: approx. 15 pages (approx. 60%)*
  - *Proposed Solution: approx. 6 pages (approx. 24%)*
  - *Conclusion: approx. 1 page (approx. 4%)*
- *98 footnotes*
  - *Introduction: 1 footnote (approx. 1%)*
  - *Background.: 77 footnotes (approx. 79%)*
  - *Proposed Solution: 18 footnotes (approx. 18%)*
  - *Conclusion: 2 footnotes (approx. 2%)*

DEFINING THE CONTOURS OF AN ETHICAL DUTY OF TECHNOLOGICAL COMPETENCE

As a descriptive phrase, this is a good example of how a title can be effectively constructed without the traditional two-part approach.

By Katy (Yin Yee) Ho

INTRODUCTION

Many blogs and articles focus on the topics of how the practice of law has been affected by technology and whether technological competence should be made an explicit ethical duty. However, in exploring the intersection of technology and the law, the issue of whether the profession needs a duty of technological competence is increasingly moot. The relevant question to ask should be: "How and to what extent should an ethical duty of technological competence be imposed?" While states have only recently begun adopting language in their rules of professional conduct that seek to implement, or to recommend, a duty of technological competence, this is merely a first step for the legal profession to catch up to societal and market norms in which technology is ubiquitous.

Right from the start, Katy makes it clear that the issue addressed in her paper is current and timely. Blogs often present ongoing conversations about timely events and her note immediately connects to the already-recognized significance of technology in law practice. But her note goes beyond that conversation by firmly explaining that the conversation should be about the content and boundaries of the duty of technological competence, rather than questioning the need for such a duty. She thus previews her thesis in this very first paragraph by reformulating the relevant question.

The rapid advancement in technology and new media, especially with the pervasive use of social media, has created beneficial tools for data storage and data sharing capabilities—and generated unique problems for legal professionals. Exploring to what extent an ethical duty of technological competence should be imposed on attorneys is important. Due to the ubiquitous nature of technology, more and more areas of legal practice are impacted by modern tools of communication, information storage, and information dissemination. Technology amplifies concerns regarding legal practice when attorneys are representing clients in a new normal in which everyone is "plugged in" and accessible—and, as a result, more prone to liability. One's data or digital fingerprints can span multiple locations and exist in various forms. This Note will explore how the legal profession is responding to the impact of technology within the legal profession, and whether the responses so far are adequate or efficient.

In this paragraph, Katy puts her paper in the greater context of technology and social media as it relates to data storage and data sharing. She again previews her thesis by concluding the paragraph with a sentence about what the Note will explore.

Technology has expanded the scope of information gathering, especially in the contexts of discovery and jury selection. In recent years, however, technology has created a space for misconduct, increased the danger of invasion of privacy, and created new areas of potential liability for both clients and attorneys. Relative to the emergence and rapid growth of technology, the legal profession has been slow to embrace this technological trend and to regulate attorney conduct from an ethical angle. Technology, especially new media, affords a broad scope for information gathering, raises serious privacy concerns, and is currently operating within legal practices and customs established before the technology boom. Given this, the profession will benefit from defining an affirmative ethical duty of competence in the use of technology by setting out explicit guidance and expectations for attorneys to navigate the intersection of the legal profession and a technological society.

This Note will briefly explore three areas of legal practice in which the impact of technology has been extensive and discuss how the legal profession has begun to respond to the need for regulation of the use of technology by attorneys. While the current Model Rules of Professional Conduct ("Model Rules") took a step forward in 2012 by adding a brief, general comment mentioning a duty of technological competence, this Note will argue that the American Bar Association (ABA) should provide more explicit guidance on this duty in order to effectively regulate the use of technology in the law and to encourage attorneys to stay up-to-date.[1] This Note will argue that clear guidance and a notice of an ethical duty of technological competence in the Model Rules will help to regulate technology use in the profession by standardizing practices, putting pressure on the twenty-three states that have not passed such a duty, keeping out external regulation of the legal profession, and keeping up with market forces in a marketplace in which clients are technologically adept and expect attorneys to be as well.

In these two paragraphs, Katy identifies specific problems with the current approach and offers additional exigency for her thesis before transitioning into her roadmap. Katy explains her focus on three areas of legal practice where technology is most significant in terms of justifying a need for a clearly-defined ethical duty of technological competence. In the introduction to Part I (below), Katy also uses a scope footnote to explain that her note limits discussion to these three areas even though there are other areas where technology might raise potential concerns. Technology-related issues present many challenges and it would not be possible to address every intersection of technology and law practice in a single Note; limiting the scope to the three most significant helped Katy keep her project manageable.

Part I of this Note will discuss the ongoing impact of technology on the practice of law, focusing on the areas of evidence gathering, jury selection, and client management. Part II will discuss the development of the duty of technological competence by examining the ABA's amendment to the Model Rules and the states that have followed its lead. Part III will argue that the Model Rules, both as proper rule-making and a normative matter, should define the contours of the ethical duty by providing specific guidance for attorneys to help define this duty and its scope.

Katy's roadmap lays out each part of the Note, following the convention used by her journal. She also states her thesis in the sentence noting the argument set forth

---

1. *See* Model Rules for Prof'l Conduct R. 1.1 cmt. 8 (2016) [hereinafter Model Rules].

in Part III: that the Model Rules should provide specific guidance to define the ethical duty. This roadmap reflects Katy's description of her Note in the immediately preceding paragraph.

I. THE IMPACT OF TECHNOLOGY ON THE PRACTICE OF LAW

An explicit adoption of an ethical duty of technological competence by the ABA and by the states is a necessary response by the legal profession to a rapidly changing, technology-based, and social-media-driven society. Technology has provided mechanisms for individuals to quickly communicate and disseminate information by creating new avenues of communication, such as social media platforms. These technological advancements in information gathering, storage, and dissemination have changed the practice of law, especially when compounded with the cultural changes within society toward an increased reliance on social networking.[2] Thus, in order to work efficiently and compete in the market effectively, attorneys are increasingly utilizing new technology and media in their practices. This trend will help attorneys to successfully fulfill their responsibilities of zealously advocating for their clients, both in and out of the courtroom.[3]

---

2. *See generally* Noor Nazzal, *Experts Warn Against Over-Dependence on Social Media*, GULF NEWS (Feb. 17, 2015), http://gulfnews.com/news/uae/society/experts-warn-against-over-dependence-on-social-media-1.1458606 [https://perma.cc/ZL89-Y5XP] (discussing society's growing dependency on social media and its effects on human relationships); Tara Parker-Pope, *An Ugly Toll of Technology: Impatience and Forgetfulness*, N.Y. TIMES (June 6, 2010), http://www.nytimes.com/2010/06/07/technology/07brainside.html [https://perma.cc/Y7WX-KALK] (discussing effects of dependency on technology); *see also* FACEBOOK NEWS-ROOM, http://newsroom.fb.com/company-info/#statistics [https://perma.cc/ZHB7-DW72] (last visited Feb. 26, 201 7) (reporting an average of 1.23 billion daily active users and 1.86 billion monthly users of Facebook as of December 2016); Katy Elle Blake, *The 2016 LinkedIn Stats You Should Know—Updated!*, LINKEDIN (Aug. 17, 2016), https://www.linkedin.com/pulse/2016-linkedin-stats-you-should-know-updated-katy-elle-blake [https://perma.cc/PN5B-UD55] (reporting a total of 433 million registered LinkedIn users of which forty percent check LinkedIn daily); TWITTER, https://about.twitter.com/company [https://perma.cc/UZG3-7D9W] (last visited Feb. 26, 2017) (reporting 313 million monthly active users).

3. *See* MODEL RULES pmbl [2] ("As advocate, a lawyer zealously asserts the client's position under the rules of the adversary system."); Daniel J. Siegel, *Lawyers Can No Longer Stick Their Heads in the Sand*, 41 A.B.A. LITIG. 1, 2 (2015), http://www.americanbar.org/content/dam/aba/publications/litigation_journal/winter2015/lawyers-cant-stick-heads-in-sand.authcheck dam.pdf [https://perma.cc/2CRQ-KL43] ("[T]echnology is an essential, inescapable part of practicing law now. Used properly, it helps you do a better job and get better results for your clients."); *see also* Am. Bar Ass'n, *TechReport 2016 Overview* (2016), http://www.american bar.org/publications/techreport/2016/overview.html [https://perma.cc/8JK2-TF6R] ("Technology is now ubiquitous in the law firm. It's almost impossible to imagine anyone effectively (or profitably) practicing law without a full range of technological devices.").

To fully understand the necessity of requiring technological competence, one must first understand the ways in which new technology has affected the practice of law. The following subparts briefly discuss three major areas of legal procedure that face challenges with the widespread use of new technology and media: evidence gathering, jury selection, and management of client liability.[4]

Here, Katy reminds the reader that her Note focuses on three legal areas. Even though footnote 4 limits the scope of her Note while acknowledging that there are other areas of concern, the reader could have benefited from some context for why Katy chose these three areas. Perhaps these are the areas where technology's impact has been most significant, or these are the places where technology presents the greatest litigation challenges. There are some indications within the following subsections that each of these areas is significant, and it would have been possible to build that into this introduction as a unifying theme for the three areas discussed.

A. THE IMPACT OF NEW TECHNOLOGY ON EVIDENCE GATHERING

The technological changes in information storage and information gathering have changed the procedural practice and scope of evidence gathering in the discovery phase of litigation. With regard to information storage, the advent of cloud storage, in which data is stored at a location remote from the end user, increased storage capacity for users. This capability allows companies to shift from paper recordkeeping to digital data storage. There is increasingly more information available for parties to reach, and to access more quickly, signifying a massive change in the ways litigators ask for and manage information during discovery.[5]

---

4. While this Note limits its discussion to these three areas, there are numerous other areas in which technology is incorporated into the legal profession, including—but not limited to—service of process, courtroom presentations, digital marketing of legal services, etc. *See, e.g.*, Angela Upchurch, *"Hacking" Service of Process: Using Social Media to Provide Constitutionally Sufficient Notice of Process*, 38 U. ARK. LITTLE ROCK L. REV. 559, 569 (2016) ("[S]ocial media provides new avenues for achieving constitutionally sufficient notice."); *Evolve to Win: The Growing Role of Technology in Law Firm Business Development*, THOMAS REUTERS (Sept. 2014), http://www.elite.com/documents/evolve-win-growing-role-technology-law-firm-business-development.pdf [https://perma.cc/8AX6-5FQK] (summarizing law firms' utilization of technology for marketing and business development); Celia W. Childress, *An Introduction to Persuasion in the Courtroom: What Makes a Trial Lawyer Convincing?*, 72 AM. JUR. TRIALS 137 (1999) (noting modern technology has affected the courtroom in areas such as examination of evidence and visual aids).

5. *See, e.g.*, Maura R. Grossman & Gordon V. Cormack, *Technology-Assisted Review in E-Discovery Can Be More Effective and More Efficient than Exhaustive Manual Review*, 17 RICH J.L. & TECH. 11, 11 (2011) (discussing cost-saving benefits of automated tools used "to prioritize and select documents for review" in e-discovery).

Furthermore, a single document can be duplicated, edited, or saved on various devices and in various forms, which creates and stores additional volume in comparison to paper documentation. In addition, there are more avenues to upload files (and potentially incriminating or impeaching evidence), such as via social media platforms (Facebook,[6] Instagram,[7] Twitter,[8] Reddit,[9] LinkedIn,[10] etc.) and digital databases (Google Drive,[11] iCloud,[12] Dropbox,[13] etc.). Technological advancements in data-sharing and data-storage expanded

---

6. Facebook is a popular social networking website that allows users to create profiles, send "friend requests" to follow other users, send messages, post status updates, upload photos and videos, and live stream videos. See FACEBOOK, www.facebook.com [https://perma.cc/NHN4-3GK9] (last visited Mar. 18, 2017).

7. Instagram is a photo-sharing mobile application, acquired by Facebook, that allows users to upload pictures and videos, send direct messages, "follow" other users, and live stream videos. See INSTAGRAM, www.instagram.com [https://perma.cc/G3ZR-8FST] (last visited Mar. 18, 2017).

8. Twitter is a social networking platform on which users can post their own messages (restricted to 140 characters), see current trending topics, and "favorite" and "retweet" other users' messages. See TWITTER, supra note 2 (giving "everyone the power to create and share ideas and information instantly, without barriers").

9. Reddit is a platform that allows members to post and share web content to a community of users. See REDDIT, https://about.reddit.com/ [https://perma.cc/KB4W-RCCU] (last visited Mar. 18, 2017) ("Reddit bridges communities and individuals with ideas, the latest digital trends, and breaking news").

10. LinkedIn is a professional networking platform that allows employers to post jobs and company information, users to post their qualifications, and users to "connect" with others' profiles. See LINKEDIN, https://press.linkedin.com/about-linkedin [https://perma.cc/UV7L-K8QF] (last visited Mar. 18, 2017) ("LinkedIn operates the world's largest professional network on the Internet with more than 467 million members in over 200 countries and territories.").

11. Google Drive is a file hosting service that allows users to store, synchronize, and share files across devices. See Get Started with Google Drive, GOOGLE, https://support.google.com/drive/answer/2424384?hl=en [https://perma.cc/5NN3-GSQX] (last visited Mar. 18, 2017).

12. iCloud is a cloud storage and computing service provided by Apple Inc. that allows users to store, share, and manage data on various Apple devices. See ICLOUD, http://www.apple.com/icloud/ [https://perma.cc/26HM-39PE] (last visited Mar. 18, 2017) ("iCloud securely stores your photos, videos, documents, music, apps, and more—and keeps them updated across all your devices. So you always have access to what you want, wherever you want it.").

13. Dropbox is a file hosting service featuring cloud storage and file synchronization. See DROPBOX, https://www.dropbox.com/about [https://perma.cc/7M5M-9GR3] (last visited Mar. 18, 2017) ("500 million people around the world use Dropbox to work the way they want, on any device, wherever they go.").

the scope of evidence gathering in unimaginable ways[14]—especially when compared to the data storage methods from the time when the Federal Rules of Civil Procedure (FRCP) Rule 26 on discovery was first enacted.[15]

Most, but not all of Katy's readers are probably familiar with these different technological platforms. Here, Katy wisely uses footnotes to describe each of them, so that readers who do not know what some or all of them are will have a complete picture without Katy sacrificing room in the text of the Note to explain each of them.

To effectively obtain information relevant and favorable to their clients, attorneys must embrace new technology. Social media, for example "has become a permanent fixture in how a large part of our society, for better or for worse, communicates,"[16] and is a "valuable discovery tool that must not be ignored."[17] Thus, it is unsurprising that regulations surrounding e-discovery have adapted to such changes.[18]

An often-cited case demonstrating how a party can use social media to their advantage in discovery is *Romano v. Steelcase Inc.*, a personal injury action in New York.[19] The plaintiff, Romano, sued alleging permanent injuries sustained

---

14. *See, e.g.*, John S. Wilson, Myspace, Your Space, or Our Space? New Frontiers in Electronic Evidence, 86 Or. L. Rev. 1201 (2007) (discussing ways in which traditional rules ineffectively address challenges brought by the technological revolution in discovery of electronic evidence); *see also* Fawcett v. Altieri, 38 Misc. 3d 1022, 1027 (N.Y. Sup. Ct. 2013) ("[W]ith the expansion of the use of mobile phones that are connected to the Internet, and the overall ease of access to broadband Internet connections at home, electronic discovery will quickly enter into actions where it was once thought irrelevant.").

15. Overall, technology creates tension with the law because "the bulk of legal authority and ethical guidance is rooted in precedent based on antecedent technologies [with] little resemblance to the emerging social centers of cyberspace." Ken Strutin, *Social Media and the Vanishing Points of Ethical and Constitutional Boundaries*, 31 Pace L. Rev. 228, 228 (2011).

16. Kevin W. Turbert, *Discoverability of Social Media Profiles in New York: How Defense Litigators Can Optimize on Disclosure*, 87 N.Y. St. B.J. 10, 11 (Oct. 2015) (approximating around seventy-four million Americans check their social network profiles daily).

17. *Id.*

18. In 2006, the FRCP was amended to provide guidance on the discovery process regarding electronically stored information (ESI). *See* Gregory D. Shelton, *Rulemaking in State Courts: A Rationale for Adopting ESI Provisions of FRCP 26*, Metro. Corp. Counsel (Mar. 1, 2009), http://www.metrocorpcounsel.com/articles/11068/rulemaking-state-courts-rationale-adopting-esi-provisions-frcp-26 [https://perma.cc/D9A8-Q3Q3] ("[C]hanges to Rule 26 [provided] additional protections to litigants who are dealing with a proliferation of computer usage, inexpensive data storage, and developments in communication technology that have changed discovery practice tremendously.").

19. *See generally* Romano v. Steelcase Inc., 907 N.Y.S.2d 650 (N.Y. Sup. Ct. 2010).

from a defective chair manufactured by the defendant that robbed her of participation in activities, such as traveling, and resulted in a loss of enjoyment of life.[20] The defendant successfully motioned for access to plaintiff's current and deleted MySpace[21] and Facebook accounts, including information from the private portions of the user's accounts (such as posts marked non-public).[22] The public portions of the plaintiff's MySpace and Facebook pages displayed various pictures revealing her active lifestyle and travels to different states during the period of claimed injuries, as alleged in the defendants' motion to be inconsistent with the nature and extent of her injuries.[23] The judge granted the discovery request, noting that the compelled productions "would not be violative of plaintiff's right to privacy, as plaintiff had no legitimate reasonable expectation of privacy given the nature and purpose of social networking sites, and any such concerns were outweighed by defendant's need for the information."[24] The evidence gathered from Romano's social media accounts was a severe blow to her case. Scenarios like this are set to become more prevalent—especially with society's increased focus on "social broadcasts"[25] that allow individuals to log daily events in real time. Accordingly, attorneys who are savvy in social media stand to benefit by being able to gather information that helps their clients.

However, with these new modes of access to evidence, the legal profession must confront potential threats to an individual's right to privacy due to the uniquely invasive nature of new media.[26] Though ultimately dismissed by the

---

20. *See id.* at 650.

21. MySpace is a social networking site "self-described as an 'online community'" that allows users to create personal profiles to communicate, post photographs, discover music, and share interests with other users. *See id.* at 653–54. Despite MySpace's success in the mid-2000s, it could not compete with the popularity of Facebook. *See* Kevin Kelleher, *How Facebook Learned from MySpace's Mistakes*, FORTUNE (Nov. 10, 2010), http://fortune.com/2010/11/19/how-facebook-learned-from-myspaces-mistakes/ [https://perma.cc/7XAT-2ZHD] (discussing the missteps that led to MySpace's demise).

22. *See Romano*, 907 N.Y.S.2d at 650.

23. *See id.*

24. *Id.*

25. Jacob Silverman, *'Pics or It Didn't Happen' the Mantra of the Instagram Era*, GUARDIAN (Feb. 26, 2015), https://www.theguardian.com/news/2015/feb/26/pics-or-it-didnt-happen-mantra-instagram-era-facebook-twitter [https://perma.cc/Q9JA-EB72] (discussing a societal focus on attention and visibility due to a "cultural premium now placed on recording and broadcasting one's life and accomplishments" in a way that creates "records of existence").

26. *See generally* Derek S. Witte, *Bleeding Data in a Pool of Sharks: The Anathema of Privacy in a World of Digital Sharing and Electronic Discovery*, 64 S.C. L. REV. 717, 738–48

judge in Romano, opposition remains to the reach of e-discovery into various social media platforms, favoring privacy.[27] Moreover, the "public" and "private" functions of social media platforms can cloud a judge's decision on privacy issues when evaluating whether particular content is within the reach of discovery.[28] It is essential for attorneys to not only be knowledgeable about social media platforms and their functions in the context of evidence gathering, but also to be aware of the risks and concerns that arise from particular platforms. The relevant inquiry should be whether the current FRCP regulations surrounding e-discovery—including prohibitions against reckless handling of electronically stored information—put sufficient pressure on attorneys to ensure they are using technology ethically and effectively; or, whether such responsibility can be further encouraged through guidance provided by an ethical duty of technological competence within the rules of professional conduct.[29]

(2013) (arguing the law must adapt to protect an individual's right to privacy when technology allows third parties to store our personal information and documents); see also Wilson, supra note 14 at 1234 (referring to leading case in modern privacy law, Katz v. United States, 389 U.S. 347 (1967), for guidance on individual privacy rights analysis for social-networking sites); Samuel D. Warren & Louis D. Brandeis, The Right to Privacy, 4 HARV. L. REV. 193, 195–96 (1890) (discussing how the changing demands of society, specifically in communication technology, call for the law's recognition and protection of an individual's right to privacy).

27. See, e.g., Fawcett v. Altieri, 38 Misc. 3d 1022, 1027–28 (N.Y. Sup. Ct. 2013) (limiting reach of closed or private social media accounts to showing of "some credible facts that the adversary subscriber has posted information or photographs that are relevant to the facts of the case at hand"); Tompkins v. Detroit Metro. Airport, 278 F.R.D. 387, 388 (E.D. Mich. 2012) (denying request for authorized release of plaintiff's Facebook account as irrelevant and overly broad by noting that defendant "does not have a generalized right to rummage at will through information that Plaintiff has limited from public view").

28. Many social media platforms provide advanced privacy settings that enable users to restrict the viewership of a given piece of content. For example, on Facebook, content marked "public" can be viewed by any Facebook user. Users can alternatively restrict posted content to be viewable by, inter alia, only "friends," "friends of friends," or other groups. The platform also offers strictly "private" functions, such as direct messaging between two users. Unfortunately for the user, discovery can reach both public and private content in certain contexts. See, e.g., E.E.O.C. v. Simply Storage Mgmt., LLC, 270 F.R.D. 430 (S.D. Ind. 2010) (allowing an employer's discovery request on an employee's social media activity set as "private" within platform settings). But see, e.g., Crispin v. Christian Audigier, Inc., 717 F. Supp. 2d 965 (C.D. Cal. 2010) (addressing subpoena of an individual's Facebook page by suggesting private information, such as direct messaging, to remain private, while public information on the platform is subject to e-discovery).

29. See infra Part III.

B. THE IMPACT OF NEW TECHNOLOGY ON VOIR DIRE

Jury selection is another legal process impacted by technology, particularly by the widespread popularity of the use of social media as a public chronicle of a person's life. Social media can be characterized as an "online self"[30] for the user because the user often shares significant aspects of her life on the Internet, thereby creating a virtual persona.[31] Individuals disseminate information about themselves not only to those within their social circles; they also relay their thoughts, ideas, experiences, and opinions to the general public. With a large audience,[32] and with modern society's normalization of over-sharing[33] and constant communication,[34] there exist more opportunities for an individual to share things about herself that are of interest to legal adversaries in the process of picking an ideal jury most favorable to their clients.

Given this, in voir dire, during which attorneys are searching for any hint of bias that could affect the outcome of their cases, attorneys have embraced the use of new media to dig up more information on potential jurors.[35] Social media searches have been recognized by courts as helpful methods to "turn up information useful to lawyers in exercising their three peremptory challenges, and, might even, in a very rare case, turn up information concealed during voir dire that could lead to a for-cause removal."[36] However, the advantage of using social media to uncover information about a particular juror—such as a juror's political affiliation, religious beliefs, litigation history, and societal

---

30. *See generally* John Browning, *It's Complicated: How to Walk the Fine Ethical Line in the Age of Social Media*, 76 TEX. B.J. 959, 962 (2013) (discussing the extent to which attorneys should probe "the online selves of prospective jurors").

31. Often times a user's followers on one social media platform also follow the same user on other platforms. Thus, the "online self" can be formed from a user's Facebook posts, pictures, and comments, and be reinforced through posts on Instagram, Twitter, and via Snapchat in real time. *See* Strutin, *supra* note 15, at 228, 247 (distinguishing social media from e-mails "because of its unique information sharing capabilities and the risks of unrestrained republication of personal data" by noting the large extent of content users share to retain "followers").

32. *See, e.g.*, Peggy Drexler, *The Problem Isn't Over-Sharing. It's Over-Following*, TIME (Oct. 24, 2014), http://time.com/3535342/oversharing-overfollowing/ [https://perma.cc/CQ3E-X58J] (discussing a widespread habit of "obsessive following" that provides a wide audience for social media users).

33. *See id.* ("[S]ocial media just makes sharing—oversharing—way too easy.").

34. *See generally* Silverman, *supra* note 25.

35. *See generally* John G. Browning, *Should Voir Dire Become Voir Google? Ethical Implications of Researching Jurors on Social Media*, 17 SMU SCI. & TECH. L. REV. 603 (2014).

36. Oracle Am., Inc. v. Google Inc., 172 F. Supp. 3d 1100, 1101–02 (N.D. Cal. 2016).

views—comes with the responsibility of remaining compliant with Model Rule 3.5's prohibition on ex parte communications with a juror.[37] The trend from courts that have allowed the use of social media seems to be a prohibition on attorneys making direct contact (such as sending "friend requests"[38] or "following" jurors) or posing as someone else.[39] Furthermore, state bars have noted that attorneys generally may only reach publicly accessible pages and content.[40]

It should be noted that a study conducted in 2014 suggested many courts that have encountered social media issues have erred on the side of caution by denying usage of social media during voir dire.[41] It is understandable why judges are so protective of juries; as one judge noted, "[I]t must pain [trial judges] to contemplate that, in addition to the sacrifice jurors make for our country, they must suffer trial lawyers and jury consultants scouring over their Facebook and other profiles to dissect their politics, religion, relationships, preferences, friends, photographs, and other personal information."[42] However, this is another prime example of how the legal profession falls behind the times. Considering social media's role as a popular form of self-expression, there must be some room for allowing its usage in voir dire from an efficiency standpoint, especially when information shared is intended for a public audience in the first place. As noted in *Johnson v. McCullough*:

> in light of advances in technology allowing greater access to information that can inform a trial court about the past litigation history of venire members, it is appropriate to place a greater burden on the par-

---

37. *See* MODEL RULES R. 3.5.

38. *See* Anita Ramasastry, *Googling Potential Jurors: The Legal and Ethical Issues Arising from the Use of the Internet in Voir Dire*, FINDLAW (May 30, 2010), http://writ.news.findlaw.com/ramasastry/20100730.html [https://perma.cc/Q8QQ-447R] (stating attorneys seeking to gain access to a juror's private Facebook account via a "friend request" are breaching their duties).

39. *See generally* Browning, *supra* note 30, at 962 (discussing New York and Oregon State Bars' caution against attorneys' direct or indirect contact with jurors in passive monitoring of jurors via social networking sites).

40. *See, e.g.*, Ass'n of the Bar of the City of N.Y., Formal Op., No. 2012-2 (2012) (allowing attorneys to read publicly available posts but not conduct research that results in communication to a prospective juror).

41. *See* Meghan Dunn, *Jurors' and Attorneys' Use of Social Media During Voir Dire, Trials, and Deliberations*, FJC (May 1, 2014), http://www.fjc.gov/public/pdf.nsf/lookup/dunnjuror.pdf/$file/dunnjuror.pdf [https://perma.cc/K6FS-H8EZ] (showing nearly twenty-five percent of judges have denied permission for attorneys to use social media during voir dire with a majority of the rest of the sample having not yet encountered these issues).

42. *See* Oracle Am., Inc. v. Google Inc., 172 F. Supp. 3d 1100, 1101 (N.D. Cal. 2016).

ties to bring such matters to the court's attention at an earlier stage [rather than] wait until a verdict has been rendered.[43]

If the duty of technological competence provides more guidance on the use of technology in voir dire, perhaps courts will more willingly allow these uses. In addressing this issue, the challenge will be to create guidelines that fairly protect individuals' right to privacy, while making room for effective information-gathering.

Throughout this subsection, Katy explains the challenges of technology in the context of voir dire. She brings that discussion to a fitting close by pointing out the opportunity for the Model Rules to balance technological advantages with individual privacy.

C. THE IMPACT OF NEW TECHNOLOGY ON CLIENT MANAGEMENT

As a practical matter, the development of technology and new media has made the role of the attorney as a legal adviser[44] to the client more challenging. As mentioned, the rise of social media has the benefit of allowing an individual to conveniently and quickly disseminate information to a large audience. However, these new channels of communication also create new opportunities for client liability by increasing exposure of clients to the public and to opposing counsel.

The use of social media has become a liability from a client management[45] perspective. Under various circumstances, a client's (and sometimes a witness') social media activity can bring an attorney's case under fire through exposure of incriminating or impeaching evidence that undermines the case. The threat of liability is further increased since "what happens on the Internet stays on the Internet."[46]

---

43. Johnson v. McCullough, 306 S.W.3d 551, 558–59 (Mo. 2010).

44. *See* MODEL RULES pmbl. [2] (explaining a lawyer's responsibilities: "[a]s advisor, a lawyer provides a client with an informed understanding of the client's legal rights and obligations and explains their practical implications").

45. For this Note, "client management" refers to the advisory role of an attorney in the context of preventing clients from exposing themselves to legal liabilities or sanctions—the risk-management aspect of an attorney-client relationship.

46. Andrew Couts, *What Happens on the Internet Stays on the Internet*, DIGITAL TRENDS (Apr. 3, 2011), http://www.digitaltrends.com/computing/what-happens-on-the-internet-stays-on-the-internet/ [https://perma.cc/3E95-5CUQ] (discussing the permanency of information posted on the Internet).

For example, *In re Jackson* illustrates how a client's Instagram activity can cause additional legal harm in a pending suit.[47] Here, debtor Curtis Jackson III (better known professionally as rapper 50 Cent) posted a series of Instagram photos showing off large stacks of bills, which invoked concerns from the judge—as well as public criticism—regarding the allegations of nondisclosure in Jackson's contemporaneous bankruptcy case.[48] Jackson's social media activity understandably brought his credibility and the legitimacy of his bankruptcy claims into question.[49] In a society where technology can track and store all sorts of information about an individual, a level of privacy that our pre-technology society had is lacking. Thus, in *In re Jackson*, the use of new media further diminished a client's privacy and increased his exposure to the public and to the judge.

Given new media's potential for profound effects on litigation, attorneys should take the cautionary approach of warning clients about their social media usage in order to avoid situations like *In re Jackson*. How far should attorneys go in limiting their clients' new media usage? Is this risk-management approach so vital to litigation in the modern context that it has become an issue of attorney incompetence if an attorney fails to warn her clients otherwise? If so, attorneys would benefit from an explicit statement of what their duties include in order to provide competent representation to their clients.

With a firm sense of three specific areas where technology presents significant challenges to attorneys, Katy's note has successfully laid a firm foundation for the next part of her paper. The next part is a mix of background and analytical criticism of the status quo.

II. DEVELOPMENT OF AN ETHICAL DUTY OF TECHNOLOGICAL COMPETENCE

As discussed above, the change in society towards a new-age, technology-driven culture has impacted the legal profession in various ways. These new technology tools have allowed attorneys to even more zealously advocate for their clients by adopting strategies that incorporate the use of technology to

---

47. *See In re* Jackson, 560 B.R. 39 (Bankr. D. Conn. 2016).

48. Jackson was characterized as "flaunt[ing] his wealth on social media" by "us[ing] stacks of money to fill buckets, redecorate his refrigerator, and spell out the word 'broke' in online pictures bragging about his wealth" despite filing for bankruptcy a year before. Victor Luckerson, *Bankrupt 50 Cent Says the Cash in His Instagram Photos Was Fake*, TIME (Mar. 11, 2016), http://time.com/4255654/50-cent-instagram-cash-bankrupt-bankruptcy/ [https://perma.cc/KV93-TU7K].

49. *See id.*

their legal advantage. However, these creative practices have also increased opportunities for ethical misconduct and professional incompetency. Driven by a need to regulate attorneys in these circumstances, and by the legal profession's longstanding preference for keeping out external regulation,[50] the legal profession has begun, albeit relatively slowly, to address issues created by the rise of new technology. This part of the Note will first discuss the 2012 addition of a duty of technological competence to the Model Rules, and then briefly survey how various states have responded to the ABA's amendment.

Katy effectively uses a roadmap to conclude this introduction to Part II and set the reader's expectations for this part. Her descriptive subheadings also help the reader.

A. ABA MODEL RULES OF PROFESSIONAL CONDUCT

In 2009, the ABA created the Commission on Ethics 20/20 to study the impact of technology on the legal profession as a whole and to propose any necessary changes to the Model Rules based on its findings.[51] In the report filed with the ABA's House of Delegates, the Commission noted a key trend in which "technology has irrevocably changed and continues to alter the practice of law in fundamental ways, ... [thus,] [l]awyers must understand technology in order to provide clients with the competent and cost-effective services that they expect and deserve."[52] In response to this study, the ABA in 2012 approved an amendment to comment 8 of Model Rule 1.1[53] pertaining to attorney competence.[54] The adopted comment 8 now reads: "[T]o maintain the requisite knowledge and skill, a lawyer should keep abreast of changes in the law and its practice, including

---

50. *See, e.g.*, Model Rules pmbl. [10] ("Although other professions also have been granted powers of self-government, the legal profession is unique in this respect because of the close relationship between the profession and the processes of government and law enforcement."); *see also* Jonathan Macey, *Occupation Code 541110: Lawyers, Self-Regulation, and the Idea of a Profession*, 74 Fordham L. Rev. 1079, 1094–98 (2005) (discussing the self-regulation of the legal profession).

51. *See* Am. Bar Ass'n Comm'n on Ethics 20/20, *Introduction and Overview* (Aug. 2012), http://www.americanbar.org/content/dam/aba/administrative/ethics_2020/20120508_ethics_20_20_final_hod_introduction_and_overview_report.authcheckdam.pdf [https://perma.cc/R6XK-VKA4].

52. James Podgers, *Come the Evolution: Ethics 20/20 Proposals Seek to Adapt Existing Professional Conduct Rules*, A.B.A. J. (July 1, 2012), http://www.abajournal.com/magazine/article/come_the_evolution_ethics_20_20_proposals_seek_to_adapt_existing_profession/ [https://perma.cc/HVC9-9KJF].

53. *See* Model Rules R. 1.1.

54. *See* Robert Ambrogi, *27 States Have Adopted Ethical Duty of Technology Competence*, Lawsites (Mar. 16, 2015), http://www.lawsitesblog.com/2015/03/11-states-have-adopted-

the benefits and risks associated with relevant technology, engage in continuing study and education and comply with all continuing legal education requirements to which the lawyer is subject."[55] The Model Rules, though non-binding,[56] serve as guidance to states in formulating their respective rules. Thus, this amendment serves as guidance for state bars to take note of the changes brought by technology, and to formulate their own duty of technological competence.[57]

B. STATES' ADOPTION OF AN ETHICAL DUTY OF TECHNOLOGICAL COMPETENCE

Following the ABA's lead, as of early 2017, twenty-seven states have adopted rules for the ethical duty of technological competence.[58] These twenty-seven[59] states are: Arizona, Arkansas, Colorado, Connecticut, Delaware, Florida, Idaho, Illinois, Iowa, Kansas, Massachusetts, Minnesota, New Hampshire, New Mexico, New York, North Carolina, North Dakota, Ohio, Oklahoma, Pennsylvania, Tennessee, Utah, Virginia, Washington, West Virginia, Wisconsin, and Wyoming.[60] The fact that more than half of the United States has adopted this rule within four years of the ABA amendment is an indication that any changes in the Model Rules are monitored closely by state bars. Hence, the ABA's amendment was indeed a positive step forward for the legal profession toward adapting to a technology-driven world in which attorneys use the tools of technology and new media to stay competitive in the legal market.

Of the twenty-seven states that have reacted to the ABA's comment 8 amendment, twenty-one of them have adopted the exact language of comment 8 in their rules.[61] Pennsylvania was one of these twenty-one states. For the 2013 amendments to the Pennsylvania Rules of Professional Conduct, the notice of the proposed rulemaking stated that the ABA amendment "reflected changes

---

ethical-duty-of-technology-competence.html [https://perma.cc/U7C2-S2X3] (discussing this "sea change in the legal profession").

55. MODEL RULES R. 1.1 cmt. 8 (emphasis added).

56. *See* Ambrogi, *supra* note 54 (stating that the *Model Rules* are just "a model" to "provide guidance to the states in formulating their own rules of professional conduct").

57. *See id.*

58. *See id.*

59. Twenty-seven states have adopted the duty of technology competence as of April 9, 2017. *See id.*

60. *Id.*

61. The twenty-one states that have adopted the language of the ABA amendment verbatim are: Arizona, Arkansas, Connecticut, Idaho, Illinois, Iowa, Kansas, Massachusetts, Minnesota, New Mexico, North Carolina, North Dakota, Ohio, Oklahoma, Pennsylvania, Tennessee, Utah, Virginia, Washington, Wisconsin, and Wyoming. *See id.*

in 21st century technology, lawyer mobility, and the legal marketplace."[62] The Pennsylvania bar noted that while its original competency rule (which mirrored Model Rule 1.1) implicitly included a duty of technological competence, the amendments made it explicit.[63] The great benefit of the ABA's 2012 amendment was to make such a duty explicit within the Model Rules, thereby placing attorneys on notice of possible violations and future sanctions.

One state—Delaware—fully adopted the ABA amendment and took it further by forming a Commission of Law and Technology.[64] The purpose of the Commission is to provide attorneys with "sufficient guidance and education in the aspects of technology and the practice of law" to facilitate compliance with the newly adopted duty of technological competence.[65] Delaware's approach recognizes the lack of specific guidance provided by the original ABA amendment, and sets up a system in which the duty of technological competence can be actively promoted among attorneys. This is a good approach because, due to the fast-paced changes in technology, the Commission can adjust the specific duties expected of technologically competent attorneys when necessary.

Some of the other states adopted minor variations to the ABA amendment. New York adopted a variation of the language by specifying that an attorney should "keep abreast of the benefits and risks associated with technology the lawyer uses to provide services to clients or to store or transmit confidential information."[66] This variation provides a bit more guidance by specifying particular circumstances of which attorneys should be aware. In New York, attorneys are thus put on notice that they should be attentive to the dangers of technology particularly when dealing with information storage or providing client services.

---

62. *See Amendments to the Pennsylvania Rules of Professional Conduct to Address the Need for Changes in Detection of Conflicts of Interest, Outsourcing, Technology and Client Development, and Technology and Confidentiality*, 43 Pa. Bull 1997 (Apr. 12, 2013), http://www.pabulletin.com/secure/data/vol43/43-15/652.html [https://perma.cc/55QY-KZDB].

63. *Id.*

64. *See* Comm'n on Law & Tech., http://courts.delaware.gov/declt/ [https://perma.cc/FPP9-LMP2] (last visited Feb. 26, 2017) ("The Commission was created by Order of the Supreme Court on July 1, 2013" to "develop and publish guidelines and best practices regarding the use of technology and the practice of law.").

65. *Delaware Supreme Court Creates New Arm of Court-Commission on Law and Technology* (July 5, 2013), http://www.courts.delaware.gov/forms/download.aspx?id=69618 [https://perma.cc/HF2F-9VHK].

66. Robert Ambrogi, *Two More States Adopt Duty of Technology Competence*, Lawsites (Nov. 11, 2015), http://www.lawsitesblog.com/2015/11/two-more-states-adopt-duty-of-technology-competence.html [https://perma.cc/AK9X-VNQP].

Similarly, Colorado's adoption of the amendment in April of 2016 differs from the Model Rules by providing further specificity. Colorado amended its rule as such: "To maintain the requisite knowledge and skill, a lawyer should keep abreast of change in the law and its practice, and changes in communications and other relevant technologies, engage in continuing study and education...."[67] Colorado appears to emphasize competence in technological communications as part of an attorney's professional responsibility. Furthermore, the amended comment cross-references the rule on confidentiality of information,[68] in effect signaling to attorneys that they should be wary of the impact of new technology on the privacy of communications and on modes of information storage.

Some state bars impose stronger ethical duties. For example, West Virginia changed the ABA language of "a lawyer should keep abreast" to "a lawyer must keep abreast."[69] This textually strengthens the duty of competence and explicitly notifies attorneys of it.

Florida took a different approach. The Florida bar added language detailing that competent representation could involve retention of "a non-lawyer advisor with established technological competence in the relevant field," as well as safeguarding any confidential information "including electronic transmissions and communications."[70] Here, Florida adopted not only an explicit duty of technological competence, but also recognized the possible need of third-party assistance to fully accommodate clients' technology needs. Florida's strengthening of the Model Rules' imposition of an ethical duty is further evidenced by its mandatory technology-related CLE courses that require a minimum of three hours of courses per three-year cycle.[71] This new CLE rule not only allows Florida to declare a standard of competence, but also to take active steps to ensure attorneys are receiving the proper training in technology to achieve this new standard. Overall, the Florida approach recognizes the need for specified guidance and training for attorneys rather than a mere declaration of a duty of technological competence.

---

67. COLO. RULES OF PROF'L CONDUCT R. 1.1 (emphasis added).
68. *See id.* ("See Comments [18] and [19] to Rule 1.6."); *see also* Robert Ambrogi, *Another State Adopts Duty of Technology Competence; Makes It 26*, LAWSITES (Dec. 28, 2016), http://www.lawsitesblog.com/2016/12/another-state-adopts-duty-technology-competence-makes-26.html [https://perma.cc/CE9V-HL78].
69. *See* W. VA. RULES OF PROF'L CONDUCT R. 1.1.
70. *In Re*: Amendments to Rules Regulating the Fla. Bar 4-1.1 and 6-10.3, No. SC16-574 (Sept. 29, 2016), http://www.floridasupremecourt.org/decisions/2016/sc16-574.pdf [https://perma.cc/T5SP-5MPD].
71. *See id.*

In contrast, New Hampshire adopted the ABA amendment with commentary that suggested a less stringent standard. New Hampshire found that "this broad requirement may be read to assume more time and resources than will typically be available to many lawyers. Realistically, a lawyer should keep reasonably abreast of readily determinable benefits and risks...."[72] This language seems to soften the technological competence requirement by recognizing practical limitations that prevent attorneys from being fully compliant. It does so by providing some guidance as to what, at minimum, attorneys should do to meet the ABA's "broad requirement," which appears to be simply an awareness of the "readily determinable benefits and risks" rather than additional research.[73]

California interestingly did not explicitly adopt the Model Rules standard. The state bar instead issued a detailed formal opinion that discussed the duty of technological competence in the discovery of electronically stored information, requiring competency in electronic document creation and storage, electronic communications, and e-discovery.[74] The opinion noted that in certain circumstances, "a lack of technological knowledge in handling e-discovery may render an attorney ethically incompetent."[75] This ethical obligation may be fulfilled by acquiring sufficient learning and skills before use, consulting with technical consultants or competent co-counsels, or declining client representation.[76] Since California, as the home of the leading social media platforms[77]

---

72. Ambrogi, *supra* note 66.

73. *Id.*

74. *See* Cal. Bar Standing Comm. on Prof'l Responsibility & Conduct, Formal Op., No. 2015-193 (2015), http://catalystsecure.com/components/com_wordpress/wp/wp-content/uploads/2015/08/CAL-2015-193-11-0004-06-30-15-FINAL.pdf [https://perma.cc/6MBG-WAH5].

75. *Id.* at 7.

76. *Id.* at 3.

77. Among others, Facebook, Instagram, Twitter, LinkedIn, Reddit, WhatsApp, and Snapchat are all headquartered in California. *See, e.g.*, FACEBOOK NEWSROOM, http://newsroom.fb.com/company-info/ [https://perma.cc/N75L-9DTD] (last visited Mar. 5, 2017) (Facebook, which owns Instagram, has its headquarters in Mountain View, CA); *About Us*, LINKEDIN, https://press.linkedin.com/about-linkedin [https://perma.cc/X8BW-MVCM] (last visited Mar. 5, 2017) (LinkedIn headquarters is located in Mountain View, CA); *Company Overview of Reddit, Inc.*, BLOOMBERG, http://www.bloomberg.com/research/stocks/private/snapshot.asp?privcapId=29927936 [https://perma.cc/Z2XE-TU3T] (last visited Mar. 5, 2017) (Reddit, Inc.'s headquarters is located in San Francisco, CA); *Contact WhatsApp*, WHATSAPP, https://www.whatsapp.com/contact/ [https://perma.cc/54K7-7YDV] (last visited Mar. 5, 2017) (WhatsApp Inc.'s headquarters is located in Mountain View, CA); *Company Overview of Snap, Inc.*, BLOOMBERG, http://www.bloomberg.com/research/stocks/private/snapshot.asp?privcapId=224055283 [https://perma.cc/B8A7-W8TS] (last visited Mar. 5, 2017) (Snap, Inc.'s headquarters is located in Venice, CA).

and a hub of the start-up technology industry,[78] encounters the intersection of technology and law more often than other states, the California approach indicates where the duty will evolve to and what measures are needed to put attorneys on notice of their ethical duties surrounding the use of technology. The ABA rule should adopt a similar approach and provide specific guidance on its duty of technological competence rather than leaving the vague language in comment 8 to be interpreted by individual state bars and attorneys.

In Katy's discussion on California's approach, she includes some analysis of how the ABA should see the California approach as a model. This is a nice transition to Part III, the bulk of the analytical part of Katy's Note.

III. THE BENEFITS OF DEFINING THE CONTOURS OF AN ETHICAL DUTY OF TECHNOLOGICAL COMPETENCE

While the ABA took a step towards catching up to the technological evolution, the amended comment in the Model Rules provides minimal guidance on the extent of the newly explicit ethical duty of technological competence. This part argues that the ABA should further define the contours of the ethical duty by specifying how attorneys can satisfy this duty and identifying particular areas and practices in which attorneys might face difficulties. While technology is fast-developing and unprecedented in its capabilities, its effect on legal practice is mostly to amplify concerns in particular areas and processes, such as confidentiality of information, communication, and the reach of discovery. The ABA should take a disciplined approach to rule-making by explicitly identifying areas in which technology amplifies concerns. By providing guidance and notice of potential ethical breaches concerning the use of technology, the ABA can balance specificity of the new rule with flexibility, allowing judges and bar associations to address new issues that arise from future technological developments. As a normative matter, setting explicit rules will help manage expectations and provide a minimum standard for attorneys to meet.

This section begins with a restatement of Katy's thesis: This part argues that the ABA should further define the contours of the ethical duty by specifying how attorneys can satisfy this duty and identifying particular areas and practices in which attorneys might face difficulties.

---

78. *See* Richard Florida, *The Global Cities Where Tech Venture Capital is Concentrated*, ATLANTIC (Jan. 26, 2016), https://www.theatlantic.com/technology/archive/2016/01/global-startup-cities-venture-capital/429255/ [https://perma.cc/NBJ3-YF3F] (noting that the Silicon Valley in California is a "tech hub" where tech venture capitals are concentrated).

A disciplined approach to rule-making involves carefully drafting a rule that both addresses current concerns and anticipates areas in which flexibility should be maintained. The new rules should properly address concerns surrounding the use of technology in practice noted by the ABA Commission on Ethics 20/20. The Commission noted two trends in its 2012 report. First, "technology has irrevocably changed and continues to alter the practice of law in fundamental ways."[79] Due to changes in communications and commerce, attorneys must gain an understanding of technology to provide competent and efficient client services.[80] Second, technology, in combination with globalization, has changed the legal marketplace "with more clients confronting legal problems that cross jurisdictional lines."[81] The current amendments do not explicitly note these concerns and instead provide general language about technological awareness.

Furthermore, disciplined rule-making requires anticipating issues and confusion surrounding the implementation of new rules. When the Commission was first created, it was tasked with "protecting the public; preserving the core professional values of the American legal profession; and maintaining a strong, independent, and self-regulated profession."[82] While its proposed amendment, which the ABA adopted, helps explicitly declare a duty of technological competence, it does not address anticipated confusion regarding the extent of the duty. The amendment lacks guidance on the contours of the duty and minimum responsibilities required of attorneys. The ambiguity surrounding the use of technology leads to a lack of standardization of attorney expectations, which in turn harms the public interest and runs counter to the legal profession's need to provide services competently.

Here, Katy criticizes the ABA's proposed amendment and sets forth the need for disciplined rule-making to avoid additional problems in trying to respond to technological change in the legal profession.

To follow the objectives above and to provide guidance for the profession, the ABA should further amend the Model Rules to define and specify the extent of the duty of technological competence. As noted by the Commission on Ethics 20/20, technology has impacted legal work in the realm of storage of confidential information, communication, discovery, legal research, and marketing of services.[83] The ABA should carefully tailor the rules to address these

---

79. Am. Bar Ass'n Comm'n on Ethics 20/20, *Introduction and Overview, supra* note 51, at 2–3.

80. *Id.*

81. *Id.* at 7.

82. *See id.* at 1.

83. *See id.*

issues and specify that the duty exists in these areas. This would outline the baseline criteria that attorneys must satisfy to fulfill their responsibilities — thereby highlighting for attorneys the areas of practice in which the usage of technology requires extra care.

This paragraph reinforces Katy's thesis and makes explicit what she wants the ABA to do and why it should do it.

There is a danger in drafting requirements that are too vague or overbroad; such rules can bring unintended consequences or unnecessarily create conflict in interpretation of the rules. Thus, while the ethical duty should not be so specific as to lose flexibility for future technology, it must be carefully tailored to provide greater guidance. Here, the current amendment's direction to keep abreast of "the benefits and risks associated with relevant technology"[84] is too vague. What technology is relevant? Does this duty require attorneys to actively research new technology and new relevant regulations prior to usage? Does simply being a user of the technology render one competent enough? What happens if an attorney mistakenly uses a new technology and gets sanctioned — what additional steps should she have taken to avoid a breach in her ethical duty of technological competence?

Here, Katy uses practical questions to illustrate the weaknesses of vague or overbroad requirements. The reader can easily imagine these questions coming up in practice and Katy's anticipation of those questions further legitimizes her argument here.

Since state bars tend to follow changes in the Model Rules,[85] the ABA should take the lead in further clarifying this ethical duty to avoid any unintended consequences or misinterpretations. Some of these rule-making concerns are analogically highlighted in John C. Coffee Jr.'s critique of a class action bill in which he discussed the drawbacks of overbroad and carelessly drafted rules.[86] The Fairness in Class Action Litigation Act of 2017 was proposed as a mass procedural reform of class action litigation.[87] Coffee criticized the Act as being "clumsily drafted" with "overbroad" reforms.[88] At the center of his critique is the provision barring a federal court from certifying a class action in which the proposed named plaintiff or representative is or formerly was a client of

---

84. MODEL RULES R. 1.1 cmt. 8.
85. *See supra* Part II.
86. *See* John C. Coffee Jr., *How Not to Write a Class Action "Reform" Bill*, CLS BLUE SKY BLOG (Feb. 21, 2017), http://clsbluesky.law.columbia.edu/2017/02/21/how-not-to-write-a-class-action-reform-bill/ [https://perma.cc/H6WU-89FQ].
87. H.R. 985, 115th Cong. (2017).
88. Coffee, *supra* note 86.

the particular class counsel.[89] Coffee also criticized the non-specificity of the Act, stating that "nothing about [this section] seems carefully drafted"[90] because there are a variety of situations that fall within the provision in which firms can be barred from representing their clients, directly conflicting with the norms of class action litigation practice. Coffee condemned the bill's language as a "breathtaking overkill" on class actions rather than merely adding procedural protections.[91] Proper rule-making should have involved careful tailoring so as to give consideration to the plaintiffs' bar and its litigation practice.

Katy's note explains why the ABA should take the lead. This analysis responds to the potential counterargument that the ethical duty should be defined state by state. In using the analogy to procedural reform in class action litigation, Katy effectively grounds her position. Even though there is no authority supporting her specific position (it's her novel idea, after all!), by drawing on another area of law where there were similar weaknesses, she adds legitimacy to her proposal.

Similarly, the ABA's ethical duty of technological competence would benefit from careful drafting and tailoring. The mere recitation of a requirement of technological competence does not provide guidance as to the scope of this duty, particularly when this requirement is likely to be adopted by most state bars and be imposed on all attorneys. The ABA, following a more disciplined approach to rule-making, should give more consideration to the current norms of practice and provide guidance as to what specific changes or areas of legal procedure an attorney should be technologically aware of. This will help avoid any misinterpretations arising from the vague text of comment 8.

As a normative matter, the ABA can better manage expectations by outlining the minimum conduct or considerations required for attorneys to be technologically competent in the areas of legal practice noted above. In contrast to Coffee's concerns surrounding the class action bill, the California state bar's latest formal opinion on e-discovery was carefully drafted to specifically outline particular areas in the discovery process in which attorneys should take greater care with the use of technology.[92] In its 2015 opinion, the California bar addressed the question of "what are an attorney's ethical duties in handling of

---

90. *Id.*

91. *Id.*

92. *See* Cal. Bar Standing Comm. on Prof'l Responsibility & Conduct, Formal Op., No. 2015-193, *supra* note 74.

discovery of electronically stored information?"[93] Rather than prescribing a general obligation for attorneys to be aware of the benefits and risks of electronically stored information and of e-discovery procedures, the California bar acknowledged areas of concern and provided examples of competent actions satisfying the ethical duties of e-discovery. For example, it specified that an ethical duty of competence in e-discovery requires attorneys to assess "at the outset of each case what electronic discovery issues might arise.[94]" If an attorney lacks the skills or resources to properly assess these issues, the attorneys should either "try to acquire sufficient learning and skill" or "consult with someone with expertise to assist."[95] Furthermore, it specified these issues could arise in areas of information preservation, information collection, performance of data searches, and production of responsive electronic evidence. While the directions maintain a degree of abstraction to preserve flexibility, the California bar provided more guidance to shape attorneys' expectations in providing competent representation in the e-discovery context.

Here, Katy explains how the ABA can respond more specifically to technological challenges. By drawing a comparison to the California state bar and its ability to be more specific in drafting guidance on e-discovery, Katy helps support her view about the need for more than the ABA's initial general guidance in the amendment as well as shows how more specific guidance is possible.

The ABA should follow a similar approach to formalizing the contours of the overall ethical duty of technological competence. Besides offering the benefits of putting attorneys on notice of potential ethical breaches, providing further guidance on the duty helps encourage attorneys to embrace technology as a tool and direct their practice in the intersection of technology and law. Furthermore, the ABA's current minimalistic approach prevents attorneys from acting as zealous advocates on behalf of their clients.[96] Attorneys cannot fulfill their duty of competence if they do not know what it entails. The ABA should help attorneys gain a general understanding of where and how technology has been impacting the practice of law and notify them of particular areas of concern. By defining the contours of an ethical duty of technological competence, the ABA can more quickly help the legal profession address the challenges brought by the incorporation of technology into the legal profession.

---

93. *Id.* at 1.
94. *Id.* at 3.
95. *Id.*
96. *See* MODEL RULES pmbl. [9].

CONCLUSION

An ethical duty of technological competence is an inevitable outcome of a technologically-driven society clashing with legal practices established in the context of paper-based documentation. The discussion in the legal community should not be focused on whether such a duty is necessary in the legal profession, but rather to what extent this duty should be defined and imposed upon an attorney. What minimum familiarity with technology is required for competence in the context of e-discovery? Can an attorney be sanctioned for not employing social media in her voir dire procedures when the societal norm is that an average citizen will likely have multiple social media profiles, all easily accessible by the attorney? Should an attorney be required to warn her clients about their use of social media and its effects on legal disputes?

The use of questions here brings the Note full circle in identifying the gaps in the existing rule. Without answers to these questions, attorneys will continue taking risks, even unknown risks. Katy has effectively reinforced the need to move past the questions about whether to craft more specific guidance and instead focus on what that guidance should be.

The ABA helped the legal profession take a step forward in 2012 by including an amended comment to Rule 1.1 acknowledging an explicit ethical duty of technological competence in the form of recognizing the benefits and risks of technology usage. This amendment helped encourage the legal profession to incorporate the use of technology in legal practice. More than half of the states have adopted some version of the model rule thus far, and it is expected that more will adopt this duty of technological competency.[97]

However, mere recognition of the importance of technology is an inadequate response. Rather, the ABA should take a larger leap forward by adopting a disciplined approach to rule-making and balancing the need to address challenges brought by technology with the necessity of maintaining flexibility to address future changes. The ABA should define the contours of an ethical duty of technological competence and provide guidelines as to the scope of the duty surround-

---

97. *See generally* Matthew Verga, *Half of States Now Have Technical Competency Requirements for Attorneys*, ADVANCED DISCOVERY (2016), http://www.advanceddiscovery.com/blog/2016/11/half-of-states-now-have-technical-competency-requirements-for-attorneys/ [https://perma.cc/GJF6-HF3T] ("With the ABA and half of all states on board, it's likely such requirements will eventually be universal."); Ambrogi, *supra* note 54 (predicting more states will adopt amended comment 8).

ing the interplay of technology and legal practice. This would provide attorneys with notice of incompetent behavior, and allow attorneys to truly be zealous advocates for their clients in a modern world. With the imminent continual rise of the ethical duty of technological competence, the ABA and state bars should keep up with the rapid changes in technology. As the Supreme Court once noted, "it is the task of the law to form and project, as well as mirror and reflect."[98]

Katy concludes by calling for action and providing the practical context for why that change is needed.

Peter Smyth's Case Note

The following annotated paper is a case note. A case note is different from a traditional law review note because the topic of a case note is limited to a single case. A case note should report the Prior Law, Background, and Court's Analysis as objectively as possible. It is in the author's Personal Analysis where he puts forward his own arguments and seeks to persuade the reader.

Peter's Paper in Brief:
- *17,138 words including footnotes*
- *47 pages double-spaced using Times New Roman 12 point font for text and Times New Roman 10 point font for footnotes*
- *6 basic parts: Introduction, Prior Law, Background, Bilski v. Kappos, Business Methods and Dualism, and Conclusion*
  - *Introduction: approx. 3 pages (approx. 6%)*
  - *Prior Law: approx. 15 pages (approx. 32%)*
  - *Background: approx. 5 pages (approx. 11%)*
  - *Court's Analysis (Bilski v. Kappos): approx. 15 pages (approx. 32%)*
  - *Personal Analysis (Business Methods and Dualism): approx. 8 pages (approx. 17%)*
  - *Conclusion: approx. 1 page (approx. 2%)*
- *326 footnotes (excluding epilogue)*
  - *Introduction: 13 footnotes (approx. 4%)*
  - *Prior Law: 114 footnotes (approx. 35%)*
  - *Background: 37 footnotes (approx. 11%)*
  - *Court's Analysis (Bilski v. Kappos): 116 footnotes (approx. 36%)*
  - *Personal Analysis (Business Methods and Dualism): 51 footnotes (approx. 16%)*
  - *Conclusion: 5 footnotes (approx. 2%)*

---

98. United States v. White, 401 U.S. 745, 786 (1971) (Harlan, J., dissenting).

A Functionalist Recommendation for Business Method Patents:
A Note on *Bilski*

*Like many scholarly legal paper titles, Peter's title contains two parts: a title and a subtitle. Both parts are descriptive, with the first telling the reader the purpose behind writing his note. The second part tells the reader his impetus for writing this paper, i.e. a recent Supreme Court decision on his topic. Furthermore, by including the case name in the title, he seeks to make his paper easily accessible to readers who are interested in the implications of this recent decision. Look to **Chapter 4** for more information on constructing your title.*

By Peter K. Smyth

Table of Contents

Introduction — App-51
I. Prior Law — App-53
II. Background — App-64
III. Bilski v. Kappos — App-67
  A. Majority Opinion — App-68
    i. Machine-or-Transformation Test — App-70
    ii. Business Method Exclusion — App-71
    iii. Abstract Idea — App-72
  B. Stevens Concurrence — App-73
IV. Business Methods and Dualism — App-78
  A. Cartesian Dualism — App-79
  B. A Functionalist View of Business Method Patents — App-82
  C. Proprietary Protection Outside of the Patent System — App-84
Conclusion — App-85
Epilogue — App-86

Peter included a table of contents for two reasons: first, to give the reader a guide to his paper, which is lengthy and second, to enable a reader who is interested only in a summary of Bilski *to jump directly to that portion of his paper.*

A process is an act, or a mode of acting. A conception of the mind, seen only by its effects when being executed or performed.[1]

Peter begins his paper with a quotation. Because his thesis concerns the application of Cartesian dualism to a legal principle, he introduces the separation

---

1. Tilghman v. Proctor, 102 U.S. 707, 728 (1881).
This is an attributing footnote. Most of Peter's footnotes are used simply to attribute to sources.

*between ideas and physical manifestations from the outset. Moreover, he found this quotation repeatedly throughout his research and decided that it was a good anchor from which to start his paper. There are several different ways to start a paper, including hypotheticals or factual narratives, to get the reader interested in what is next. See **Chapter 4** for different approaches to creating an interesting opening.*

Introduction

In re Bilski identified the inherent dualism in business method patents.[2] *Bilski v. Kappos* rejected the outright dualist, machine-or-transformation test as the exclusive means to decide patentability of processes, and attempted to return business method patent ("BMP") applications to a monist framework—that a process is a process no matter what the invention is—but gave no direction for how an unembodied idea could be patented under the historically machine-based Patent Act.[3]

Philosophy and psychology have studied the merits of both monism and dualism for hundreds of years.[4] One of the main problems with Cartesian dualism is the inability of *res cogitans* to communicate with *res extensa*.[5] Because the dualist communication problem is very similar to the problem posed by process patents and the machine-or-transformation test,[6] the Court of Appeals for the Federal Circuit uncovered a fundamental flaw in allowing statutory protection for unembodied processes.[7] By looking to the centuries-old discussion of the mind-body problem, a solution can be found to the inadequacy of the Patent Act with regard to unembodied process patents, especially business method patents.[8]

Peter has both a philosophy and a patent background so he has chosen a thesis that incorporates both fields. Writing his note on how philosophical and psychological theories could inform the law in this area helped Peter to maintain interest

---

2. *In re* Bilski, 545 F.3d 943 (Fed. Cir. 2008).
3. Bilski v. Kappos, 130 S. Ct. 3218 (2010).
4. *See infra* Part IV(A).
   The journal for which Peter wrote has a convention of citing nearly every sentence. For that reason, and to allow the reader to jump forward for more information on the cited sentence before moving on, he has included "infra" citations indicating where the reader can find more information on the sentence within this paper.
5. *See infra* text accompanying note 283.
6. *See infra* Part III(A)(i).
7. *See infra* Part IV(B).
8. *See infra* Part IV.

*in his note over the many months that it took to write. Refer back to **Chapter 2** for advice about picking a topic and thesis that can maintain your interest in this way.*

Supreme Court attempted to solve the problem by fleshing out the language of the Patent Act itself in *Bilski v. Kappos*.[9] The Court, however, punted the ultimate issue of how to handle BMPs by rejecting the machine-or-transformation test without providing a suitable replacement for use by patent examiners and appellate courts.[10] The solution is to hold unembodied processes nonstatutory altogether, as the concurrence suggests, because it is efficient as a practical matter and patent safeguards to BMPs are unnecessary.[11]

The Court implicated the mind-body problem by recognizing that there are abstract ideas which are novel and useful, but unpatentable because not tied to a machine. BMPs raise the mind-body dilemma because they toe the line between abstract ideas and physical. Past cases seem to have drawn the line in such a way as to make BMPs unpatentable,[12] but the current Court is apparently not comfortable with this line due to advances in technology. The Court's recent decisions have shifted the line to make business methods patentable but have not satisfactorily determined how to hold unembodied process like BMPs patentable and still conform to *stare decisis* and the purpose of the Patent Act. The Court should draw on other disciplines, including philosophy and psychology to resolve the BMP problem in favor of unpatentability.

In his opening paragraph, Peter jumps right into the problem with which he is most concerned. It may have been a better choice for him to reorganize his Introduction to ease his readers into the topic by beginning with the paragraphs that explained briefly what the Court was deciding in Bilski, *what the dualist dilemma is, and how the dilemma is implicated in* Bilski. *Although all of those pieces are included in his introduction, the reader would have been better served by a more methodical organization.*

Part I is a recitation of the history of the prosecution of process patent applications. Part II shows the background of the prosecution of the Bilski patent application. Part III gives the Supreme Court's analysis and decision concerning the patentability of Bilski's invention. Part IV begins with a brief discussion of Cartesian dualism and then highlights the short-comings of dualism with

---

9. *See infra* Part III(A).

10. *Cf.* Bilski v. Kappos, 130 S. Ct. 3218, 3231 (2010).

11. *See infra* Part III(B).

12. *See* discussion of Justice Stevens's concurrence in *Bilski*, 130 S. Ct. 3218, *infra* Part III(B).

regard to BMPs. It then gives reasons why business methods do not need patent protection, and argues that allowing BMPs would be overly administratively burdensome.[13]

*A roadmap is included here, at the end of the Introduction, so that the reader has an idea of the progression of the rest of the paper. A roadmap makes it easier for the reader to follow the text because he has an idea of what is coming next. Look back to **Chapter 4** for a discussion of how to construct these types of roadmaps.*

I. Prior Law

Patent protection in the United States has its roots in the Intellectual Property Clause of the Constitution.[14] The power given to Congress to grant limited monopolies to inventors was meant for the purpose of promoting innovation.[15] Allowing an inventor an exclusive right to a particular new tech-

---

13. This paper presumes a minimum understanding of the patent system. For a brief introduction to patents refer to the Berkman Center for Internet and Society at Harvard Law School's abbreviated summary at General Patent Information, http://cyber.law.harvard.edu/ilaw/BMP/patent_background.html (last visited Feb. 3, 2011), or a slightly more complete summary at Michael Neustel, *Patent Information*, http://www.patent-ideas.com/Xpatents.htm (last visited Feb. 3, 2011) (including some basic legal advice on patent protection and a flow chart for basic patent prosecution). The official requirements for patents are given in the Patent Act, 35 U.S.C. § 100, et seq., and the Regulations, 37 C.F.R § 1.51, et seq.

Because Peter was writing for a particular audience he did not explain the patent system in the text of his paper. Rather, in this footnote, he limits the scope of his paper, directing readers to additional sources in case they would like additional background information. If he knew his audience was likely to be unfamiliar with the patent system, he might have included more specific information in this footnote. See Chapter 4 for more information about how to craft footnotes.

14. U.S. Const., art. I, §8, cl. 8 ("The Congress shall have Power ... To promote the Progress of Science and useful Arts, by securing for limited Times to Authors and Inventors the exclusive Right to their respective Writings and Discoveries...."). This is often referred to as the Patent Clause, but the scope of the power granted to Congress goes beyond patents to include protections such as trademarks and copyrights. *Cf.* Robert P Merges, *As Many as Six Impossible Patents Before Breakfast: Property Rights for Business Concepts and Patent System Reform*, 14 BERKELEY TECH. L.J. 577, 584 (Spring, 1999) (referring to the Intellectual Property Clause).

15. Federalist No. 43 (Madison wrote, "The utility of the clause will scarcely be questioned. The copyright of inventors has been solemnly adjudged, in Great Britain, to be a right of common law. The right to useful inventions seems with equal reason to belong to the inventors. The public good fully coincides in both cases with the claims of the individuals.")

nology which was invented by him protected an inventor's investment in the creation of the technology.[16] Without any such safeguard, products and processes which required extensive front-end investment would be inhibited by the fear of opportunism by those who would adopt recently invented technology for their own gain without investment and without any fear of recourse from rightful inventors.[17] By allowing an inventor to reap any benefits from technology he created, to the exclusion of all others, he was ensured that no one could be unjustly enriched by using the invention at the inventor's expense.[18] Protection spurred innovation and provided legal recourse against infringers.[19]

In this paragraph, Peter introduces the reader to the origin of patent protection in the United States and why it was necessary, and in the following paragraphs he shows the limitations that have been placed on the initially expansive patent protections. Peter returns to these themes later in the Court's Analysis and Personal Analysis sections and ultimately relies on these historical limitations to prove his thesis.

Congress was well aware of the power of limited monopolies and instituted wide-ranging, but not unlimited parameters on what was patent-eligible.[20] The Patent Act of 1790 stated that any "useful art, manufacture, engine, machine, or device, or any improvement therein" could be given patent protec-

---

16. *See* David S. Olson, *Taking the Utilitarian Basis for Patent Law Seriously: The Case for Restricting Patentable Subject Matter*, 82 Temp. L. Rev. 181, 231 (Spring 2009) (noting the up-front costs associated with pharmaceutical development).

  Including an explanatory parenthetical is a good idea in a "see" cite because it fills the gap between what has been stated in the text and the authority it relies on. If there is no gap, then it may be better to omit the "see" signal altogether.

17. *See id.* (explaining the types of expenses necessary to market a new drug).

18. *See* Festo Corp. v. Shoketsu Kinsoku Kogyo Kabushiki Co., 535 U.S. 722, 730–31 (2002) (stating that "the monopoly is a property right" like any other property right).

19. 35 U.S.C. § 281.

20. *See* Merges, *supra* note 14, at 585–86 (discussing abuses by the Crown as the reason for the British Statute of Monopolies); British Statute of Monopolies of 1623, 21 Jac. 1, c. 3 (1623) (available at http://www.statutelaw.gov.uk/legResults.aspx?LegType=All+Legislation&searchEnacted=0&extentMatchOnly=0&confersPower=0&blanketAmendment=0&sortAlpha=0&PageNumber=0&NavFrom=0&activeTextDocId=1518308) (generally condemning monopolies except for particular items which were given exclusive rights of use by their inventor for 14 years). *See also, generally,* Edward C. Walterscheid, *The Early Evolution of the United States Patent Law. Antecedents (Part 3 Continued)*, 77 J. Pat. & Trademark Off. Soc'y 847 (1995) (discussing early patent law in the United States).

tion.[21] Since the enactment of the first Patent Act, numerous changes have been made,[22] but Congress maintained that protection of patents should be widely inclusive.[23] The most recent act, the Patent Act of 1952, enumerated four classes of statutory subject matter: processes, machines, manufactures, and compositions of matter.[24] "The statutory class of 'process' differs fundamentally from the other three classes."[25] Machines, manufactures, and compositions of matter can be categorized collectively as products, whereas processes are seen as something intangible.[26] Generally, products have been much more easily understood by the courts than processes and have posed fewer conceptual problems.[27]

Peter uses quotations twice in this paragraph, each for a different purpose. The first quotation captures the exact language of the statute, which is important because the Court's purpose in Bilski *is to interpret the meaning of that language. The second quotation, although perhaps unnecessary, is used to identify language from the preeminent treatise on the topic that is addressed in the paper. The quotation here tells the reader that there is something about "processes" that is important to the author and he wants to reader to pay attention to it. Be careful, however, not to overuse quotes because they can become burdensome or distracting. Look back to* **Chapter 7** *for a discussion of appropriate use of quotations and the problem of over-quoting.*

Early on, courts found several types of categorically unpatentable subject matter.[28] In 1853, the Supreme Court explained that no abstract principle, original cause, nor motive could be patented because they should be available to every-

---

21. First Congress, Sess. II, ch. 7, 110 (1790) (available at http://memory.loc.gov/cgi-bin/ampage?collId=llsl&fileName=001/llsl001.db&recNum=233).

22. The Patent Act had undergone nearly 50 changes before the 1952 version. Bilski v. Kappos, 130 S. Ct. 3218, 3245 (2010) (Stevens, J., concurring). *See generally* Ladas & Parry, LLC, *A Brief History of the Patent Law of the United States*, http://www.ladas.com/Patents/USPatentHistory.html (last visited Jan. 14, 2011) (giving a brief history and timeline of the Patent Act).

23. *See* Committee Reports, S. Rep. No. 82-1979, at 5 (1952) (stating that Congress intended statutory subject matter to "include anything under the sun that is made by man").

24. 35 U.S.C. § 101.

25. Chisum on Patents § 1.03, 1–109 (Rel. 105-9/2006 Pub. 525) (Mathew Bender & Co., Inc., 2010).

26. *See id.* (stating that "[a] process is not a structural entity but rather an operation or series of steps leading to a useful result").

27. *Id.*

28. *See, e.g.*, Le Roy v. Tatham, 55 U.S. (14 How.) 156, 175 (1853) ("A principle, in the abstract is a fundamental truth; an original cause; a motive; these cannot be patented, as no one can claim in either of them an exclusive right.").

one.[29] The notion against patentability of abstract ideas was stated very succinctly in *Rubber-Tip Pencil Co. v. Howard*: "An idea of itself is not patentable."[30]

In one of the earliest cases on the patentability of a process, the Court sought to determine what was unique about processes apart from the machine needed to carry out the process.[31] *Corning* stated:

> The term machine includes every mechanical device or combination of mechanical powers and devices to perform some function and produce a certain effect or result. But where the result or effect is produced by chemical action, by the operation or application of some element or power of nature, or of one substance to another, such modes, methods, or operation, are called process.... The arts of tanning, dyeing, making water-proof cloth, vulcanizing India rubber, smelting ores, and numerous others, are usually carried on by processes, as distinguished from machines.[32]

The *Corning* court separated the mode of producing a certain useful result from the machine that was used to carry out the mode, and found that the machine in question was patentable, but not the mode.[33] Specifically, the Court found that the roller machine used to press impurities out of iron was patentable subject matter, but the general process of pressing them out was not.[34] Therefore, any other process used to press impurities out of cast iron that did not use the patented machine was not an infringement on the patent, because the inventor's roller machine was merely a useful improvement on the already common practice of pressing out impurities by compression through the use of other means.[35]

---

29. *Id.*
30. Rubber-Tip Pencil Co. v. Howard, 87 U.S. (20 Wall.) 498, 507 (1874).
31. Corning v. Burden, 56 U.S. (15 How.) 252, 267 (1853). Part of the necessity for definition of a process arose because, at this time, the term "process" was not included in the Patent Act. Thus, the Court relied on an implicit inclusion of processes in the "useful arts" that were enumerated in the Patent Act of 1790. *See id.* (stating that "[a] process, eo nomine, is not made the subject of a patent in our act of Congress. It is included under the general term 'useful art'"). *See also* Expanded Metal Corp. v. Bradford, 214 U.S. 366, 382 (1909) (clarifying that "the word 'process' has been brought into the decisions because it is supposedly an equivalent form of expression or included in the statutory designation of a new and useful art").
32. *Corning*, 56 U.S. (15 How.) at 267–68.
33. *Id.* at 268 ("It is well settled that a man cannot have a patent for the function or abstract effect of a machine, but only for the machine which produces it.").
34. *Id.* at 269.
35. *Id.* at 268 (the Court gives examples of methods for removing impurities from molten iron, including "tilt hammers and alligator jaws" and other simple machines which

The year following *Corning*, a patent was granted for a process using electromagnetism to produce distinguishable signs for telegraphy.[36] The Court, however, declined to allow the inventor's claim to an exclusive right to any future mechanisms which "mark[ed] or print[ed] intelligible characters, signs, or letters, at any distances" via electromagnetism.[37] This was essentially an attempt to patent any machine that involved a process using electromagnetism.[38] The Court recognized that to grant this claim would preclude any future inventions using electric current, even if the new invention was less complicated, less expensive in construction and in its operation, or was composed of an entirely different machine.[39] To allow this sort of monopoly would have been too broad and therefore not patentable.[40]

---

produced the same results that Burden's roller machine produced, but which required more time and energy, so Burden's machine was patentable because it was a useful improvement over earlier techniques, but the idea of pressing impurities out of iron was not).

36. O'Reilly v. Morse, 56 U.S. (15 How.) 62, 112 (1854). The inventor in *O'Reilly v. Morse* was Samuel Morse, inventor of the telegraph and namesake of Morse code. Wikipedia, http://en.wikipedia.org/wiki/Telegraphy (last visited Jan. 14, 2011). Electromagnetism is magnetic force produced by the flow of electricity through a wire (electric current). Ron Kurtus, *Electromagnetism*, Apr. 3, 2005, http://www.school-for-champions.com/science/electromagnetism.htm (last visited Jan. 14, 2011). Using electromagnetism, one can turn a magnet on and off by turning on electricity or stopping the flow of electricity respectively. Using pre-determined sequences of electric flow that correspond to the alphabet, one can send messages over long distances as long as there is a continuous wire capable of conducting electricity connecting the sender to the receiver. *See* Wikipedia, http://en.wikipedia.org/wiki/Telegraphy (explaining telegraphy). For this reason, telegraphs were often called "wires." Wikipedia, http://en.wikipedia.org/wiki/Telegraphy.

Here is an example of an explanatory footnote. The electromagnetism case in the text is concerned with the far-reaching legal implications of the patent claim. Peter included a footnote explaining electromagnetism here to help the reader understand what was at issue in the case referred to in the text without distracting from the legal argument. Because Peter has included the additional information in a footnote, the reader is free to focus solely on the legal argument presented in the text or to engage with the footnote and gain additional information for a fuller understanding.

Peter cites to Wikipedia in this footnote. Although the information found on the cited Wikipedia web page is correct, be wary of using this informal authority. The paper would probably have been better served if Peter had used Wikipedia as a jumping off point, ultimately citing a more reputable authority.

37. *Morse*, 56 U.S. (15 How.) at 112.

38. *Id.*

39. *Id.* at 113.

40. *Id.*

In 1877, the Supreme Court refined the definition of process given in *Corning*, stating that a process is "an act, or a series of acts, performed on the subject-matter to be transformed and reduced to a different state or thing."[41] The Court left open the possibility that a process could be patentable subject matter apart from any machine used to implement the process, but in the immediate case it ruled that the contested process was again too broad and was not tied to a particular piece of machinery.[42] The process sought to be protected would have precluded even the use of a "pestle and mortar" for grinding meal into "superfine flour."[43]

Shortly thereafter, the Court stated:

> [a machine] is visible to the eye, an object of perpetual observation. [A process] is a conception of the mind, seen only by its effects when being executed or performed. Either may be the means of producing a useful result. The mixing of certain substances together, or the heating of a substance to a temperature, is a process.[44]

In a patent application for a process, at least one mode of implementing the process must be shown,[45] but in order to receive protection for exclusive use of a process it is not necessary to describe every possible application of the process.[46]

Drawing on the previous cases, the Court in *Expanded Metal Co. v. Bradford* found that although one could not patent the effect produced by a machine, the process used to produce that effect was not automatically nonstatutory.[47] Process patents were not, therefore, limited to chemical processes, as might have been concluded from the language in *Corning*, and processes for "mechanical operations" could be statutorily valid for patentability.[48]

---

41. Cochrane v. Deener, 94 U.S. 780, 787–88 (1877) (finding process unpatentable).

42. *Id.*

43. *Id.*

44. Tilghman v. Proctor, 102 U.S. 707, 728 (1881).

45. *See* 35 U.S.C. §112 (stating that one of the requirements of a valid patent specification is that "the specification shall contain ... the manner and process of making and using it").

46. *Tilghman*, 102 U.S. at 728.

47. Expanded Metal Co. v. Bradford, 214 U.S. 366, 383 (1909) ("the mere function or effect of the operation of a machine cannot be the subject-matter of a lawful patent[, b]ut it does not follow that a method of doing a thing, so clearly indicated that those skilled in the art can avail themselves of mechanism to carry it into operation, is not the subject-matter of a valid patent.").

48. *Id.* at 385–86 (granting a patent for the process of making expanded sheet metal. "An invention or discovery of a process or method involving mechanical operations, and producing a new and useful result, may ... entitle the inventor to a patent for his discovery.")

The previous paragraphs recount the early evolution of process patent claims chrono-logically. This organization works for this paper because it shows how difficult it has been for the Court to define what a "process" is as technology has advanced. The definition of process is what is at issue in the Court's Analysis section, so understanding the foundation for the Court's decision is important. Other scholarly articles can be effectively organized by issue or some other method that makes more sense for that particular topic. Remember that there are many ways to organize your paper, and your topic will help dictate which method will most effectively transmit your ideas to your reader. You may rethink your organization following your earliest drafts. See **Chapter 5** *for more information on evaluating your organizational choices.*

The middle of the twentieth century brought new challenges for patentability with increased innovation in computer and information technology.[49] In 1972, the Court found that an algorithm useful for programming a digital computer was not patentable subject matter under 35 U.S.C. § 101.[50] In *Gottschalk v. Benson*, the inventor sought patent protection for an algorithm that would use a general purpose digital computer to convert binary-coded decimal form ("BCD") to pure binary.[51] That is, from ordinary Arabic numerals to a series of "ones" and "zeros."[52] The conversion from BCD to pure binary could be performed by hand by using a table created by the inventors; however, the process was much faster when aided by a computer.[53]

---

49. *See generally* President's Commission on the Patent System, To Promote the Progress of Useful Arts in an Age of Exploding Technology (U.S. Gov. Printing Office 1966) (discussing the Patent Act in the midst of technological advancement).

50. Gottschalk v. Benson, 409 U.S. 63, 73 (1972). The four categories of statutory subject-matter are processes, machines, manufactures, and compositions of matter. 35 U.S.C. § 101. For a general definition of "algorithm" see Wikipedia, http://en.wikipedia.org/wiki/Algorithm (last visited Jan. 8, 2011).

51. *Benson*, 409 U.S. at 65. By using algorithms, digital computers are able to make complex calculations very quickly that would take a person much longer to do manually "by head and hand." *Id.*

52. *Id.*

53. *Id.* at 66–67.
To encode a decimal number using the common BCD encoding, each decimal digit is stored in a 4-bit nibble:

Decimal:	0	1	2	3	4	5	6	7	8	9
BCD:	0000	0001	0010	0011	0100	0101	0110	0111	1000	1001

Thus, the BCD encoding for the number 127 would be:
0001 0010 0111
Whereas the pure binary number would be:
0111 1111
Wikipedia, http://en.wikipedia.org/wiki/Binary-coded_decimal (last visited Jan. 24, 2011).

This paragraph begins with a transition sentence alerting the reader to the changing nature of processes and bringing him from the early problems associated with mechanical devices into the modern era for this topic. Eventually, as the claims at issue become more abstract and less tied to machinery, Peter will present the case at the center of this note, Bilski, giving the reader a nice background from which to examine the Supreme Court's decision.

The Court analogized Benson's process claim to the rejected process claim in *O'Reilly v. Morse*.[54] To allow Benson a patent on the use of the mathematical algorithm would "cover both known and unknown uses of the BCD to pure binary conversion" because it was not tied to a particular machine and could be "performed through any existing machinery or future-devised machinery or without any apparatus" at all.[55] To narrow the effects of patenting a process the court stated that "[t]ransformation and reduction of an article to a different state or thing is the clue to the patentability of a process claim that does not include particular machines."[56] The court held that because the algorithm did not transform any physical matter into another state or thing and the algorithm was not tied to a particular machine it was unpatentable as merely an idea.[57] The Court was sure to point out, however, that it had no intention to "freeze process patents to old technologies, leaving no room for the revelations of the new, onrushing technology," and left open the possibility of process patents if they conformed to the requirements set forth in earlier case law.[58]

Parker v. Flook placed additional restrictions on process patents, reigning in what seemed an ever expanding definition until *Benson*.[59] Flook sought to patent a process which used a mathematical algorithm to determine "alarm limits" that would alert an operator to abnormal conditions or danger in the catalytic conversion process.[60] The key component of the patent claim was the use of the algorithm, but in order to use it certain data was needed—i.e. "the original alarm base, the appropriate margin of safety, the time interval that should elapse between each updating, the current temperature (or other process variable), and the appropriate weighting factor to be used to average the

---

54. *Benson*, 409 U.S. at 68. *See supra* n. 36–40 and accompanying text.
55. *Id.*
56. *Id.* at 70 (internal quotation marks omitted).
57. *Id.* at 71–72.
58. *Id.* at 71.
59. Parker v. Flook, 437 U.S. 584, 589–90 (1978).
60. *Id.* at 585.

original alarm base and the current temperature."[61] As in *Benson*, once someone has all the necessary data the calculation can be done through any number of mediums, including by hand, and was not limited to a particular machine.[62] Unlike Morse, who sought to preempt any use whatever of electromagnetism for long distance transmission, Flook sought patent protection for the use of his invented algorithm only in the field of catalytic conversion of hydrocarbons.[63] This restriction would have covered a broad range of uses in the petrochemical and oil-refining industries, but allowed application of the formula in any other industry.[64]

Flook argued that the use of the algorithm for a particular "post-solution activity" made it patentable, but the Court found that Flook's process was not patentable because the only parts of the application that were novel with regard to prior art was the algorithm itself.[65] The Court pointed out, however, that use of a mathematical formula was not alone fatal to a patent application, and the patent application should be taken as a whole.[66] Flook's invention, "once [the] algorithm is assumed to be within the prior art ... contains no patentable invention."[67] "[I]f a claim is directed essentially to a method of calculating, using a mathematical formula, even if the solution is for a specific purpose, the claimed method is nonstatutory."[68] So, "post-solution activity" by itself will not make a previously unpatentable algorithm patentable.[69]

Diamond v. Diehr implemented *Flook's* rule of looking to an entire patent application, rather than looking at each claim independently, to determine patentability.[70] Using "the [machine-or-transformation] clue" articulated in *Benson*,[71] although the application included a mathematical algorithm as one of its key components, the invention was statutory because the algorithm was connected to a machine.[72] In distinguishing its finding from *Benson* and *Flook*,

---

61. *Id.* at 585–86.
62. *Id.* at 586 (1978).
63. *Id.*
64. *Flook*, 437 U.S. at 586, n. 4.
65. *Id.* at 594–95.
66. *Id.* at 593–94 (1978).
67. *Id.*
68. *Id.* at 595 (1978) (quoting *In re* Richman, 563 F.2d 1026, 1030 (1977)).
69. *Flook*, 437 U.S. at 594–95 (1978).
70. Diamond v. Diehr, 450 U.S. 175, 184 (1981).
71. *See* Gottschalk v. Benson, 409 U.S. 63, 70 (1972) (adding to the definition of process in Cochrane that "[t]ransformation and reduction of an article 'to a different state or thing' is the clue to the patentability of a process claim that does not include particular machines").
72. *Diehr*, 450 U.S. at 184.

the Court explained that Diehr was not attempting to patent a mathematical formula, but rather a process for curing synthetic rubber.[73] The process of curing rubber using the invented press could have been done without the use of the algorithm but the incorporation of Arrhenius' equation "significantly lessen[ed] the possibility of overcuring or undercuring" the rubber, so its use in conjunction with the machine did not render the entire invention unpatentable.[74] This ruling effectively extended the patentability of processes from chemical actions[75] to machines[76] to computer-aided inventions as interpreted by the Court of Customs and Patent Appeals in later opinions.[77]

A two part analysis arose out of the *Flook* and *Diehr* decisions to determine whether a process patent application which included a mathematical formula was unpatentable as a fundamental scientific principle, law of nature, idea, or mental process.[78] The test was deemed the Freeman-Walter-Abele test after the three cases which fleshed out the rule introduced by the Supreme Court in *Benson*, *Flook*, and *Diehr*.[79] To apply the Freeman-Walter-Abele test:

> It is first determined whether a mathematical algorithm is recited directly or indirectly in the claim. If so, it is next determined whether the claimed invention as a whole is no more than the algorithm itself; that is, whether the claim is directed to a mathematical algorithm that is not applied to or limited by physical elements or process steps. Such claims are nonstatutory. However, when the mathematical algorithm is applied in one or more steps of an otherwise statutory process claim, or one or more elements of an otherwise statutory apparatus claim, the requirements of § 101 are met.[80]

---

73. *Id.* at 187.

74. *Id.* at 187, 188.

75. Corning v. Burden, 56 U.S. (15 How.) 252, 267–68 (1853).

76. Expanded Metal Co. v. Bradford, 214 U.S. 366, 385–86 (1909).

77. Arrhythmia Research Tech. Inc. v. Corazonix Corp., 958 F.2d 1053, 1057 (Fed. Cir. 1992).

78. *Id.* at 1057–58.

79. *In re* Freeman, 573 F.2d 1237 (CCPA 1978), *In re* Walter, 618 F.2d 758 (CCPA 1980), and *In re* Abele, 684 F.2d 902 (CCPA 1982), were decided in the Court of Customs and Patent Appeals seeking to create a workable rule for examining patents consistent with *Flook* and *Diehr*. The U.S. Court of Appeals for the Federal Circuit explained the construction of the rule in *Arrhythmia*. 958 F.2d at 1058. Until 1982, the United States Court of Customs and Patent Appeals had jurisdiction over appeals of patents until the CCPA was disbanded and its docket transferred to the Federal Circuit. Wikipedia, http://en.wikipedia.org/wiki/United_States_Court_of_Customs_and_Patent_Appeals (last visited Feb. 3, 2011).

80. *Arrhythmia*, 958 F.2d at 1058.

This test was not meant to be the exclusive test for determining statutory subject matter,[81] and even if a claim failed the test it may still have been patentable.[82] The key was to look at "*what* the claimed method steps do rather than *how* the steps are performed."[83]

The Bilski *case that Peter focuses on in this note did not use the Freeman-Walter-Abele test. However, Peter includes a discussion of the test because the Supreme Court mentions the test in its opinion as one of several tests that can be helpful to practitioners. The discussion of this test could have been relegated to a long footnote with only a brief reference to it in the text. However, Peter includes it in the text because he wants to make sure that his readers have an understanding of how past courts have handled process cases before they are discussed in the Court's Analysis part. Without having learned about prior tests, the reader could have difficulty understanding the holding of the Supreme Court in* Bilski.

Applying the Freeman-Walter-Abele test to the *Arrythmia* heart monitor application, the court found that the process described was statutory under 35 U.S.C. § 101. The first step was to determine if a mathematical algorithm was recited in the claim.[84] *Benson* defined an algorithm as a "procedure for solving a particular mathematical problem."[85] *In re Iwahashi* interpreted that to mean that any step-by-step process, whether mechanical, electrical, biological, or chemical involved an "algorithm" in the broader sense of the term.[86] *Arrythmia* relied on the broad usage given in *Iwahashi* and summarily presumed that an algorithm was included in the subject matter of the process claims.[87]

The court then determined whether the process claimed in the application would be statutory in case it did not include the algorithm.[88] If the algorithm was "applied in any manner to physical elements or process steps" and the physical elements contribute more than a field of use limitation or non-essential

---

81. *In re* Meyer, 688 F.2d 789, 796 (CCPA 1982).
82. *In re* Grams, 888 F.2d 835, 839 (Fed. Cir. 1989).
83. *Arrhythmia*, 958 F.2d at 1058 (quoting *Ex Parte* Logan, 20 U.S.P.Q.2d 1465, 1468 (PTO Bd. Pat. App. And Interf. 1991)).
84. *Arrhythmia*, 958 F.2d at 1058.
85. Gottschalk v. Benson, 409 U.S. 63, 65 (1972).
86. *In re* Iwahashi, 888 F.2d 1370, 1374 (Fed. Cir. 1989); *See also See* Wikipedia, http://en.wikipedia.org/wiki/Algorithm (last visited Jan. 8, 2011) (discussing a wide variety of types of algorithms).
87. *Arrhythmia*, 958 F.2d at 1058–59.
88. *Arrhythmia*, 958 F.2d at 1059.

post-solution activity, then the process claim would be statutory.[89] That is to say, that if the process was statutory without the mathematical formula—albeit less efficient or even inoperative—then it was statutory when the formula was included.[90] The claims in *Arrythmia* sought to patent a method for analysis of electrocardiographic signals taken from a patient shortly after he had suffered a heart attack.[91] Based on the findings of the doctor who analyzed the signals, the doctor could administer certain drugs which were only necessary in certain instances to prevent further medical problems.[92] The court found that the signals in the claim were not abstractions, but rather tangible things "related to the patient's heart function"—physical, electrical signals.[93] Because the process was physical, limited to the particular use for analyzing electrocardiographs, and merely employed an algorithm for efficiency, the process claims satisfied the Freeman-Walter-Abele test and were statutory.[94]

The Court of Appeals for the Federal Circuit, in *In re Alappat*, noted that the Freeman-Walter-Abele test could be useful in determining whether a claimed process was statutory, but instead relied directly on *Diehr* to decide "whether the subject matter as a whole is a disembodied mathematical concept ... which in essence represents nothing more than a law of nature, natural phenomenon,

---

89. *In re* Abele, 684 F.2d 902, 907 (CCPA 1982) (quoting *In re* Walter, 618 F.2d 758, 769 (CCPA 1980)).

90. *Abele*, 684 F.2d at 907.

91. *Arrhythmia*, 958 F.2d at 1054.

92. *Id.*

93. *Id.* at 1059. The court summarized the steps in the claimed process:
The electrocardiograph signals are first transformed from analog form, in which they are obtained, to the corresponding digital signal. These input signals are not abstractions; they are related to the patient's heart function. The anterior portion of the QRS signal is then processed, as the next step, by the procedure known as reverse time order filtration. The digital filter design selected by Dr. Simson for this purpose, known as the Butterworth filter, is one of several known procedures for frequency filtering of digital waveforms. The filtered signal is further analyzed to determine its average magnitude, as described in the specification, by the root mean square technique. Comparison of the resulting output to a predetermined level determines whether late potentials reside in the anterior portion of the QRS segment, thus indicating whether the patient is at high risk for ventricular tachycardia. The resultant output is not an abstract number, but is a signal related to the patient's heart activity. *Id.*
As in the **Morse** *footnote, above, Peter included this block quote to help the reader understand the process that is being described, because it is not important enough to be included in the text. If the reader is uninterested in this side point, he may move on without learning the specific facts of* **Arrhythmia**.

94. *Id.*

or abstract idea."[95] If Alappat's claims fell into any of those three categories, the claims would be unpatentable.[96] Like in *Arrhythmia*, the court found that although the process utilized a mathematical formula, the formula was used incidentally to the physical aspects of the application.[97] The claimed process was a means for "creating a smooth waveform display in a digital oscilloscope."[98] The court found that the oscilloscope's display was representative of actual physical phenomena—a specific machine to produce a "useful, concrete, and tangible result"—and was, therefore, patentable statutory subject matter.[99]

Another test is introduced here because it is mentioned in the Court's Analysis. By including it in the Prior Law part, Peter lays the foundation for its mention later in the paper.

The Federal Circuit continued to use the "useful, concrete, and tangible result" test in *State Street Bank & Trust Co. v. Signature Financial Group, Inc.* where the court found patentable a method for pooling multiple mutual funds' assets in an investment portfolio organized as a partnership to take advantage of the benefits of administering multiple investments simultaneously with the tax advantages of a partnership.[100] The court found that the transformation of data representing actual dollar amounts using a mathematical algorithm was

95. *In re* Alappat, 33 F.3d 1526, 1544 (Fed. Cir. 1994).
96. *See* Funk Brothers Seed Co. v. Kalo Inoculant Co., 333 U.S. 127, 130 (1948) (stating that the concepts covered in these exceptions are "part of the storehouse of knowledge of all men ... free to all men and reserved to none"); Mackay Radio & Tel. Co. v. Radio Corp. of Am., 306 U.S. 86, 94 (1939) (finding that "while a scientific truth, or the mathematical expression of it, is not a patentable invention, a novel and useful structure created with the aid of knowledge of scientific truth may be").
97. *Alappat*, 33 F.3d at 1544.
98. *Id.* at 1537. To learn more about oscilloscopes see, NIHAL KULARATNA, DIGITAL AND ANALOGUE INSTRUMENTATION: TESTING AND MEASUREMENT 165–208 (Institution of Engineering and Technology 2003).
99. *Alappat*, 33 F.3d at 1544.
100. State Street Bank & Trust Co. v. Signature Fin. Group, Inc., 149 F.3d 1368, 1370 (Fed. Cir. 1998), *cert. denied*, 525 U.S. 1093 (1999). The Federal Circuit's holding was considered by some to be the first allowable business method patent in decades, overturning a general prohibition on BMPs. Larry Downes, editor, *Supreme Court Hedges on Business Method Patents*, CNET, http://news.cnet.com/8301-13578_3-20009046-38.html; William Fisher and Geri Zollinger, *Business Method Patents Online*, THE BERKMAN CENTER FOR INTERNET & SOCIETY AT HARVARD LAW SCHOOL, http://cyber.law.harvard.edu/ilaw/BMP/ (stating that prior to the *State Street* decision, business methods were widely assumed to be unpatentable).

statutory because it produced a "useful, concrete, and tangible result" in the form of a final share price.[101]

Furthermore, the court called into question the categorical statutory exclusion of business methods.[102] Instead of excluding all business methods as nonstatutory *per se*, the court found that business method processes should be subjected to the same scrutiny as other process patent applications.[103] Quoting Judge Newman's dissent in *In re Schrader*,[104] the court stated:

> [The business method exception] is ... an unwarranted encumbrance to the definition of statutory subject matter in § 101 that [should] be discarded as error-prone, redundant, and obsolete. It merits retirement from the glossary of section 101.... All of the "doing business" cases could have been decided using the clearer concepts of Title 35. Patentability does not turn on whether the claimed method does "business" instead of something else, but on whether the method, viewed as a whole, meets the requirements of patentability as set forth in sections 102, 103, and 112 of the Patent Act.[105]

State Street noted that business method claims have not been held unpatentable as business methods but rather on grounds of nonpatentability of abstract ideas, so their categorical exclusion was unnecessary.[106] The court defended its position by finding that the decision credited with creating the business method exception, *Hotel Security Checking Co. v. Lorraine Co.*,[107] was based on lack of novelty and not because of its status as a business method.[108] The court points to the 1996 deletion of language in the Manual of Patent Examining Procedures (MPEP) which rejected business methods as nonstatutory.[109] Moreover, the 1996 Examination Guidelines for Computer Related Inventions acknowledged examiners' difficulty with the business method exclusion and ad-

---

101. *State Street*, 149 F.3d at 1373.
102. *Id.* at 1375.
103. *Id.* at 1375, n.10.
104. *In re* Schrader, 22 F.3d 290, 298 (Fed. Cir. 1994) (Newman, J., dissenting).
105. *State Street*, 149 F.3d at 1375 n.10.
106. *Id.* at 1375.
107. Hotel Security Checking Co. v. Lorraine Co. 160 F. 467 (2d Cir. 1908).
108. *State Street*, 149 F.3d at 1376.
109. *See* MANUAL OF PATENT EXAMINING PROCEDURE § 706.03(a) (United States Patent and Trademark Office 1994) (explaining that "[t]hough seemingly within the category of process or method, a method of doing business can be rejected as not being within the statutory classes").

vised that "[c]laims should not be categorized as methods of doing business. Instead such claims should be treated like any other process claims."[110]

AT&T v. Excel Communications adopted *State Street*'s rejection of the business method exclusion stating, "[W]e consider the scope of § 101 to be the same regardless of the form—machine or process—in which a particular claim is drafted."[111] The claimed process of "using subscribers' and call recipients' PICs as data ... to create a signal useful for billing purposes"[112] was found to be statutory because it employed a mathematical algorithm merely for the production of a "useful, concrete, and tangible result" because the produced signal was representative of a non-abstract thing used for billing purposes.[113] The court rejected a restrictive meaning of "physical transformation" which would only include substances like synthetic rubber[114] and extended the definition to include representations of physical things, like visual monitors which represent a patient's heart activity.[115] Indeed, in 2006, the Supreme Court of the United States held a business method patent valid which "facilitate[d] the sale of goods between private individuals" in an electronic market (the internet) by "establishing a central authority to promote trust among participants."[116]

The State Street *and* AT&T *decisions were the latest innovation in courts' decisions concerning process patents prior to* Bilski. *As noted earlier, full understanding of these decisions is only possible where the reader understands the earlier decisions concerning process patents so the chronological organization is probably the right way to go. The reader has now been brought up to the current day and the paper transitions to a discussion of the recent Supreme Court decision.*

Continued confusion led the Supreme Court to hear *Bilski v. Kappos* in an attempt to determine the proper treatment for business method patents under the Patent Act.[117]

---

110. Examination Guidelines, 61 Fed. Reg. 7478, 7479 (1996).

111. AT&T Corp. v. Excel Comm., Inc., 172 F.3d 1352, 1357 (Fed. Cir. 1999).

112. *Id.* at 1358.

113. *Id.*

114. *See, e.g.,* Diamond v. Diehr, 450 U.S. 175, 184 (1981) (claiming "[t]hat respondents' claims involve the transformation of an article, in this case raw, uncured synthetic rubber, into a different state or thing cannot be disputed").

115. *AT&T,* 172 F.3d at 1358–59. *See, e.g.,* Arrhythmia Research Tech. Inc. v. Corazonix Corp., 958 F.2d 1053, 1059 (Fed. Cir. 1992) (finding that representations of a patient's heart function displayed on a monitor was sufficiently concrete for patentability).

116. EBAY, Inc. v. Mercexchange, LLC, 547 U.S. 388, 390 (2006).

117. Bilski v. Kappos, 130 S. Ct. 3218 (2010).

A transition sentence is used here to indicate to the reader that he has been given all of the background information he needs to understand the Bilski case and the important issue that the case will resolve.

II. Background

Bilski v. Kappos[118] arose from a patent application filed April 10, 1997, entitled *Energy Risk Management Method*.[119] Bernard L. Bilski and Rand A. Warsaw sought patent protection on a method of commodities hedging where market participants of a commodity and consumers of a commodity would employ an intermediary, referred to as a commodity provider.[120] Using the method thereby sheltered all the parties from the consumption risks associated with a commodity whose price fluctuated.[121]

> For example, coal power plants (i.e., the "consumers") purchase coal to produce electricity and are averse to the risk of a spike in demand for coal since such a spike would increase the price and their costs. Conversely, coal mining companies (i.e., the "market participants") are averse to the risk of a sudden drop in demand for coal since such a drop would reduce their sales and depress prices. The claimed method en-

---

118. *Id.*

119. *In re* Bilski, 545 F.3d 943, joint app. A-3 (Fed. Cir. 2008). The Bilski patent application number was 08/833,892, and claimed priority to a provisional patent application filed April 16, 1996 with application number 60/ 015,756. *Id.* at joint app. A-5 n.1.

120. *Id.* at 949–50. Only two of the patent's eleven claims are independent claims: claims one and four. Bilski v. Kappos, 130 S. Ct. at 3223. Claim one is the textual description of the method, whereas claim four is the concept of claim one presented as a mathematical algorithm. *Id.* Claim one reads:

1. A method for managing the consumption risk costs of or a commodity sold by a commodity provider at a fixed price comprising the steps of:

(a) initiating a series of transactions between said commodity provider and consumers of said commodity wherein said consumers purchase said commodity at a fixed rate based upon historical averages, said fixed rate corresponding to a risk position of said consumers;

(b) identifying market participants for said commodity having a counter-risk position to said consumers; and

(c) initiating a series of transactions between said commodity provider and said market participants at a second fixed rate such that said series of market participant transactions balances the risk position of said series of consumer transactions.

Ex parte Bilski, No. 2002-2257, 2006 Pat. App. LEXIS 51, 2006 WL 5738364, at *2 (B.P.A.I. Sept. 26, 2006). *See* Bilski v. Kappos, 130 S. Ct. at 3223–24.

121. *Ex parte* Bilski, 2006 Pat. App. LEXIS 51, at *2.

visions an intermediary, the "commodity provider," that sells coal to
the power plants at a fixed price, thus isolating the power plants from
the possibility of a spike in demand increasing the price of coal above
the fixed price. The same provider buys coal from mining companies
at a second fixed price, thereby isolating the mining companies from
the possibility that a drop in demand would lower prices below that
fixed price. And the provider has thus hedged its risk; if demand and
prices skyrocket, it has sold coal at a disadvantageous price but has
bought coal at an advantageous price, and vice versa if demand and
prices fall.[122]

*Peter does a good job here introducing the reader to the patent at issue in his note.
By using a block quote from the appellate court in the case, Peter explains the patent
in the way that the court understands it. This allows the reader to examine the
issue from the same perspective as the court and puts the reader in the best position
to analyze the case as if he were deciding it himself. (In reality, Peter attempted to
construct an example of his own to avoid having another massive block quote since
his prior law is replete with them. But in the end, he decided that it was better that
he get the scenario right, rather than risk an example that didn't quite work.)*

The patent examiner rejected all eleven of the *Bilski* application's claims as
unpatentable subject matter under 35 U.S.C. § 101.[123] The examiner rejected
the claims on the grounds that the method was not within the "technological
arts" because it was not tied to a computer or any other "specific apparatus,"
and "merely manipulate[d] an abstract idea and solve[d] a purely mathematical
problem without any limitation to a practical application."[124] The examiner
provided a definition of technology as described in the Guidelines for Computer-Related Inventions.[125] Technology is the "application of science and en-

---

122. *In re* Bilski, 545 F.3d at 949–50.
123. *Id.* at joint app. A-216. *See* 35 U.S.C. § 101 (2010) (limiting patentable inventions
to processes, machines, manufactures, and compositions of matter).
124. *In re* Bilski, 545 F.3d at joint app. A-216.
125. *Id. See* U.S. Patent and Trademark Office, *Examination Guidelines for Computer
Related Inventions: Final Version*, http://www.uspto.gov/web/offices/pac/dapp/pdf/ciig.pdf
(last visited Sept. 16, 2010) (stating that computer programs as such are not physical "things"
nor are they statutory processes because they are not "acts" being performed, whereas "com-
puter-readable medium encoded with a computer program defines structural and functional
interrelationships between the computer program and the medium which permit the computer program's functionality to be realized, and is thus statutory").
    *Again Peter uses an attributing footnote, explaining to the reader the original basis
    for the patent claim's rejection that initiated the* Bilski *litigation.*

gineering to the development of machines and procedures in order to enhance [or] improve human conditions, or at least to improve human efficiency in some respect."[126]

Bilski was somewhat confused by the rejection based on a computer related definition because he had clearly stated that the invention need not be tied to a computer.[127] Whether the invention was considered computer-related or not, the inventors submitted that the same analysis should have been used to determine statutory subject matter of a process whether or not a " 'useful, concrete, and tangible result' ensued from the application of the process."[128] Bilski argued that through the use of a mathematical algorithm, the process calculated fixed rates that an intermediary could use to determine his "risk position."[129] That risk position could then be used to set prices with the market participant and the consumer in such a way that the commodity provider would offset his risk of unforeseen changes in the market.[130] Both the fixed rates and the risk position were concrete, tangible and useful results similar to the share price calculated in *State Street*[131] which was sufficiently statutory.[132] Bilski further claimed that the court in *AT&T* did away with the "physical limitation" requirement for a process claim, therefore no "specific apparatus," such as a computer, was needed to make the process statutory.[133]

---

126. *In re* Bilski, 545 F.3d at joint app. A-216; COMPUTER DICTIONARY 384 (Microsoft Press, 2d ed. 1994).

127. *In re* Bilski, 545 F.3d at joint app. A-216 ("It is unclear why the Examiner insists on applying the Guidelines to this invention, especially because the Appellants have made it clear that a computer is *not* part of the invention.") (emphasis in original).

128. *Id.* at joint app. A-216-17; *See* AT&T Corp. v. Excel Comm., Inc., 172 F.3d 1352, 1359 (Fed. Cir. 1999); State Street Bank & Trust Co. v. Signature Fin. Group, 149 F.3d 1368, 1374 (Fed. Cir. 1998), *cert. denied*, 525 U.S. 1093 (1999).

129. *In re* Bilski, 545 F.3d at joint app. A-217.

130. *See id.* It should be noted that although the method claimed by the inventors could be used in various commodities and futures trading forums this application particularly targeted energy commodities, such as coal. *Id.*

By illuminating the limitations of the patent claims, Peter is objectively stating what Bilski sought to protect. Further, the reader now knows that the Court's Analysis broadens the scope of the issue from Bilski's claims to business method patents generally.

131. *See State Street*, 149 F.3d at 1374 (holding that a process which produced "a final share price momentarily fixed for recording and reporting purposes and even accepted and relied upon by regulatory authorities and in subsequent trades" was a "useful, concrete, and tangible result," rendering it statutory).

132. *In re* Bilski, 545 F.3d at joint app. A-217.

133. *Id. See AT&T*, 172 F.3d at 1359 ("Since the claims at issue in this case are directed to a process in the first instance, a structural inquiry is unnecessary.").

The first sentence of this paragraph characterizes the plaintiff as "confused." It may be better for Peter to avoid this sort of characterization, but he explains his basis by using a quote in the explanatory parenthetical following his footnote. Normally a reader will not question that the cited authority actually supports the proposition put forward in the text. However, where the reader may have some misgivings, a quote can quickly dispel them.

You can see that the patent examiner was concerned with at least two tests: the "useful, concrete, and tangible result" test and the "specific apparatus" test. Had Peter not included discussions of them in the earlier Prior Law section, the reader might be confused about the tests' relevance and why the examiner relied on them to reject Bilski's application.

The Board of Patent Appeals and Inferences reversed the Examiner's decision insofar as it was based on "technological arts."[134] The Board agreed with Bilski that the process need not be performed on a specific apparatus because a process may still be patent eligible if "there is a transformation of physical subject matter from one state to another."[135] Discussing the prior case law, the Board claimed that "the cases do not imply that a process is not in the technical arts if it is not performed on a machine."[136] However, the Board maintained the Examiner's rejection of the claims because the process was "nothing but an [sic] disembodied 'abstract idea.'"[137] Because the steps of "initiating a series of transactions" and "identifying market participants" were overly broad, they would have preempted any implementation of the steps by another, either by hand or through a machine, and were therefore nonstatutory.[138] Lastly, the Board rejected Bilski's contention that the process was "useful, concrete, and tangible."[139] Although the invention described in the application was "useful," the Board found that it did not recite a "practical application" or produce a "concrete and tangible result" and was therefore nonstatutory under 35 U.S.C. § 101.[140] Bilski timely filed an appeal of the Board's decision.[141]

---

134. *Ex parte* Bilski, No. 2002-2257, 2006 Pat. App. Lexis 51, 2006 WL 5738364, at *41 (B.P.A.I. Sept. 26, 2006).

135. *Id.* at *42.

136. *Id.*

137. *Id.* at 46.

138. *Id.* at 42. *See generally* 35 U.S.C. § 112 (2010) (setting out the requirements for the specification of a patent application, including that the written description be in "full, clear, concise, and exact terms").

139. *Ex parte* Bilski, 2006 Pat. App. Lexis 51, at *49–50.

140. *Id.*

141. *In re* Bilski, 545 F.3d at 950.

The U.S. Court of Appeals for the Federal Circuit reviewed the case *de novo*, determined to find the proper test for discerning what a process was under § 101.[142] Because claims one and four were the only independent claims, and claim four was merely an algorithmic depiction of claim one, the court focused its analysis on the process outlined in that claim.[143] The court looked to the Supreme Court's rulings in *Benson*,[144] *Flook*,[145] and *Diehr*[146] for guidance.[147] The Court of Appeals found that the proper test was the "machine-or-transformation" test as stated in *Benson* and reaffirmed in *Diehr*.[148] The court went on to dispatch as insufficient several other tests, including the Freeman-Walter-Abele test,[149] the "useful, concrete, and tangible result" test,[150] and the "technological arts" test,[151] and concluded that "the machine-or-transformation test is the only applicable test and must be applied, in light of the guidance provided by the Supreme Court and this court, when evaluating the patent-eligibility of process claims."[152] Applying the machine-or-transformation test, the Court of Appeals affirmed the Board's rejection of Bilski's patent claims.[153]

The United States Supreme Court granted *certiorari*.[154]

---

142. *See id.* at 950–52 ("[The] underlying legal question thus presented is what test or set of criteria governs the determination by the Patent and Trademark Office or courts as to whether a claim to a process is patentable under § 101 or, conversely, is drawn to unpatentable subject matter because it claims only a fundamental principle.").

143. *Id.* at 951 ("[The] issue before us involves … how to determine whether a given claim—and Applicants' claim one in particular—is a 'new and useful process.'")

144. *See* Gottschalk v. Benson, 409 U.S. 63 (1972) (algorithm for converting BCD to pure binary unpatentable).

145. *See* Parker v. Flook, 437 U.S. 584 (1978) (algorithm limited to petro-chemical industry unpatentable).

146. *See* Diamond v. Diehr, 450 U.S. 175 (1981) (algorithm patentable when limited to use with a particular machine).

147. *In re* Bilski, 545 F.3d at 952–55.

148. *In re* Bilski, 545 F.3d at 955. *See supra* Part I (giving a history of process patent holdings).

149. *See supra* notes 79–80 and accompanying text.

150. *See supra* note 99 and accompanying text.

151. *See supra* note 124 and accompanying text.

152. *In re* Bilski, 545 F.3d at 958–64.

153. *Id.* at 963–64 ("[Claim one] does not involve the transformation of any physical object or substance, or an electronic signal representative of any physical object or substance. Given its admitted failure to meet the machine implementation part of the test as well, the claim entirely fails the machine-or-transformation test and is not drawn to patent-eligible subject matter.").

154. Bilski v. Doll, 129 S. Ct. 2735 (2009). Following the grant of *certiorari*, a flood of amici briefs were filed due to the potential impact of the Court's ruling.

III. Bilski v. Kappos

*Peter began his research for this note by reading the recent Supreme Court decision, Bilski, and through developing his horizontal and vertical knowledge realized that the history of process patents closely tracked the progression of philosophical theories concerning dualism. Refer back to **Chapter 3** for more information about horizontal and vertical knowledge.*

The Court's Analysis section tracks very closely to the Bilski opinion itself. Peter maintains his objectivity throughout this part and seeks to report the opinion as it was written.

The Supreme Court broadened the issue at hand to whether a patent could be issued for a claimed process invention designed for the business world — that is, a business method patent.[155] The majority opinion and the Stevens concurrence reached the same conclusion that Bilski's process claims would not be given patent protection but for very different reasons.[156] While the majority relied on its finding that Bilski sought protection for an abstract idea, the concurrence argued that business methods were *per se* nonstatutory.[157]

This opening paragraph does a nice job of laying out the issue that the Court was deciding and stating the holding and the main reasons for the Court's holding. Both defining the issue and stating the holding up front provide a foundation for the reader. Moreover, a reader may only be interested in the holding of the case, so putting it in the opening paragraph may save that reader from having to sift through the rest of the discussion.

The opening paragraph also provides a mini-roadmap, stating that there is a majority opinion and a concurrence. Peter then discusses the sub-parts individually, setting each off with its own heading.

---

155. Bilski v. Kappos, 130 S. Ct. 3218, 3223 (2010).
   Generally, short citations with shortened case names should be used after a long-form citation has been presented to the reader. However, because there are many "Bilski" citations that refer to opinions at various points in the litigation, Peter chooses to include entire case names to avoid ambiguity. He could also have devised a short-form system, such as Bilski I, Bilski II, etc. as long as he was consistent. The main purpose for citations is to allow the reader to quickly find the authority upon which the text relies.

156. Bilski v. Kappos, 130 S. Ct. 3218 (2010).

157. *Compare* Bilski v. Kappos, 130 S. Ct. at 3231, *with* Bilski v. Kappos, 130 S. Ct. at 3257 (Stevens, J., concurring).

A. Majority Opinion

The Court ultimately rejected Bilski's invention as nonstatutory, and an attempt to patent an "abstract idea."[158] However, the Court left open the possibility that business methods may be given patent protection,[159] and rejected the appellate court's decision that the machine-or-transformation test was the *sole* test for determining what inventions constitute a "process" as enumerated in § 101.[160] Furthermore, the Court refused to endorse the Court of Appeals' limiting interpretation of § 101, allowing for the possibility of reviving the use of previous tests, and permitting creation of new tests as long as they were within the purpose of the Patent Act.[161]

Again, Peter states the holding of the majority and Court's main reasoning to provide a foundation for the rest of the discussion in this sub-part.

The Patent and Trademark Office offered three arguments that Bilski's invention was not statutory subject matter: (1) it was not tied to a machine and did not transform an article; (2) it involved a method of conducting business; and (3) it was merely an abstract idea.[162] In laying the foundation for the Court's analysis it began with the text of the controlling statute, 35 U.S.C. § 101:

> Whoever invents or discovers any new and useful process, machine, manufacture, or composition of matter, or any new and useful improvement thereof, may obtain a patent therefor, subject to the conditions and requirements of this title.[163]

The Court noted the use of the term "any" and concluded that Congress contemplated that the Patent Act should be widely inclusive,[164] and further noted

---

158. Bilski v. Kappos, 130 S. Ct. at 3223, 3231 (majority opinion).

159. *See id.* at 3228 ("[A] business method is simply one kind of "method" that is … eligible for patenting under § 101.").

160. *Id.* at 3227.

161. *Id.* at 3231.

162. *Id.* at 3223.

163. 35 U.S.C. § 101 (2010).

164. Bilski v. Kappos, 130 S. Ct. at 3223; Diamond v. Chakrabarty, 447 U.S. 303, 308 (1980). Chakrabarty found that a human-made, genetically engineered bacterium was statutory as a "manufacture" or a "composition of matter" even though bacteria in general are products of nature, because the Charkrabary bacterium did not occur naturally. *Chakrabarty*, 447 U.S. 303. Therefore, by construing "any" liberally, the Court found that even biological substances were patentable manufactures. *Id.*

that "ingenuity should receive a liberal encouragement."[165] Congress, therefore, took a permissive approach to patent eligibility.[166] However, the bounds of patentability are not limitless. The Court's precedents provide three specific exceptions to § 101's broad patent-eligibility principles: "laws of nature, physical phenomena, and abstract ideas."[167] It was acknowledged that these exceptions were not explicit in § 101 but were consistent with the statutory requirement that an invention be "new and useful."[168] Further, these exceptions had been recognized for 150 years[169] and were "part of the storehouse of knowledge of all men ... free to all men and reserved exclusively to none."[170] With regard to patentability, it was also restated that just because an invention goes to subject matter within the statute doesn't mean that it is patentable.[171] An invention must also satisfy the conditions and requirements of the Patent Act, including that the invention is novel,[172] nonobvious,[173] and fully and particularly described.[174]

Bilski's claims were undisputedly directed to a process so the court sought to determine the meaning of the term "process" in § 101.[175] In § 100(b) a process is described as "[a] process, art or method, and includes a new use of a known process, machine, manufacture, composition of matter, or material."[176] Because this circular definition was not particularly helpful on its own, the Court again looked to past law to find its true meaning.[177] The Court began with the lower court's dispatch of several tests previously used to determine process.

The transition sentence here tells the reader that there are going to be additional, discrete discussions below. However, only the first section deals with the Court's analysis of previous tests, whereas the second and third sections concern other parts of the Court's argument. Peter could have done a better job of roadmapping what

---

165. *Chakrabarty*, 447 U.S. at 308–09 (quoting 5 Writings of Thomas Jefferson 75–76 (H. Washington ed. 1871)).
166. Bilski v. Kappos, 130 S. Ct. at 3225.
167. *Id.*; *Chakrabarty*, 447 U.S. at 309.
168. 35 U.S.C. § 101.
169. Le Roy v. Tatham, 55 U.S. 156, 174–75 (1853).
170. Bilski v. Kappos, 130 S. Ct. at 3223 (quoting Funk Brothers Seed Co. v. Kalo Inoculant Co., 333 U.S. 127 (1948)).
171. *Id.* at 3225.
172. 35 U.S.C. § 102 (2010).
173. 35 U.S.C. § 103 (2010).
174. 35 U.S.C. § 112 (2010).
175. Bilski v. Kappos, 130 S. Ct. at 3225.
176. 35 U.S.C. § 100(b) (2010).
177. Bilski v. Kappos, 130 S. Ct. at 3225.

the sections are by instead stating that the Court confronted three arguments and explicitly noting the headings to each argument in the roadmap.

i. Machine-or-Transformation Test

The Supreme Court rejected the appellate court's finding that the machine-or-transformation test was the "sole test" for what constitutes a process, and rather should be used as an "important and useful clue."[178] The Court stated that one should be cautious about reading limitations and conditions into the patent laws which had not been expressly included.[179] The Court has previously used common usage and plain meaning of terms in §101.[180] Indeed, in *Chakrabarty*, the Court read the term "manufacture" in accordance with dictionary definitions,[181] and "composition of matter" consistent with common usage.[182] The Court recognized that some opinions have deviated from ordinary meaning when interpreting the Patent Act, but maintain that that was only in cases where ordinary meaning encompassed some unpatentable subject matter, such as laws of nature, physical phenomena, and abstract ideas.[183] These exceptions to ordinary meaning do not open the door for other limiting or exclusionary tests "that are inconsistent with the text and the statute's purpose and design."[184]

In light of ordinary meaning, the Court found that the appellate court had gone too far in pronouncing the limiting machine-or-transformation test as the only determination of a §101 process.[185] In looking to the definition of process as defined by that statute[186] the Court found no "ordinary, contempo-

---

178. *Id.* at 3226.

179. *Id.*

180. *See* Diamond v. Diehr, 450 U.S. 175, 182 (1981) (stating that "[unless] otherwise defined, 'words will be interpreted as taking their ordinary, contemporary, common meaning.'" (quoting Perrin v. United States, 444 U.S. 37, 42 (1979))).

181. Bilski v. Kappos, 130 S. Ct. at 3226. *See* Diamond v. Chakrabarty, 447 U.S. 303, 308 (1980) (using the pre-1931 CENTURY DICTIONARY quoted in American Fruit Growers, Inc. v. Brogdex Co., 283 U.S. 1, 11 (1931)).

182. Bilski v. Kappos, 130 S. Ct. at 3226. *See Chakrabarty*, 447 U.S. at 308 (relying on 1 A. DELLER, WALKER ON PATENTS §14, at 55 (1st ed. 1937)).

183. Bilski v. Kappos, 130 S. Ct. at 3226; Parker v. Flook, 437 U.S. 584, 588–89 (1978).

184. Bilski v. Kappos, 130 S. Ct. at 3226.

185. *Id.*

186. "The term 'process' means process, art or method, and includes a new use of known process, machine, manufacture, composition of matter, or material." 35 U.S.C. §100(b) (2010).

rary, common meaning of the definitional terms 'process, art, or method' that would require these terms to be tied to a machine or to transform an article."[187] When a term was defined by the statute, there was no reason to go outside of the ordinary meaning to impute meaning on the term.[188] Furthermore, the appellate court's reliance on *Benson* as authority for exclusive use of the machine-or-transformation test was misguided.[189] *Benson*'s statement that "[t]ransformation and reduction of an article 'to a different state or thing' is *the clue* to the patentability of a process claim that does not include particular machines"[190] was softened with that caveat that *Benson* did not hold that "no process patent could ever qualify if it did not meet [machine-or-transformation] requirements."[191] Six years after *Benson*, it was again stated that it was possible for a process to be patentable even though it didn't meet the machine-or-transformation test.[192] Thus, although the Court continued to regard the machine-or-transformation test as "an investigative tool" it was not the only test, and Bilski's process patent claims could not be rejected solely because they were not tied to a particular machine or apparatus and they did not transform a particular article into another state or thing.[193]

ii. Business Method Exclusion

Drawing on its analysis in the previous section, the Court similarly rejected the PTO's contention that business method patents were categorically excluded from statutory subject matter.[194] The Patent Act's definition of process includes "methods" and does not therefore exclude business patents on the Act's face.[195] Moreover, the Court claimed that it had not found any argument that excluded business methods from the term "method".[196] The Court was also hesitant to categorically exclude business method patents because it was unsure exactly

---

187. Bilski v. Kappos, 130 S. Ct. at 3226 (some internal quotation marks omitted).

188. *Id. See* Burgess v. United States, 553 U.S. 124, 130 (2008) ("When a statute includes an explicit definition, we must follow that definition" (internal quotation marks omitted)).

189. Bilski v. Kappos, 130 S. Ct. at 3226–27.

190. Gottschalk v. Benson, 409 U.S. 63, 70 (1972) (emphasis added).

191. *Id.* at 71.

192. Parker v. Flook, 437 U.S. 584, 588 (1978).

193. Bilski v. Kappos, 130 S. Ct. at 3226–27.

194. *Id.* at 3228.

195. *Id. See also, e.g.,* WEBSTER'S NEW INTERNATIONAL DICTIONARY 1548 (2d ed. 1954) (defining "method" as "[a]n orderly procedure or process ... regular way or manner of doing anything'; hence, a set form of procedure adopted in investigation or instruction").

196. Bilski v. Kappos, 130 S. Ct. at 3228.

what was considered a "business method," which might include technology or other things for conducting business efficiently.[197]

The Court looked to other sections, beyond § 100(b), for clarification as to what sorts of processes might be patentable.[198] The Act specifically mentions prior use of "a method of conducting business" as a defense for claims of infringement bases on "a method of a patent."[199] The language in § 273 acknowledged that there may be business method patents, and without changing the meaning of § 100(b), was merely a clarification that a business method is one type of "method" that was eligible for patent protection under § 101.[200] The Court defended this interpretation with the "canon against interpreting any statutory provision in a manner that would render another provision superfluous."[201] To exclude business patents altogether would violate this rule by rendering § 273 meaningless.[202] Though § 273 was enacted some time later than § 101[203] the rule must be followed.[204] The Court, therefore, declined to reject Bilski's claims based on status of business method alone, but it limited inclusion of BMPs by stating that *Bilski v. Kappos* should not suggest wide patentability of business methods.[205]

iii. Abstract Idea

Although the Court found that business method patents were not categorically excluded from patenting and they may even be patentable if they failed the machine-or-transformation test, the Court rejected Bilski's claims as unpatentable processes because they were attempts to patent abstract ideas.[206] The Court decided the claims were nonstatutory narrowly on the basis of *Benson*, *Flook*, and *Diehr*.[207]

---

197. *Id.*

198. *Id.* at 3228–29.

199. 35 U.S.C. § 273(a)–(b) (2010).

200. Bilski v. Kappos, 130 S. Ct. at 3228.

201. *Id.* at 3228–29; Corley v. United States, 129 S. Ct. 1558, 1560 (2009).

202. Bilski v. Kappos, 130 S. Ct. at 3228.

203. Section 101 was enacted with most of the other provisions in the Patent act in 1952, whereas, § 273 was enacted much later, in 1999, as a Congressional response to *State Street*. *See infra* note 241 and accompanying text (concerning congressional responses to *State Street*).

204. Bilski v. Kappos, 130 S. Ct. at 3228–29. *See also, e.g.*, Hague v. Committee for Industrial Organization, 307 U.S. 496, 529–30 (1939) (Stone, J.) (enforcing the canon when two provisions of the same act were enacted at different times).

205. Bilski v. Kappos, 130 S. Ct. at 3229.

206. *See id.* at 3229–30.

207. *Id.*

"A principle, in the abstract, is a fundamental truth; an original cause; a motive; these cannot be patented, as no one can claim in either of them an exclusive right."[208] The *Benson* court declined to patent Benson's use of a mathematical formula for converting BCD into pure binary code because to do so would "wholly pre-empt the mathematical formula and in practical effect would be a patent on the algorithm itself."[209] The Court extended the exclusion of abstract mathematical formulas in *Flook*,[210] where it was found that an unpatentable mathematical formula would not become patentable simply because its use was limited to a "particular technological environment" or added "insignificant postsolution activity."[211] *Diehr* rounded out the rule by explaining what uses of mathematical algorithms would be allowable.[212] That Court found that because the invention was not "an attempt to patent a mathematical formula, but rather [was] an industrial process for the molding of rubber products," it was statutory subject matter under § 101.[213] *Diehr* distinguished between purely abstract ideas, laws of nature, or mathematical formulae and the "*application* of a law of nature or mathematical formula to a known structure."[214] The court also emphasized that upon examination the claims of an invention must be considered as a whole, and not dissected into old and new elements."[215] By combination of previously well known constituents a process may thereby be novel and useful in a way never before invented.[216]

Peter is able to quickly run through the Court's application of Benson, Flook, *and* Diehr *because he has already discussed each case in some detail previously*

---

208. Gottschalk v. Benson, 409 U.S. 63, 67 (1972) (quoting Le Roy v. Tatham, 55 U.S. (14 How.) 156, 175 (1853)).

209. *See Benson*, 409 U.S. at 72. *See supra* Part I for a fuller discussion of the history of process claims.

210. Parker v. Flook, 437 U.S. 584, 590 (1978).

211. Diamond v. Diehr, 450 U.S. 175, 191–92 (1981). *See Flook*, 437 U.S. at 594–95 (attempting to patent the use of a mathematical algorithm when used in the field of petrochemical and oil-refining industries).

212. *See generally Diehr*, 450 U.S. 175 (finding that the process was patentable subject matter because the claimed invention did not preclude other inventions from using the mathematical algorithm incorporated in Diehr's application).

213. *Id.* at 192–93.

214. *See id.* at 187 (emphasis in original); Mackay Radio & Telegraph Co. v. Radio Corp. of America, 306 U.S. 86, 94 (1939) ("While a scientific truth, or the mathematical expression of it, is not a patentable invention, a novel and useful structure created with the aid of knowledge of scientific truth may be.").

215. *Diehr*, 450 U.S. at 188.

216. *Id.*

in the Prior Law section. In the event that a reader was unsatisfied with the coverage of those cases here, he could return to the previous part for additional discussion.

In *Bilski v. Kappos*, the Court held that the claims were unpatentable abstract ideas in the same way as the mathematical algorithms were in *Benson* and *Flook*.[217] "Allowing petitioners to patent risk hedging would pre-empt use of this approach in all fields, and would effectively grant a monopoly over an abstract idea."[218] Moreover, a limited monopoly on the use of the algorithm for hedging within energy markets was analogous to *Flook*'s denial of post-solution activity in a specific field and was therefore not patentable.[219]

This paragraph succinctly puts forward the Court's final analysis of the case. By this time, the reader has developed a thorough knowledge of the facts and the law that govern the case at hand so the reader can easily understand how the Court applied that law.

By relying on the decisions in *Benson*, *Flook*, and *Diehr* and holding Bilski's claims unpatentable under the abstract idea exclusion, the Court was able to avoid further definition of a "process" beyond what was given in § 100(b).[220] The Court did not foreclose, however, that tests may be developed for guidance about what a process was, as long as they were consistent with the text of the Patent Act.[221]

This section ends by stating the majority's conclusion. Additionally, it tells the reader the limitations of the Court's holding. Peter will address some of the limitations in his Personal Analysis section, so he briefly alerted the reader to their existence here.

B. Stevens Concurrence

The concurrence written by Justice Stevens agreed that Bilski's application was directed to unpatentable subject matter because it was an abstract idea, and agreed also that the machine-or-transformation was not the exclusive test to determine patentability of a process although it was reliable in most cases.[222] The concurrence stated, however, that the opinion was not clear in its analysis and rather than decide *Bilski* because it concerned an abstract idea it should

---

217. Bilski v. Kappos, 130 S. Ct. at 3231.
218. *Id.*
219. *Id.*
220. *Id.*
221. *Id.*
222. Bilski v. Kappos, 130 S. Ct. at 3231–32 (Stevens, J., concurring).

have rejected the application as merely describing a method of doing business which did not qualify as a "process" under § 101.[223]

This sub-part again begins with the sub-part's conclusion and goes on to describe the concurring opinion objectively.

Originally, Peter was only going to discuss the consequences arising from the majority opinion, but late in the writing process decided that the concurrence was important to the argument he makes in his Personal Analysis. Although the Prior Law part discusses much of the law that the concurrence relied upon, there are some gaps that should have been addressed in the earlier part. Writing a scholarly article is a recursive process so it is important to update the entire paper when revisions are made, to avoid disconnect between parts. Refer to **Chapters 5 and 6** *regarding the process of Refining.*

Instead of attempting to understand the meaning of process by plain meaning, the concurrence looked to both the legislative history of the Patent Act and prior case law concerning business method patents.[224] The concurrence began its analysis of process by noting that the ordinary lay meaning of process was far too broad and the Patent Act never intended the term to encompass "*any* series of steps or any *way* to do any *thing*."[225] The concurrence also rejected the PTO's assertion that process should be construed in accord with the other categories of statutory subject matter—machines, manufactures, and compositions of matter—which would limit processes to technological and industrial methods; eliminating business methods as statutory.[226] Terms in patent law are specialized terms of art and should not be given ordinary, lay interpretations, nor should they be dismissed because of associated words in a statute.[227] For these reasons, the con-

---

223. *See id.* at 3232–35 (stating three particular complaints: (1) the Court does not actually apply plain meaning because to do so purely would lead to absurd results, (2) the opinion does not make clear that the machine-or-transformation test will still be an effective test for most processes, and (3) the Court's analysis of abstract idea is confused and conflates portions of § 112 and § 102 considerations in its § 101 analysis).

224. *Id.* at 3236–50.

225. *Id.* at 3237 (stating that under the "anything under the sun" approach a number of patents for obviously unintended processes could receive protection, including a process for "training a dog, a series of dance steps, ... or a method of shooting a basketball").

226. *Id.*

227. Bilski v. Kappos, 130 S. Ct. at 3237–38 (Stevens, J., concurring). *See also* Barber v. Gonzales, 347 U.S. 637, 641 (1954) ("While it is true that statutory language should be interpreted whenever possible according to common usage, some terms acquire a special technical meaning by a process of judicial construction.").

currence outlined a history of the Patent Act from its commencement to gain clearer insight into the judicially tailored meaning interpretation of processes.[228]

The original Patent Act of 1790 did not include the term "process."[229] It was not until the Act was amended in 1952 that process replaced the term "useful arts."[230] That amendment was not meant to alter the scope or meaning of the term "art" as it had been used in case law prior to 1952, and was a made for clarity in an attempt to keep the Act up to date.[231] During the framing of the Act and its early amendments[232] "art" was considered to be related to technology as we now understand it.[233] Indeed, days before the Constitutional Convention a list was made concerning progress in the useful arts which included ships, potash, gunpowder, paper, stone work, and harnesses.[234] It was highly unlikely that arts included business patents because the Constitution's framers were wary of private monopolies on areas of commerce which were abolished in England by the Statute of Monopolies.[235] The concurrence also made note that although there were great innovations in business methods during the Revolutionary era very few were patented, and those that did have patent protection were likely self-registered.[236]

As the drafter of the 1793 Patent Act, Thomas Jefferson recognized the difficulty in deciding what should be patentable, and left most of the decision making to the courts.[237] Congress agreed with Jefferson and although it modified the Patent Act, Congress intentionally left to the courts broad discretion to "keep pace with industrial development."[238]

The *Bilski* concurrence claimed that throughout the history of judicial decisions concerning business method patents they have consistently been rejected

---

228. Bilski v. Kappos, 130 S. Ct. at 3236–50 (Stevens, J., concurring).

229. *See id.* at 3242 (quoting the Patent Act of 1790 as allowing patent protection for one who "invented or discovered any useful art, manufacture, engine, machine, or device, or any improvement therein not before known or used ...").

230. *Id.* at 3247.

231. *Id.*

232. *See* Walterscheid, *supra* note 20 (discussing early patent law in the United States).

233. Bilski v. Kappos, 130 S. Ct. at 3243 (Stevens, J., concurring).

234. *Id.* at 3244.

235. *See id.* at 3242 (giving an introductory history on the English treatment of patents prior to the United States Constitution). Moreover, writings from the framers at the time distinguished between the useful arts and the "science of finance" and commerce. *Id.* at 3244.

236. *Id.* at 3241–42, 3246 n.35.

237. Bilski v. Kappos, 130 S. Ct. at 3245 (Stevens, J., concurring).

238. *Id.* (quoting Herman Berman, *Method Claims*, 17 J. Pat. Off. Soc. 713, 714 (1935)).

as unpatentable.[239] The concurrence cited several opinions dating from 1893 to the present concerning patent applications whose proposed business plans were explicitly rejected because they claimed business methods.[240] In addition to the case law, several leading patent treatises considered business methods unpatentable.[241]

Judicial opinions in the mid-1900's explained art by using "method, process, system, or like terms."[242] The concurrence reasoned that because process was meant to be given the same judicial interpretation as art, it should have been construed in line with previous decisions such as *Hotel Security Checking Co.* and *Loew's Drive-In* which explicitly held business methods nonstatutory.[243] The concurrence also claimed that the *State Street* decision did not in fact open the possibility of statutory business methods and asserted that the Court found State Street Financial's process patentable based on its mechanical components and not its unembodied theory.[244] The *State Street* decision merely stated that "an otherwise patentable process [was] not unpatentable simply because it [was] directed toward the conduct of doing business,"[245] e.g. a machine that makes complex calculations necessary to the business of an accounting firm. Following *State Street*, BMPs continued to be of "suspect validity."[246]

---

239. *Id.*

240. *Id.* at 3246. *See, e.g.*, Hotel Security Checking Co. v. Lorraine Co., 160 F. 467, 469 (2d Cir. 1908) ("A system of transacting business disconnected from the means for carrying out the system is not, within the most liberal interpretation of the term, an art"); *In re* Patton, 127 F.2d 324, 327–28 (CCPA 1942) ("a system of transacting business, apart from the means for carrying out such system is not an art within the meaning of the patent law, nor is an abstract idea or theory, regardless of its importance or ... ingenuity"); Loew's Drive-In Theaters, Inc. v. Park-In Theatres, Inc., 174 F.2d 547, 552 (1st Cir. 1949) ("[A] system for transacting business ... however novel, useful, or commercially successful is not patentable apart from the means for making the system practically useful, or carrying it out").

241. Bilski v. Kappos, 130 S. Ct. at 3246 (Stevens, J., concurring) (listing treatises and articles including WALKER ON PATENTS from both 1937 and 2009 that "considered well established that [business] methods were non-statutory"). *See also id.* at 3251 n.41 (quoting Congressmen in the aftermath of *State Street* stating that they thought business methods were unpatentable).

242. *Id.* at 3247 (internal quotation marks omitted).

243. *See id.* (stating that the provisions in the 1952 Act should be treated as a codification of judicial precedent); *supra* notes 231–33 and accompanying text.

244. Bilski v. Kappos, 130 S. Ct. at 3248 n.40 (Stevens, J., concurring).

245. *Id.*

246. *Id.* at 3249; EBay Inc. v. MercExchange, LLC, 547 U.S. 388, 397 (2006) (Kennedy, J., concurring).

The concurrence defended the unpatentability of business methods by stating that § 273 was not meant to introduce business methods as statutory subject matter.[247] The First Inventor's Defense Act of 1999, codified as 35 U.S.C. § 273, was a response to the *State Street* decision which provoked wide-spread confusion about what was patentable, and meant to mitigate the potential fallout from litigation concerning BMPs.[248] Thus, the concurrence rejected the majority's interpretation to retroactively impute business methods as statutory under the 1952 Patent Act based on the 1999 statute.[249]

The concurrence's last argument leveled a public policy concern against BMPs as too costly both literally in dollars needed for commercial innovation and metaphorically for their effects on society.[250] The Constitution has given power to Congress to "promote the Progress of ... useful arts."[251] The clause was meant to encourage innovation by giving protection to those who invented new, useful inventions.[252] When protection no longer encourages innovation it will have exceeded the bounds of the framer's intention.[253] The courts were therefore given the difficult task of balancing the need for "promot[ion] of innovation and the recognition that imitation and refinement through imitation are both necessary to invention itself."[254] The concurrence recognized that not all business method patents would have the same effect on society, but maintained that a categorical approach was warranted to give clear guidelines about patentability.[255]

The concurrence stressed that protection for BMPs was not in line with the motivating purposes behind granting patent monopolies. Part of the balance of patentability was determination whether a patent monopoly was necessary

---

247. Bilski v. Kappos, 130 S. Ct. at 3250–52 (Stevens, J., concurring).

248. *Id.* at 3250 (illuminating that businesses which had used a presupposed unpatentable business method for years could become liable to another who received a newly minted patent). *See infra* Part IV(C).

249. Bilski v. Kappos, 130 S. Ct. at 3252 (Stevens, J., concurring).

250. *Id.* at 3252–57.

251. Art. I, § 8, cl. 8.

252. Bilski v. Kappos, 130 S. Ct. at 3252 (Stevens, J., concurring).

253. *See id.* (stating that the clause was meant to avoid monopolies that would stifle competition without resulting progression of the useful arts). *See also* Quanta Computer, Inc. v. LG Electronics, Inc., 553 U.S. 617, 626 (2008) (stating that the primary purpose for patents was the promotion of science and the useful arts and not the creation of private fortunes).

254. Bilski v. Kappos, 130 S. Ct. at 3252–57 (Stevens, J., concurring).

255. *Id.* at 3253. *See* Diamond v. Diehr, 450 U.S. 175, 219 (1981) (Stevens, J., dissenting) (stating that it was necessary to have "rules that enable a conscientious patent lawyer to determine with a fair degree of accuracy" what is patentable).

to "motivate the innovation."[256] Factors to be taken into account were cost, risk, and reward attached to an invention, or category of invention.[257] The concurrence showed that many commentators doubt that patent protection was necessary for innovation among business methods.[258] It also proffered that there were other advantages to business innovation beside patent protection including advantages in the competitive marketplace from first-mover rewards such as lockins, branding, and networking effects, notwithstanding the risk that others may copy efficient schemes.[259] Moreover, innovation in business methods rarely required the same kind of front-end investment of labor and resources that technology did, so the same protection was not needed to recoup investment costs.[260]

Patents were granted in return for publication of inventions.[261] Publication was meant to benefit society by allowing an inventor to improve on another's invention.[262] Because businesses normally operate in public, the concurrence argued that publication of business methods was unnecessary for disclosure to the public.[263] The concurrence asserted that allowing BMPs would increase costs of business by necessitating increased searches of prior art before a business implemented a more efficient business method, attainment of complex licensing agreements, and threat of litigation among competitors.[264] An even greater concern than the cost to businesses was the cost to the public. Because business methods tended to be broad they were the "basic tools of commercial

---

256. Bilski v. Kappos, 130 S. Ct. at 3253 (Stevens, J., concurring) (quoting Pfaff v. Wells Electronics, Inc., 525 U.S. 55, 63 (1998)).

257. *Id. See generally* W. LANDES & R. POSNER, THE ECONOMIC STRUCTURE OF INTELLECTUAL PROPERTY LAW 13–15 (2003) (discussing economic influences on patent decisions).

258. Bilski v. Kappos, 130 S. Ct. at 3253 (Stevens, J., concurring); Dan L. Burk et al., *Policy Levers in Patent Law*, 89 VA. L. REV. 1575, 1618 (2003).

259. Bilski v. Kappos, 130 S. Ct. at 3254 (Stevens, J., concurring). *See infra* Part IV(C).

260. Bilski v. Kappos, 130 S. Ct. at 3254 (Stevens, J., concurring). *See* Burk et al., *supra* note 258 (stating that "[b]ecause business methods do not generally require substantial investment in R&D, the prospect of even a modest supracompetitive reward will provide sufficient incentive to innovate").

261. 37 U.S.C. § 122(b) (maintaining that a patent application will be published within 18 months from its earliest priority date).

262. *See, e.g.*, Bilski v. Kappos, 130 S. Ct. at 3256 (Stevens, J., concurring) (stating that "imitation and refinement through imitation are both necessary to invention itself" (quoting Bonito Boats, Inc. v. Thunder Craft Boats, Inc., 489 U.S. 141, 146 (1989))); Brenner v. Manson, 383 U.S. 519, 533 (1966) (discussing the effect of publication on scientific progress and "increasing the fund of scientific knowledge").

263. Bilski v. Kappos, 130 S. Ct. at 3254–55 (Stevens, J., concurring).

264. *Id.* at 3255. *See* Olson, *supra* note 16 (stating that undue expense may result from lawsuits and settlement between competing businesses with potentially conflicting patents).

work."[265] "Think how the airline industry might now be structured if the first company to offer frequent flyer miles had enjoyed the sole right to award them."[266] Businesses may be inhibited from implementing new business conduct that could be beneficial to consumers because of added costs of pre-implementation searches to avoid the possibility of infringement of broadly worded BMPs.[267] The concurrence argued that this problem was particularly difficult for business methods because they were normally not directed to a kind of good and thus vaguely written claims made discovery of prior art costly and time consuming, not to mention costs to negotiate licenses for use of BMPs.[268] Increased start-up costs were especially damning to small businesses and may come into direct contention with antitrust laws.[269]

Because the concurrence found that the history of patent law precluded patentability of business methods, and BMPs were not only unnecessary to protect proprietary business practices, but might in fact be harmful, the concurrence maintained that the Bilski application was nonstatutory for very different reasons than the majority opinion.[270] The Supreme Court's disparate analyses highlight the difficulty surrounding the issue of business method patents. Part IV below proposes a solution by drawing on historical discussions of unembodied mental processes in philosophy and psychology.

The final paragraph of this section states the conclusion of the discussion about the concurring opinion and the conclusion to the entire section. It ends with a transition sentence that tells the reader the problem raised by the Court's analysis and that the next part will offer a solution to the problem.

Footnote 270 tells the reader that there was a second concurrence. Peter relegated that concurrence to the footnotes because it was not particularly important to

---

265. Bilski v. Kappos, 130 S. Ct. at 3255 (Stevens, J., concurring).
266. *Id.* at 3255–56 (quoting Rochelle Cooper Dreyfuss, *Are Business Method Patents Bad for Business?*, 16 SANTA CLARA COMPUTER & HIGH TECH. L. J. 263, 264 (May 2000)).
267. Bilski v. Kappos, 130 S. Ct. at 3256 (Stevens, J., concurring).
268. *Id.*
269. *Id.* at 3256–57, 3257 n.59.
270. *Id.* at 3257. Justice Breyer also wrote a concurrence, agreeing with Justice Stevens, but wrote separately to highlight the agreement between Members of the Court: (1) the text of § 101 is not inclusive of unlimited statutory subject matter, (2) both courts maintain that the machine-or-transformation test is a reliable landmark for determining patentability of processes, (3) the machine-or-transformation test is not the sole test for determining patentability of processes, (4) the "useful, concrete, and tangible result" test is also not the only metric for determining patentability. Bilski v. Kappos, 130 S. Ct. at 3257–58 (Breyer, J., concurring).

his argument and he did not want to distract the reader by including it in the text.

IV. Business Methods and Dualism

The history of the Court's decisions concerning patentability of processes versus that of products clearly indicates that a process could be patentable subject matter under 35 U.S.C. § 101 if it met the other requirements of the Patent Act, namely novelty and utility.[271] However, the Court has not, in the over 200 years since the first Patent Act was enacted, determined the proper means by which to give process patents the technological validity that is seemingly requisite to patentability, especially for business methods which are often a mode of conducting business not necessarily tied to any physical constraints.[272] The Federal Circuit in *In re Bilski* highlighted what seems to be the most problematic issue pertaining to business method patents by adopting the machine-or-transformation test.[273] In its rejection of the test, the Court attempted to avoid inherently dualist problems by including processes for conducting business — or steps taken in a consistent, orderly and predictable fashion — within the bounds of statutory subject matter under 35 U.S.C. § 101 rather than accepting that some process patents could be novel and useful but overly broad because not tied to a particular application.[274] Under the current structure of patentable subject matter it will be impossible for any purely mental process, including business methods as such, to meet the requirements of patentability without being embodied in some way by a tangible mechanism.[275] Scholarship in philosophy of mind and psychology has thoroughly explored the same problem faced by the Court: Cartesian dualism. By aligning itself with conclusions made in these other fields and adopting a functionalist approach to business method patents the Court could avoid much confusion about what is statutory.[276] Maintaining that unembodied processes are non-statutory would alle-

---

271. *See supra* Part I.

272. *See generally*, *e.g.*, Bilski v. Kappos, 130 S. Ct. at 3242–50 (Stevens, J., concurring) (recounting judicial history that has not found business methods patentable).

273. *In re* Bilski, 545 F.3d 943, 951 (Fed. Cir. 2008).

274. Bilski v. Kappos, 130 S. Ct. at 3242–50 (Stevens, J., concurring). Some of the difficulty with finding a proper test for processes no doubt stems from the likelihood that previous tests were designed for tangible technology.

275. *See*, *e.g.*, Bilski v. Kappos, 130 S. Ct. 3218 (2010) (finding method for hedging investments unpatentable); Gottschalk v. Benson, 409 U.S. 63 (1972) (finding method for converting BCD to pure binary unpatentable).

276. *See supra* Part III(B).

APPENDIX

viate practical difficulties and those seeking BMPs would still maintain proprietary protection through other means.

Part IV is Peter's Personal Analysis on Bilski. *He begins this part with a quick recap of the legal landscape surrounding the case, and then introduces his critique. Moreover, the law does not exist in a vacuum. Peter tells the reader what he will encounter in the remainder of the part by asserting in his opening paragraph that because those extra-legal areas had already faced the dilemma that the Court was trying to resolve in* Bilski, *the Court should resolve that issue similarly.*

A roadmap would be helpful here to guide the reader on how the rest of the part will proceed. One of the reasons that Peter includes a Table of Contents at the beginning of his article is to tell the reader the progression of the article, but it is unlikely that the reader is going to return to the Table as he is reading the article. A roadmap should be included each time there are sub-parts. **Chapter 4** *discusses roadmaps in more depth.*

A. Cartesian Dualism

Dualism is the theory that reality consists of two disparate and discrete parts.[277] Dualism is exhibited in many areas, but each contains the same dilemma: the existence of two (or more) discrete "substances" apparently creates an unbridgeable gap in communication between the substances.[278] The lack of communication is the essence of their discreteness.[279] Taken on its face, the incommensurability of substances is unproblematic, but becomes para-

---

277. THE CAMBRIDGE DICTIONARY OF PHILOSOPHY 244 (2d. ed. 1999) [hereinafter CAMBRIDGE DICTIONARY]. Distinctive parts of a whole have been described in numerous ways pertaining to the area which is being discussed. For instance, Descartes referred to the parts as distinct "substances" whereas Leibniz called them "monads." *See generally* THE RATIONALISTS (Anchor Books 1974) (compiling notable works from Descartes, Spinoza, and Leibniz). Use of different terminology generally signifies that the theorist is categorizing the parts in a different way than someone with a different lexicon, even if the theorists' discussion takes place in the same arena. *See, e.g.,* JOHN COTTINGHAM, THE RATIONALISTS (Oxford University Press 1988) (discussing basic tenets of early rationalist philosophies and the employment of different terminology to distinguish one theory from another).

278. *See* CAMBRIDGE DICTIONARY, *supra* note 277 (listing a number of different areas in which philosophers have uncovered the existence of dualism).

279. Leibniz contended that there must be simple, indivisible substances because there were "composite" substances which can be divided into smaller parts. At some point, the parts must be indivisible so as to be the "true Atoms of nature" that are the building blocks of composite substances. Gottfried Wilhelm Freiherr Von Leibniz, *The Monadology, in* THE RATIONALISTS, *supra* note 277, at 455 (George Montgomery, with revisions by Albert R. Chandler, trans.) (1714).

doxical when two substances are the constituents of a whole, i.e. a rational universe.[280] The whole seems to be completely functional so the difficulty arises in explanation of how two completely separate substances function in combination without the ability to act on one another.[281]

This sub-part provides background on Cartesian dualism. Like the Prior Law part provides a foundation for the Court's Analysis, this sub-part gives the reader a foundation for the claims that are made concerning dualism and business method patents. The reader now knows the pertinent law and this section develops the reader's knowledge of dualism that is necessary to understand the thesis shown in Peter's Personal Analysis section.

Descartes, in his *Meditations*, introduced the mind-body problem.[282] Descartes identified two discrete "substances" which made up his reality: *res cogitans* (or thinking stuff) and *res extensa* (or extended stuff).[283] The principle difference between the two substances was that the mind was an unextended, thinking substance and the body was a passive unthinking extension.[284] These two substances were independently existent, but both were necessary to explain our ordinary, everyday existence.[285] The mind-body problem is two-fold: (1) how can the unextended mind influence the body to act, and (2) how can sen-

---

280. CAMBRIDGE DICTIONARY, *supra* note 277.

281. Causation is being conflated with communication here to emphasize that the problem with dualism is not that there can be no outside external observance by one substance of another (although this is likely the case), but rather that the communication between two substances of a whole would be causation because the substances would be informing each other of circumstances which would have an effect on the circumstances of the other, inducing a reaction by the latter by the action of the former. *See* Robert H. Wozniak, *Mind and Body: Rene Descartes to William James*, http://serendip.brynmawr.edu/Mind/17th.html (1995) (stating that the kind of interaction needed for causation in the Cartesian system is impossible where the substances are completely distinct from each other).

282. Rene Descartes, *Meditations on the First Philosophy: In Which the Existence of God, and the Real Distinction of Mind and Body, Are Demonstrated*, *in* THE RATIONALISTS, *supra* note 277, at 112 (John Veitch trans.) (1641). The notion that the soul is separate from the body was explored at length by Plato and has been present throughout the history of philosophy, but Descartes has been credited as the "father of the modern mind-body problem." CAMBRIDGE DICTIONARY, *supra* note 277, at 684.

283. COTTINGHAM, *supra* note 277, at 115–24 (discussing Descartes' argument that mind and matter were distinct substances).

284. CAMBRIDGE DICTIONARY, *supra* note 277.

285. Descartes, *supra* note 282, at 165. *See also* COTTINGHAM, *supra* note 277, at 119–20 (discussing Descartes' assertion that mind and body were able to exist independently of one another, but the mind was "intimately conjoined and intermingled with the body").

sations felt by the extended body impress upon the mind?[286] For a substance
to have any effect on another there must be a causal connection—one that is
apparently lacking in dualist theories.[287]

*Because this paper is a legal critique, Peter moves through his philosophical dis-
cussion much more quickly than he did his legal discussion. In the text he
includes only what he thinks bears on his argument and relegates deeper discussion and helpful authority to the footnotes. If he were writing an article for
a philosophical journal, he might focus more on nuances that have been glossed
over here.*

Many theories have been presented in an attempt to explain apparent mind-
body causation including miraculous intervention from God, occasionalism,[288]
and parallelism.[289] Other philosophers rejected dualism and theorized instead
that there was only one substance and the mental and physical were actually
representations of a single substance.[290] Gilbert Ryle held that it was a mistake
to speak about the mind as a discrete substance, and the mind, rather than
being subject to verbage used to describe physical phenomena, was simply a

---

286. CAMBRIDGE DICTIONARY, *supra* note 277.

287. *See id.* at 125 (discussing causation). Psychophysical causal interaction has been
the subject of serious academic and practical inquiry in (among others) the field of psychology, especially as advancement in technology has revealed connections between before-
thought-of mental states and physical brain states. *See generally* Wozniak, *supra* note 281,
at http://serendip.brynmawr.edu/Mind/ (giving a history of the mind-body problem and
its proposed solutions).

288. Wozniak, *supra* note 281 (explaining Nicolas Malebranche's argument that mind
and body do not actually interact but God makes it appear that way).

289. Wozniak, *supra* note 281 (explaining Gottfried Wilhelm Leibniz's "pre-established
harmony" where God created the world in such a way that mind and body never actually
interacted, but rather were on parallel tracks making it appear as though there was some
causation between the two when there actually was not). Substantial additional problems
are raised by dualist explanations of Cartesian interactionism (reciprocal causal influence
between discrete substances), including proving the existence of God and fatalist implications
contradicting self-determination through volition. CAMBRIDGE DICTIONARY, *supra* note
277, at 685. The problem of volition arises in later theories, including epiphenomenalism
which claims that sensory input affects the mind, but that the mind cannot influence the
body. *Id.* at 685–86.

290. *See, e.g.,* Benedict de Spinoza, *The Ethics, in* THE RATIONALISTS, *supra* note 277,
at 179–261 (John Veitch trans.) (showing by proofs that God is the only substance, and He
is comprised of an infinite number of representations). *See also* CAMBRIDGE DICTIONARY,
supra note 277, at 686–92 (describing other theories of monism).

body that had a certain capacity or disposition.[291] More specifically, the mind was not a "thing" in itself, but rather a physical state which could be observed.[292] This theory was criticized on the grounds that one can have a mental state and not exhibit it behaviorally.[293] Likewise, some behavior could be physically manifested without the corresponding mental state, e.g., lying or faking that one is in pain when he is not.[294] Despite monist theories that would eliminate the dualist problem of causation, monist theories have their own problems[295] and Western philosophy continues to be predominantly dualistic.[296] Over time philosophers of mind seemed resigned to the difficulties posed by both dualism and monism and compromised with functionalism.[297] Functionalism concedes that there may be mental states which are separate from physical states, but that mental states can only be realized by exhibition in the physical world.[298] Functionalism does not answer the problem of Cartesian Dualism, but it does narrow the focus as to what is meaningful in the physical world, namely that a mental state is only of consequence when exhibited by some physical phenomenon.[299]

291. CAMBRIDGE DICTIONARY, *supra* note 277, at 686. Ryle introduced the term "category mistake," claiming that Cartesian dualists used terminology reserved for physical phenomena as if it were applicable to a non-physical substance. The mistake was that mental phenomena and physical phenomena do not have the same attributes so they cannot be described the same way without misunderstanding what is being talked about. *Id.* at 123. For a more in-depth treatment of category mistakes see GILBERT RYLE, THE CONCEPT OF MIND (University of Chicago Press 1984) (1949).
292. CAMBRIDGE DICTIONARY, *supra* note 277, at 686.
293. *Id.*
294. *Id.* at 686–87.
295. *See id.* at 686–92 (discussing different theories of monism and their flaws).
296. *Id.* at 245.
297. *See generally* CAMBRIDGE DICTIONARY, *supra* note 277, at 684–92 (reciting a short history of the struggle between dualist and monist theories of mind).
298. *Id.* at 691–92. Functionalism is not an entirely novel idea and was implied by Hume in his writings because he held that one could never truly know the effect of some cause. *See generally* David Hume, *An Enquiry Concerning Human Understanding, in* THE EMPIRICISTS 316–46 (Anchor Books 1974) (1748). Hume, after showing that an effect could never truly be shown to be connected with its cause until after the cause had been observed, purported that humans are able to function in the world through custom and habit. *Id.* at 336. As a matter of custom, one could assume that where a past cause had produced some effect, a similar cause would produce a similar effect. *Id.* Without the ability to predict an effect, one would never be able to seek an end through the use of some means, which is not the case with humans, so it follows that although one can never be sure that some cause will produce the desired effect, he must rely on custom and habit if he is to achieve his desired end. *Id.* at 345–46.
299. *Cf.* CAMBRIDGE DICTIONARY, *supra* note 277, at 692 (illuminating functionalism's possible susceptibility to mental misinterpretations).

B. A Functionalist View of Business Method Patents

Like functionalism, the Patent Act should be concerned only with the physical exhibition of an invention as it is maintained in an inventor's application for patent. In fact, this is the reason for the specificity requirement in § 112 and the formal claims requirements—to limit the inventor to protection of inventions that have actually been stated and not what the inventor wanted to invent.[300] Section 112 is a safeguard against granting patent protection for concepts which have not been articulated with sufficient specificity.[301] If patent application claims are rejected for being overly broad when they meet the requirements of § 112,[302] certainly concepts which are not claimed in the form of a physical manifestation cannot meet the purpose of the requirements.

The opening sentence to this sub-part does a good job of succinctly stating the importance of functionalism and why it bears on business method patents.

The Court has recognized the existence of concepts which are *prima facie* unpatentable because to allow an individual a monopoly on them would preclude others from using the building blocks of science.[303] But the Court has also maintained that the use of those concepts may be patented when to do so would not preclude others from their use except in the particular invention claimed in the patent.[304] The *Diehr* process claims were statutory if, and only if, they were tied to a machine.[305] By attempting to extend *Diehr*'s "limited use" treatment to business method patents, the Court has encountered the age-old dilemma of dualism because a patent on an unembodied process would not be limited by any machine.

---

300. 35 U.S.C. § 112 (2010); 37 C.F.R. § 1.51 (2010) (specifically identifying the requirements for patent application).

301. 35 U.S.C. § 112.

302. In order to pass the preliminary stages of the patenting process, one would have had to satisfy the § 112 requirements. *Benson* and *Flook* both satisfied § 112, but were deemed nonstatutory nonetheless as fundamental principles. *See supra* Part I.

303. *See, e.g.*, Gottschalk v. Benson, 409 U.S. 63 (1972) (algorithm for converting BCD to pure binary); Parker v. Flook, 437 U.S. 584 (1978) (algorithm measuring conditions in a catalytic converter); Diamond v. Diehr, 450 U.S. 175, 188 (1981) ("a scientific truth, or the mathematical expression of it, is not a patentable invention ..."). *See also In re* Bilski, 545 F.3d 943, 1012–13 (Fed. Cir. 2008) (Rader, J., dissenting) (arguing in Part II of his opinion that Bilski's invention is unpatentable as an abstract idea).

304. *See, e.g.*, *Diehr*, 450 U.S. at 187 (allowing patenting of an algorithm's use in a machine to cure rubber).

305. *See supra* note 72 and accompanying text.

A business method is a way by which one should conduct himself or his operations in order to reach a desired result.[306] This is merely an algorithm that describes a series of steps that should be performed—no different from the algorithms used in mechanical or computer-related inventions.[307] In cases where algorithms were found patentable, they were tied to specific physical embodiments and the patent was for the physical embodiment and not for the algorithm.[308] The algorithm may have played an integral role in the functioning of the machine, but if the physical elements of an invention were the object seeking patent protection, and not just post-solution activity, then the algorithm could have been patented for use within the narrow scope of the physical embodiment.[309]

Peter recognized that it may have been quite some time since the reader read the Prior Law part on algorithms. He reminds the reader here of their significance because he is about to apply them in his argument against allowing business method patents. Peter does a good job including relevant material in the text while using a variety of footnotes to help the reader, including an explanatory footnote, a "see" cite with an explanatory parenthetical, and a "supra" cite to aid the reader in jumping back to previous text within the note.

A business method need not be tied to a machine.[310] This is evidence that a business method is a discrete, unextended substance within the Cartesian definition because it is not dependent upon any extended substance for its existence.[311] An unembodied business method can no doubt be novel and useful,

---

306. *See* Wikipedia, http://en.wikipedia.org/wiki/Algorithm (last visited Jan. 8, 2011) (discussing a wide variety of types of algorithms); *infra* text accompanying note 307.

307. An algorithm need not have a definite start and end point. Many algorithms are designed to incorporate randomness, acknowledging that the result of using a particular algorithm may not be foreseen upon commencement of the algorithm. *See* Wikipedia, http://en.wikipedia.org/wiki/Algorithm (last visited Jan. 8, 2011).

308. *See, e.g., Diehr,* 450 U.S. at 187 (allowing patenting of an algorithm's use in a machine to cure rubber).

309. *Id.*

310. *See, e.g., supra* pp. 18–20 (discussing *State Street* and *AT&T*).

311. *See* COTTINGHAM, *supra* note 277, at 119 (explaining that when some thing is able to exist wholly apart from another substance, then it is its own substance); Expanded Metal Co. v. Bradford, 214 U.S. 366 (1909) ("[T]he patentability of the process in no degree depends upon the characteristic principle of the machine, although machinery is essential to the process, and although a particular machine may be required.") (quoting GEORGE TICKNOR CURTIS, A TREATISE ON THE LAW OF PATENTS FOR USEFUL INVENTIONS: AS ENACTED AND ADMINISTERED IN THE UNITED STATES OF AMERICA, § 14 (4th ed. 1873)). *See also supra* notes 283–86 and accompanying text.

and even described with sufficient specificity that a patent on the method could be limited to particular instances, but the true parameters of the method are unknowable without physical substance.[312] The courts have followed the philosophical progression of the treatment of the mind-body problem even so far as to allow processes which "refer" to physical substance.[313] The Court should, therefore, adopt a functionalist approach as a practical matter, and hold business method patents non-statutory *per se* because they are not embodied by a physical mechanism.

This paragraph is the crux of Peter's Personal Analysis. It is in this paragraph that all of the Prior Law and the discussion of Cartesian dualism finally come together to prove his thesis. It may seem rather anticlimactic, but the proof of his thesis is only one of Peter's goals in his article. He provides a comprehensive history of process patents in this arena that others may draw upon, he summarizes Bilski, *the most recent Supreme Court decision on business method patents, and he shows how decisions concerning business method patents can be improved by cross-disciplinary analysis.*

The last sub-part of Peter's article is a summary response to criticism; a sort of "damage control" paragraph to assure hesitant readers that there are other protections available to business methods absent patent protection.

C. Proprietary Protection Outside of the Patent System

The Court is understandably hesitant to adopt any test which would result in too narrow a limitation on patentability due to the nature of invention.[314]

---

312. *See, e.g.*, O'Reilly v. Morse, 56 U.S. (15 How.) 62 (1854) (machine using electromagnetism to transmit information patentable). *But see, e.g.*, *Benson*, 409 U.S. 63 (formula for converting BCD to pure binary unpatentable); Cochrane v. Deener, 94 U.S. 780 (1877) (method for bolting flour unpatentable).

313. *See generally, e.g.*, Arrhythmia Research Tech. Inc. v. Corazonix Corp., 958 F.2d 1053 (1992) (finding a process using a monitor to represent a patient's heart activity patentable because a sufficient physical representation of a patient's condition). The referential theory of language was proposed decades ago to attempt to explain how discrete minds could convey meaning to one another through the use of language because both the speaker and the listener referred to the same physical object in the real world by the same term. *See* CAMBRIDGE DICTIONARY, *supra* note 277, at 673–74 (listing hypotheses as to the nature of the meaning of words). For more in-depth discussion of referential theories of language see Hilary Putnam, *Meaning and Reference*, *in* 70 THE JOURNAL OF PHILOSOPHY 699, 699–711 (1973) and SAUL KRIPKE, NAMING AND NECESSITY (Harvard University Press 1980).

314. *See* Bilski v. Kappos, 130 S. Ct. 3218, 3227–28 (2010) (expressing concern that a too narrowly restrictive test would inhibit granting patents for legitimate inventions).

The Patent Act is designed to protect invention, not to stifle it by limiting protection of new technology to old forms.[315] But business methods have not suffered for lack of innovation because of the unavailability of patents, and should not be subject to that concern in the same way that other processes might be.[316] Justice Stevens's *Bilski v. Kappos* concurrence[317] illuminates many other ways to protect proprietary ways of doing business including trade secret and first-mover marketplace advantages.[318] These alternative means to protect business methods may be spoiled by the allowance of BMPs. For one thing, patents must be published for the good of the public by allowing inventors to piggyback off of one another's patented inventions.[319] By exposing business methods to this sort of publication, trade secrets may be compromised and proprietary methods exposed for an even greater likelihood of use by competitors.[320] In this scenario, the only method for protecting one's intellectual property may be increased litigation.[321] This is far from the beneficial result that patents are supposed to bestow upon the public.

---

315. *Benson*, 409 U.S. at 71.

316. *See* Merges, *supra* note 14, at 585–86 (noting the success of business despite lack of patent protection).

317. *See supra* Part III(B).

318. Merges, *supra* note 14, at 585–86 (Spring, 1999). *See* Burk et al., *supra* note 258 (discussing rewards that result from innovation regardless of patent protection); Mark A. Lemley et al., *Encouraging Software Reuse*, 49 STAN. L. REV. 255, 274–75 (1997) (discussing first-mover benefits in the marketplace by getting a jump-start on imitators, including establishment of production and distribution facilities). *See also* THE SOCIAL NETWORK (Columbia Pictures 2010) (showing how Mark Zuckerberg's Facebook was able to gain an insurmountable market advantage over Winklevoss brothers' ConnectU by delaying ConnectU's launch until after Facebook had entered the market). Congress recognized the dangers associated with BMPs shortly after *State Street* and responded by enacting the First Inventor's Defense Act to protect businesses which had not published their operating procedures, but nonetheless should not have been subject to patent infringement by one who later received a business method patent. 35 U.S.C. §273(b) (2010). Indeed, if a business were apprehensive about subjectivity to an infringement suit from an outside firm it may subject itself to patent infringement by patenting its currently functioning business method.

319. *See Brenner*, 383 U.S. at 533 (discussing the effect of publication on scientific progress and "increasing the fund of scientific knowledge").

320. *See* Fisher et al., *supra* note 100 (observing that business methods were commonly kept secret to reserve an advantage over competitors).

321. *See* Brent Kendall et al., *Door Left Open to Business Patents*, THE WALL STREET JOURNAL (referring to amicus briefs wary of increased litigation); Downes, *supra* note 100 (stating that there are so many business patents pending in the USPTO that "the creation of a new online product or service today would likely infringe as many as 4,000 patents").

This paragraph alerts the reader to additional considerations surrounding
business methods, but does not delve deeply into them. Instead, they are offered
as counter-evidence to criticism against Peter's thesis. To discuss the consequences
of these additional types of intellectual property protection would greatly expand
the scope of Peter's paper so it is better that they are left for some other article
to discuss.

Conclusion

Bilski v. Kappos successfully evaded defining what types of unembodied
processes qualify as patentable subject matter under § 101 by finding Bilski's
claimed process unpatentable as an abstract idea.[322] Maintaining that business
methods may be patented without satisfying the machine-or-transformation
test triggers the dualist dilemma—abstract ideas are unpatentable but unembodied processes may be. This position is untenable, and gives no guidance to
inventors, drafters, or patent examiners. As it stands, business method patent
applications are unadministrable and the Court must either adopt a functionalist
approach, whereby only physical embodiments of processes are patentable, or
hold BMPs nonstatutory subject matter *per se* based on precedent. The latter
approach seems the more palatable because it would not preclude entirely that
an unembodied process is unpatentable (leaving room for expansion of technology[323]) while adhering to the innovative purpose of the Patent Act because
the business world does not require patent protection to spur innovation.

Justice Stevens's analysis in *Bilski v. Kappos* categorically excluding BMPs
was better than the majority's analysis because there is no way to give BMPs
adequate patent protection without great harm to society.[324] In the past, the
Court found that to grant monopoly over an idea not attached to a machine
was overly broad.[325] To grant a patent on an abstract idea under the guise of
business method would truly be a "monopoly" in the pejorative sense.[326]

In his Conclusion, Peter sums up the main arguments that he presents in his note,
offering the two solutions that would solve the problem raised by the Bilski *decision*

---

322. Bilski v. Kappos, 130 S. Ct. 3218, 3231 (2010).

323. *See* J.E.M. Agric. Supply, 534 U.S. 124, 135 (2001) (stating that historical
conceptions of patentable subject matter must not entirely restrain interpretations of the
Patent Act because the Act must be open to new forms of technology).

324. *See supra* Part III(B).

325. *See supra* p. 8–9 (discussing limits on Morse's use of electromagnetism). Reliance
on § 112 specificity may be able to fix scope issues, but consistent, accurate patenting
decisions from examiners may not be possible without clearer guidance from the Court.

326. *See* Merges, *supra* note 14 at 585 (discussing the British Statute of Monopolies).

and propounding that his argument proves the better is to hold business methods nonstatutory per se. The note's final sentence refers the reader back to the origins of the Patent Act at issue, urging the reader that Peter's solution is supported both by practical necessity and by the history of the law.

Epilogue

The America Invents Act was signed into law on September 16, 2011.[327] The patent law reform made significant changes to the patent law, but it does not appear that the changes affect the arguments advanced in this note.[328]

Between the time that Peter completed work on his note and its inclusion in Scholarly Writing, *Congress passed and the President signed into law a patent reform bill. When writing about emerging issues, it is not uncommon for some event to occur between the time the scholarly article is finished and the time of publication that could affect the article's claims. In Peter's case, the new law does not affect his arguments, but he includes an epilogue to relieve the reader of having to do any research to make sure. Review* **Chapters 2 and 3** *for more discussion about emerging issues, preemption, and keeping your research updated.*

---

327. 112 P.L. 29, 125 Stat. 284 (LEXIS 2012).
328. *Id.*

INDEX